Preventive Conservation for Historic House Museums

AMERICAN ASSOCIATION FOR STATE AND LOCAL HISTORY BOOK SERIES

ABOUT THE SERIES

The American Association for State and Local History Book Series publishes technical and professional information for those who practice and support history, and addresses issues critical to the field of state and local history. To submit a proposal or manuscript to the series, please request proposal guidelines from AASLH headquarters: AASLH Book Series, 1717 Church St., Nashville, Tennessee 37203. Telephone: (615) 320-3203. Fax: (615) 327-9013. Web site: www.aaslh.org.

ABOUT THE ORGANIZATION

The American Association for State and Local History (AASLH) is a nonprofit educational organization dedicated to advancing knowledge, understanding, and appreciation of local history in the United States and Canada. In addition to sponsorship of this book series, the Association publishes the periodical *History News*, a newsletter, technical leaflets and reports, and other materials; confers prizes and awards in recognition of outstanding achievement in the field; and supports a broad education program and other activities designed to help members work more effectively. To join the organization, contact: Membership Director, AASLH, 1717 Church St., Nashville, Tennessee 37203.

Preventive Conservation for Historic House Museums

Jane Merritt and Julie A. Reilly

with chapter contributions by
Lucy Lawliss and Rebecca L. Stevens

AltaMira Press
A Division of
ROWMAN & LITTLEFIELD PUBLISHERS, INC.
Lanham • New York • Toronto • Plymouth, UK

Published by AltaMira Press
A division of Rowman & Littlefield Publishers, Inc.
A wholly owned subsidiary of The Rowman & Littlefield Publishing Group, Inc.
4501 Forbes Boulevard, Suite 200, Lanham, Maryland 20706
http://www.altamirapress.com

Estover Road, Plymouth PL6 7PY, United Kingdom

British Library Cataloguing in Publication Information Available

Library of Congress Cataloging-in-Publication Data
Merritt, Jane, 1952–
Preventive conservation for historic house museums / Jane Merritt and Julie A. Reilly.
p. cm. — (American Association for State and Local History book series)
Includes bibliographical references and index.
ISBN 978-0-7591-1216-2 (hardcover : alk. paper) — ISBN 978-0-7591-1217-9 (pbk. : alk. paper) — ISBN 978-0-7591-1941-3 (electronic)
1. Historic house museums—United States—Management. 2. Historic house museums—Collection management—United States. 3. Historic buildings—Conservation and restoration—United States. 4. Dwellings—Conservation and restoration—United States. 5. United States—Antiquities—Collection and preservation. 6. Historic preservation—United States. I. Reilly, Julie A., 1957– II. Title.
E159.M527 2010
363.6'9—dc22 2009029946

∞™ The paper used in this publication meets the minimum requirements of American National Standard for Information Sciences—Permanence of Paper for Printed Library Materials, ANSI/NISO Z39.48-1992.

Printed in the United States of America

Contents

Foreword

HISTORIC HOUSES PLAY a vital role in making available the history and art of our nation. They tell us about how our ancestors lived, what they accomplished, the challenges with which they dealt, and the legacy that they willed to us. Those who oversee the well-being of historic houses have the responsibility to care for their collections, historic structure(s), and landscape so that future generations will be able to appreciate and learn from and about them.

To meet this responsibility and reduce the cost of conservation treatments and major structural repairs, *Preventive Conservation for Historic House Museums* is an essential resource for the many thousands of historic houses in our country. As Benjamin Franklin said, "An ounce of prevention is worth a pound of cure."

I first learned about preventive conservation when the Museum Program of the National Endowment for the Arts was initiated in 1973. As director of program development and management, I was responsible for coordinating the development of grant guidelines. Leading conservators who acted as our consultants recommended that the guidelines place an emphasis on preventive conservation. While I was director of the American Association of Museums in 1984, our Commission on Museums for a New Century chose promoting preventive conservation as one of its five most important recommendations. Joining Heritage Preservation in 1988 gave me the opportunity to devote my energies to developing programs that promote and support preventive conservation.

For more than thirty years, Heritage Preservation has been one of the leading advocates for promoting preventive conservation measures. Our books *Caring for Your Collections* and *Caring for Your Historic House* were the first broadly available sources of information for individuals. The authors of *Preventive Conservation for Historic House Museums* have integrated the information from these books and, very importantly, expanded upon them to address the unique issues that face historic house museums. After long careers assisting historic house museums, Jane Merritt and Julie Reilly are exceptionally qualified to fulfill this task.

LAWRENCE L. REGER, PRESIDENT
HERITAGE PRESERVATION

Acknowledgments

THE AUTHORS ARE GRATEFUL for the support and encouragement they received from their employers, colleagues, and friends while writing this book. They would like to acknowledge substantial financial support from the Samuel H. Kress Foundation through the FAIC Samuel H. Kress Conservation Publications Fellowship and the National Park Foundation, which supported the photography.

The authors would like to recognize the contributions and thank:

The Nebraska State Historical Society and Jim Potter for support of the book project;

The National Park Service, Harpers Ferry Center, and its director, Don Kodak, Interpretive Planner Mary Mallen, and the staff of Media Assets, with particular thanks to Alice Newton.

The National Society of the Colonial Dames of America, Nebraska Chapter, for their encouragement and interest in the book;

Rebecca L. Stevens for a comprehensive overview of historic house museum structures;

Lucy Lawliss for a great discussion of the cultural landscape of the historic house property;

Mary Coughlin for research and contributions on light dosimeters;

Darryl Herring for his fabulous photographs;

Richard Kerschner for his review of the chapter on environmental control;

Lisa Metzger Grotrian, Debbie Long, Jessica Waite, and Lorrie Monteiro for their help and patience in reading many, many drafts;

The many curators at NPS historic house sites; and Pam West for providing us with images of disasters and emergencies;

And all the staff and volunteers who have ever worked to preserve the historic house museums of America.

Introduction

THERE IS NO ELEMENT OF professional activity in the historic house that protects and preserves the house and its contents more than preventive conservation.

Preventive conservation is the holistic discipline that looks to the events and environments that surround material culture with an eye to slowing the pace of deterioration and preventing damage, wear, and decay. Preventive care includes areas of focus such as the control of environmental conditions like type and levels of light and the amount of relative humidity, and the use of inert housing, storage, and display materials in proximity to collections. These and a number of other elements form the sphere of influence of preventive care. There is no question within the museum profession today of the value of preventive concepts in the practice of conservation, just as there is no question as to the value of preventive health care in the medical profession. Concepts of preventive care are vital to the practice of professional conservation.

Preventive conservation in the context of the historic house museum looks equally to the protection of the historic structure itself, as well as of the items displayed within that structure. The Association for Preservation Technology International (APT) and the American Institute for Conservation of Historic and Artistic Works (AIC), two professional organizations dedicated to the preservation of built heritage and material culture, worked together to create the "New Orleans Charter for the Joint Preservation of Historic Structures and Artifacts" of 1992. This groundbreaking document formalized the complex problems and team decision-making processes that confront the professional museum community when working with historic sites that house material culture. These two organizations continued their collaboration and in 1998 issued "Guidelines for Light and Lighting in Historic Buildings That House Collections." These two documents are found at the end of this introduction.

It is now widely recognized that maintaining and preserving the historic house and its fabric is as important as and may, in some instances, be more important than preserving the collections held within. The extent of interdependence of preventive collection conservation and preventive site conservation should not be underestimated. Solutions to the complex problems that arise from this relationship require an interdisciplinary approach to their problem solving. Historians, engineers, curators, interpreters, conservators, architects, and maintenance professionals involved in working in a historic house context must act together to preserve the sites and collections that constitute our historic house museums.

Preventive care involves investigating and determining aspects of both the intellectual control and the physical control of collections and sites. Intellectual controls include administrative and management policies and procedures that ensure the protection of the site and its contents, such as governance, mission statements, house management policies, emergency response plans, collection management policies, and interpretive plans. Physical controls include security and safety precautions, routine maintenance and cleaning practices, environmental control, pest control, exhibit practices, educational activities, and storage practices.

Many different museum and other professionals are a necessary part of the preventive care team that address all of the intellectual and physical controls needed to care for a site and a collection. The expertise of the team members, and the policies and practices for intellectual and physical controls they develop, should be integrated into one clearly written preventive care plan or Preservation Master Plan for each site. The members of the preventive care team can use the plan to lay out the goals of preservation, determine priorities in care and ascendancy of parts of the site or collection, set down environmental parameters, delineate maintenance schedules, describe cleaning methods and materials, explore the interdependence of public programming and preservation, and provide reference materials for more information. The plan should be reviewed regularly and updated, and it can be used as an effective tool in training staff and board members and informing outside consultants.

This book will introduce preventive care concepts in the context of the historic house setting and develop them to a more advanced level. It will propose a collaborative and informed approach to preservation planning that is based on interdisciplinary research, critical thinking, and observation rather than on rote maintenance schedules and everyday residential cleaning practices. The authors and other colleagues that have contributed to this book embody the knowledge, experience, and practice necessary to synthesize a dynamic, proactive approach to preservation planning for historic sites and their collections.

NEW ORLEANS CHARTER FOR THE JOINT PRESERVATION OF HISTORIC STRUCTURES AND ARTIFACTS

The New Orleans Charter is the product resulting from two symposia on museums in historic buildings held in Montreal, Quebec (1990), and New Orleans, Louisiana (1991), cosponsored by the American Institute for the Conservation of Historic and Artistic Works (AIC) and the Association for Preservation Technology International (APT). This charter has been officially adopted by the boards of directors of both AIC and APT. It was subsequently adopted by the National Council of State Historic Preservation Officers (NCSHPO) at its annual meeting in Washington, D.C., in March 1992; the American Institute of Architects (AIA) Committee on Historic Resources at its spring meeting in April 1993; and the board of directors of the American Association of Museums (AAM) in December 1993:

- Arising from a concern for the coexistence of historic structures and the artifacts within them;
- Recognizing our responsibility as stewards to provide the highest levels of care for the structures and other artifacts placed in our care;
- Recognizing that many significant structures are used to house, display, and interpret artifacts;
- Recognizing that historic structures and the contents placed within them deserve equal consideration in planning for their care;
- Recognizing that technologies and approaches will continue to change; and
- Recognizing that those involved in preservation are part of a continuum, and are neither the first nor the last to affect the preservation of historic structures and artifacts:

We, therefore, adopt these principles as governing the preservation of historic structures and the artifacts housed in them:

1. Institutions' statements of mission should recognize the need to preserve the unique character of both the historic structure and artifacts.
2. The preservation needs of the historic structure and of the artifacts should be defined only after study adequate to serve as the foundation for the preservation of both.
3. Requisite levels of care should be established through the interdisciplinary collaboration of all qualified professionals with potential to contribute.
4. Appropriate preservation must reflect application of recognized preservation practices, including assessment of risk before and after intervention, and the expectation of future intervention.
5. Measures which promote the preservation of either historic structure or the artifacts, at the expense of the other, should not be considered.
6. Regarding public use, the right of future generations to access and enjoyment must outweigh immediate needs.
7. Appropriate preservation strategies should be guided by the specific needs and characteristics of the historic structure and artifacts.
8. Appropriate documentation of all stages of a project is essential, and should be readily accessible and preserved for the future.
9. The most appropriate action in a particular case is one which attains the desired goal with the least intervention to the historic structure and the artifacts.
10. Proposed preservation strategies should be appropriate to the ability of the institution to implement and maintain them.

GUIDELINES FOR LIGHT AND LIGHTING IN HISTORIC BUILDINGS THAT HOUSE COLLECTIONS

On 5–7 November 1998, the Association for Preservation Technology International (APT) and the American Institute for the Conservation of Historic and Artistic Works (AIC) hosted their third symposium on museums in historic buildings as part of APT's thirtieth-anniversary conference in Williamsburg, Virginia. This event focused on the theme of light and lighting in historic buildings that house collections, and included a number of presentations and discussions on this topic. It concluded with a lively forum during which the draft guidelines that were distributed to participants at the beginning of the symposium were reviewed, debated, and refined. The comments made during this forum have since been integrated into the guidelines that follow.

Problems of light and lighting in historic structures that house collections have often been seen as someone else's concern. Collections conservators make recommendations for visible and UV light levels and for filtration. Architectural conservators work on repair or replacement of windows and on historic fixtures. Curators search for historic fixtures, and ask for "better" or more light. But there is rarely a combined effort, or even much discussion, about the function of light in a particular structure or collection, or about the role light may have played in the original design and enjoyment of a particular space. In rare circumstances, when the wishes of the architect or designer are easily known, there may be an automatic reaction against changing anything, even when the preservation of the artifacts housed within is endangered. Then a situation is created where the collections conservator takes a stance on one side, to "protect the collections," and those advocating for the structure take the opposing stance, to "protect the structure" and its original design.

As in other areas where there may be differing opinions and different requirements, the New Orleans Charter may serve as a framework for the resolution of potential conflict.

1. Initially the institution must recognize that light, and the many functions it may play in an interior, are of critical importance to the mission of the institution. These may include the portrayal of the interiors in a state as close to their original appearance as possible, the preservation of original artifacts and structural fabric, and the interpretation of these materials to the public.
2. Adequate study of all aspects of the problem is essential. This does not mean just an understanding of the deleterious effects of light on artifacts, but a deeper investigation into the particular needs of the specific artifacts under discussion, as well as a careful investigation into the original appearance of the interiors and the role light may have played in that appearance.
3. Participation by a variety of individuals is necessary to address these different aspects of the task. Curator, lighting designer, collection and architectural conservators, interpretive staff, and so on should be included.
4. The dedication to "original appearance" must be balanced against the known risks associated with light exposure. Especially important is the need to include the possibility of shifts in natural light, or the possibility that light (levels, color, etc.) should be changed to accommodate a variety of needs.
5. The needs of visually impaired visitors must be accommodated, while understanding that this accommodation may involve temporary changes rather than permanent ones.
6. Plans to provide or control natural and artificial light must be designed to answer the specific needs of a situation rather than based on a generalized plan developed from other situations.

Figure 1.1 Arlington House, Robert E. Lee Memorial, U.S. National Park Service, Arlington, Virginia. Parged exterior of the Greek revival–style home of the Custis and Lee families.

CHAPTER 1

Preventive Conservation and the Historic House Museum

As an individual, community, and nation we care for and preserve those things that have value to us, most often starting with our own homes and possessions. In nineteenth-century America, activists recognized that there was a need to preserve houses and their contents and buildings of architectural, historical, and cultural significance that were threatened by neglect or the encroachment of the modern world. Thus began a movement to create historic house museums and to open them to the public. In doing so the stories of our past and our identities as a people are shared, communicated, and preserved. To ensure that the maximum information from the past is passed on to future generations, an approach of preservation, retention, maintenance, repair, and conservation is advocated.

Preventive conservation, or preventive care, is the mitigation of deterioration and damage to cultural property through the formulation and implementation of policies and procedures for all of the activities that are fundamental to a museum that can affect the preservation of the site and the collection.[1] It supports the primary function of a museum to protect collections so they may be enjoyed by the generations to come.

Preventive conservation has proven to be a cost-effective means to extend the life of a cultural property and reduce the need for interventive treatments. It involves a continuous process of developing and implementing policies and procedures; their ongoing assessment and review; and inspection, monitoring, and revision. This book advocates a holistic approach to the management of the historic house site, in which the structure, landscape, systems, and collections are considered an integrated resource to preserve through the preventive conservation approach. A key benefit from using this holistic approach is that you create and work in teams and use the resources of many specialists and practitioners in the preservation activities, not unlike the original owners and occupants of historic properties.

To create an effective preventive care program at your institution, you will need to involve all staff and volunteers. Each will play a role and have a perspective based on his or her experience and area of work that will shape policy documents and procedures. The process most often begins with an evaluation of current conditions through an assessment. Ideally this assessment is performed by a team of professionals with

Figure 1.2 Furnished parlor of Arlington House, Robert E. Lee Memorial, U.S. National Park Service, Arlington, Virginia.

various areas of expertise, who visit the site and evaluate the facilities, collections, planning documents, procedures, and staffing. The team identifies the threats to the museum and its collections and tries to evaluate the severity of the risk in order to set priorities for corrective actions. From this information, the museum can set goals and develop a strategy for success. Some corrections may be able to be made almost immediately, while others may take years to effect and may require a capital fund-raising campaign to accomplish the work. This initial assessment begins the process of creating a Preservation Master Plan for the museum.

THE PRESERVATION MASTER PLAN

Every historic house museum needs a written Preservation Master Plan in which all of the institution's activities are considered in the context of preservation. It puts together in one document all of the concerns and threats to the museum, delineates and determines the risk and potential for damage, prioritizes required actions, and finally, highlights the benefits realized from a preventive care approach. Just as every museum and its collections are unique, the Preservation Master Plan will be specific and unique to the institution.

Preventive care has long been recognized as the most effective means of mitigating damage and deterioration of a house and its contents. As you proceed through this book you will note that many of the techniques that are advocated here have their foundations in traditional housekeeping practices. What the profession of conservation brings to this arena is a methodical approach, in which the care processes are based on scientific research and are well documented.

HISTORY OF CARE AND CLEANING

In their day, historic houses and their contents were maintained and cleaned by their contemporary owners, occupants, and in many cases, servants and slaves. Depending on the period of the structure, the time of its occupation, and the prevailing social norms, care and upkeep involved different levels of cleanliness and presentation using a variety of methods, tools, and materials. The emphasis of housekeeping was to keep house interiors and family possessions in a state of usefulness and preserved aesthetics for as long as possible. Care involved protection, cleaning, repair, and seasonal rotations—techniques, in fact, that form the basis of many of our preventive conservation practices today.

Care procedures emphasized protection and prevention. For example, a house would be sited where water would not seep inside. It was graded so rainwater drained away from the foundation. Gutters aided in this process, and they were inspected and cleaned out on a regular basis. Covers protected the furnishings from wear and light. Precious carpets were covered by a lightweight and durable fabric, usually made of linen. These covers also facilitated cleaning routines. Graphic representation in paintings and drawings, the written word, and oral traditions all inform today's caretakers of the practical approach to housekeeping taken in the past.

From the mid-seventeenth century onward, the people who cleaned the homes or managed the tasks of the servants who cleaned the homes had specific guidance from published manuals. Housekeeping recommendations were referenced in ladies' letters and diaries, and the first printed instructions began to appear in books as early as the late 1400s.[2] By the nineteenth century, the writing of these instructional manuals on the management or maintenance of a household was a flourishing industry and a tradition that continues today. Homemakers read these manuals and enlisted the assistance of a range of practitioners in keeping the house and gardens well run, neat, and tidy. It is a recent concept to have these buildings, grounds, and furnishings converted to museums to be maintained by formally trained museum professionals.

Social, religious, physical, economic, and technical forces have affected the evolution of housekeeping and changed the definition of "clean." Understanding the contemporary definition of cleanliness and its importance to the human condition affects the amount and type of care expended on a structure and its contents. Today we buy soaps that are antibacterial, toilet brushes that eject and flush, and surface wipes that are disposable and sanitary. This raises the level of hygiene of our homes and simplifies cleaning tasks, but it may complicate our perception and expectation of cleanliness in the historic house museum and lead to well-meaning but misinformed overcleaning and potential damage to collections.

For example, water is an essential element in most house care activities today. The availability of a supply of clean water for housekeeping activities has had a tremendous effect on the methods, materials, and labor required to perform a specific cleaning task. In America, the ready availability of potable water was, until fairly recently, the primary challenge for those responsible for keeping houses clean. Water was usually carried in buckets from wells, requiring much labor to keep a house supplied with water, and therefore dry systems of cleaning were devised. In the eighteenth century, sand rather than water was used to clean floors. The sand was spread on the floor and then swept up. It absorbed grease and oil deposits and lightly abraded the wood surface. Occasionally, sand was dampened to offer additional cleaning benefit, but actual wet cleaning was rare. Finely powdered sand was sometimes spread on the floors and left to absorb grease and to prevent dirt and spills from staining the wood. Mixtures of leafy herbs such as tansy, mint, and fennel were strewn on the bare floors and rubbed or swept about to deodorize and freshen the floors.[3]

Another critical element that altered house care practices was the installation of electricity in the home. Homekeeping technologies soon developed that took advantage of this new power source. Machines that captured household dust, such as sweepers, were invented and perfected. The vacuum cleaner was invented in the early twentieth century, and it remains one of the most employed cleaning tools in the home. It continues to undergo improvements to include better filtration, variable suction, to weigh less, and most recently adding a supplementary dust collection/polishing cloth to the vacuum. Electricity also led to the introduction of bright, clean, on-demand lighting in homes, which meant one could see the dirt more clearly and there were now more available lighted hours inside to spend on housework. These new technologies provided faster means to do this work.

It is important to understand that we cannot bring our twenty-first-century perception of a clean house to the historic house interior. Rather, the level of cleanliness we seek to sustain in the historic house needs to be appropriate to the interpretive period of the site, the economic resources of the occupants, and their personal preferences, if known.

THE TRANSITION FROM HOME CARE TO PREVENTIVE CONSERVATION

Most historic houses have gone through great periods of change, and many were at some point abandoned or neglected for a time before being converted to museum use. Some were commandeered by militia for campaign headquarters or hospitals, or divided into multiple-unit dwellings and later converted back to single-family units. Others were used for nonresidential purposes such as storage locations, offices, and businesses. Some were inhabited until the moment they became historic house museums.

Whatever the history of the house, the transition from home care or housekeeping to preventive care as a museum has an impact on the structure's condition and preservation. Sometimes caretakers stay on at the property as it transitions into a museum. There can be both benefits and challenges to such a situation. Their knowledge of family, home, and collection history and their care and commitment to the site is incomparable. On the other hand, the transition to professional museum practices can be difficult for seasoned caretakers. Inherited pre-museum practices are often continued in instances where housekeeping staff is retained as museum staff.

It can also be difficult for academically trained museum professionals, who may never have cleaned their own rooms, let alone an entire house, to take charge of a historic house museum. If they have experience in home care, it is often limited to the style or approach used in contemporary living spaces with modern materials and methods. Such housekeeping practices may not transfer to the historic house or to the materials and technologies of historic decorative arts and collections. Respect for and knowledge of historic approaches to housekeeping are important in developing a sound approach to preventive care in the historic house setting. Understanding the housekeeping methods of the period is integral to the development of a responsible approach to preventive care and maintenance for the property today.

A HOLISTIC APPROACH

The care and preservation of historic house sites requires a holistic approach and constant communication among those sharing this task. All aspects of preventive care in a historic house setting are deeply intertwined and cross many disciplines. Successful preventive care is a team activity. Each team member, from the site custodian to the museum director, brings unique and specialized information and problem-solving skills to the process. Architects, conservators, curators, educators, engineers, maintenance staff, docents, exhibit staff, and sales shop personnel all have a contributory role on the preventive care team. Once staff understands the advantages to this approach, the museum will benefit in ways that only time will fully reveal. While the preventive care strategy is one that will pay off in the short term, the greatest benefits will come year after year as major interventions at the site or with the collections are rarely necessary.

Trusted with the preservation of heritage, the stewards of each historic house need to act responsibly and provide the best possible care for the property that experience and budget permits. It is a continuous struggle, because deterioration is an ongoing process. We know today that adopting the tenets of preventive conservation will bring long-term benefits to the museum and its collections. Developing a Preservation Master Plan for your site will ensure your success.

Figure 2.1 Scotty's Castle, Death Valley National Park, Death Valley, California.

Evolution of the Historic House Museum

HISTORIC HOUSE MUSEUMS help to build cultural identity. Here visitors participate in the ideas, people, events, politics, and society that shaped a region, a people, a nation. Once a house is established as a museum, its functions change and it is used in a way rarely intended by the original owners or builders. It is the job of the present-day caretakers to preserve the site given these new and changing circumstances. To accomplish this goal, it is essential to develop a preventive care program that encompasses all aspects of site activities from care of the building and interiors to living history programs to research and documentation.

HISTORIC HOUSES

The custom of visiting great houses is centuries old. In Britain and elsewhere in Europe, visitors to estates viewed grand galleries decorated with works of fine art, often collected by the owner while traveling to foreign countries. Accounts of these visits exist in letters and diaries and are described in literature. It is not a great leap from wanting to visit stately homes to wanting to preserve and establish them as museums.

Societies need to develop and hold on to a social or national identity. One means of doing this is to protect heritage, which records changes during the passage of time and documents the ravages of war and revolution. America began to preserve important historic sites early in its history. The Jonathan Hasbrouck House in Newburgh, New York, was the earliest house museum established in the United States. The site was the military headquarters of George Washington during the Revolutionary War. It was purchased by New York State in 1850 and became the first government-funded historic house museum. In 1853, the Mount Vernon Ladies' Association was founded to save and restore Mount Vernon, the Virginia home of George Washington. It was opened to the public in 1860 as the first privately funded historic house museum. Those early advocates seeking to preserve a site were generally women of means who volunteered their time for an important cause. Today the preservation field consists of professional historians, architects, and facility managers, among others, who work in government and in the private sector to preserve historic places. However, the volunteer is still the backbone of many institutions and in particular the small historic house museum.

THE HISTORIC PRESERVATION MOVEMENT IN THE UNITED STATES

In 1933 Laurence Vail Coleman, director of the American Association of Museums, wrote:

> Some buildings are distinguished from the moment they are finished, and the future may destroy them only at great loss. Some buildings achieve importance by withstanding the assaults of time and so gaining values that they did not have while in company with many of their kind. Other buildings have greatness thrust upon them by acts of man that create hallowed associations.[1]

Sites are saved because of their association with famous owners, architects, U.S. presidents, authors, warriors, industrialists, and significant events. In the United States, we have many laws and regulations that protect our natural and cultural heritage at the federal, state, and local levels. Natural sites of great beauty were already coming under state or national protection by the middle of the nineteenth century. As early as 1906, Congress acted to protect historic and prehistoric ruins and monuments on federal lands by passing the Antiquities Act (16 U.S.C. 431-433), which was signed into law by President Theodore Roosevelt.

The cultural, societal, and technological changes that occurred during the twentieth century had a profound effect on how Americans lived and spent their leisure time. It is not surprising that the preservation movement sought to preserve and protect our natural and cultural heritage from loss so that it could be enjoyed by the citizens. After World War II, highways began to cross the country and motoring became a recreational pastime. Scenic parkways were established where the speed (low) was controlled so that a visitor could experience a leisurely drive through natural wonders (figure 2.2). Automation and the workers' rights

Figure 2.2 Purgatory Mountain Parking Widening (mile 92.2), U.S. National Park Service, Blue Ridge Parkway, Virginia. Photographer: Abbie Rowe, 1940s; NPS Historic Photograph Collection, Harpers Ferry Center, Harpers Ferry, West Virginia.

movement were also contributing to the increase in leisure time, and this leisure time could now be spent driving to a historic site and experiencing the past or a significant event. Coleman also made the observation that automobiles and historic house museums multiplied during the same decades.[2] As people traveled in their cars for recreation with the ability to go to areas that were not served by train lines, they were ready to visit sites that were scattered across the country. Writing at a time when Americans' interest in house museums was increasing, Coleman advocated the creation of a national system of historic houses.

At the same time, Americans were moving from the cities into newly created suburbs. The cities saw jobs and populations leave and neighborhoods and buildings deteriorate. A popular solution to deal with the decay of the cities was to create urban renewal projects that tore down many older neighborhoods—and with them many historic structures. A national concern was developing that unchecked development would endanger our built heritage and would change the look of the country if it were not subjected to controls. Congress responded to this concern and in 1966 passed the National Historic Preservation Act. The outcome of this legislation was a national historic preservation program implemented by the Department of the Interior and the National Park Service (NPS).

The NPS devised a system that delegates the identification, documentation, and preservation of historic properties to State Historic Preservation Offices (SHPOs), using guidance from the NPS and the Secretary of the Interior. Since the 1960s, federal, state, tribal, and private programs have cooperated to preserve historic sites. It is essential to know that legislation exists to help with preservation activities at historic houses and to keep work performed at sites within regulations to protect properties and to prevent lawsuits.

The National Historic Preservation Act also authorized the creation of the National Register of Historic Places, which is the nation's official list of cultural resources that have been evaluated using set standards and have been determined to have significance and be worthy of preservation. Listed sites are eligible for some federal benefits. This program is also administered by the NPS.

States and local governments have also enacted legislation to protect the historic nature of their community. Some of these laws may have stricter requirements than the federal laws. It is important for any institution to consult all applicable laws—be they federal, state, or local—when seeking information or funding support or looking to perform work on the site.

The cadre of skilled preservation professionals that exists at the federal, state, and local level includes historic architects, archaeologists, and historians. They can help a site understand and apply relevant preservation and environmental laws, policies, standards, and guidelines to short-term and long-range planning and operations. Their expertise should be sought to inte-

TWO KEY RELEVANT FEDERAL REGULATIONS

The National Historic Preservation Act (NHPA), Section 106

NHPA established a federal program to identify, preserve, and protect historic resources. A key part of this act that is particularly applicable to historic house museums is Section 106, which involves the impact that a change to a property may have on the integrity of that property. Section 106 applies to properties on or eligible for the National Register of Historic Places. All potential changes or modifications proposed for a historic resource must be studied and approved by government employees in the SHPO or other government office.

A large historic site with many buildings wished to make one of their houses wheelchair accessible. The house is a brick colonial with the front door facing out onto a quiet estuary. Without consulting the applicable authorities, the staff constructed a long ramp out of pressure-treated lumber, which started at the side of the house and extended along much of its front to the doorway. The impact of this addition was significant and dramatically changed the appreciation of the site. Eventually a different solution was found to make the house wheelchair accessible and the wooden ramp was removed. Consultation with the applicable government office would have saved this site the expense of constructing the ramp.

National Environmental Policy Act (NEPA), Section 102

While NHPA protects built heritage, NEPA (42 U.S.C. 4321) was passed by Congress to create a national policy to protect, maintain, and enhance the environment. It was conceived to preserve our environment by requiring protections for wetlands and shores (invasive species management coordinated with site landscape) and requires an environmental impact statement for projects that receive federal funds. This law too can have an effect on the house museum and should be understood by those seeking to modify the landscape.

A colonial-style house had a small stream running past it. A previous owner decided to stem the stream to create a pond in front of the home. The pond thrived and became a sanctuary for many types of local fauna and flora. But as the decades passed, the site's water table rose and became a problem for the house itself, with water seeping into the basement. The logical repair is to lower the water table by permitting the stream to flow again, but recent development blocks what would be the path of the stream. The site cannot drain the pond either without complying with NEPA regulations, as it is classified as wetlands.

grate federal accessibility laws and sustainable design practices into work projects. While a site may be privately owned, it must still comply with certain federal regulations. If a site obtains federal funds to use for projects that involve historic resources, there are additional requirements that must be met in order to maintain eligibility for federal funding. Preservation professionals can help work through these regulations, and they are necessary members of a stewardship team.

ORGANIZATIONS THAT SUPPORT THE PRESERVATION OF HISTORIC HOUSE MUSEUMS

Professional organizations have recognized the unique attributes of the historic house museum and have created specialized interest committees to help staff at historic houses understand their challenges and to provide guidance. The American Association of Museums (AAM) has the Historic House Museum Professional Interest Committee to assist historic house museums with issues that are common to all museums and with issues unique to historic houses. In 1998 the International Council of Museums (ICOM) created the committee DemHist, where members meet periodically to explore themes and issues relevant to historic site museums. The American Association for State and Local History (AASLH) created the Historic House Initiative. Membership in one or more of these groups is recommended.

DIVERSITY OF HISTORIC HOUSE MUSEUMS

The range of preserved sites has broadened appreciably, reflecting the many peoples who have built our past. Today someone can visit an elegant house (figure 2.3), a pioneer cabin, slave quarters (figure 2.4), the inner-city tenement house of an immigrant, a house of worship, or a school.

Figure 2.3 Hampton National Historic Site, Towson, Maryland.

Figure 2.4 Slave quarters at Melrose Mansion, Natchez National Historical Park, Natchez, Mississippi.

Historian Patricia West makes the case that while these sites are there to bring history to their visitors, they are equally the product of the political trends of the period of their establishment.[3] Institutions are recognizing that their history may not be as simple as once interpreted, and there is a trend to broaden the perspectives of the stories they tell.

As sites become more inclusive, the routines of daily life and those who supported those routines have an increased role in a site's interpretation. Many houses now open their kitchens, laundry rooms, or dairies (figure 2.5). Visitors tend to find an immediate connection with the tools and items displayed here, perhaps recognizing a gadget from their childhood. They marvel how people managed without so many of our modern conveniences. The time when visitors typically entered a house through the front door as a guest has given way to using the entrance that most suits the interpretive theme of the site.

Hampton National Historic Site is a property with a Georgian mansion (previously owned by a prominent first family in Maryland), agricultural lands and buildings, and living quarters of the African slaves and servants who supported the family and their businesses. The interpretation of the site has expanded over the years to tell the stories of all the inhabitants of Hampton and to preserve the extant structures, whether mansion, farm, or slave quarters.

Figure 2.5 Kitchen at Johnson Farm at Blue Ridge Parkway, U.S. National Park Service, North Carolina.

EXPANSION IN FUNCTIONS

Just as the politics or trends of interpretation of the house museums change, so do the functions. House museums are central to the life of a community. They may host holiday events or founder's day activities, or offer a purpose to those who wish to contribute time and expertise as volunteers and members of a board of directors. Visiting a site reaches far beyond seeing the collections and learning the story of the occupants to understanding the life and era of its occupation. Educational programs and activities inform the visitor about the past—the hardships as well as the luxuries. Students on school trips make up a significant number of the visitors to many sites. Programs about period cooking, farming methods, and medical practices, or leisure activities such as dancing and musical events are often scheduled at sites (figure 2.6).

Figure 2.6 Musical program at Blue Ridge Parkway, U.S. National Park Service, North Carolina.

Some sites may have farm animals that are there to emphasize their importance to the original occupants, making these sites particularly popular destinations for children.

Visiting house museums has always been a leisure-time activity, and heritage tourism is now a significant portion of today's leisure market. Sites often serve refreshments or meals, and rent out space for parties and receptions; some accept overnight guests, and there are destination villages such as Colonial Williamsburg where visitors can "experience" life in the eighteenth century. Many of these activities are driven by a need

Figure 2.7 Sheep shearing during Celebrations Museum Day at the Textile Museum, Washington, D.C.

to raise funds to maintain the site and keep it open and staffed. It is critical for all staff to communicate and work together on most aspects of operations, and this need is even more critical when a site begins to expand its activities beyond the act of receiving visitors for an exhibit or house tour (figure 2.7). The diverse nature of this category of museum necessitates management guidelines that reflect their complexity. Operational standards need to be clearly defined, based on the sound principles of preventive care that will prepare the site for more changes that will undoubtedly come for the historic house museum.

CHAPTER 3

Principles of Preventive Conservation

An Overview

THOSE WHO WORK IN THE historic house museum may not have had formal training in the actual processes of conserving and preserving their collections. Only a handful of academic programs have classes or courses in preventive or interventive conservation, and even fewer of those discuss the processes by which conservation of collections occurs. Many institutions do not have conservators on staff, and many more have never engaged the services of one for any conservation activity, consultation, or treatment. Therefore, how does the staff at a small museum begin the process of conservation of the collection? The first step is to understand how the conservation profession defines itself and its work.

DEFINITIONS

Conservation (also referred to as *artifact conservation* or *object conservation*) describes activities that preserve and protect cultural resources. These activities include object examination, documentation, treatment, stabilization, restoration, and preventive care. Conservation seeks to minimize physical and chemical damage to collections through both preventive care practices and actual conservation treatments. There are several fundamental tenets of conservation that include the need to preserve the significance and contextual information of an object. Much of what is discussed in this book is in the arena of preventive conservation, as it is the most efficient and cost-effective means of protecting cultural heritage.

Preventive conservation (used interchangeably with *preventive care*) seeks to protect collections from deterioration and damage through the formulation and implementation of policies and control procedures dealing with environmental conditions, object handling, storage, exhibition, use (including consumptive

Figure 3.1 Textile conservator wet-cleaning an embroidered sampler.

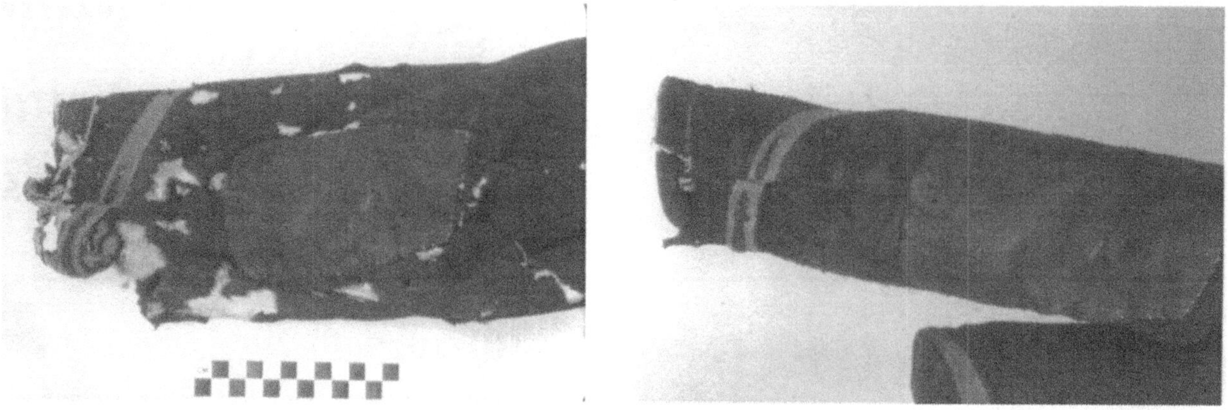

Figure 3.2 *Left*: Detail from the sleeve of a Civil War uniform jacket before undergoing conservation treatment. *Right*: Detail of the same sleeve of a Civil War uniform jacket after conservation treatment. Photos by Susan Schmalz.

use), integrated pest management, packing, transport, emergency preparedness and response, reproduction, reformatting, and duplication. The goal of preventive conservation is to diminish the daily stresses on collections that build up over time and to avoid catastrophic damage or loss.

Conservation treatment is the intentional intervention or alteration of the physical and/or chemical state of cultural resources to extend their existence (figure 3.2). Treatment may seek to stabilize the object without affecting its integrity. Stabilization seeks to minimize further deterioration. When treatment is performed to return an object to an original or known state, it is called *restoration*. Usually, this requires the addition of nonoriginal materials to the object. Paintings, tapestries, carpets, and furniture are among the types of objects that are routinely restored. Conservation treatments are thoroughly documented in a written report, with images and a detailed list of materials that were used to effect the treatment.

When preventive care practices are effective, conservation treatments will rarely be necessary. In order to develop a preventive conservation program your institution needs to understand the responsibility it has to preserve its resources. This means that the institution must have its foundation documents in order.[1]

A *conservator* is someone who through training, knowledge, and professional experience furthers the work of conservation—a practitioner skilled in both the theories and practices of preventive conservation and conservation treatments. Generally, a person will specialize in specific types of materials (e.g., books, photographic materials, fine and decorative arts, textiles, etc.). Generally the role of the conservator is to assess the condition of objects, perform treatments, survey the condition of collections, identify signs and causes of object deterioration, provide information and advice about the environment and object handling, recommend preventive care practices, and conduct research.

The American Institute for Conservation of Historic and Artistic Works (AIC) is a national membership organization for conservators that advances and promotes the importance of the preservation of cultural property. This organization has categories of membership based on interest, qualification, and fitness to further the purposes of the AIC. Professional associate and fellow members agree to practice conservation in accordance with a Code of Ethics and Guidelines for Practice established by the membership. The AIC maintains a membership list of conservators by geographic region, area of specialization, and category of membership.[2]

DETERMINING THE NEED FOR CONSERVATION

A site needs to fully understand its purpose as a collection-holding institution and its collections policies before undertaking conservation work. Is your collection important for its aesthetic qualities? Is it a research collection? Is the collection unique? Does it have historic significance? Individual objects in a collection may be important for one or all of these reasons. The "place" of an artifact in a collection will determine its conservation needs. Archival collections with items that are important for their historic and cultural content often do not receive extensive cosmetic conservation procedures; instead, efforts are directed toward preserving the content and not necessarily the appearance of the original materials. Objects in research collections are conserved with the intent to prevent interference with their research potential. Art collections often receive more attention to cosmetic or aesthetic condition problems. Ethnographic and folk art collections are often stabilized, but not restored to previous appearances. The nature of the collection is an important determinant in its conservation.

LAYING THE FOUNDATIONS FOR CONSERVATION

The policies and procedures adopted and enforced by a collection-holding organization constitute an important line of defense in protecting the collections and the historic structure from inadvertent or accidental damages and loss. Referred to as "intellectual controls," they are usually written and managed, for the most part, by the curatorial department or administrative staff. They can include the mission statement, scope of collections statement, organizational goals and objectives, historic house policies, collection management policies, and other written documents that form the intellectual framework of the organization.

Among all of an institution's foundation documents, it is the Collections Policy or Collections Management Plan that best describes and supports the preventive conservation activities. This document sets down in writing the institution's professional standards and practices, which should follow standards set by the American Association of Museums. A good plan includes information about the history of the site and collection, the scope of the collection, cataloguing and documentation systems, records management, security, environment, storage, exhibits, routine and cyclic maintenance, access and use, staffing, planning, programming, and funding. When all of these topics are addressed, the resulting document becomes the manual for the care and preservation of the institution's cultural resources. With a clear idea of the depth and breadth of a collection and an understanding of the importance and priority of the collection to the institution, the process of collection conservation can begin.

Physical controls in tandem with the intellectual controls contribute to the preservation of collections and structures. They include methods to mitigate the effects of temperature, relative humidity, poor storage materials, and pest infestation on our cultural heritage. They prevent the chemical and physical sources of damage in the environment surrounding an object or structure from adversely affecting collections and structures.

THE CONSERVATION ASSESSMENT

In the United States there is a formalized process to assist with determining the conservation needs of museums and obtaining support, which is supported by professional organizations such as the American Association of Museums and the American Institute for Conservation and by governmental funding institutions. The first step in the conservation process is to complete a Conservation Assessment, a tool designed to help institutions learn about their current ability to care for their collection and meet current standards for professional practice through both intellectual and physical controls.[3] A Conservation Assessment offers prioritized recommendations for both short- and long-term collections care activities, and forms the baseline for the development of a long-term conservation plan. The assessment ends with a detailed written report on the policies, practices, and conditions within an institution that impact collection survival. It should include the following nine areas:

1. General information about the site and the collection
2. Staffing for collection care and site maintenance
3. Sites and structures
4. Climate control and environment at the site
   - temperature/relative humidity
   - pollutants and particulates
   - illumination
   - pest control
   - housekeeping
5. Collections and collections policies
6. Exhibition of collections
7. Storage of collections
8. Emergency preparedness for the site and collection
9. Security and safety of the collection and site

The goal of a Conservation Assessment is to assist and inform the on site staff, board, and volunteers about the state of preservation at a site and to recommend priority actions to improve collection care and conservation for the collection.

The Conservation Assessment Process

The Conservation Assessment is conducted through a pre-visit questionnaire, an on-site visit, and the completion of a written report describing, summarizing, and prioritizing the findings of the investigation.

The pre-visit questionnaire is filled out in advance by the staff of the institution and returned to the assessor so the conservator can prepare for the upcoming visit. It is about sixteen pages long and will take some effort to complete if there is little institutional information already compiled. The questions cover the areas listed above and may require the input of more than one staff member.

The on-site visit usually lasts one to three days, depending on the size of the collection and extent of the site. During the visit, the assessor and museum staff will visit each room in each structure and will visit each collection area. The assessor will be looking for and asking about all nine areas covered by the assessment.

After the site visit, the conservator will prepare a written draft report that covers the findings of the assessment and will be thirty to forty pages long. The draft will be sent to the site staff for review and comment before a final report is prepared. The final assessment report should have a one- to two-page executive summary attached that can be shared with board members, community leaders, and the press, if desired.

If you have a historic building(s), the assessment process should include an architectural assessor as well as a conservator/collection assessor. The architectural assessor will represent the needs of the historic structures under the institution's care. The recommendations of the architectural assessor should be integrated with those of the conservation assessor.

Obtaining a Conservation Assessment

Conservation Assessments are performed by experienced assessors and can be arranged through a technical assistance program of the Institute of Museum and Library Services (IMLS) called the Conservation Assessment Program (CAP).[4] CAP is managed by Heritage Preservation[5] and is noncompetitive in that awards are made on a first come, first served basis. There is no required match for the program awards, but a minimal amount of financial contribution is required by the institution to cover all the assessment costs.

To find out more about the CAP program, call Heritage Preservation or visit the Heritage Preservation website. You can get a sample of a completed successful application and the application forms from them. It is best to complete the application as soon as possible and have it ready to submit on the day the award deadline is announced. This will ensure that your application gets to Heritage Preservation as soon as possible.

Conservation Assessments are also completed outside of the CAP program. A conservator and/or architectural assessor can be engaged directly by your institution. Funding can come from operational sources or donations or from other grant programs such as the IMLS Conservation Project Support (CPS) grants. CAP grants are designated for smaller institutions, but CPS grants can be awarded for assessments of larger institutions. Assessments usually cost around $4,000 per assessor, plus travel and other expenses.

Selecting an Assessor or Conservator

The best way to find a conservator is through personal references from your colleagues. If you are in an area with fewer conservators, you can find the nearest conservator by using the AIC referral list on the AIC website. This website also offers a pamphlet called *Selecting a Conservator* that can be downloaded. Heritage Preservation will send a list of approved and experienced assessors for you with the announcement of your CAP award.

However you find conservators for the work you would like to have done, you should ask for a resume and a list of references. The conservator should be able to send samples of work completed that is comparable to the project you have in mind. You should talk with the conservator over the phone or meet with him or her in person to ensure a good fit between you, your institution, and the conservator.

THE ASSESSMENT AS PLANNING TOOL

The Conservation Assessment report should be used to develop the Preservation Master Plan. Staff from different departments or areas of the institution should be drawn together to form a conservation planning group to blend institutional priorities and integrate the assessment recommendations. As with all long-range planning, efforts can be advanced on several fronts simultaneously, taking into account long-range and short-range improvements. The conservation/preservation plan should be in written form and should elucidate assumptions, rationales, and goals. The items in the long-range plan may include both intellectual control improvements (inventory, cataloguing, photo-documentation) and physical control improvements (environmental conditions, storage, exhibition methods).

The Conservation Assessment report and the long-range plan should detail preventive measures to undertake to preserve the collection, and indicate which parts of the collection are most significant to the institution and which parts are likely to be in the most need of conservation. The planning process will also determine which parts of the collection should be the first to receive a Conservation Collection Condition Survey.

CONSERVATION COLLECTION CONDITION SURVEY

A Conservation Collection Condition Survey is a tool that examines individual objects for their specific conservation needs. The process involves examining each object in the collection or portion of the collection for condition, treatment needs, housing needs, exhibition recommendations, and storage methods. For example, a textile conservator can be engaged to evaluate all or part of the textiles in your collection, or an objects conservator can be engaged to survey the objects. In general, a Conservation Collection Condition Survey covers a discrete portion of a collection (figure 3.3), although in some cases complete collection surveys are undertaken.

Prior to the survey visit, the conservator should prepare a survey form in consultation with the curatorial staff of the institution, taking into account the specifics of the collection. The form will determine the data to be collected. The data collected should be able to answer the questions prompting the survey. Each item is individually examined unless the collection is prohibitively large, in which case random sampling is used to select items for individual examination, or groups of similar objects are examined and reported en masse.

The survey data should be used to summarize the needs of the collection. Roughly 10 percent to 15 percent of the average collection will require interventive conservation treatment by a conservator for preservation. A large majority of objects usually require preventive measures for long-term survival, and many of the needed procedures can be performed by on-site staff. Surveys are often done using database software so that a variety of information can be generated for all or parts of the surveyed group. The survey data will indicate which items, at what priority, require what kind of conservation work by what kind of practitioner. The data should include time estimates for the recommended work.

OBJECT TREATMENT

After conservation assessment, preservation planning, and a collection survey, it is finally time for individual object treatments. Ironically, many museum professionals and board members think conservation treatment of individual objects is "conservation of the collection," when in reality it is one step in a long process and not a final step at that.

The conservation treatment process must begin with an examination report and a treatment proposal. The examination report should describe the object, its materials, manufacture, maker/artist, appearance, and condition. The treatment proposal should systematically recommend treatment procedures, ideally with options, to correct condition problems and to preserve and conserve the object. An examination report and treatment proposal is required by current conservation professional practice standards prior to the start of any work on the object. The treatment proposal must be signed and approved by the owner or an agent for the owner before any work is undertaken. The proposal should also come with a clear estimate of the time and costs for the work. After the conservation treatment is completed, the conservator sends the owner a treatment report detailing the work done, including the materials and techniques used, and before and after treatment photo documentation.

Figure 3.3 On-site survey project in which two conservators examine firearms.

This is the basic course for responsible conservation for collections. Clearly, one must have the advice and input of consultants in different specializations to make this process a success. Financial resources are required and can come from many sources: grant awards such as the National Endowment for the Humanities Preservation Assistance Grant program (PAG) and the Institute for Museum and Library Services, Conservation Project Support program; donations; and operational funds (established through dedicated budgetary line items). Staff, volunteers, and board members must be available to assist with assessments, conduct strategic planning, and implement preservation recommendations.

Museums are chronically underfunded, but this sound sequence of assessments and planning activities makes excellent use of limited resources. Every step along the way is positive progress, ensuring that scarce resources are used efficiently toward the activities that will best preserve the collections. Each achievement, however small, should be celebrated and shared. Each realistic goal set and each goal achieved is a step in the right direction.

RISK ASSESSMENT AND MANAGEMENT

This discussion on preventive conservation should conclude with a note regarding risk assessment and management—the process of identifying vulnerabilities, analyzing risk, and implementing controls. A set of tools is used that evaluates risk and helps manage its impact. These tools have been used extensively in medicine, biology, engineering, ecology, insurance, and business and are now finding increasing application in the preservation of cultural heritage. There are many methods and systems in use for risk assessment and decision making, from simple decision trees to mathematical predictive models that require sophisticated computers for analysis and determination. The most simplistic methods can be and are being applied to the museum context. In general, they serve to remind us of the information we should keep in mind when assessing risks to collections and the thought processes that we should be using when making decisions about risk management in our collection environments.

Conservators in England and in Canada have been extrapolating risk assessment and management tools from other disciplines and applying them to the museum environment.[6] These works remind us to consider the relative probability that a hazard will occur, the relative potential for damage that a hazard may present, the relative effects on collection materials that a hazard may create, and the relative ability to manage the effects of the hazard. For example, the probability that a fire may occur may be small, but the potential for damage or total loss to a collection from a fire is huge and the effects are generally irreversible. However, we have developed systems of fire detection and suppression that are considered standard for museum environments, which can be effective and significantly reduce the potential for damage from a fire. If the most sophisticated systems are too expensive, there are less expensive alternatives that may provide less protection. Cost-benefit analysis can help determine the most cost-effective solution for the risk associated with fire hazards for your specific museum environment. These tools remind us that rote solutions to potential risks to collections are never the most informed answers. These tools will most likely continue to be developed for museum application and should result in changes in how preventive conservation solutions are chosen by those charged with the care and preservation of collections.

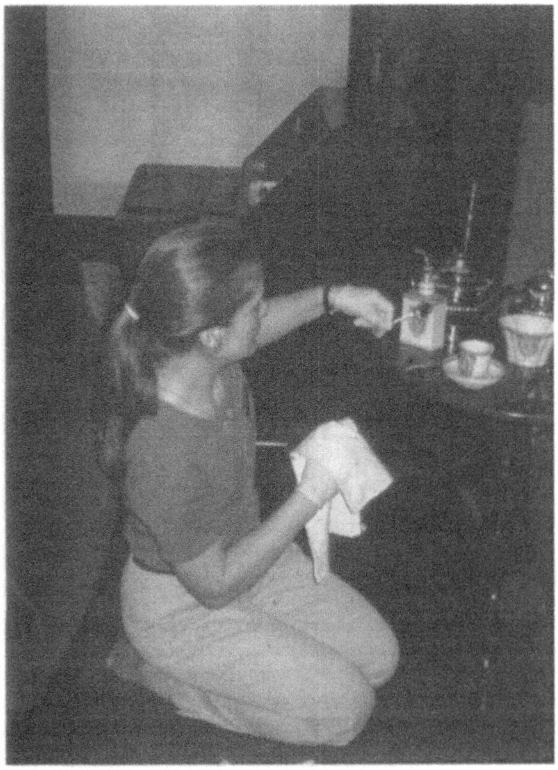

Figure 3.4 Curatorial assistant dusting in furnished room at Adams National Historical Park, Quincy, Massachusetts.

Intellectual and Physical Controls

INTELLECTUAL CONTROLS

Intellectual controls include the broad statements of intent that define an organization and the collections it holds in trust. The highest tier of organizational paperwork might include articles of incorporation, tax status documentation, donors' wills, bylaws, and documentation of county, state, and/or federal legislation. From these written documents, the fundamental purpose of the organization and mission statement should be clearly defined.

A variety of resources are needed to develop foundation intellectual controls. Many institutions have an advisory council or a board of directors who guide and support the institution by donating time, funds, or expertise. Most often these advisers are professionals and members of the community who can review policies and offer recommendations and guidance. For example, a lawyer would be a helpful trustee to review a donation and gift policy. A public collection–holding organization must meet legal and fiduciary obligations, and it is often the trustees who can provide assistance to staff in these areas. It is important for a museum to have an organizational structure that supports the development of policy documents.

There are several ways to reinforce the foundation principles and documents for an institution. The American Association of Museums (AAM) offers a series of internal and external assessments called the Museum Assessment Program (MAP), which evaluate and provide guidance for institutions with incomplete foundation documents or for institutions undergoing change. They include the following:

- Institutional MAP Assessment (IMAP). This assessment looks at institutional mission, planning, governance, administration, finance, collections stewardship, interpretation, presentation, marketing, public relations, membership, and community support.
- Collections Management Assessment (CMAP). This assessment focuses on mission, governance, finance, interpretation, marketing, collections stewardship, scope of collections, acquisitions, deaccessioning, legal and safety issues, documentation, backlog, inventory, and risk management.
- Public Dimension Assessment (PDA). This assessment looks at public perception, public experience, communication, collaboration, audiences, marketing, public relations, audience development, and exhibitions.
- Governance Assessment (GMAP). This assessment focuses on governing authority structure, roles, responsibilities, mission, and effective institutional planning.

More information about these tools can be found by visiting the AAM website (www.aam-us.org).

Mission Statement

Generally a mission statement, founding legislation, and perhaps the will that created the institution are the basis for policy development. In an efficient organization, each policy document builds from and supports the next. Consequently, the ideals voiced in the mission statement, the most essential foundation document, will be reflected in all the other written policies.

The mission statement for any organization is the cornerstone of the institutional foundation. It should clearly reflect the purpose and intent to preserve and protect the cultural resources managed by the organization. If the mission statement does not include this express intent, it should be rewritten to include this wording. It is best if preservation is listed as the first or at least the second element of the statement. An institution trusted as a repository for the preservation of collections and historic structures must formally accept the responsibility for their care, and this responsibility should be expressed in the mission statement.

The mission statement should also clearly delineate the relationship between the historic structure and any furnishings or collections used within the structure. If either the collection or the historic structure has primacy of significance over the other, this should be clearly indicated. In the case that a compromise is needed in preserving one over the other, this relationship should be expressed in the mission statement and will be a significant element of decision-making processes.

Long-Range Institutional Plan

Among the numerous planning documents that provide direction and facilitate the management of a historic site, the long-range institutional plan, sometimes called a general management plan, is key. It details the use and preservation of a historic site based on its mission statement or founding legislation. This document should evaluate all aspects of a site's operations, establish institutional goals, and define the conditions necessary for preservation and protection of site resources, both cultural and natural, over time.

The topics that should be found in the document begin with a delineation of the resources themselves and then move to how they will be managed, interpreted, and preserved. Visitor enjoyment, participation, education, and appreciation of those resources should be a strong focus of the plan. For example, if the site intends to seek listing in the National Register of Historic Places, expand visitor services, improve or rehabilitate facilities, and acquire additional properties, the details of these activities and their execution should be discussed. The level of support that is required to sustain these activities should also be addressed, including management, staffing levels, and funding strategies.

The document should be based on sound research, technical and scientific information, and the involvement of outside experts. These plans are most successful when all stakeholders have input, particularly neighbors and the community. How programs will be managed, implemented, and evaluated is included. The goals and programs should be realistic, and the financial impact of proposals and their sustainability considered.

Comprehensive historic preservation planning needs to be addressed within the long-range institutional plan or a subsidiary document. Preservation goals for the property within its historic context should be established. It should define how the property's preservation program would be directed, based on activities such as rehabilitation, stabilization, or restoration. A more complete discussion of these activities is found in chapter 12, "Preventive Conservation and the Historic House Structure."

While the long-range institutional plan is meant to be broad in scope and vision, it is not meant to be static. All planning is dynamic. This plan (as all others) should be reviewed regularly and changed when appropriate. Examples of institutional plans can be found at the following websites:

San Bernardino County Museum Strategic Plan: www.sbcounty.gov/museum/media/StrategicPlan2004.pdf

State Historical Society of North Dakota Strategic Long-Range Plan: www.nd.gov/hist/LRPlan.htm

RESOURCE ALLOCATION The mission statement and institutional long-range plan can be used as yardsticks to ensure that resource distribution, including staffing as well as funding, reflects the mission and goals of the institution. If preservation is important and expressed in the mission statement and long-range institutional plan, adequate resources should be directed to preservation activities, including an appropriate number of employees, adequate space, and adequate funding for preservation. Employees or volunteers who are responsible for preservation in a historic house should be given specific indications that care of the collection and structure is an important part of their job duties. Preservation should be part of the official performance plan for these employees/volunteers. Often the distribution of staff in different divisions at a historic site museum does not reflect a significant focus on preservation. The site may have ten people in the education and interpretation department and only one person assigned to preserve the historic structure and the collection. Often the exhibits department is larger than the collections department. Careful thought should be given to the distribution of resources for care and preservation.

Those responsible for preservation should be qualified to provide this protection. If not, they must receive training appropriate to their level of responsibility. In the event that the staff of the organization is very small and there are no trained preservation or conservation professionals on staff, the institution should seek to develop relationships with outside preservation architects and conservators. A long-term relationship with an outside professional can be effective and rewarding. The outside consultants can provide information, answer inquiries, and provide training for the staff, volunteers, board, and community. Relationships of this type can often develop as the result of a Conservation Assessment Program grant from the Institute of Museum and Library Services through Heritage Preservation as discussed in chapter 3, "Principles of Preventive Conservation: An Overview." The assessors selected for the Conservation Assessment can make excellent long-term consultants because they will have an in-depth understanding of the historic structure, collection, and organization as a result of their work on the assessment. They will also be familiar with staff and volunteers at the site. If a conservation assessor is not an option, there may be local museum organizations or a larger museum or library nearby that could provide an entrée to local preservation and conservation professionals.

Allocation of space and operating funds are critical to preservation of the site and collections. There is always competition for space and funding within historical site operations. Is public access more important than preservation? Is educational programming more important than building maintenance and preservation? Preservation needs are often deferred in order to divert funding to programs and public events. Deferred maintenance of historic structures and collections has become a significant problem for small and large cultural institutions, necessitating emergency restoration and repair campaigns. Planned maintenance and ongoing preservation programs can avert crises of this scale and help historic house museums address future large project expenses. The question of relative importance of projects often plagues historic sites, many of which are already seriously underfunded. Solid intellectual controls that clearly delineate institutional purposes and goals can help avoid crises and destructive internal competition for resources.

Collections Management Manual

The next tier of organizational documentation includes the Collections Management Manual. Collections Management Manuals are comprised of a series of policies that address concerns and priorities relating to all aspects of the management of collections, including the historic structures. These policies should include discussion of the intent and rationale for a variety of activities, some of which are listed below. Each policy can be a simple statement or a lengthy exposition relating to the activity.[1] The size and complexity of the collection and the organization will determine the length and depth of the policy. Sources for sample policies can be found below.

CODE OF ETHICS. The Collections Management Manual focuses on the movable collections and should include a code of ethics (conflict of interest, NAGPRA, ESA, UNIDROIT).[2] This policy should define the organization's position in relation to ethical issues affecting the collection and historic structure. Many professional museum entities such as the American Association of Museums and professional groups such as the Registrars' Committee and the American Institute for Conservation have prepared examples of ethical statements. The following websites give examples of codes of ethics:

American Association of Museums (AAM): www.aam-us.org/museumresources/ethics/coe.cfm
American Institute of Conservation (AIC) (search for core documents): www.conservation-us.org
Endangered Species Act (ESA): www.nmfs.noaa.gov/pr/pdfs/laws/esa.pdf
International Council of Museums (ICOM): icom.museum/other-codes_eng.html
Native American Graves Protection and Repatriation Act (NAGPRA): www.nps.gov/nagpra/mandates/index.htm
National Alliance of Preservation Commissions (NAPC): www.uga.edu/sed/pso/programs/napc/pdfs/Code%20of%20Ethics.pdf
United Nations Educational, Scientific and Cultural Organization (UNESCO): portal.unesco.org/culture/en/ev.php-url_id=13095&url_do=do_topic&url_section=201.html
International Institute for the Unification of Private Law (UNIDROIT): www.unidroit.org
Wyoming State Museum Code of Ethics: wyomuseum.state.wy.us/policies

STATEMENT OF VALUES (INSTITUTIONAL VALUES). Value statements usually indicate the principles, ideals, or standards most important to the organization. Examples might include honesty, high professional standards, and diversity, but they may also reflect organizational orientation. An Underground Railroad museum may want to select community involvement as an important value. A museum of large machinery may select functionality as an important value. Examples of value statements can be found at the following websites:

Museum of Northern Arizona: www.musnaz.org/trustees/mvv.html
Wilton House Museum: www.wiltonhousemuseum.org/
World War II Victory Museum: www.wwiivictory.org/about

COLLECTING POLICY, SCOPE OF COLLECTIONS (WHAT, WHY, HOW MUCH). A collecting policy indicates what the institution will collect, why it collects, and how much of a specific material it will collect. For example, a county historical society in a historic home may collect items relating to the history of the county and to the history of the house (i.e., families that lived in the house or activities that occurred in the house). The collecting policy may also indicate that the historical society will not collect items duplicated elsewhere (at the state historical society or archives) and will not collect duplicate items that are already in the collection. This policy may specify that only items in good condition will be collected. In general, the collecting policy should clearly delineate what one could expect to find in the collection and perhaps which areas are the focus of ongoing collecting, as do the following examples:

Franklin Historical Commission Collection Policy: www.franklin.ma.us/auto/town/historical/museum/muescol/default.htm
Smithville Historical Society Collecting Policy: www.wisconsinhistory.org/localhistory/articles/written_policy.asp
University of St Andrews Museum Collection Policy: www.st-andrews.ac.uk/media/CollPol02.pdf

ACCESSION AND DEACCESSION POLICIES AND PROCEDURES (COMMITTEES, LEGAL ISSUES). These policies indicate how items can enter and permanently leave the collection and usually include the establishment of a committee to advise or vote on specific items proposed for inclusion or removal from the collections. Accession and deaccession forms should be developed to ensure that these decisions are made with appropriate information and consideration. Legal aspects of accessions and deaccessions are also discussed in this policy. Examples of these policies can be found on the following websites:

The Cambridge Historical Society Collections Policy: www.cambridgehistory.org/HLN_House/HLN_Library/Collections_policy.htm
Digital Library for Earth System Education (DLESE): www.dlese.org/documents/policy/collections_accession.html
Montana Heritage Preservation and Development Commission, "Accession Policy": www.montanaheritagecommission.com/Policies/AccessionPolicy.asp
William R. and Clarice V. Spurlock Museum, University of Illinois at Urbana-Champaign: www.spurlock.uiuc.edu/policy/deaccessions.html

RIGHTS AND REPRODUCTION POLICY (CREDIT BYLINES, ETC.). This policy should address copyright issues and actions relating to the use of collection images and items in publications. If digital images are involved, there may be other topics that need to be touched upon, such as using a protective watermarking to prevent misuse. If the organization has a reproduction program or a gift shop operation that sells house- or collection-related items, this may introduce other trademark-related topics. Excellent examples of policies can be found on these websites:

George Eastman House, "Image Rights and Reproduction": www.eastmanhouse.org/inc/collections/rights.php
Museum of Modern Art, "Research Resources: Image Permission": moma.org/research/permissions
The Rights and Reproduction Information Network: www.panix.com/~squigle/rarin/01rcsite.html

NUMBERING AND LABELING POLICIES (WHAT NUMBERS, WHERE, HOW). These policies specify the standardized numbering system used to identify and inventory the collection and structures. Often a year designation, donor designation, collection type designation, and object number designation is indicated by the numbering system. Archaeological specimens are often numbered with their provenance; buildings and sites may have geographically linked identification numbers or street addresses. This policy should also describe where and how the numbers are to be affixed, applied, or associated with the item. Reference to numbering and labeling can be found at:

Collections Link: www.collectionslink.org.uk/manage_information/labelling_marking/marking_intro
The Royal Air Force Museum's "Policy for the Labeling and Marking of Artifacts": www.rafmuseum.org/london/policy-performance/documents/collecting_policy/Labelling%20and%20Marking%20Policy.doc
William R. and Clarice V. Spurlock Museum, University of Illinois at Urbana-Champaign: www.spurlock.uiuc.edu/policy/numbersystems.html

INVENTORY PROCEDURES (WHO, WHEN, HOW). Inventory is one of the most important activities at a cultural institution. It is critical to know what the institution holds in its care. This information is needed for insurance, security, and many other purposes. In order for items to be used in exhibits, research, loans, conservation surveys, and other activities, each piece must have a number that is clearly assigned to that object. Inventory procedures are fairly straightforward and can be found in the body of literature for the museum profession. They are completed by staff on a regular schedule and may be done through random or comprehensive means. The inventory should be checked by a different staff member from the one(s) who performed the inventory as a backup against internal theft. Inventory policies and procedures are discussed at the following website:

William R. and Clarice V. Spurlock Museum, University of Illinois at Urbana-Champaign: www.spurlock.uiuc.edu/policy/inventorypolicy.html

CATALOGUING PROCEDURES (NOMENCLATURE, INFORMATION COLLECTED). Cataloguing procedures are sometimes confused with inventory, but they are very different. Cataloguing involves recording detailed information about each object or group of objects in the collection such as date of manufacture, maker, artist, place of origin, historic association, and so on. The catalogue record for the collection should be written using consistent professionally established nomenclature and recording conventions. Different collection categories have different conventions for catalogue nomenclature. For example, biological collections are catalogued following the typologies established by the parent scientific discipline. Elements of the historic structure should also be catalogued (and inventoried), particularly if the elements can be or have been removed from the structure. Examples include lighting devices, drapery hardware, and other decorative or removable elements. Sources for vocabulary include:

Robert G. Chenhall's system for classifying man-made objects.[3]

The J. Paul Getty Trust's "Art and Architecture Thesaurus" (AAT): www.getty.edu/research/conducting_research/vocabularies/aat/index.html

The Library of Congress Prints and Photograph Division's "Thesaurus of Graphic Materials I: Subject Terms" (TGM I): www.loc.gov/rr/print/tgm1

English Heritage "Building Materials Thesaurus": thesaurus.english-heritage.org.uk/thesaurus.asp?thes_no=129

English Heritage MDA "Archaeological Objects Thesaurus": www.collectionstrust.org.uk/archobj/archcon.htm

It is possible that a Historic Structure Report for a building could be used as the catalogue record for the structure. Excellent discussions of cataloguing policies and procedures and standard historic structure reports can be found at these websites:

Federal Preservation Institute: "Historic Structure Report": www.historicpreservation.gov/web/14501/28

New Jersey Department of Environmental Protection, Historic Preservation Office, "Historic Structure Reports and Preservation Plans: A Preparation Guide": www.state.nj.us/dep/hpo/4sustain/preparehsr.pdf

Office of Historic Preservation, California State Parks, "Historic Structure Report Format": www.ohp.parks.ca.gov/pages/1072/files/historic%20structure%20report%20format.pdf

DOCUMENTATION POLICIES (PHOTOGRAPHY, RECORD KEEPING). These policies determine the extent and types of documentation kept for the collection items and the structure. Black-and-white photographic negatives or prints, color transparencies, color prints, written records, digital images, copies of receipts, and other materials should be kept on file. Certain files should be duplicated and a copy kept off-site in the event of a disaster that destroys the original records. This documentation policy should establish and describe the standard records to be kept regarding the collections and structures. More information on documentation and record keeping can be found on the following websites:

SPECTRUM (the UK and an international standard for documentation and information management about collections): www.collectionstrust.org.uk/spectrum-terminology/index

William R. and Clarice V. Spurlock Museum, University of Illinois at Urbana-Champaign: www.spurlock.uiuc.edu/policy/cdihr.html#overview

INSURANCE POLICIES (INVENTORY, COVERAGE, LIABILITIES). Information on the insurance policies that cover the collections and the structures can be very complicated and involved. The registrar or another staff member or volunteer will have this information and should be able to indicate how it can impact the care of the collections and sites. Excellent references on museum insurance policies and requirements are on the following websites:

Massachusetts Institute of Technology Museum: web.mit.edu/museum/pdf/Manual-text5.pdf

William R. and Clarice V. Spurlock Museum, University of Illinois at Urbana-Champaign: www.spurlock.uiuc.edu/policy/insurance.html

GIFT AND DONATION POLICIES AND PROCEDURES (LEGAL ISSUES, CONTROL, DISPOSITION). Gift and donation policies delineate how gifts and donations can be received by the organization. They determine what legal and other information is required from the donor. They limit the restrictions that the donor can place on the management and use of the items or structure. They indicate the tax benefits the donor can claim as a result of the gift. In the case of real estate, this policy should specify the covenants, easements, and codicils that are permitted or required for the gift or donation. For good sources for information relating to gifts and donations see:

Log House Museum: www.loghousemuseum.org/donate.php

Massachusetts Institute of Technology Museum: web.mit.edu/museum/pdf/Manual-text2.pdf
Old State House Museum: www.oldstatehouse.com/collections/donate_collections.asp

APPRAISAL POLICIES (LEGAL STANDARDS, CONFLICT OF INTEREST). Appraisal policies address some of the legal and professional issues involved in acquiring good valuations for the items and structures in the collection. Only qualified appraisers in the appropriate area of specialization should be used. Appraisers with any personal or financial interests in the items should be avoided for ethical conflict-of-interest reasons. For a good discussion of appraisals and appraisers, see the following:

Charles M. Schultz Museum: www.schulzmuseum.org/appraisal.html
Old State House Museum: www.oldstatehouse.com/collections/appraisal_policy.asp
William R. and Clarice V. Spurlock Museum, University of Illinois at Urbana-Champaign: www.spurlock.uiuc.edu/policy/appraisal.html

HANDLING POLICIES (WHO, HOW, WHY). Handling guidelines and policies are essential to the safe movement and examination of the collection. They should specify why and how items can be moved and who has authority to handle collection pieces. There are many good handling guidelines that can be used as the starting point and adapted to the organization's specific needs, such as these:

University of Colorado Museum: cumuseum.colorado.edu/Research/Botany/Pemberton/policies.html
William R. and Clarice V. Spurlock Museum, University of Illinois at Urbana-Champaign: www.spurlock.uiuc.edu/policy/handlingpolicy.html

SECURITY AND ACCESS POLICIES (WHO, WHEN, HOW, MONITORING METHODS, KEY CONTROL). Security and access policies form the baseline for the security of the collection. They should indicate who has access to the collection at what specific times and for what specific purposes. These policies delineate how access is to be gained and from whom. Monitoring methods such as access logs and key card monitors should be described. The key control system should be specified. An excellent reference of security and access for historic site museums can be found on the following websites:

National Park Service: http://www.nps.gov/history/museum/publications/MHI/Appendix%20G.pdf
Phoebe A. Hearst Museum of Anthropology: hearstmuseum.berkeley.edu/collections/policies_collections.html
William R. and Clarice V. Spurlock Museum, University of Illinois at Urbana-Champaign: www.spurlock.uiuc.edu/policy/collectionsaccess.html

PACKING AND SHIPPING POLICIES (PROFESSIONAL STANDARDS). This policy should specify packing and shipping information and restrictions for the collection items. Often they are fairly general references to standard museum practice for packing and shipping. They may indicate when couriers are required, which countries objects can be sent to, and what kind and how much insurance is required. A number of excellent references are available on this topic, including the following:

Department of the Interior, Department Manual, "Museum Property Handbook": www.doi.gov/museum/policy/pdf/mphi-8.pdf
William R. and Clarice V. Spurlock Museum, University of Illinois at Urbana-Champaign: www.spurlock.uiuc.edu/policy/packingpolicy.html

CONDITION REPORTING POLICIES (WHEN NEEDED, WHO CAN REPORT, TERMINOLOGY). This policy should spell out when condition reports are required and who is qualified to complete them. Reports are generally done before and after any object is moved, exhibited, loaned, or used. Any preferred format for the report should be described, as should any specific terminology or glossaries that should be used to describe features and condition elements. There are many examples of condition report forms and formats. These can be found on the following websites:

Museum of Florida History: www.flheritage.com/museum/programs/trex/policies.cfm#conditionreports
Te Papa, National Museum of New Zealand: www.tepapa.govt.nz/NR/rdonlyres/AD8BFA1C-D492-45CB-8822-E1360408DCA6/0/conditionreporting.pdf

STORAGE POLICIES (FURNITURE, HOUSINGS, ACCESS, ENVIRONMENT). Storage policies should delineate the desired conditions for collection storage, including the types of furniture and housing materials, environmental conditions, and access parameters for storage areas. Indication that current professional best practices are desired is essential in setting up and maintaining good storage. This policy may also indicate when a structure is to be mothballed or closed up for a season and what steps need to be taken to do this safely. See the Canadian Conservation Institute Notes for more information about storage and closedown information.[4] Also see the following websites:

National Park Service Museum Management Program: www.nps.gov/history/museum/publications/MHI/CHAP7.pdf
Northern States Conservation Center: www.collectioncare.org/cci/ccis.html

EXHIBITION POLICIES (LENGTH, PROTECTION FOR OBJECTS, SECURITY). The exhibition policy should indicate why and what exhibitions can be planned for an institution. The process of choosing a topic and developing the exhibition from object selection to design should be described. The staff needed on the exhibition team should be listed. Each critical step for the exhibit process should be specified. A statement should be included to indicate that safe exhibition practices are to be used to protect the collection and the structure from intrusive measures. Guidelines for exhibit conservation developed by the National Park Service are available for purchase as a CDRom.[5] Discussion of exhibits in historic houses can be found in chapter 6, "Preventive Conservation and Exhibits in the Historic House," and on the following websites:

The British Museum: www.britishmuseum.org/pdf/Display.pdf
Collections Link: www.collectionslink.org.uk/organise_exhibitions/exchanging_exhibitions/feasibility/policy_lender/policy_notes
Douglas County (IL) Museum: www.docomuseum.org/policy_exhibition.htm

CONSERVATION/PRESERVATION POLICIES (PROFESSIONAL STANDARDS). Conservation and preservation policies must detail the wishes of the institution to follow current professional best practices for care and preservation of the collection. Formal documents such as the American Institute for Conservation Code of Ethics and Guidelines for Practice and the APT/AIC New Orleans Charter for the Joint Preservation of Historic Structures and Artifacts (see Introduction) must be referenced and copies appended to the Collections Management Manual. Information should also be assembled on how to choose a preservation or conservation professional for consultation or work. Sample documents can be found at these websites:

"Alabama State Historic Preservation Plan": www.nps.gov/history/hps/pad/stateplans/alabama.htm
Carleton University Art Gallery: www.carleton.ca/gallery/policies3.html
"Development of a Preservation Plan for the Sterling-Moorman House, Cheney, Washington": www.cityofcheney.org/documents/planning/RFP%20Moorman%20House%20Pres%20Plan.pdf
William R. and Clarice V. Spurlock Museum, University of Illinois at Urbana-Champaign: www.spurlock.uiuc.edu/policy/preservation.html

PEST CONTROL POLICY (INTEGRATED PEST MANAGEMENT). The pest control policy should indicate that an integrated pest management approach to pest control is followed. Integrated pest management (IPM) is the professional standard for pest control in museums and on sites around the world today. See chapter 10, "Preventive Conservation and Integrated Pest Management," for a detailed discussion of IPM in historic houses. Excellent references for this can be found on the websites listed below.

Historic New England: www.museumpests.net/resources/samples/Hist_New_England_IPM.pdf
Minnesota History Center: www.museumpests.net/resources/samples/MinnesotaIPM_PROC.pdf
Northern States Conservation Center: www.collectioncare.org/cci/ccip.html
William R. and Clarice V. Spurlock Museum, University of Illinois at Urbana-Champaign: www.spurlock.uiuc.edu/policy/pestpolicy.html

ENVIRONMENTAL CONTROL POLICY (TEMPERATURE, RELATIVE HUMIDITY, LIGHTING, POLLUTANTS). An environmental control policy details the environmental conditions that are acceptable for the site. It should state temperature levels, relative humidity levels, light levels, percentage of particulate filtration levels, and range of gaseous pollutant levels that are acceptable. It should also delineate the ways in which the levels can be adjusted or changed seasonally. It should specify who has authority to override the controls (e.g., change the thermostat) and why, and who has the responsibility to monitor conditions. An excellent reference to environmental control is Garry Thompson's *The Museum Environment.* Also see chapter 8, "Preventive Conservation and Light," and chapter 9, "Preventive Conservation and Environmental Control." The following websites offer detailed discussions of light and environmental control in historic house museums:

Chicora Foundation, Inc., "Managing the Museum Environment": 206.180.235.135/byorg/chicora/chicenv.html

National Park Service, "Heating, Ventilating, and Cooling Historic Buildings": www.nps.gov/history/hps/tps/briefs/brief24.htm

"The New Museum Climate: Standards and Technologies": 206.180.235.135/byorg/abbey/an/an20/an20-4/an20-411.html

EMERGENCY PREPAREDNESS AND RESPONSE PLAN. Emergency preparedness is an essential element of collections management. It is even more critical for sites with historic structures with aging infrastructure, as the structure cannot be perceived solely as the protective envelope for the collection and must also be protected. Many emergency preparedness plans address staff and visitor safety but neglect the safety of historic structures and collections. The historic structures and collections must be specifically addressed in the emergency plan. See chapter 13, "Preventive Conservation and Emergencies, Safety, and Security," for information on emergency preparedness for historic site museums. Excellent Web references include:

Heritage Emergency National Task Force: www.heritagepreservation.org/programs/taskfer.htm

Museum SOS: www.museum-sos.org/htm/res_menu_docs.html

National Park Service, "Be Prepared: Develop a Museum Emergency Operations Plan": www.nps.gov/history/museum/publications/conserveogram/21-09.pdf

MANAGEMENT POLICIES FOR THE STRUCTURE. Policies specific to the protection and preservation of the historic structure and immovable collections should include discussion of the need to protect and preserve original building fabric, adequate documentation of the structure, nonintrusive maintenance procedures, and safe use policies for parties and public events. Much of the damage to the historic structure can result from well-intentioned but inappropriate repairs, "remodeling," or redecorating. The organization should develop written guidelines for these activities. The APT/AIC New Orleans Charter of 1992 and the Secretary of the Interior's *Standards for the Treatment of Historic Properties* set forth guidelines that provide a sound starting point for these policies. More specific guidelines will be needed for use of the structure for nonmuseum activities. Some historic structures include living spaces, office spaces, classrooms, and so on. Protective guidelines should be developed for these uses. See discussions and/or sample policies at these websites:

Farmington Historic Plantation: www.historichomes.org/farmington/event_rentals.html

National Park Service, "Cultural Resource Management Guideline, Management of Historic and Prehistoric Structures": www.nps.gov/history/history/online_books/nps28/28chap8.htm

National Park Service, "Rehabilitating Interiors in Historic Buildings: Identifying and Preserving Character-Defining Elements": www.nps.gov/history/hps/tps/briefs/brief18.htm

Philbrook Museum of Art: www.philbrook.org/experience/facility/guidelines.cfm

Science Museum of Virginia: www.smv.org/aboutus/special_events_policies.pdf

HISTORIC STRUCTURE USE POLICIES: MODIFICATIONS FOR OFFICE USE. When a historic structure is used for office space, there are many potential opportunities for damage and loss to the structure, particularly when oversight of modifications is not in the hands of someone sensitive to and aware of preservation issues. It is not uncommon to find that the will to satisfy the office workers' needs may overcome ideas of preservation. Even simple items like switch plates and plug covers should not be replaced without sufficient cause and only when absolutely necessary for safety reasons. Written policies that discuss and limit modifications are needed to prevent this sometimes subtle form of attrition. Policies should exist to address modifications for:

- The installation and use of special equipment
- The installation of phones, computers, and fax machines
- The need for extra outlets and other electrical modifications
- The need for safe and secure access for clients and staff
- The need for installation of Internet and other communication lines

HISTORIC STRUCTURE USE POLICIES: ACCOMMODATIONS FOR LIVING SPACES. When historic properties are used for living spaces, other areas for potential loss and damage to the property arise, both in terms of initial modifications, and also in terms of use, wear, and misuse by tenants. Written policies should be in place to address:

- The rules for pets (types and numbers allowed, liabilities for damages)
- The need for modifications for cable and phone access
- The desire of tenants to decorate, paint, carpet (what is allowed, who does the work)

- The need for safe and secure access to the property for tenants

ACCOMMODATIONS FOR PARTIES, SOCIAL USE, AND EVENTS. When historic properties are used for parties, social gatherings, and other public events, a number of potential risks of loss and damages occur. It should be clear which staff member(s) has the authority to arrange and approve events, and specify details for events at the site. It should also be clear which staff members will be present at events to monitor the activity and to provide the security needed to protect the house and the collections within. No exceptions should be permitted. Historic sites that have been hosting social events for years have learned through trial and error that fairly simple rules and policies help prevent much damage. Policies that have been found helpful include:

- The limitation of certain activities such as games, dancing, loud music or bands, smoking, the use of grills, and the use and distribution of alcohol
- The prohibition of high or spike heels from properties (which damage floors and carpets)
- The requirement that only light-colored beverages are served (to minimize staining when spilled on textiles, floors, etc.)
- The restriction of food to specific areas to reduce stains and pest infestation potential
- The control of rental service activities for delivering and setting up tables, chairs, and dining service, and for the safe removal of same
- The control of food service caterers (Contracts should specify, in writing, the need for caterers to be aware of the care of the historic structure and the need to clean up after themselves.)
- The need for diligent cleanup and trash removal immediately after events
- The potential desire to open windows and/or doors for ventilation
- The potential desire of the renters to tape, tack, or hang decorations and other items

GENERAL POLICIES. A number of general building policies can help prevent risks and accidents. These include policies relating to building repair and maintenance work. They might include:

- An open-flame policy that requires all heat-generating activities to be undertaken with a "buddy" to watch for smoke and flame. Many museum and historic-structure fires are caused by torches used in repair work.
- A ladder-use policy that requires all workers using ladders in historic house interiors to have a spotter to make sure the ladder is not swung into any building elements or fixtures.

A routine maintenance schedule is an important policy for the structure and the landscape. See chapter 12, "Preventive Conservation and the Historic House Structure," and chapter 11, "Preventive Conservation and the Historic House Landscape," for a more detailed discussion.

DOCUMENTATION POLICIES. Documentation policies, much like those established for the collection items, should be established for the building structure, landscape, and all removable elements. These policies might specify:

- Baseline photographic and written records describing the site
- Photographic and written records required to document all alterations
- Retention of all samples taken for paint analysis or wood analysis
- Retention of all materials removed during repair or maintenance

ETHICAL POLICIES RELATING TO REPAIR AND RESTORATION. The APT/AIC "New Orleans Charter" and the Historic American Buildings Survey / Historic American Engineering Record (HABS / HAER) "Guidelines" lay down the fundamental ethical and decision-making parameters for the repair or restoration of historic structures. Local legislation regarding registered or designated historic properties may also entail specific regulations or guidelines that should be integrated into the building policies of the historic site:

Association for Preservation Technology International/American Institute for Conservation (APT/AIC) "New Orleans Charter for the Joint Preservation of Historic Structures and Artifacts": www.apti.org/resources/charters1.cfm

Historic American Buildings Survey / Historic American Engineering Record (HABS/HAER) "Guidelines": www.nps.gov/history/hdp/standards/index.htm

Review of Policies

There are a number of professional groups and granting agencies that provide assistance with the development and review of policies. More information about professional organizations and their programs can be found at the following websites:

American Association of Museums (AAM): www.aam-us.org

American Association for State and Local History (AASLH): www.aaslh.org
American Institute for Conservation (AIC): www.conservation-us.org
Association for Preservation Technology (APT): www.apti.org
Heritage Preservation (HP): www.heritagepreservation.org
National Park Service (NPS): www.nps.gov
National Trust for Historic Preservation: www.preservationnation.org
State Historic Preservation Offices (SHPO): www.cr.nps.gov/nr/shpolist.htm

Granting agencies that work with historic site museums and their websites include the following:

Getty Grant Program: www.getty.edu/grant
Institute for Museum and Library Services (IMLS): www.imls.gov
National Endowment for the Arts (NEA): www.nea.gov
National Endowment for the Humanities (NEH): www.neh.gov

Implementation of Intellectual Controls

The policies discussed above form the bulk of the contents of the Collections Management Manual. They include fundamental institutional documents, policies for the protection of the collection, and policies for the protection of the structure, and they form the essential framework within which all physical activity involving the historic resources occurs. This framework must be strong and clear. All staff, volunteers, board members, and other stakeholders must be aware of the intellectual controls and must be encouraged to support them wholeheartedly. The "culture" of the organization should embrace a vital preservation mind-set. If all three levels of the organization—the board, the administration, and the staff—do not support this approach but undermine preservation policies, everyone (including the community) will become confused and frustrated, and the cultural resources or the organization will suffer. Often staff members try to support preservation initiatives in the absence of administrative or board cooperation. In other cases, it is the lower-level staff that undermines the preservation culture through passive resistance to policies. It is important that all staff is enfranchised in the culture of preservation of the organization.

The discussion above serves as a reminder that the preservation of the collection and the structure is a team activity. The support of members of all levels of staff and all departments or divisions is necessary for effective preventive care and preservation. When board members and all levels of staff are included in training and team-building activities, the result is positive and productive. Let no one minimize the potential contribution of any stakeholder in the fight to preserve the collections and the historic structures that house them. Let no one minimize the ability of strong, clear intellectual controls to significantly affect the preservation of cultural resources.

PHYSICAL CONTROLS

The bulk of preventive conservation practices involves "physical controls" that manage the risks found in the physical environment around the collection or the structure. In order for the physical controls to be effective, they must be born of effective intellectual controls. For example, one of the most common recommendations found in the Conservation Assessment report for small historic house museums is that a complete inventory of items in the collection is needed. If the organization does not know what it has in its collection, how can it responsibly preserve it? By the same token, good, solid pest-prevention measures will not be successful unless they are mandated by a written and enforced museum pest-control policy. Restriction of food and coffee stations throughout a historic structure is useless if open trash receptacles containing food waste are left standing overnight in the neighboring custodial closet or hallway. The intellectual controls form the latticework on which the physical control portions of the preventive conservation plan will be built.

With clear, written preservation-oriented foundation documents developed, the organization can begin to institute some of the collection and historic building policies that will protect historic resources. These policies should include discussion of the intent and rationale for the activities that take place in the historic structure and with the collection. The "policies" can be simple statements of intent or focus that are one sentence long, or they can be lengthy expositions on the potential impact of the activity and the measures taken to prevent damage. The size and complexity of the collection and the organization will determine the length and detail of the written policies.

An example of the importance of the intellectual underpinnings of collections management can be found at a beautiful historic house in the central Midwest. The house and its furnishings were left, by the donor, to a nonprofit group to establish a historic house museum to honor the accomplishments of the initial residents. The furnishings in the house were inventoried and catalogued, but many of the seasonal items like patio furniture, holiday decorations, and household linens were not deemed important enough at the time of initial accessioning. As the years passed, these ancillary items became more important or could no longer be replaced, and the staff began to worry about them. The curator sought conservation treatment for several of the items, only to find that conservation expenditures were limited by the foundation documents to accessioned collection items only. The curator had to eventually have the existing scope-of-collections policy rewritten so that these previously less-valued items could be accessioned into the collection and receive collection care resources.

Policies specific to the protection and preservation of the historic structure can include preservation plans that detail the need for protection and preservation of original building fabric, adequate documentation of the structure, nonintrusive maintenance procedures, and safe use policies for parties and public events.

Much damage to historic structures can result from well-intentioned but inappropriate repairs. As an example, several historic buildings on a large historic house property were used as living quarters for senior staff. The decision was made to install dishwashers in the kitchens of these structures. The building maintenance staff felt the vendor providing the machines could handle this activity, as installation was included in the price paid for the appliances. In the process of installing the dishwashers, the installers cut and removed all of the mid-seventeenth-century wood trim that impeded the dishwasher installation. They also removed all the "debris" from the "job" and dropped it off at the landfill on the way back to their shop. None of the pieces were recovered.

Mechanisms of Deterioration

The physical controls enacted for preservation constitute the foundation of preventive conservation and care. The physical surroundings of an object or structure can contribute to deterioration, halt or slow deterioration, or remain a neutral influence on deterioration. Preventive conservation aims to provide surroundings that halt or slow deterioration or, at the very least, act as a neutral influence.

It is in the nature of all materials to deteriorate due to natural forces of physics and chemistry. The scientific law of entropy states that systems, including molecular structures, will tend toward a state of maximum disorder, or in other words, minimum energy. Disordered systems require less energy than ordered systems. Deteriorated materials are less ordered than un-deteriorated materials. This natural order of things means that all materials will deteriorate, through chemical or physical mechanisms.

Physical damages are caused when "work" energy, from handling, moving, bending, flexing, and other manipulations, is transferred to the structure of a material like wood or metal. This energy causes wear, tearing, fraying, and other breakage that result in damage to the physical structure of the material.

Chemical mechanisms for deterioration involve chemical reactions that break down the molecular structure of materials. For example, light damage that results in fading of dyes and colorants is a chemical reaction. The loss of color occurs because the light provides energy that causes certain chemical reactions to progress. Colorant compounds such as dyes, pigments, and inks have a chemical structure composed of many fully bonded double bonds. Electrons can race back and forth along the chemical backbone of this type of structure. The constant movement of electrons, also called resonance, creates an energy that is emitted and detected by the parts of our eyes.

The wavelength of the energy emitted determines the color that we see. Exposure to light energy from the sun or a lamp causes breakage of the double bonds that contribute to the resonance. Once the bonds are broken, the electron resonance is impaired and the wavelength of the energy produced by the electrons is altered, resulting in a perception of color change. Highly colored materials may begin to look pale; white or off-white colors appear to become more yellow. This is the basic chemical mechanism for fading.

Other chemical reactions that cause material deterioration include attack by water or moisture (hydrolysis) and attack by acids. As an example, newsprint fibers are attacked by the acids from the manufacturing process in the newsprint and become brittle and yellowed within a few days after the paper is made.

Chemically induced deterioration often results in physical changes in the material. The increased acidity in aged newsprint makes it brittle and weak; the green corrosion seen on a metal artifact may be the result of an oxide produced on the surface. Physically induced deterioration does not necessarily change the chemical makeup of a material undergoing alteration. The worn surface of a wool carpet is still wool. Only the physical properties of the material change (strength, tear resistance, fold endurance, length of the fibers), not the chemistry of the material.

Chemical changes that occur during deterioration alter the actual chemical makeup of the materials. Physical changes as a result of deterioration, on the other hand, do not necessarily change the chemical makeup of a material undergoing alteration. If you tear a piece of paper, it doesn't change the chemical nature of the paper. Both kinds of changes are permanent and cannot be reversed.

It is not possible to stop deterioration or to reverse changes that have already occurred in the materials of collections and structures. It is only possible to use preventive methods, both intellectual and physical, to interfere with the process of deterioration and slow it down. This preventive interference is positive in that it slows the deterioration process. Interference can also be negative and can accelerate deterioration.

Positive interference involves efforts to reduce the chemical and physical energy available for deterioration reactions by controlling the temperature, controlling exposure to light, managing use, eliminating wear, and excluding those chemicals needed for deterioration reactions.

Negative interference involves adding chemical and physical energy and chemicals needed for deterioration reactions. Any action that changes environmental moisture or water content outside the optimal range for the materials, changes temperature outside the optimal range, increases light levels, increases use or wear, or contributes chemicals needed for deterioration reactions will accelerate deterioration. Positive interference in deterioration is preventive conservation or preventive care.

Some side issues to this discussion of the nature of deterioration are of interest. For example, all collection materials have a finite life span. Collection care professionals, as temporary caretakers of structures and collections, do not know how far along its limited life span a material, object, or element has already progressed. Often there may be clues like fragmentation or evidence of wear, but this is not always the case. This uncertainty affects our ability to make responsible decisions about what stresses may be safe to subject a particular part or object to at a particular point in time.

Deterioration cannot be reversed and damage is costly to repair. Some visual and structural effects can be reduced, but in the attempt to correct the effects of the damages, a treatment may cause other kinds of physical or chemical changes that may be harmful. We can also use conservation methods to minimize the effects of what has already occurred.

Some materials have built-in "inherent vice" and will cause their own deterioration. Inherent vice refers to instabilities in the physical or chemical makeup of an object that ultimately causes its deterioration. Newspaper is one example. Weighted silk, too, is a very problematic material in many house museum collections that displays inherent vice. The precious silk filaments were treated with metallic salts to make the silk heavier and therefore go further in the weaving process. However, the metallic salts accelerate the deterioration process. For that reason many garments and drapes in museums are very fragile and they shatter when touched.

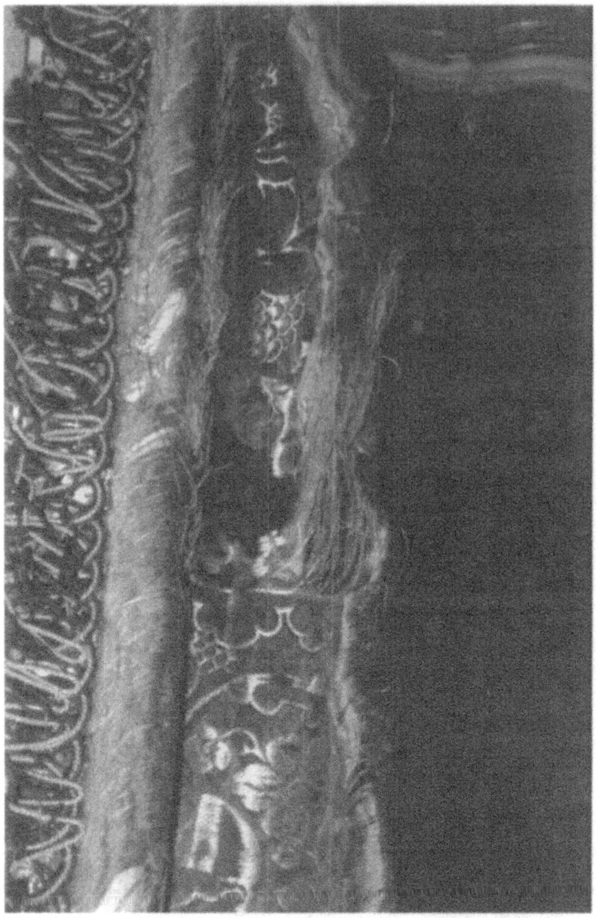

Figure 4.1 Detail of a shattered silk drape.

Some chemical reactions are "autocatalytic"; that is, their deterioration process is self-perpetuating without any outside help. Autocatalytic reactions produce byproducts that cause the reaction to start all over again and continue until all the materials are converted to the deterioration product; they unzip. A good example of autocatalyzed deterioration can be found in the deterioration of cellulose nitrate. Nitrogen groups in the parent molecule become detached and combine with moisture in the environment to form nitric acid, which attacks the cellulose nitrate molecules and releases more nitrogen groups, causing continued deterioration. Celluloid or cellulose nitrate is a familiar material in house collections, whether as a hair comb, eyewear, or knife handles. When the deterioration process begins, it is self sustaining, making celluloid items difficult to protect. Cellulose nitrate plastics also produce active deterioration products that attack neighboring objects.

Deteriorating collection materials can affect neighboring materials and accelerate deterioration of nearby items. Many deterioration products are chemically active, including hydrochloric acid, nitric acid, and sulfuric acid. These acids will attack neighboring materials. They are often emitted as gases that can migrate through the air and through storage materials like tissue to cause accelerated degradation of nearby materials.

PHYSICAL AND INTELLECTUAL CONTROLS TO PREVENT DETERIORATION

Physical controls, then, are those that control the physical spaces and chemical environments surrounding an object, a material, or a structure with the aim of preventing deterioration. Intellectual controls establish the foundations on which the physical controls can be effective. The desired result of enacting intellectual and physical controls on a collection is the prevention and slowing of deterioration and the preservation of the site's resources.

Figure 4.2 Melrose Mansion, Natchez National Historical Park, Natchez, Mississippi.

Figure 5.1 Costumed interpreter winds clock as part of her care routines. Note gloves are worn when performing this task. George Washington Birthplace National Monument, Washington's Birthplace, Virginia.

Interpretation and Preventive Care

INTERPRETATION IS A CORE function of museums of material culture. For the historic house museum it may be the dim "candle" light, the costumed interpreter, and the spindle-legged furniture that looks like it cannot support the weight of a grown man that take the visitor into a past century. The ambience now set, the guides and exhibits strive to make the experience authentic to the period of interpretation. As stated by the American Association of Museums (AAM), a museum carries out its mission and educational role through interpretation, the process of communication between the site and the audience. Interpretive media and activities include exhibits, tours, websites, classes, school programs, publications, and public outreach.[1]

Historic house museums can provide very powerful experiences as the spaces where the famous lived, worked, and died or where significant historical events took place. They can make our shared history more real to us when we visit the home of a farmer or a slave. Interpretation at historic sites has moved beyond telling a narrow (and perhaps upper-class) story, where collections in a house are regarded solely as art objects. Expanded histories and stories now tell the roles of black and white, male and female, slave, soldier, servant, citizen, or immigrant.

The tangible assets like the collections may rest mute, however, without explanation and interpretation. How a site relays its story and history—what view of politics, society, or economics to present to the public—is a considered choice developed and written in its interpretive plan. A significant change has occurred in how sites are visited and interpreted since the preservation movement began in the United States. Many sites have transitioned from interpreting important people or events to also relating the tales of ordinary life. Contemporary visitors want to hear about the role and work of women and slaves, or how children lived and played. The challenge today is to explain the past to an increasingly multicultural audience with diverse interests and to examine critically what message to deliver that makes a difference and expands the world of the visitor.

The active use of tangible assets such as the collections adds depth to the interpretive message and provides evidence of the past. Staff must be mindful of the collection's care and preservation needs. It is recommended that preventive care practices, both the modern routines in use and the historic systems, be part of the interpretation program. Care routines are as much an integral part of the history of the house as any other aspect of domestic activity. Historic methods and materials for housekeeping are interesting and can be used as tools to illuminate many facets of social and economic history at different times during the occupation of the site. Housekeeping activities can be successfully demonstrated and make excellent activities for first-person interpretation.

PREVENTIVE CARE AND INTERPRETATION

The interpretation of the historic house will impact the practices of preventive care, and vice versa. Consider the entrance to a site to understand this interdependence. To keep dust and dirt from entering the house, doormats are recommended. However, they may not be accurate for the house—but a metal boot scraper is. If the boot scraper is used, the housekeeping staff may have to initiate cleaning practices that are more intensive at the entrance than if doormats were used, and the interpreter guides may have to request that all visitors use the scraper.

The dilemma posed by needing to maintain historical accuracy while preserving collections is acutely illustrated in the furnished rooms on the second floor of the Russian Bishop's House, Sitka National Historical Park, in Sitka, Alaska. The house was built in 1842, and the second floor contains an office, library, and sleeping quarters that are furnished with original artifacts, period antiques, and reproductions. When the history of the site was researched and a Historic Furnishings Report developed, there was no oral or written notation of any type of window treatment or structural coverings such as shutters. Nor was there any physical evidence that they existed. Consequently, light

Figure 5.2 The Russian Bishop's House, Sitka National Historical Park, Sitka, Alaska. Interior of room in which the windows have no coverings and no evidence that coverings ever existed. Photograph by Sue Thorsen.

levels in the furnished rooms are very high. The most basic options for light control—shutter, curtain, or shade—are inaccurate for the furnished interior. Object-level housekeeping techniques such as placing covers over chairs (which are used in some rooms and are referenced in the furnishings report) will help to preserve these collections.

Figure 5.3 A simple cotton cover is placed over the furnishings during all hours when the Russian Bishop's House is not open to visitors. In other rooms, historically accurate checked covers protect furnishings. Photograph by Sue Thorsen.

CARING FOR THE HOME

Written documents and letters throughout history speak to the care of personal possessions. In the past, people were more aware of the importance and value of preventive care for items in their homes than we are in the twenty-first century. They understood the damage that light, dust, and pests caused and what protections to employ. They noted how to preserve their important belongings in journals, shared the information, and passed it on. Perhaps this was due to the fact that furniture, dishes, clothing, and other household goods were handmade and cost relatively more than the mass-produced goods we furnish our homes with today. Fewer household items were disposable; they were investments expected to last for a lifetime and generations.

Women, who were heads of their households, wrote letters home while visiting and traveling, instructing the servants and employees at home about details of housekeeping. Some of these passages included exhortations to the servants to remember to close the blinds or curtains in specific rooms at certain times of the day to prevent light from falling on a treasured piece of furniture, upholstery, or painting. They included instructions not to polish metal items too harshly. Clearly, the details of housekeeping were well known to the managers of early homesteads and households, and some of the writings are almost tutorials. Englishwoman Susannah Whatman may be one of the most noted household mistresses who wrote about her management responsibilities. In a book she began in 1776 during the first year of her marriage, she put down quite specific housekeeping instructions for her servants to follow.[2]

"How to" books about housekeeping methods and household management were first written and published in the late 1500s.[3] There was a rapid increase in the numbers of these treatises in the mid-nineteenth century. The prevalence of books of household hints and techniques can be related to the increasing number of women and girls who could read and write and the determination of what constituted a proper course of study for a young lady. As more girls and women had the opportunity to learn to read and write, more materials were written. The number of books and periodicals about housekeeping and cleanliness increased with the focus on sanitation and disease during the late 1800s and early 1900s.

Today, the number of books and publications addressing housekeeping and home care has diminished. Little is written about the technical aspects of care of household goods and homes, even in magazines and periodicals focusing on home life and techniques for mindful living. A few television programs and publications have taken a holistic and scientific approach to the care of things, but many more print articles with household hints focused on tips ands tricks and "old wives' tales" rather than suggestions based on research, quality materials, and safe, careful methods. Perhaps the current boom and interest in collecting and the desire to pass on family possessions to the next generation will spur more interest in the gentle, thoughtful care of things.

SEASONAL HOUSEKEEPING CYCLES AND SEASONAL CHANGE EXHIBITS

Interpretive themes and programs can highlight seasonal differences in the management of the household and the life of the occupants. In an area such as the Northeast, the routines of winter were very different from those of summer. In winter, a family would focus most activities around the fire or stove. Furnishings that were located elsewhere in the house may have been brought to the warmed room, and house exhibits may be planned to reflect this fact. Other necessities of winter such as bed-warming pans and foot stoves should be rotated off display in warm weather months. The terms *summer dress* and *winter dress* refer to seasonal differences in house furnishings (figure 5.5). Once winter passed and the fires that deposited soot on the furnishings were no longer lit, the house was cleaned and prepared for the warm temperatures of summer. Spring cleaning entailed washing walls and windows, taking up carpets, putting away thick drapes, and cleaning fireplaces. Heavy bed curtains came down, to be replaced by gauze netting that protected the sleeper against mosquitoes. Mirrors and chandeliers were draped in netting as well, to keep the flies off.

While many of the rigors of changing exhibits are not recommended, a site can dress rooms seasonally, using reproduction covers and selecting furnishings in good condition that are candidates to move, and can monitor the effects of such a routine with diligence.

Figure 5.4 Netting at Clara Barton National Historic Site, Glen Echo, Maryland.

Figure 5.5 ***Left:*** **Music room at Hampton National Historic Site, Towson, Maryland. Furnishings as they appear during the winter months when the yellow silk showcovers are displayed.** ***Right:*** **During the warm weather, floral-patterned cotton slipcovers are placed over the silk. There are many summer-weight slipcovers in the collections at Hampton Mansion, showing that slipcovers were used over many years at the mansion.**

Such seasonal routines show visitors how real people ate, played, worked, slept, and lived together at a time when the exterior environment had more of an impact on indoor life than it has today.

INTERPRETING HISTORIC CLEANING AND CARE PRACTICES

The domestic guides written in the eighteenth and nineteenth century are excellent references for historic cleaning and maintenance methods. Any attempt by a site to interpret historic cleaning practices needs to be thoroughly researched in primary and secondary historic literature sources related to the period and occupancy of the site. The goal is to pass accurate information about housekeeping methods, materials, and motivations to the public. There are good primary references and scholarly discussions about housekeeping and domestic economy in the literature. Many relate to specific documentation from specific historic sites. Institutions that have conducted research in this area include the Colonial Williamsburg Foundation, the Henry Ford including Museum and Greenfield Village, the H. F. du Pont Winterthur Museum, and the National Park Service.

THE LEVEL OF CLEANLINESS

One aspect of housekeeping that should be addressed in the interpretive plan for a site is the conscious choice of the level of cleanliness to which the site is presented. An example of this decision-making process can be found at Carl Sandburg Home National Historic Site in Flat Rock, North Carolina. The home of author Carl Sandburg is interpreted as it was when Mr. Sandburg was living in the house (with his wife) and writing. He was a fairly disordered person, and his work and living environment reflected this quality. To interpret this part of his personality and lifestyle, the National Park Service has maintained the piles of periodicals, magazines, correspondence, and (basically) stuff stacked here and there throughout the house just as it was left by the Sandburgs. The curators catalogued and inventoried the stacks of papers. They try to protect the stacks from visitors and guests who are enticed to reach out and touch (or worse, to straighten) the piles. The difficulties for collections care at this site are less evident than the interpretive gains. It is difficult to dust and clean a home interpreted in a very lived-in state. It is also difficult to maintain an integrated pest management program in a cluttered home. The curators and interpreters do not want to present the house as a spotless, shining example of domestic enterprise, but clearly there is a significant effort that is needed to maintain it in this state.

The Carl Sandburg Home is a clear example of the conscious, informed decision to represent a site at a specific level of cleanliness that relates directly to its interpretive mission. Other sites may not be as straightforward. For many years the floors of eighteenth-century house museums were stripped, sanded, and varnished, and kept shiny and clean. Research over time has shown that these floors were more likely not sanded and varnished but often uncoated, porous, raw wood. They were cleaned by scouring with sand. As we learn more about past home maintenance practices, we adjust and modify our current maintenance and collection care approaches. There is much yet to learn and there are many unanswered questions. Should an eighteenth-century house be shown at a twentieth-first-century level of cleanliness? What is a realistic presentation, valid for the period of interpretation? How does visitor safety influence the level of cleanliness at a site? How do our twentieth-first-century perceptions of cleanliness and "responsible care" or good housekeeping affect the ways we present our historic properties? The answers will be different for each site, determined through research and careful consideration and explained in the interpretive plan.

THE COST OF CARE

Routine cleaning is a necessity. Vacuuming the visitor-use carpets, for example, will keep dust levels down in the furnished rooms and may result in reducing the frequency that the collections are dusted. This routine of cleaning may be done frequently. Cleaning the collections, however, is different from this kind of cleaning and has to be considered very carefully. Cleaning is ultimately an invasive act. Surfaces are scratched and worn by any dusting method. The risk of breakage due to the handling associated with cleaning is very real. Breakage due to housekeeping activity can be a major source of damage to collection objects. Cleaning should be performed only when actually necessary. A modern sense of "clean" is most likely more extreme than the sense of cleanliness prevalent during the period of use or interpretation of a historic house.

INTERPRETATION OF COLLECTIONS CARE

Care activities practiced in museums can be used as effective interpretive tools. When collections care work is conducted in historic house spaces during the hours that the structure is open to the public, it can be used as a discussion point of current professional practices in the care of collections. Visitors can ask questions about the care of their own things, which serves to make safe collections care relevant to their families, homes, and everyday lives. Interpretation of collections care activities can be ad hoc and can occur as questions arise from the public, but the information given out must be accurate. Care routines can also be thoroughly developed and scheduled as part of the interpretive programming for the site. Rather than trying to hide or disguise these essential activities, they can be effective tools for interpretive and educational programming.

REPRODUCTIONS

Reproduction objects can offer visitors the opportunity to see things that are too fragile or deteriorated to be exhibited. They can accurately represent objects that are so damaged that they no longer reflect their state during use in the historic house. Visitors can handle an object unfamiliar to us in the twenty-first century through a reproduction. A reproduction kitchen where demonstrations are scheduled may permit a visitor to touch items that do not exist in his or her kitchen, with its electric mixer and microwave oven. They can offer visitors the opportunity to use and experience an object firsthand, without any risk to an original historic object.

Reproductions can be expensive and should receive adequate preventive care. For example, the textiles in a furnished room should be monitored for pests and displayed in diminished light levels. But sometimes reproductions are treated as if they were accessioned museum objects and are brought to conservators for treatment. The care of reproductions should not supersede the care of the original objects that were copied.

Occasionally reproductions acquire an interpretive value of their own. Reproduction rugs commissioned by the Hubbell Trading Post National Historic Site were woven at a time when there was a resurgence in interest and skill in Navajo weaving. Today these rugs fill a gap in the continuum of that weaving history and have acquired a historical value never imagined when they were purchased. Depending on the mission of a site, it is conceivable that a reproduction could eventually enter a collection. It is important that reproductions be clearly marked as such and that their value be fully understood.

ON-SITE SPECIAL EVENTS

Demonstrations

Demonstrations of housekeeping, cooking, weaving, candle making, and other domestic and commercial activities are common at historic sites and are well received by visitors. They often take place in reconstructed outbuildings or outdoors, but they may be performed in original structures near collection objects as well. One should keep in mind the effect these demonstrations can have on the archaeological record of the site, on remnants of any original structures or their foundations, on safety and health risks to guests and employees, on fire risks that may affect nearby original structures, and on the potential to damage original architectural elements and objects. Demonstrations should be done using accurate reproduction objects, never original historic collections. They should be closely monitored for safety and health risks. Items created during demonstrations—for example, fireplace reproduction tools forged by the site's blacksmith—should not become confused with the collection originals. A clearly written protocol for dealing with such materials (perhaps selling them in the museum shop) needs to be included in the management documents.

Figure 5.6 Quilting demonstration in front of Mathew's Cabin, Blue Ridge Parkway, U.S. National Park Service, North Carolina. This very popular activity brings to life the homekeeping skills of Appalachian women. The park has permitted visitors to participate and try their hand at quilting. Some visitors have embroidered their names on some of these demonstration quilts, adding another level to the visitor experience.

Entertainment

Performances of music, dance, singing, and theatrical productions in historic structures attract visitors to the site and expand the support base in the community. They can also create potential risks for the structure and the collections. Risks represented by the programs, from increased visitors to increased electrical demands, should be evaluated and preventive measures taken to eliminate or reduce the risks. These programs should be able to be presented without serious risk to the spaces, structures, and collections. The key ingredients in safely presenting performances in historic settings are the earnest cooperation and team spirit of the performers and the collections staff in creatively finding solutions to mitigate any risks.

Special or Seasonal Events

Holiday decorating using garlands and trees, parties, receptions, performances, special exhibits, and social events mark the seasonal calendars of historic site properties. These events, as well as annual fairs or festivals, can present huge risks to the buildings and collections (figure 5.7), but they may also be the most important times for increasing visitation and visibility of the organization. Obviously, creative compromise is essential for safe seasonal activities. Staff must evaluate the potential risks from each event and take needed preventive measures to protect the cultural resources of the organization.

Awareness of all the benefits and risks presented by a special program or event on the part of all the stakeholders (including curators, educators, trustees, housekeeping staff, performers, collections care staff,

Figure 5.7 Pine floor showing stains from sap from the holiday decorations and the pine Christmas tree dragged across the floor each year.

building managers, historians, and community leaders) is critical. Protection of the structures and collections is essential.

If our historic properties are to engage, educate, and entertain the public, we must preserve the integrity of the house's link to the past and protect the collections within. Interpretation helps historic house sites communicate about the past in context. A strong relationship between the educational and preservation missions must exist. As stated repeatedly in this volume, the staff must work closely together to accomplish these mutual goals.

Figure 6.1 Dining room at Hampton National Historic Site, Towson, Maryland.

CHAPTER 6

Preventive Conservation and Exhibits in the Historic House

EXHIBITS ARE THE TRADITIONAL method of communicating ideas, stories, and themes about a site to visitors. In the historic house where the interior is furnished with possessions of the occupants, the exhibits offer a tangible connection to a person or an event that deepens the visitors' understanding and appreciation of the site's story. An intimacy is created when personal possessions are seen in the context of where they were used, rather than in the glass case of a museum gallery.

A distinguishing feature of historic house museums is that the exhibits are on open display, and for most sites they are on permanent open display. Objects are rarely in cases; rather they are arranged in a room setting in order to give the impression that the house occupants have just stepped out for a moment. However, the seeming familiarity or casualness of a room setting may make visitors feel they can approach and touch collections.

A host of physical threats needs to be combated in order to keep collections from irreparable damage. The display environment is usually hostile, with too much light, dust, and extremes of temperature and relative humidity. Well-meaning caretakers may overclean sensitive materials. The layout or constraints of the house may pose a problem. Objects may be in close proximity to the tour route and at risk of getting bumped or jostled. Visitors' use and handling of items is always a concern, as is theft. Therefore, exhibition techniques used in the historic house must be creative and always keep preservation goals at the forefront. Caretakers balance the competing need for long-term collection presentation with the need to provide access and interpretation.

Americans have been preserving historic houses since the middle of the nineteenth century, but these efforts are rarely supported by an endowment, nor do they have strong financial support for their operations. In addition, there is not a cadre of professionals who operate the institution, as many houses are community supported and run by volunteers. How an institution is staffed and funded impacts the story of the site, the cohesiveness of collections, and what the visitor learns from the visit.

Figure 6.2 Hallway at Adams National Historical Park, Quincy, Massachusetts. Visitors are not permitted to pass down this narrow hallway during the guided tour.

DEVELOPING EXHIBITS: THE FURNISHINGS PLAN

Objects are selected for display in a variety of ways. The typical historic furnished interior is an assemblage of site-associated and site-appropriate furnishings set within a room that has architectural features and finishes. The ideal situation is that the site has

Figure 6.3 Dining room displaying the collections of the former home owners, Albert Mussey Johnson and his wife Bessie. Scotty's Castle, Death Valley National Park (Grapevine Canyon), Death Valley, California.

accomplished this exhibit through a well-researched Historic Furnishings Plan that was written by a curator and other specialists.

A suggested list of contents for a historic furnishings plan and a website where examples may be found is at the end of this chapter. In the plan, the function and content of the rooms is established through written documentation such as inventories, bills, diary entries, letters, and graphic sources such as paintings or historic photographs. Architectural details within a room are examined to provide clues to the history and the use of the space. The plan dictates the date and function of each room for furnishing and interpretation. Objects are specific to one room and may also have a specific location within that room. Generally, the preserved furnished interior that we interpret today depicts the sequence of changes to a space over a specific period of time (the period of interpretation). The furnishings plan helps the site to inform the visitor about life in another time or place. Too often, historic houses display objects without a clear interpretive theme, choosing to display only the most highly styled objects or merely the collection they have, which may span many time periods.

At the end of the nineteenth century, the "Colonial Revival" period had a significant impact on the style of historic house interiors. The centennial celebrations of 1876 generated a renewed interest in America's colonial past, which became a dominant style in domestic designs in the twentieth century. At the same time, an increasing number of homes of architectural distinction or owned by noted Americans were established as historic house museums and opened to the public. These houses tended to be furnished in a style reflective of the times and not always as accurate to the period and the way their eighteenth- and early-nineteenth-century inhabitants lived. Rooms tended to be more cluttered with furnishings and objects rather than simply furnished, which is historically accurate. Research has given us a better understanding of the history and evolution of furnishing styles and décor.

Since the 1970s there has been a change in perspective about the ways houses are interpreted. Supported by a well-developed furnishings plan based on documentation and an examination or reexamination and scientific analysis of physical evidence in a house, our historic house interiors have been undergoing changes so that they more accurately reflect their period of interpretation.

A commonly seen practice is to display the contents of a historic house just as the owners left them before the site became a museum, as is the case at the Harry S. Truman National Historic Site in Independence, Missouri. When visitors walk into the kitchen of the home the president shared with his wife, Bess, they may notice aprons hanging on the hooks behind a door and a dishcloth at the sink, just where Mrs. Truman left them. This is a powerful interpretive technique that preserves and displays a moment in time, and it may result in a variety of décor styles to be displayed within one room. Other sites may determine that a room setting will be reflective of a particular time period and select objects from the collections that date only to that period.

Figure 6.4 Furnished interior, Andrew Johnson National Historic Site, Greenville, Tennessee. Photograph by Alice Newton.

For still other sites, the house may be a collection of antiques and donated items that are representative of a geographic region. Whatever approach a site takes, the exhibits should be researched and planned; otherwise, they are merely an accumulation of objects and no true interpretive theme is delivered to the visitor.

MANAGING THE EXHIBITS

To adequately preserve collections on open display, a conservator should be a full participant in the exhibit process, assisting with decisions about object integrity, security, placement, use, care and maintenance, rotation, reproduction, and retirement. Only objects in good condition can withstand the stresses of long-term open display. Some objects may need extensive conservation treatment before they are displayed. Furniture may need regluing, flaking paint or gilt may need stabilization, and structural damage will need repair. This work should be performed by a conservation professional.

Exhibits need to be well documented. All objects on display should be accessioned and catalogued. Objects on loan should have an appropriate loan agreement, insurance if required, and they should also be documented. Items should have catalogue numbers firmly attached. An inventory should exist for each room or space, which is reviewed on a regular basis. By locating objects on a floor plan, it becomes an easy task for staff and volunteers to check spaces for missing or moved items.

There should be a condition assessment for each object, which includes photographic documentation. It is important to have a baseline condition assessment for an object when it goes out on display in order to evaluate the impact that display has on it. The information will enable site staff to track changes that occur over time and make alterations to the display environment or remove an object from display if necessary. Note all structural and surface conditions such as losses, tears, accretions, fading, and so on. Objects may need cleaning, stabilization, or extensive conservation treatment before going out or continuing on display. Treatment should be performed by a qualified conservator and be documented.

An object may need additional preparation for exhibit. For example, a print may need framing, a family Bible may need a book mount to support its open pages, or a dress may need a mannequin (figure 6.5). Mounts are an important part of preparing objects for display, and they need to be made of stable materials that are designed to adequately support and protect the collections. Seek assistance from a professional mount maker or conservator for recommended techniques and materials rather than improvising a support at the site when you are about to install an object.

Carpets will need preparation and protection. A polyester underlayment needs to be placed underneath both installed and area rugs (figure 6.6). Caster cups or small squares of acrylic or archival board should be used under furniture legs, and rolling casters to distribute the weight of the legs and reduce the directed stress that will crush pile (figure 6.7).

If deterioration in the condition of an object is noted, intervene quickly. Try to determine the cause of

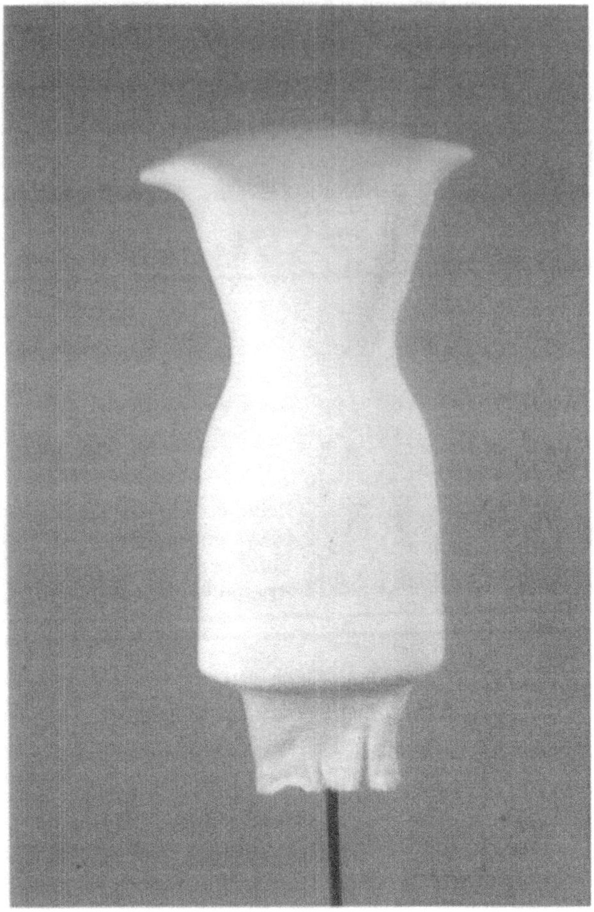

Figure 6.5 Mannequin under construction.

Figure 6.6 Polyester underlayment for carpet.

Figure 6.7 Caster cups protect carpet from the weight of furniture.

the change and correct the situation. If it is a conservation concern, talk with a conservator. Perhaps the display mount is not providing adequate support. Maybe visitor backpacks and bags are scratching a surface of a piece of furniture. The site staff need to work together to alter the tour route, move the object, or have visitors check their bags at the entrance.

If it is not possible to quickly correct the condition causing the problem, you may have to remove the item until a solution can be found. Maintaining the exhibits is a team effort. The more eyes that observe the displays, the greater the probability that loss or damage will be noted quickly and that areas will be kept clean and well maintained. Remember that open and continuous display causes significant stress on collections, and that regular object review and condition evaluations are essential. A morning security walk through the house is recommended. Routinely review the inventory of the rooms and assess collection condition. Write down your observations for the files and sign and date your notations.

SUSTAINING THE EXHIBITS: PROTECTION OF SENSITIVE MATERIALS

Sensitive materials may need to be displayed under special conditions. Traditionally, blackout covers were pulled over precious objects so that dust, flyspecks, and light would not be a continuous problem. The cover was pulled back or removed when the objects were to be enjoyed or admired (figure 6.8).

Sites should consider limiting the time of display for sensitive materials by showing them only at certain times of the year. For example, a silk and lace wedding dress worn by Elizabeth McMurran is displayed for six weeks each spring at Melrose Mansion (Natchez National Historical Park) in Natchez, Mississippi. The dress, which needed extensive conservation treatment before it could be displayed, is brought out during "Pilgrimage," when site visitation is at its highest and the interior environment is the most stable before arrival of the summer heat and high humidity (figure 6.9). After Pilgrimage, it is returned to storage. The fact that the display period for the dress is limited means that

Figure 6.8 Painted banner protected by a blackout cover. Ravena-Coeymans Historical Society Museum, Ravena, New York.

Figure 6.9 Wedding dress of Elizabeth McMurran on display during Pilgrimige at Melrose Mansion, Natchez National Historical Park, Natchez, Mississippi.

its annual return to the parlor at Melrose is announced in the local newspaper.

OBJECT ROTATION

A site should consider limiting the total exposure time of an object by rotating it with a similar object from the collection. In this way the damaging effects of permanent display are distributed among two or more objects rather than the consumptive use of one object. However, it should be noted that the philosophical decision to expose several objects to display conditions and therefore some level of deterioration versus consumptively using one object is one that the site administrators need to make and set as part of the collections policy.

When a site does not have additional original materials to rotate within the exhibits, reproductions can be very effective. Photocopy machines, digital cameras, and computer-based printing techniques make reproducing historic photographs, watercolors, textiles, original documents, and so on easy and relatively inexpensive. The reproduction can be placed on permanent display or rotated with the original, which is displayed for a limited time. In the case of a print or a sampler, the reproduction can be framed similarly to the original so that the room interior is not changed and an effective preventive care routine is established.

REPLACEMENTS AND REPRODUCTIONS

As research reveals more of the history of the site and its collections, the curator may find that what currently exists in the house should be replaced with something that is more accurate for the interpretive period or more appropriate to the setting. An industry exists specializing in the manufacture of reproduction period items. Lighting fixtures, furnishing fabrics, glass, and carpets can all be purchased easily through these firms. Custom-made reproductions can also be commissioned from craftsmen.

Another method to replace what is missing from a room is to buy a period piece. The piece should be in good condition, as conservation treatment dollars should be

Figure 6.10 Reproduction hand-painted floorcloth placed over the original hand-painted floorcloth at Melrose Mansion, Natchez National Historical Park, Natchez, Mississippi. An acrylic viewing window is set over a portion of the original floorcloth to provide visual access to a portion of the original.

reserved for the collections. Treatment would also significantly increase the cost of the object to the institution. A period replacement will have the same preservation needs as an original artifact and its usefulness on display and its exhibition life will be limited based on its condition.

When objects, particularly textiles such as drapes and carpets, are too deteriorated to continue on display, the site needs to plan to retire the object and obtain a replacement. How accurately the object is reproduced is largely dependent on documentation, availability of materials and sometimes manufacturing equipment, and funds. Reproductions custom-made to match an original object can be extremely expensive and may not always be possible. For example, it may not be possible to duplicate a sumptuously patterned colored silk because the particular type of loom used to weave the fabric may no longer be in operation. A somewhat simplified fabric may have to be made, but one that still has the spirit of the original.

It is recommended that the site award the same level of care to a replacement or reproduction (such as regularly removing dust and maintaining appropriate light levels) as it does to an original. The logic behind this recommendation is that the cost for a replacement purchase and for custom-made reproductions is very high. Good preservation practices protect that investment.

PROTECTING OBJECTS ON OPEN DISPLAY

Coatings

Objects on open display need protection from the deleterious environmental conditions of too much light, accumulation of dust, and damage that can occur during cleaning routines and from visitors and staff. Protection from some of these conditions is discussed elsewhere in the book (see chapter 8, "Preventive Conservation and Light," and chapter 9, "Preventive Conservation and Environmental Control"). At the object level, some measure of protection is practical. For example, a coat of wax on the surface of a table protects the surface during dusting routines and against light surface scratches.

Metals, especially silver, can be protected from tarnish while on display through the application of a coating. Wax and oils were used to delay the onset of corrosion. Today a clear acrylic coating is often applied to polished metal by a professional conservator. A conservator should be consulted before applying any type of a coating to an object.

Covers

Historically, cloth was used to protect the surface of tables and furniture. Dinner was served on a table completely covered by a cloth, and runners were set atop serving sideboards (figure 6.11). The cloths were decorative, often embellished with lace or embroidery or intricately patterned (such as linen damask), but their function was to protect the wood or marble surface. Fitted case covers were placed over chairs and remained on the furniture until a formal occasion necessitated their removal (figure 6.12).

Period housekeeping practices that protect objects should be incorporated into displays whenever possi-

Figure 6.11 Dining room at Arlington House, Robert E. Lee Memorial, U.S. National Park Service, Arlington, Virginia.

ble and can enhance the interpretive message. Netting was wrapped over gilt frames and chandeliers in summer to keep flyspecks off surfaces. Advice and instructions on keeping a household have been printed and circulated since the fifteenth century, and housekeepers were well versed in practices that protected furnishings from light and dust. Most home keepers used some of these techniques, and visitors find them fascinating.

Installed features such as floorcloths and wall coverings need protection. Sheets of Mylar or acrylic are typically placed against vulnerable locations on walls to protect wallpapers or fabrics. Floorcloths, which can be a defining feature for a room but may also need to be walked upon, need to have a visitor-use carpet over the surface. One of the most successful projects to protect a room-size installed floorcloth occurred at Melrose Mansion, Natchez National Historical Park. The floral-pattern-painted floorcloth was analyzed, and a reproduction of the pattern woven of modern materials that could withstand frequent use and cleaning. It was installed over the original floorcloth, which was protected by a layer of Tyvek placed between it and the reproduction (figure 6.13).

When applicable, it is important to install visitor-use carpets inside a house (figure 6.14). They reduce wear on historic materials by helping to direct and keep vis-

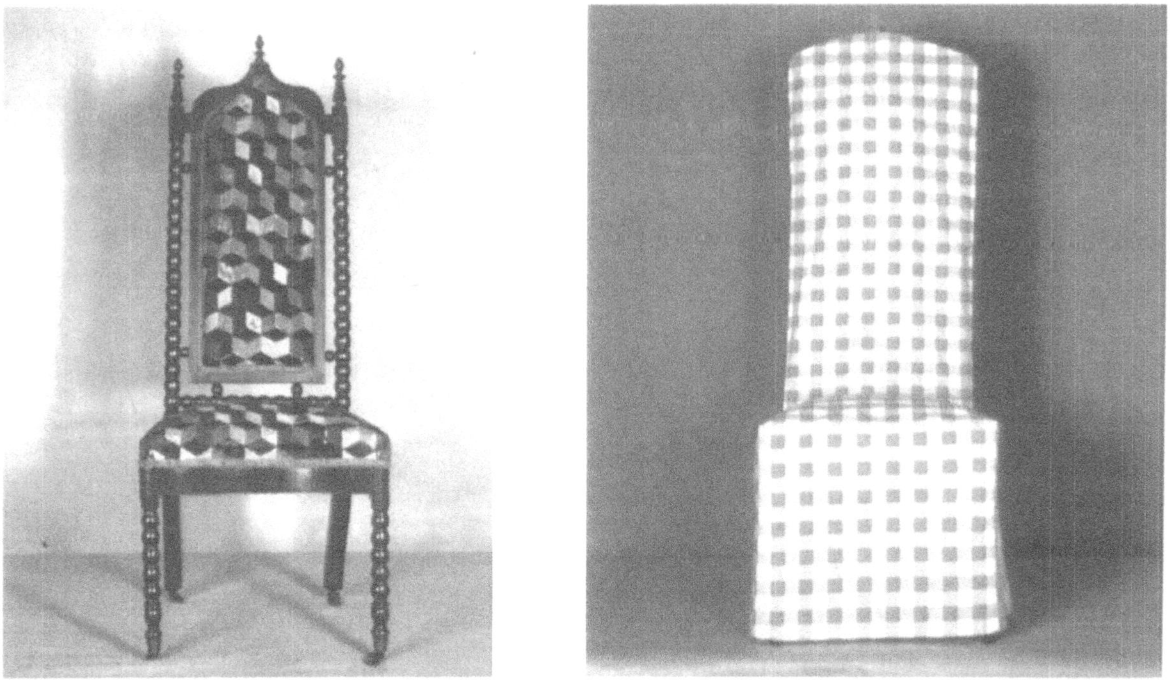

Figure 6.12 ***Left***: Dining room chair from the collection of Lincoln Home National Historic Site, Springfield, Illinois. ***Right***: The chair with original silk patchwork show cover received conservation treatment and was then fitted with protective checked covers for display at the site.

Figure 6.13 Custom-made visitor-use woven floral-patterned reproduction carpet placed over original hand-painted floor cloth (at left) at Melrose Mansion, Natchez National Historical Park, Natchez, Mississippi.

itors' feet where they will not harm collection carpets or historic floors. They also reduce the dust and grit that enter the rooms. They should be made from a high-quality carpeting material that can withstand frequent cleaning. They should have a stain-resistant finish and low volatile organic compounds (VOCs), environmental pollutants that are a health concern. A barrier layer should be installed between original materials and the visitor-use rugs (figure 6.15).

SECURITY AND THEFT

Protection is linked with preservation and exhibition. Collections need protection from physical as well as environmental damage. How a site organizes tours and restricts the flow of visitors will dictate security protections at not only the site level, but at the room and object level. Guided tours afford collections the best level of protection against breakage and theft. A well-trained staff is an invaluable asset when they note problems in the tour route and report them. The issue may be that an object is too close to the visitor path or that there are problematic vibrations in a room that cause objects to move across surfaces. When guided tours are not offered, a range of barriers need to be incorporated into displays to protect collections.

Figure 6.14 Visitor-use carpet is placed over the installed reproduction carpet at the site. Lincoln Home National Historic Site, Springfield, Illinois. Harpers Ferry Center Historic Furnishings Slide Library.

Figure 6.15 Truman Home floors are covered with a fitted carpet in which the dark gray color directs and defines the visitors' space within the furnished rooms.

Physical Barriers

Many historic houses do not permit visitors to enter a furnished room. Exhibits are viewed from a doorway, blocked by a barrier such as a metal gate (figure 6.16), braided ropes (figure 6.17), acrylic, and so on (figure 6.18). A more substantial barrier will give greater protection to the collections. A rope does little more than keep out adults, while children easily tuck under it. And while a barrier may keep people out of a room, if collections are within reach of someone who is standing at the barrier, they are vulnerable to breakage or theft.

When visitors do walk through rooms, there may be items within that space that need a barrier. For example, collection chairs may be mistaken as a place to sit, so those along the tour route are often marked off with a cotton tape to discourage sitting (figure 6.19). Bookcases may have an acrylic sheet over the face to prevent books from being casually removed from a shelf. Ropes and stanchions may surround a table and carpet to direct visitors' pathway around them. Barriers can be very effective at a site, and when designed with care and sensitivity to the interiors, they will be minimally intrusive.

Ultimately, however, particularly fragile or valuable objects should be displayed in a case to provide maximum protection. Period curios work well for smaller items, as do bookcases and breakfronts (figure 6.20).

Figure 6.16 Iron and brass gate close off furnished room at George Washington Birthplace National Monument, Washington's Birthplace, Virginia.

Attachment Techniques

Many rooms are decorated with small items that can be lost or stolen if they are not secured in some manner. Items can be attached to one another using nylon monofilament thread. Movable items are often

Figure 6.17 Cloth ropes define how far into the Rose parlor a visitor can walk at Melrose Mansion, Natchez National Historical Park, Natchez, Mississippi.

Figure 6.18 Wooden barriers close off rooms.

tied to a secure point such as a table leg. There is a danger, however, that if the object is picked up forcefully when it is secured using this system, the table and other items displayed on it could be upended.

Nonporous materials such as china and glass can be stabilized using a conservation-grade wax, if they are on surfaces that will not be stained or otherwise damaged by the wax.

Alarms and Detectors

A variety of alarms on the market can help to keep losses at a site to a minimum. A range of weight sensors (figure 6.21), magnetic contact sensors, pressure sensors, and motion detectors can be set within a static exhibit so that any disturbance is noted.

PROPS IN THE EXHIBITION

Most historic houses must deal with the issue of displaying food, flowers, firewood, and similar materials to give the impression that the house is in use. These materials can be problematic from a preservation perspective, as introducing such materials can increase the risk of a pest infestation. It is strongly recommended to use imitation foodstuffs (figure 6.22) and

Figure 6.19 A tape barrier alone on a chair may not be enough of a deterrent to prevent visitors from sitting in it.

silk flowers (figure 6.23), and to treat firewood before bringing it into the house.

Visitor education and enjoyment is enhanced by seeing collections in context in historic houses. Providing this glimpse of history, however, puts stresses on collections and requires a vigilant preservation regime. If staff focus on preventive care practices to ensure that the site can continue to convey its story with minimum impact on the collections, the collections and the visitors will be well served.

Figure 6.20 Bookcase used to display/protect vulnerable objects.

Figure 6.21 Alarmed weight set inside basket.

Figure 6.22 Examples of fake foods produced for exhibits. Photograph by Alice Newton.

Figure 6.23 Example of artificial flowers produced for exhibits. Photograph by Alice Newton.

HISTORIC FURNISHINGS REPORT

Description

A Historic Furnishings Report details the contents and look of a historic furnished space based on research and documentation. Ideally, all furnished historic interiors are studied to create a document that guides a site to develop a historically accurate appearance or atmosphere in its furnished structures. This gives the visitor the opportunity to enter "real spaces of history," where they can experience the taste and sense the personalities of the occupants or be "witness" to a historic event.

Houses, military outposts, lighthouses, and taverns are among the frequently studied structures. Ultimately, a site undertakes a historic furnishing study to install an accurately furnished historic exhibit. Work is typically performed by a curator or historian, who begins the process by becoming familiar with the site, its history, and how it is interpreted and visited. The curator conducts research using primary and secondary sources to confirm interpretive period and themes or recommend something that is more applicable or accurate. This work includes examining the collections to determine if they are suitable for the furnished exhibits. The curator may also suggest that the site obtain period pieces or purchase reproductions.

Contents

Harpers Ferry Center, the Media Center of the National Park Service, has formalized the Historic Furnishings Report process and placed this process on its website at www.nps.gov/hfc/products/furnish/furnish-plan-hfr-guide.htm. They recommend a report contain the following elements:

Table of Contents
Acknowledgments (if appropriate)
Administration (Report Summary)
History of the Structure
Historic Occupancy
Evidence of Room Use
Furnishings Plan
List of Recommended Furnishings
Related Media (if appropriate)
Illustrations
Appendixes
Bibliography

This outline can be used by a site to decide what goals to create for a Historic Furnishings Report. It can also be used to assist in developing a contract for a curator or other specialist to develop this report.

Preventive Conservation and Storage

PROPER ARTIFACT STORAGE is an aspect of preventive conservation that results in long-term preservation of museum collections. Museum professionals consider collection storage in two ways. It is both the physical location where artifacts are stored, and the process and systems of their storage. Well-designed storage areas and systems of storage prolong the life of collections. In addition to offering protection from the agents of deterioration, a storage area should be well organized for efficient inventorying, tracking, retrieval, and security of collections.

Often portions of the historic house that are not open to the public are used as storage spaces without applying basic preservation standards. Curators of historic houses usually have many more collection items than places to display them and therefore look to store objects in the closets, within the exhibition furniture, in passageways, and in the attic and basement. It is necessary to apply good preventive care practices when such spaces are used.

Finding space means that sometimes places that are not ideal environments get used for storage. When storage is sought outside of the house, outbuildings such as stables and barns are frequently used. These spaces are converted to storage without adequate insulation, air-conditioning, or light control. Very often these structures are themselves historic and cannot be altered significantly to make them into suitable storage facilities. Also, storage spaces removed from the center of museum activities can suffer from infrequent visits and inspections of the building exterior and interior.

In such situations there is an imperative need to employ safe collection storage techniques using high-quality materials. The storage areas must be rigorously monitored, kept clean, be free of pests (IPM program), have a high level of security, and have a relatively stable environment. Less-than-ideal environmental conditions can be compensated for by selecting less sensitive materials for deposit in attics (figure 7.4), basements, and outbuildings, and by creating micro-climate environments for categories of collection items. Institutions are obligated to care for their collections, and those items in storage should be considered equally as important as those objects on display.

Collections are not the only items needing safe storage in the house museum. House archives, accession records, inventory records, policies, studies, reports, library, and now digital data need to be retained in a

Figure 7.2 Collections and supplies are protected in containers, archival boxes, and with dust covers in an upstairs storage space.

Figure 7.3 Storage in a walk-in closet at a historic site.

safe, protected environment. If there is a current landscape documentation program, botanical specimens may need to be stored and in a manner so as to not attract pests.

Stored photographic materials need to be assessed to determine if there is any cellulose nitrate and cellulose ester film. These materials were in wide use from 1910 to 1950 and need to be stored at very low temperatures so they do not become unstable. Deteriorated nitrate film is both a health and a fire hazard. Nitrate film should not be stored in the general museum areas, in offices, or in the archives. It needs cold storage that is monitored on a frequent basis to ensure the equipment is fully functioning and the film has not become unstable.[1]

The facility manager will have documentation records and product literature from repairs and maintenance of the buildings that need to be retained and therefore stored. These records are rarely thought of as needing storage space other than a file cabinet in the maintenance area. But they are vital records of current and past treatment practices that can be used to diagnose systems or fabric deterioration. Therefore permanent retention, cataloguing, and storage of all maintenance documentation is important.

The collections care staff will need to keep their supplies close to where they need them (figure 7.5). The cleaning and maintenance supplies have the potential to be flammable, hazardous, or toxic and will need special storage spaces, well organized and properly labeled (figure 7.6).

In the United States, a Material Safety Data Sheet (MSDS) is a report that provides information on the physical and chemical properties of a particular product or substance. Data such as boiling point, reactivity, or handling instructions, and first-aid response procedures are among the types of information that may be included in an MSDS. These sheets provide employers, employees, and emergency responders with information on safe handling and storage of dangerous materials. Manufacturers are required to provide MSDSs for industrial products, and employers must have these sheets available to staff.

Figure 7.4 Less vulnerable inorganic materials are stored in the attic at Hampton National Historic Site, Towson, Maryland.

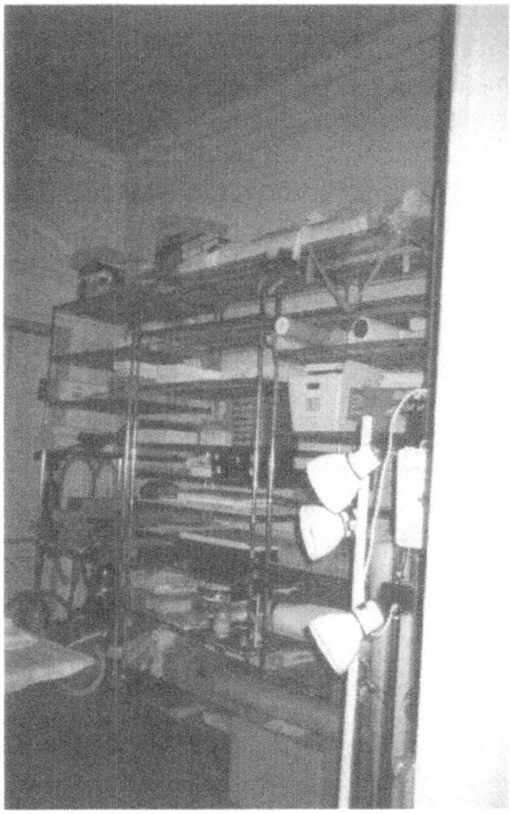

Figure 7.5 Dedicated storage for curatorial needs.

Decorations for special events, interpreters' costumes, ingredients for cooking demonstrations, and tools and equipment are among the many items that compete for space. It is imperative that the administration recognize the need to store these items properly, or they could create a hazard for the collections and the structure. Open foodstuffs will bring pests, so they need to be stored in sealed containers; special-event decorations may be a fire hazard; and the vacuum and cleaning supplies must be accessible or they will not be used regularly.

THE PHYSICAL AND STRUCTURAL REQUIREMENTS FOR SAFE STORAGE

Storage decision making is guided by organizational needs and functions, scope and size of the collections and their potential for growth, staffing, budget, and the amount and types of available space. The preservation process begins by evaluating the collection storage system, defined by the National Park Service as "the protective envelope surrounding the collections."[2] Included in this envelope is the facility or space (the structure, spaces within the structure, and the mechanical, electrical, and utility systems), the equipment (cabinets, shelving, specialized furniture, and racks), and the containers (folders, tubes, mats, mounts, and supports). Approaching a storage system in this way means that collections actually have layers of protection that shield them from the agents of deterioration.[3]

The museum field has developed standards for collections storage. A basic criterion is that collections should be in dedicated space; there should not be mixed use of the space such as office or research work areas. The space should be in a safe location—for example, not near a stream that floods. The environment should be controlled. It should not contain potential hazards to collections such as water pipes. The space needs to be sufficient so that objects are stored safely without damage, and it needs to allow for growth. The objects need to be stored on or in equipment such as shelves, cabinets, or racks that will provide support without causing damage. Collections need to remain

Figure 7.6 Dedicated storage cabinet containing well-labeled hazardous materials.

accessible. Racking and cabinets should be arranged so that there is an aisle created that is at least four feet or more wide. Security and fire protection are essential for collection storage spaces.

The better designed and built a storage space is, the better it will protect collections. Construction materials should be fire-resistant or fireproof. The space should be well insulated to maintain a stable environment; in some spaces, vapor barriers may be required. There should be few windows. The space should be well sealed against pests.

In historic house museums, most of the significant holdings are on display in the furnished rooms, with many more artifacts in storage. If a site has the opportunity to design a purpose-built storage building, the National Park Service has developed an architectural package that outlines the requirements for such a space. It considers everything from site selection (not within a hundred-year flood plain) to design features, to building materials, to interior finishes. For example, museums commonly use a water-based emulsion latex paint with a low-VOC-emission rating, but the document goes beyond that to recommend a paint that contains titanium dioxide pigment to help absorb ultraviolet light.[4] The supplied information will also be helpful if the site needs to renovate an outbuilding. Another widely used option for developing space in an outbuilding is the interior installation of an insulated modular structure.[5] A prefabricated building system made of insulation materials and metal-clad panels can be placed inside another structure. The NPS Preservation Tech Note *Museum Collections Storage in an Historic Building Using a Prefabricated Structure* discusses this option in detail (www.nps.gov/history/museum/publications/conserveogram/04-07.pdf).

Collections can also be stored in an off-site commercial storage facility. In this case, a regular inspection of the facility by museum staff is necessary. By far the more common solution to storing collection materials is to use the spaces that are available in the house, primarily the basement, attic, closets, and spare rooms that are not open to the public. In these instances storage equipment and containers become a critical protective component of the preservation plan.

ASSESSING THE COLLECTION TO UNDERSTAND STORAGE NEEDS

Developing a storage plan and requirements should be based on a collection assessment. The museum needs to know the number, type, size, and condition of the objects in the collection. The quantity and format of site documentation and research, archival, and operational information need to be included when planning for storage needs. The assessment should result in information about the overall space requirements, as well as recommend storage equipment such as type and quantity of cabinetry, shelving, and so forth. There should also be recommendations for storage methods and suggestions of objects that need special storage considerations such as containerization. Recommending environmental conditions based on material type should be a part of the assessment.

SPACE REQUIREMENTS

Once the assessment is completed, upgrading existing space to museum standards often takes resourcefulness and creativity. Improvements to the physical space may include making environmental upgrades, adding fire protection and/or security systems, rerouting pipes, and installing vapor barriers or insulation. Making such decisions should involve a team of staff members, especially the facility manager. It is important that access to plumbing, ductwork, mechanical systems, filters, and utility meters is kept clear. It is also important that the structure can bear the load of any planned shelving, cabinets, and racks. Space should be capable of sustaining a live floor load of 150 pounds per square foot, and compacting storage units need a live floor load of 200–250 pounds per square foot.[6] Spot load supports may be required, but a structural engineer should be consulted for evaluating load capacity. Windows may need to be blocked, but there needs to be enough light in the space to see, handle objects, and move about safely.

Once the space is prepared, storage furniture needs to be selected with care (figure 7.7). Some general considerations for the furniture are access, door placement, accommodation of structural load capacity, weight, mobility, and quantity of materials to house. Manufacturers will recommend load capacity for their cabinets, but as a general rule of thumb, the weight placed in a museum cabinet drawer should be less than fifty pounds.[7] Compacting storage fixtures can maximize space. To protect collections from flooding, cabinets should be raised off the floor at least four to six inches. This also helps when cleaning floors and inspecting for pests.

FUNDAMENTALS OF STORAGE

Related objects should be housed together by material, by provenance, by species, et cetera. Prepare objects with inert, archival, or compatible materials that protect the object from danger and do not contribute to its deterioration. Do not use any materials that may

Figure 7.7 Museum-quality shelving is designed, purchased, and arranged to make the most efficient use of attic space at Hampton National Historic Site, Towson, Maryland.

rust, off-gas, attract pests, and so on. Storage units should not be placed against exterior walls.

There should be a receiving area so that loan items or new acquisitions are separated from the storeroom until they are determined to be pest free. A system should be established to monitor who goes in and out of the storage area. The system may be as simple as a sign-in sheet or as complex as an electronic swipe card.

The Environmental Requirements

The damaging nature of uncontrolled humidity and temperature has already been discussed (see also chapter 9, "Preventive Conservation and Environmental Control"). Like the exhibit areas, the storeroom should have relative humidity levels that are stable. New construction and insulated modular structures should be equipped with modern heating and ventilation systems that can control the environment to the recommended levels stated in chapter 9, "Preventive Conservation and Environmental Control." In the closets and spare rooms that are so often used in the historic house, there can be dead zones for air circulation that can promote outbreaks of microorganism growth or other pests.

The storage area should be dark unless people are in the space. The visible light levels should be low but high enough to work effectively. The ultraviolet and infrared output should also be low. Ideally, light should be in zones, and only those areas where work is taking place should be lit. The placement of the light respective to the cabinets should allow for adequate viewing of interior contents. Curtains, screens, or dust sheets will reduce light exposure of objects on open racking.

Vigilance against pests is a key component of a preventive conservation program and is described in chapter 10, "Preventive Conservation and Integrated Pest Management." Many storage areas are not accessed regularly, making them dark and peaceful harbors for museum pests and making the IPM program even more critical to collection protection. Regular cleaning and room inspection are essential. Storeroom environmental monitoring must be included with the program in place for the exhibits area, and remedial actions should be initiated when problems are discovered. Periodic inspections inside cabinets and the storage containers themselves are critical to keeping storage areas pest free. An interesting proposal by Stephen L. Williams suggests using heat panels for controlling crawling insects in storage areas.[8] The low heat level (150°F–180°F) deters dermestids from passing through a metal doorway over a cement floor. Such a technique may be a solution that can be accomplished on a small budget and with a small staff.

Storage Furniture

A wide range of storage cabinetry is on the market. Specialized cabinets have been designed for many different media (maps, clothing, herbs and plants, insect collections, guns, etc.), with drawers, shelves, trays, or hanging rods that vary in materials and construction. Standing museum cabinets for objects such as ceramics and glass can have glass front doors for viewing contents, which leads to a reduced frequency of opening and closing. Otherwise, solid doors are preferred to limit exposure to light. Cabinets should be sealed from dust and lockable (figures 7.8 and 7.9).

Well-built cabinetry provides physical and environmental protection. Doors and drawers should open easily without causing unnecessary vibration. Stainless steel, chrome-plated metal, and aluminum with an inert oxide coating (powder coat) on the surface are recommended storeroom cabinetry materials. Units should

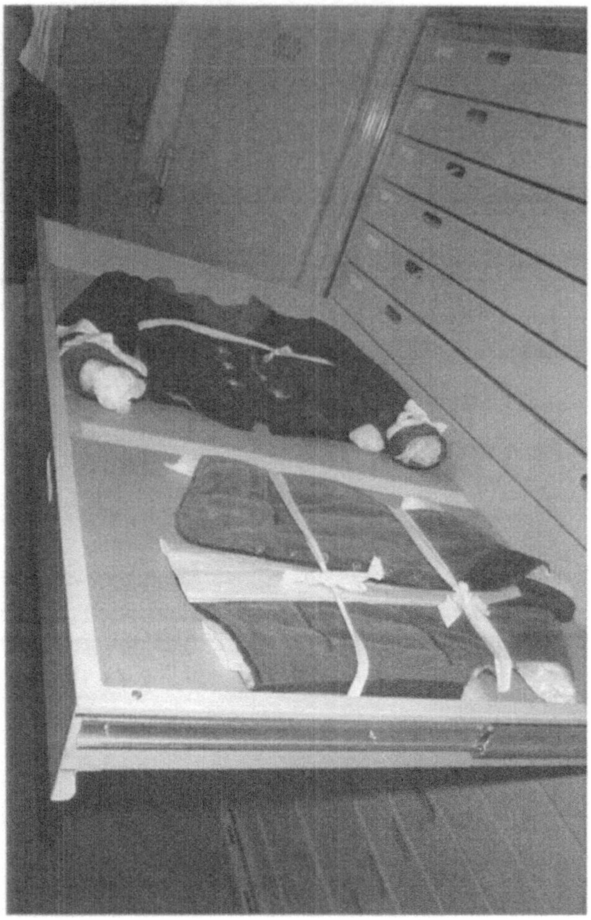

Figure 7.8 Well-sealed museum cabinet with individual customized storage support mounts for garments.

Figure 7.9 Well-sealed museum cabinet for hanging garments, which are protected by individual dust covers.

have doors with conservation-quality gaskets or covers to reduce the entry of dust, pollution, pests, and light. There should be no sharp edges, flaking paint, or rust. Wood cabinets and plywood shelves are common storage units in house museums, often made by staff members and volunteers. These may outgas acetic and formic acids. Materials such as plywood and fiberboard may include other volatile compounds such as formaldehyde. Within categories of materials, some are better to use than others. If plywood must be used, a marine grade exterior plywood is preferred. Wood should be sealed to reduce emissions. An in-depth reference on storage furniture and materials is found in the *Textile Specialty Group Catalogue*, chapter 8.[9]

Storage Management

All units in the storeroom should be clearly labeled on the exterior for easy assess to collections. The boxes, drawers, and shelves that are within or on the unit should also be labeled. A well-organized storage area will include an inventory of the objects by accession number on a particular shelf or within a box or drawer. Ideally, a photographic image of the object is attached to the container of any item that is obscured by its storage materials.

Storage areas should be tracked so that the museum knows who went into the space, when, and for how long he or she stayed. It is not unusual for maintenance staff to have keys to storage areas and to enter these spaces for routine monitoring of equipment and systems. An imperfect understanding of why they would need to sign into a space to do their jobs can lead to friction. An explanation of curatorial responsibility for monitoring all spaces where collections reside will usually help change attitudes and result in compliance with this request.

Visitors to storage need to be supervised and given parameters for note taking, object handling, and photography. For example, is there space and power to accommodate a computer in the research room, or would the site prefer that only paper and pencil be used for taking notes?

Preparation of Museum Collections

Storage materials used to support, wrap, pad, and tie or are otherwise placed in direct contact with an artifact need to be selected carefully. They should be archival or inert, compatible with artifact surface characteristics so the object is not scratched or abraded; they should provide support and not react chemically with a component of the object. There are many materials that meet these criteria, including paper products, plastics, foams, and fabrics. Materials to avoid are paper-based products such as newsprint, gift-wrapping tissue, corrugated cardboard, and other similar products that release acid, and certain fabrics that release formaldehyde, acetic acid, and sulfur compounds.

Archival-quality materials include paper-based products that are acid free, meaning that the pH is 7.0 or higher. Today, paper is most often made from wood fibers that contain lignin. Lignin produces acid, weakening the paper and potentially migrating to the collection materials in contact with it. Therefore, acid-free/lignin-free papers and cardboards are preferred. Usually these are made from an alpha cellulose base. Ideally the products are sulfur free as well.

Archival paper materials sold by museum supply companies may be buffered or unbuffered (neutral). Calcium carbonate and/or magnesium carbonate are common buffering materials that are added to papers to raise the pH to about 7.5–8.5. Buffered materials are most commonly used with paper-based collections such as books, maps, prints, and drawings. They absorb acids, and their alkaline reserve will exhaust over time.

Unbuffered materials have a pH of 7.0–7.5, which means that they may be mildly alkaline but they do not have an alkaline buffer added to them. These papers will absorb acids from the environment, and their pH will drop. It is important to surround collection materials with pH-appropriate materials. Material selection is based on the chemistry of the materials to be stored, the condition of the object, and the properties of the materials. For example, proteinaceous materials such as wool, silk, leather, and the like should not be stored with buffered papers.

Storage Techniques

Storage preparation techniques fall into basic categories such as flat, hanging, encapsulated, framed, and rolled. Housing includes boxes, trays, drawers, papers and boards, tubes, containers such as bags, folders, enclosures, and jars, among others. Archival-quality boxes and tubes come in sizes to suit a variety of media. Cardboard boxes are made of acid-free, buffered board. There are also inert corrugated polypropylene or polyethylene boxes and sheets on the market for smaller items.

An excellent resource on storage techniques is *Storage of Natural History Collections: Ideas and Practical Solutions.*[10] Storage technique selection is based on the physical and condition traits of the artifact, space considerations, and accessibility requirements. Collections should not be compressed or overcrowded in the storage furniture. They should not be stacked so high that handling them is dangerous.

Microclimates can be created in storage spaces to protect objects on open shelving units from environmental

Figure 7.10 Selection of storage materials and systems.

fluctuations, as well as from dust and pests. Polyethylene sheeting is used; instructions to create such systems can be found in Conserve O Gram 4/4.[11]

Pollution Management

In addition to environmental pollution, collection materials degrade and can release products that are detrimental to other materials in the storeroom. Buffered and unbuffered products are available to absorb acids and need to be replaced when they themselves become acidic. The history of the development of archival storage materials is interesting.[12] In the 1990s pollution scavengers came on the market; they offer another level of protection that can be afforded to the stored object. Activated carbon (porous graphite) in combination with a molecular sieve (zeolite) selectively traps certain molecules that are known pollutants. Contaminant molecules trapped by these products include acetic and formic acids, phenols, aldehydes, oxidizing gases such as hydrogen peroxide, acidic gases such as sulfur dioxide and nitrogen dioxide, and hydrogen sulfide.[13] Commonly available as paper-based sheets or rolls, the molecular sieve when set within an enclosure absorbs airborne environmental pollutant gases and degradation products released by the artifact.

Emergencies

Hazards such as fire, theft, and water incursions are just a few of the emergencies that need to be planned for and may affect the selection or placement of cabinetry in storage areas. A thorough knowledge of the natural disasters that can threaten a site, such as seismic activity or hurricanes, will influence how high cabinets are stacked, whether they are bolted into walls or floors, and how high they should be raised off the floor. For example, shelves may need padding and a barrier device such as a cord or a padded bar attached to the edges to keep objects from falling off during earth tremors.

Any hazardous materials need to be labeled. Specimens stored in fluids, collections treated with pesticides, and rocks and minerals that may be radioactive all need a health/safety insignia on the cabinets so both the staff and emergency responders know that there are potential risks to handling these materials.

Remote storage areas need to be regularly visited and inspected. A smoke alarm, sprinkler system, intrusion alarm, and water-detection alarm should be within the space. Ideally the alarms report to a central monitoring station.

HISTORIC HOUSE ISSUES

A practice that seems to be widespread in historic house museums is to use collection items for storage. A bureau, desk, or sideboard will often contain objects that cannot fit into museum cabinets. This practice, while understandable, needs to be recognized as undesirable. Even if objects are containerized in archival materials they are still vulnerable to vibration, theft, and infrequent inspection, and they cannot be tracked or accessed easily. Often items are forgotten. There is also the issue of having to open and close the furniture—an object that may be more valuable and fragile than the items housed inside it. Collections need safe, dedicated spaces.

Food used for demonstrations, costuming, and seasonal decorations may be stored in clear-sided polyethylene containers fitted with tight lids, which are available at most discount and home-remodeling stores. The containers should be labeled, and in the case of the foodstuffs the contents should be dated. Such containers are also good for storing emergency supplies such as a blanket for a sick visitor, especially if the site is remote.

STORAGE HOUSEKEEPING

A doormat should be placed at the entrance to the storage area. Smoking, eating, and drinking should be prohibited in storerooms. The storeroom ceiling, walls, floors, cabinets, and shelving should be dusted using an electrostatic cloth and vacuumed on a regular schedule. The room may need an annual cleaning, but shelving units may need monthly dusting. The frequency of dusting will depend on the physical features of the storeroom and its environmental systems.

Archival materials should be changed when they become soiled or acidic. Curtains and dust covers should be clean. Unbleached muslin is most often used as a cover material because it is inexpensive and readily available. Before use, it should be washed in hot soapy water to remove sizing and other finishes and thoroughly rinsed.

Storeroom inspections are critical. Ideally someone should enter the storeroom every day to check the environment, look for leaks or other potential problems, and inspect insect traps on a predetermined schedule. Working within the limitations of space and resources, a historic house museum can still create optimum storage conditions for collections through the use of thoughtful preventive care practices.

Preventive Conservation and Light

LIGHT IS ESSENTIAL FOR SIGHT and the perception of color and texture. Unfortunately, it is also a significant cause of deterioration to museum collections. Light is a form of energy that fuels chemical reactions which cause structural changes, embrittlement, and color loss in materials. Faded drapes or a bleached wooden tabletop are evidence that the sources of light and the amount of exposure to it need to be measured and controlled to protect collections and structures from damage. Control involves three components of light: the wavelength, the intensity, and the duration of exposure. To disregard light control or to focus control procedures on just one of these three components will mean that collections are at risk and will deteriorate.

THE NATURE OF LIGHT

The Electromagnetic Spectrum

The electromagnetic spectrum of radiation illustrates a continuum of energy waves that extend from cosmic rays at one end to radio waves at the other end. One end of the spectrum represents energy of very short wavelengths (strong energy waves); the other end represents energy of very long wavelengths (weak energy waves). Light can be described as a wave of energy that has a specific measurable wavelength. The wavelength spans from the top of one wave to the top of the next wave. This distance, or wavelength, describes the size of the wave in nanometers (nm) and the strength of the energy carried by the wave. Shorter wavelengths have more energy, are stronger, and can penetrate materials more deeply. For example, infrared radiation may be strong enough to heat the surface of human skin, but it cannot enter cells of skin. Ultraviolet radiation is stronger and has a shorter wavelength. It can enter the cells of human skin and cause tanning, and can also cause changes in cells that may lead to skin cancer. X-rays have an even shorter wavelength and are more energetic and stronger. They can pass through all of the soft tissues in the human body but are blocked by the higher density of the minerals in bone.

Electromagnetic radiation is arranged on the spectrum according to wavelength. The shortest waves are known as cosmic rays and can pass through entire planets. Radio waves have one of the longest wavelengths of energy, up to many kilometers in wavelength. Visible light is the portion of the spectrum that has a wavelength of light that can be detected by the rods and cones of our eyes, enabling the human eye to see. The energy that enters these components is transmitted to the brain, where "sight" is perceived. The wavelengths of visible light fall into a narrow portion of the spectrum from 0.4 microns (μ) or 400 nm (blue) to 0.7 μ or 700 nm (red).

When white light is passed through a prism, it splits into colors, based on wavelength: violet, blue, green, yellow, orange, and red. Waves of different wavelengths travel through the prism and are refracted through different angles by the prism. Ultraviolet (UV) light can be found just below violet light at the short end of the visible portion of the spectrum, at wavelengths between 1 and 400 nm. The longest wavelengths of visible light are near the infrared (IR) portion, which can be sensed as heat. Many light sources that we use to illuminate our spaces emit infrared and ultraviolet radiation, in addition to the visible light we need to see.

Quantum Theory

In the twentieth century, Albert Einstein proposed that light could also be understood in the form of small energy packets that he called *quanta*. The term *photon* is used to describe a unit of light energy, or a *quantum* of light. Photons are elementary particles that cannot be split into smaller particles. Photons have no mass or charge, but they do have energy and possess the characteristics of momentum.[1] The wave and quantum theories of light form our current understanding of the properties of light.

Color Perception

Brill describes color as "the sensation produced in the eye and brain by different wavelengths and intensities of

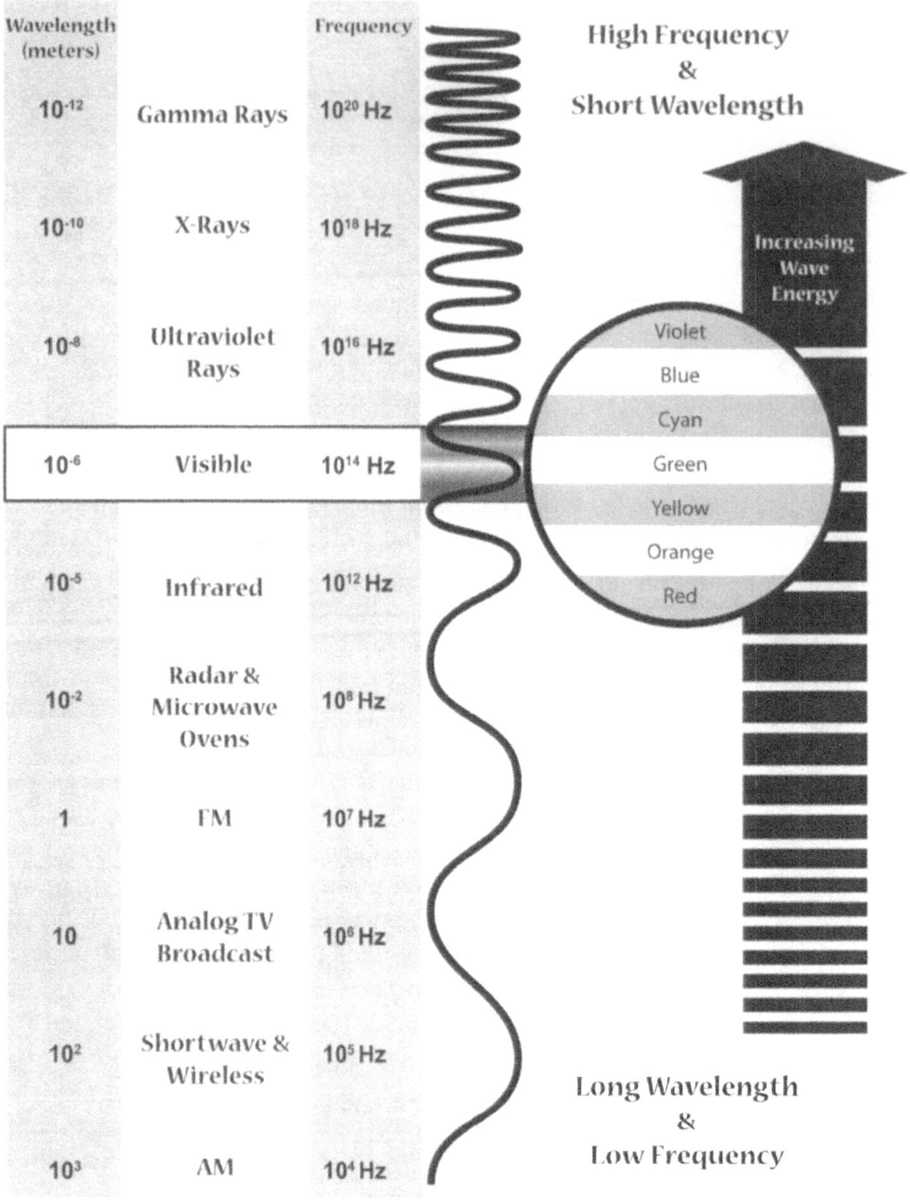

Figure 8.1 Electromagnetic spectrum. Illustration by Tom Sain.

visible light or by different energies of light to which the eye responds."[2] Color is perceived as a result of selective reflection of the wavelengths of light that fall on a colored surface. When a full spectrum of light illuminates the blue in the canton of a flag, the blue material in the flag absorbs most of the wavelengths of the spectrum except those wavelengths that correspond to what we perceive as blue, which are reflected by the fabric canton and absorbed by our eyes. Using a light with more energy in the blue range of the spectrum would make the canton look even bluer.

A simplified way of understanding color perception can be found in the color wheel. The color wheel relates colors that are absorbed by an object on one side of the wheel to the colors that are reflected by the object on the opposite side of the wheel. As an example, if the color observed is a yellow-orange, then the complementary color absorbed will be blue at the wavelength of 430 to 490 nm, which is located opposite the perceived color on the wheel.[3]

Two colors must reflect the same amount of light at every wavelength to truly "match" under all types of light sources. Two colors that reflect in this identical way are said to have the same spectral reflectivity. A phenomenon known as *metamerism* occurs when two similar colors have different spectral reflectivity. The two colors may seem to match under one light source but do not match under a different light source. Historically, art restorers knowledgeable of this phenomenon have tried to match color repairs under full spectrum daylight to avoid *metameric shifts* that occur more often under other light sources. Green and blue colors often show metameric shifts.

Light Levels and Duration of Exposure

The fundamental dilemma in museum lighting is that we need light for visitors to see our collections, while the same light that visitors need to see causes damage to our objects: visibility vs. vulnerability.[4] Generations ago, professionals set recommended lighting levels for museum collections at 50 lux based on lighting requirements determined for visibility to humans. Levels were adjusted below that baseline for more sensitive materials.[5] For many years now, conservators have indicated that textiles and paper objects should be exposed to no more than 50 lux of light, and oil paintings and furniture to no more than 200 lux of light.

When museums make lighting decisions, they should consider the reciprocity law: An object exposed to low light levels for extended periods of time will incur as much damage as if exposed to high light levels for brief periods.[6] In other words, light exposure is cumulative, and the damage doesn't "go away" or "recover" when the object is removed from the light or placed in the dark. The damage cannot be undone by periods of nonexposure. If an object is exposed to light levels higher than the 50 or 200 lux recommendation for a shorter duration, the total light exposure would be the same as if the object were exposed to lower levels for the equivalent longer period of time. The balance of exposure level versus exposure time can be manipulated by museum professionals when choosing what to exhibit for how long and under what specific lighting conditions. These calculations can also be used to help others understand why and how we must control light exposure for our collections. Literature published by the National Institute of Standards and Technology (NIST) on the factors that affect light damage can be used to help predict the damaging effects of light on vulnerable collections.[7] See also the light damage slide rule (figure 8.8) on page 70.

Damage Caused by Visible, Ultraviolet, and Infrared Light

Objects that are particularly susceptible to damage from light include watercolors, textiles, photographs, inks, paper, leather, other skin products, and wooden items. In general, organic materials as a class are more light-sensitive than inorganic materials. That notion has led to the misconceptions that uncontrolled light levels are acceptable for other materials such as ceramic and glass and that high levels are acceptable for oil paintings.

Another misconception regarding light damage involves the role played by UV filtration of light sources. Many managers administering historic house museums have the false impression that the presence of some form of UV filter on a window or a lamp means that the collections are protected from light damage. This is certainly not the case. The clear message that must be communicated is that all light is damaging and needs to be controlled: type, intensity, and duration of exposure.

As light shines on an artifact, physical or chemical changes are initiated at the exposed surface. Light energy is absorbed by the material and can cause a photochemical change. For damage to occur, the energy from light has to break molecular bonds in the object's materials, chemically changing the nature of the material. This damage can be rapid and severe, as in the case of sensitive dyes on textiles, or it may be as slow as the slight fading that occurs in paint layers over time. Light fades coloring materials such as dyes; materials lose breaking strength; some materials such as wool may yellow, while some such as wood fade. (Excellent references that discuss the deterioration process, fading rates of materials, and physical damages caused by light are listed in the bibliography.)

Our eyes cannot perceive UV wavelengths less than 400 nm, so they are not needed to see our collections and should be excluded from the museum environment. We still need to consider UV wavelengths when discussing museum light sources, because many sources emit UV light, which is very destructive. Typically, window glass and the glass of lamp bulbs filter UV radiation between 300 and 325 nm. Therefore, for the purposes of collection preservation, we need to be concerned with UV wavelengths in the range between 325 and 400 nm, which freely pass through glass. The UV component of visible light is not necessary for vision or color perception, and it is very deleterious to collections. For this reason, it should be removed from both daylight and artificial light sources through the use of films and filters.

Infrared radiation (IR) has a longer wavelength than visible light (between 750 nm and 1 mm). It is most readily perceived by humans as heat. A lamp emitting IR in close proximity to an object may warm the object, causing materials to dry. Too much IR generated by lamps in a furnished room may increase the ambient temperature. When considering what lamps to choose for your site, make sure you know how much warmth they will generate and select lamps with low IR output.

LIGHT AND ENERGY

Units of Measure

When light falls on a surface, the energy received by that surface is measured in *joules* using the International System of Units (SI). The amount of light generated by a light source is called *luminous flux*, and the unit used to measure it is called the *lumen*. *Watts* measure energy exposure per unit of time (joules per second). In order to monitor light levels, a light meter is used, which measures *illuminance*. Illuminance can be measured over a period of time to give the *total illumination* and is an accurate means of quantifying light exposure. Illuminance is measured in either *lux* (SI unit) or *foot-candles*. One lux is equal to one lumen per square meter and one foot-candle (fc) is equal to one lumen per square foot. One foot-candle therefore equals 10.76 lux or lumens per square meter. Collection caretakers need to know the energy exposure per unit of time and use the unit of joules per second or watts to measure energy absorbed per second. Terry T. Schaeffer presents an excellent discussion on the measurement of light energy in the book *Effects of Light on Materials in Collections*.[8]

Ultraviolet rays are measured as a fraction of the luminous flux in microwatts per lumen (mW/lm). It is widely published in the conservation literature that 75 mW/lm is an acceptable maximum level of UV for museum collections. However, the availability of low-UV lamps on the market, in addition to effective UV-absorbing films and filters, means that 10 mW/lm can and should be readily achieved.

Sources of Light and Their Color

Daylight is the most common light source used in historic house museums. Sunlight is said to render color accurately, although subtle qualities of daylight can vary with time of day, geographic location, and atmospheric conditions. Light in the north sky is considered to be bluer than light exposure from other directions. We describe white (full-spectrum) light as "cool" when it has these blue qualities as opposed to having reddish, yellow, or "warm" tint. This perception of warmth or coolness relates not only to the color of the light but also to its energy: A cool tint (shorter wavelength) has more energy than a warm light (longer wavelength). These attributes are used to classify light sources and are quantified using a numerical scale called "color temperature." A piece of metal that is heated will eventually begin to glow. As the temperature of the metal is increased, the color will change, passing through a sequence of colors from red to orange to yellow to blue-white. The color of the metal is characteristic of its temperature as measured in the unit Kelvin (K). Sunlight has a color temperature of 5500K. A lamp with a color rating of 4000K will give a cool tint, while lamps that are 3200K and lower give a warm tint.

Artificial light sources that are used in exhibits are selected for various reasons, including their ability to render color well—i.e., in a manner similar to daylight. The primary type of lamp used in museums is incandescent. These lamps have a metal filament enclosed in

Figure 8.2 Furnished interior at Harpers Ferry National Historical Park, Harpers Ferry, West Virginia.

a glass bulb or lamp. When electrical energy passes through the filament, it heats up and begins to glow or incandesce, producing light. Tungsten metal is used for most filaments because it has a high melting point. With use, tungsten atoms are released from the filament and the filament thins and eventually breaks. During this thinning of the filament, the glass bulb may blacken from the released metal atoms, output (lumens) will decrease, and the color temperature will change.

A tungsten-halogen lamp is a modification of this bulb configuration, where the tungsten filament is enclosed in a halogen gas that helps it remain more stable. The glass does not blacken during deterioration of the filament. The color temperature and lumen output of the lamp are stable for the life of the lamp.

Fluorescent lamps are also commonly used at sites. They consist of a glass tube coated with a layer of phosphors and filled with an inert gas and a small amount of mercury to produce mercury vapor. When an electric charge passes through the tube, UV energy is generated, exciting the coating and producing light. There are many fluorescent lamps on the market and their characteristics vary considerably. They appear in numerous shapes; some can have a high UV content, and some render color poorly while others render color well. They are energy efficient, do not generate much infrared radiation (heat), and have a long life. They require a ballast to operate, which can fail and produce an acrid smoke.

Compact fluorescent lamps (CFL) are a type of fluorescent bulb that is designed to be an energy-efficient replacement for incandescent lamps. They are of a size and format that fits into most light fixtures. Like other fluorescent lamps, they consist of phosphors, an inert gas, a small amount of mercury, and an electronic or magnetic ballast. Use of these lamps is encouraged by governments and environmentalists. They do not render color as well as incandescent lamps, but great improvements are being made to this technology and these lamps may be usable in the museum setting in the future. Fluorescent and CFL lamps should be recycled. If one is broken, the mercury must be handled appropriately. The Environmental Protection Agency recommends specific steps to take if you break a fluorescent bulb.[9] Read the product literature from the manufacturer before selecting lamps to know their attributes and how they will affect your collections.

A LIGHT-MONITORING PROGRAM

A light-monitoring program begins with an evaluation of site conditions, including the types of natural and artificial light in use, the movement of sunlight in the rooms throughout the day, the movement of sunlight in the rooms over the seasons, and available light control mechanisms. At the same time, it is important to consider the ambience of the rooms and their interpretation to the visitor. The collected information describes the lighting for each space and highlights significant or sensitive objects to determine whether any preventive measures are required, such as the use of shutters or additional filtration. A site evaluation will also determine the locations at which light readings should be taken and the times of the day that they should be recorded.

A monitoring program requires adequate equipment and a sound documentation system. There are light-measuring instruments for every budget. Measurements of light exposure can be recorded on a floor plan or in a log format. The recording sites may need to change or be augmented if lighting conditions change or if more sensitive or important objects are placed on exhibit. The same measurements should be taken each time with the same sensors and recorded in the same units. Regularity will allow interpretation from the data and will ensure consistency in the monitoring program.

Measuring Light Exposure

Every institution should measure light levels in collections spaces, exhibit areas, and in storage. At the most basic level, light intensity should be measured (in lux) and recorded as part of a routine program. A wide variety of light meters and data loggers is marketed to perform this task. A visible light meter can be purchased at a relatively low cost. It will measure the visible portion of the electromagnetic spectrum. Choose a meter that measures in lux and has a good degree of accuracy for lower levels (20 to 50 lux with 10 percent or greater accuracy) (figure 8.3). An ultraviolet meter measures UV levels in microwatts per lumen. It can be purchased as a stand-alone unit (Crawford is the standard unit used in museums) or wrapped into a complete environmental monitoring instrument (UV and visible light, temperature, and relative humidity, such as manufactured by Elsec) (figure 8.4). (See also Supplier Resources.)

Light meters operate on the basic principle that an internal sensor records the light as perceived by the eye and displays the measurement of the total exposure in either lux or foot-candles.[10] The measuring procedure should be standardized. The sensor should be oriented toward the light source, parallel to the object, where the light rests on the surface of the object. The sensor

Figure 8.3 Light meters.

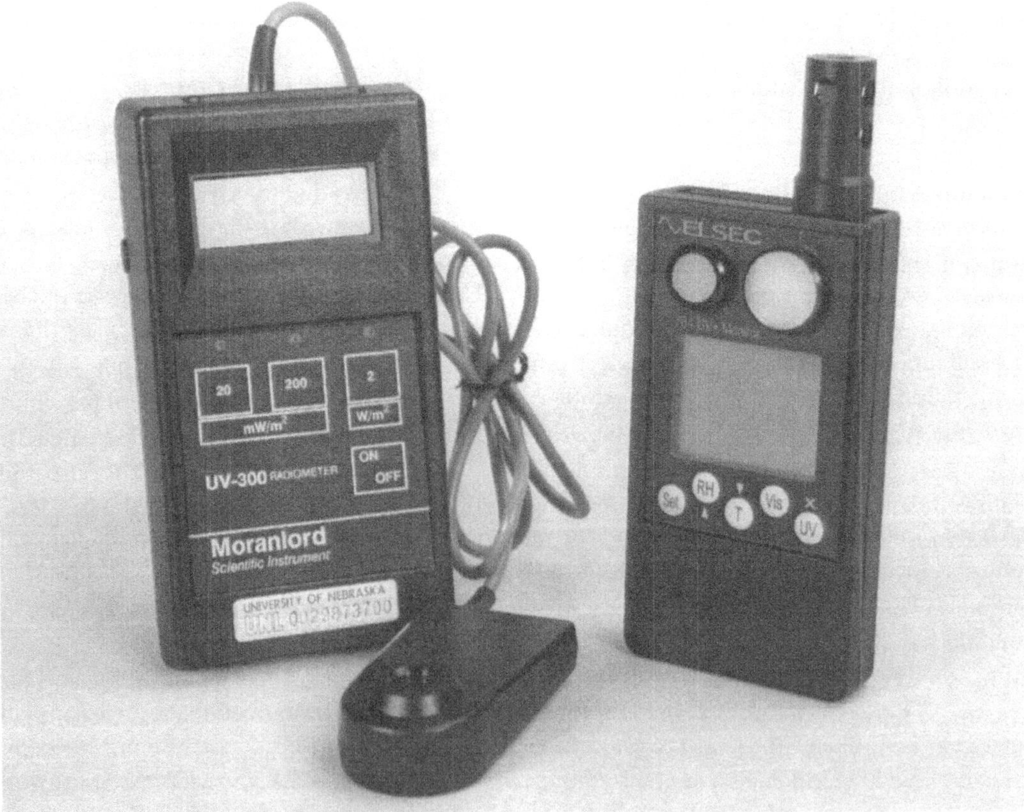

Figure 8.4 UV and environmental monitoring meters.

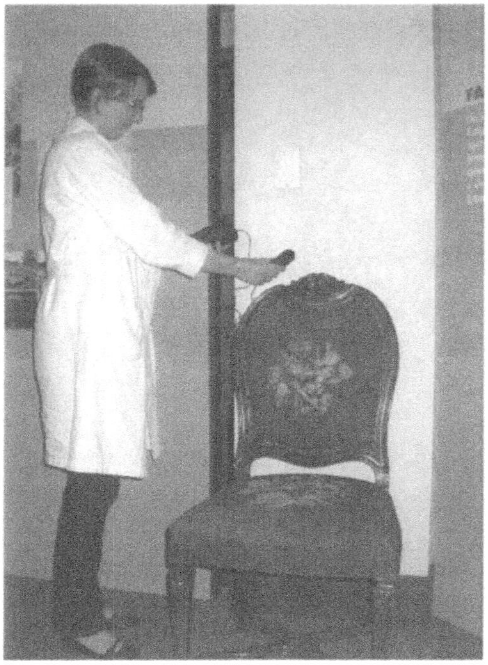

Figure 8.5 Person taking a light reading.

should not be placed in any areas of shadow, particularly those created by the body or the sensor during recording. If the object is large or unevenly shaped, a series of readings over the surface should be taken and recorded into the documentation system. Any changes in the type, location, lamps, filtration, or orientation of the light source should be noted in the documentation records along with the measurements from the meter.

Monitoring Light Damage

Today museums have the tools to take light monitoring of museum collections beyond the simple action of entering a room and checking the light levels with a meter and recording the data. There is also the ability to predict the damage the collections receive from the light exposure and take corrective actions. Predictive tools can help inform a housekeeping plan, adapt a rotation schedule, or determine when an object should be retired from display.

LIGHT DOSIMETERS Since historic house museums have mixed collections and often more ability for direct sunlight to enter (namely, through windows), these institutions face lighting concerns not always encountered in purpose-built, nonhistoric museums. Many museums will periodically measure and record the visible and ultraviolet light levels in a room; however, these spot measurements do not give an indication of the cumulative effect of light. Light levels will vary depending on the weather, the time of day, and the season. It is therefore important to measure the additive effect of light during a given period in order to get an indication of the overall effect of light on the collection. Dosimeters are that tool, as they collect light energy and reflect a measure of the damage that the light energy is causing. They permit caretakers to monitor/predict the alteration of a colored surface after a known exposure time at a specific light exposure.

Light dosimeters are relatively small, light-sensitive tools that can indicate the cumulative effect of light in a room. In general, dosimeters consist of a substrate coated with a light-sensitive material that changes color in varying degrees, depending on the amount of light exposure. In order to be predictors of light damage, dosimeters need to respond more rapidly to light than the objects. Each dosimeter is designed and tested to respond (i.e., fade) at a known rate in order to better interpret the results and apply the findings to the collection. Dosimeters are a good predictor for collective light exposure in a given space and serve as a useful visual tool to explain to staff and visitors the effects of light.[11]

There are a variety of light dosimeters available, and some are geared for specific materials. Generally, the most light-sensitive objects in a historic house collection tend to be organic materials, dyed textiles, works on paper, watercolors, and early or color photographs. Light dosimeters are designed to provide a relative indication of the lightfastness of these materials, but some dosimeters are more light sensitive than others.

ISO Blue Wool Standard. The dosimeter most frequently used in historic houses is the International Organization for Standardization (ISO) Blue Wool Standard.[12] The ISO Blue Wool Standard is a small card with eight specifically dyed bands of blue wool representing different levels of light sensitivity from 1 (fugitive) to 8 (good lightfastness). Each dyed band takes approximately twice as long to fade as the band below it. For example, band 2 takes twice as long to fade as band 1. This dosimeter tool is placed next to a collection object on display, with half of each band on the card covered by a lightproof cover and therefore not exposed to light. The fading rate of the object is determined by looking at the fading rate of the supplied Blue Wool standard set, and extrapolating similar damage to the object. Collection materials can be graded for lightfastness using the Blue Wool scale of 1 (fugitive) to 8 (lightfast).

The card and collection material are routinely checked for the first signs of fading. When fading is

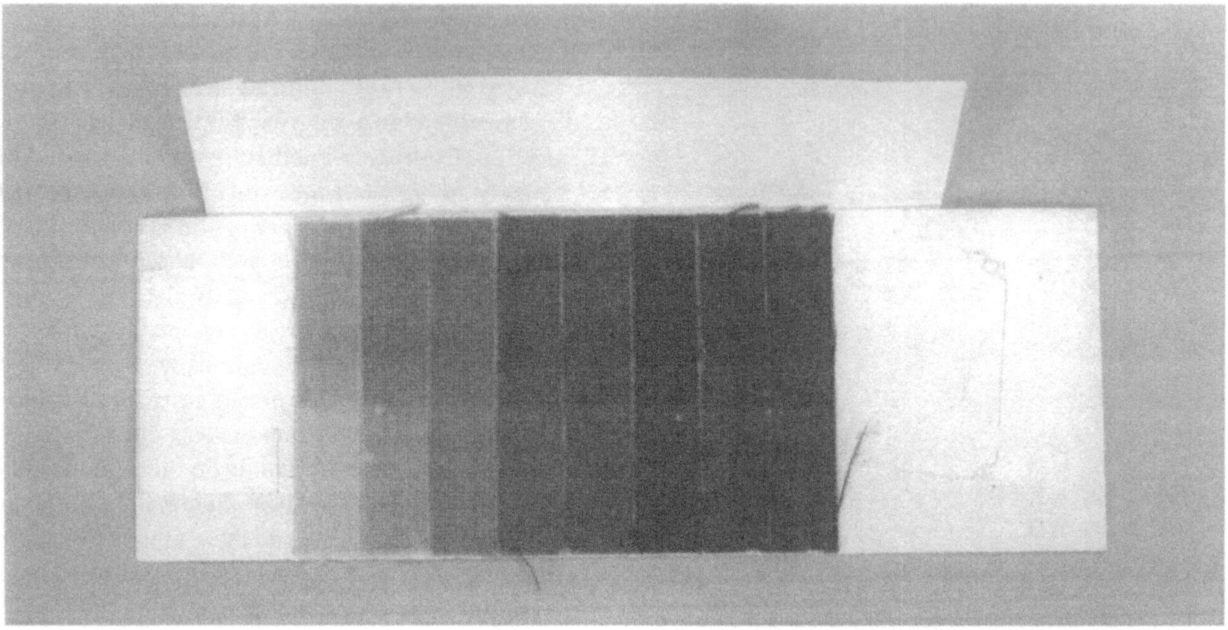

Figure 8.6 ISO Blue Wool Standard.

Figure 8.7 ISO Blue Wool Standard used on a carpet to record fading.

noted on the collection item and then compared to the card, the item can be classified as unstable or fugitive, intermediate, or excellent as categorized by Feller.[13] Feller made his assumption based on visible light exposure in a well-illuminated gallery (considered to have an annual daylight exposure of 150,000 foot-candle hours per year).[14] That daylight exposure level is likely to be too low for the historic house museum context. Feller also assumed a controlled museum environment, and few historic houses have rigorously controlled relative humidity (RH). Because RH affects fading rates and often accelerates them, this assumption would make his fading rates conservative. He also assumed that there were no UV filtration controls, which would also accelerate fading. Many historic house museums do have UV filtration in place, which would slow fading. These assumptions make Feller's rating scale less accurate for the historic house setting, but nonetheless a useful tool in evaluating light damage to collections.

The ISO Blue Wool Standard provides a means for assessing light damage that is determined through a subjective means, which is the color perception of the viewer reading the cards. Color change can be measured using instrumentation (such as a colorimeter) and yield much more accurate data and better interpretation of the results. However, instrumentation is costly and often not available to staff in historic houses.

Monitoring can be used effectively to gain support for better light control, whether it is observed as the contrast between exposed and protected surfaces on the Blue Wool Standard or as numbers on a chart. Each graphically represents the damage light can cause.

The ISO Blue Wool Standard cards do have some limitations. They were developed for technical applications to determine the lightfastness of dyes used for textiles and, as a result, are not light sensitive enough for some other applications. Low light levels that can damage very fragile objects, such as early or color photographs, will take at least a year to register on the cards.[15] While changes from low light levels may not be visible on the cards, damage to extremely fragile objects may already have taken place. This does not mean that ISO Blue Wool Standard cards are obsolete. Unless the collection is full of early or color photographs or other extremely light-sensitive objects, the ISO Blue Wool Standard will still provide a good indication of light exposure before light damage is visible on most objects found in historic house collections.

Tempera-Painted Dosimeters. The environmental effects of light, temperature, and air pollutants on paintings have been examined in several studies by using tempera-painted dosimeters.[16] The premise of the studies was to evaluate the effects of the indoor environment on paintings by using dosimeters that mimicked the structure of paintings. In one study, the tempera dosimeters were constructed using Melinex (polyethylene terephtalate) as the substrate and then painted with tempera paint and cut into strips.[17] Two sets of each of the paints were either artificially aged or placed in a museum or gallery for exposure to natural conditions. The tempera strips were then analyzed to monitor color changes in the paint. In both of the studies it was found that the chemical composition of the museum atmosphere affects the appearance of the painted samples and may amplify the degree of fading. These dosimeters provide a good indication of the damage incurred by exhibited paintings, but the tempera paint may not be light sensitive enough to be a useful dosimeter for other objects.

LiDo (LightCheck). A more sensitive light dosimeter prototype was developed and patented by The Research Center for the Preservation of Graphic Documents (CRCDG) in France[18] and is sometimes referred to as the Blue Pink Scale (BPS).[19]

The dosimeter consists of a mixture of photosensitive compounds embedded in a polymer matrix and applied to a paper substrate. The dosimeter will react to lower light levels than the ISO Wool Standards. The dosimeter changes from blue, to pink, and finally to white based on the level of exposure. Since the dosimeter is on a paper substrate, it can be cut to small sizes, even a few millimeters. The flexibility in sizing would allow the dosimeter to better fit the needs of a collection and would offer minimally obtrusive monitoring.

The potential of the Blue Pink Scale led to sponsorship by the European Union for further development, testing, and eventual production of these light dosimeters. Research began on February 1, 2001, testing dosimeters on both paper and glass substrates.[20] Both types of dosimeters were tested in climate chambers and in the field at museums in London, Paris, Prague, and Florence in order to monitor the effects of various environments. The first experiments indicated that results are visible in one to four weeks depending on conditions.[21] So far, it has been found that the glass-based dosimeters are less sensitive than the paper-based version; therefore, each type will be useful for different applications depending on the specific needs of a collection.[22] The experiments have also reiterated that relative humidity accelerates the fading effects of light. This further highlights that the environment as a whole affects the collection. The potential of this type of dosimeter to be able to respond to a variety of light levels, including very low levels, makes this a useful light-monitoring tool.

Analyzing Results. Most light dosimeters can be analyzed in several ways. The easiest way to analyze many dosimeters is to open one after the testing period and compare the exposed and unexposed sides or compare it to a standardized reference set. The dosimeters can be further analyzed by using a colorimeter to obtain instrumental chromatic values using an international system (Commission Internationale de l'Eclairage or CIE L*A*B*). In the CIE L*A*B* system, color values are calculated for the different parameters of L* for lightness, A* for red-green scale, and B* for blue-yellow.[23] Using a colorimeter will help quantify the results and remove some of the subjectivity of comparing color changes. Whether the results are compared visually or with instrumentation, a good indication of light damage can be determined by light dosimeters.

UV DOSIMETERS Ultraviolet light dosimeters also exist. They consist of a polymethyle methacrylate (PMMA) film doped with a mercury-dithizone complex.[24] The dosimeters are orange and change to various shades of blue depending on the level of exposure. Unfortunately, their use as a UV dosimeter for museum collections would be negligible, because the dosimeter's maximum sensitivity is between 270 and 315 nm, and radiation in that range is normally filtered by standard window glass.[25]

Predicting Damage from Light Exposure

The Canadian Conservation Institute (CCI) developed a slide rule to determine light damage as a collection care tool to calculate the predicted damage to artifacts from light.[26] The slide rule uses the intensity of light exposure plus the duration of the exposure to calculate the damage that will result from the combination of these two factors. The slide rule gives predicted fading in time increments and in relative severity. The instrument can be used to predict light damage to an artifact and to select appropriate light sources for the display environment (figure 8.8).

THE PHILOSOPHY OF LIGHTING FOR HISTORIC INTERIORS

For centuries daylight was the primary lighting source for a home. Depending on the date of a historic property, most furnished interiors used daylight coming through a window for illumination. Burning candles or oil supplemented the daylight when necessary. A fireplace added light to a room in the evening. The occupants of a house sat, read, wrote, and performed as many activities as possible near windows or in doorways to take advantage of the daylight. They also knew that light was harmful to furnishings, so they protected them through the use of cloth covers, and they kept rooms closed off and windows shuttered and/or drapes closed when not in use.

Museums today want to present these interiors to the public as they were used and enjoyed by their owners. Skillful introduction of daylight and control of its distribution in a period room can accommodate the visitors' need to see and enjoy the display while preventing damage to collections. Lighting control is a juncture where interpretive and preservation staffs need to work closely to develop a lighting plan that allows for both visitor enjoyment and collections preservation. In 1998, the Association of Preservation Technology and the American Institution for Conservation collaborated to develop "Guidelines for Light and Lighting in Historic Buildings That House Collections" in which this reasoned approached is recommended (see Introduction).[27]

Many housekeeping techniques that protected items from light damage and were commonplace in the seventeenth to the nineteenth centuries were abandoned in the twentieth century. Much of the damage seen in interiors today is a result of overexposure to light when the daily routine of closing shutters, pulling down shades, and placing slipcovers on furniture gave way to permitting uncontrolled penetration of sunlight into the interior because houses no longer had a staff to maintain these systems of control. While historic light control methods were being discontinued, a changing aesthetic valued light-filled rooms of historic furnishings. At the same time, the furnishings were being mass-produced for reduced costs. These factors combined to increase the rate of light damage of historic house furnishings during the twentieth century. Rein-

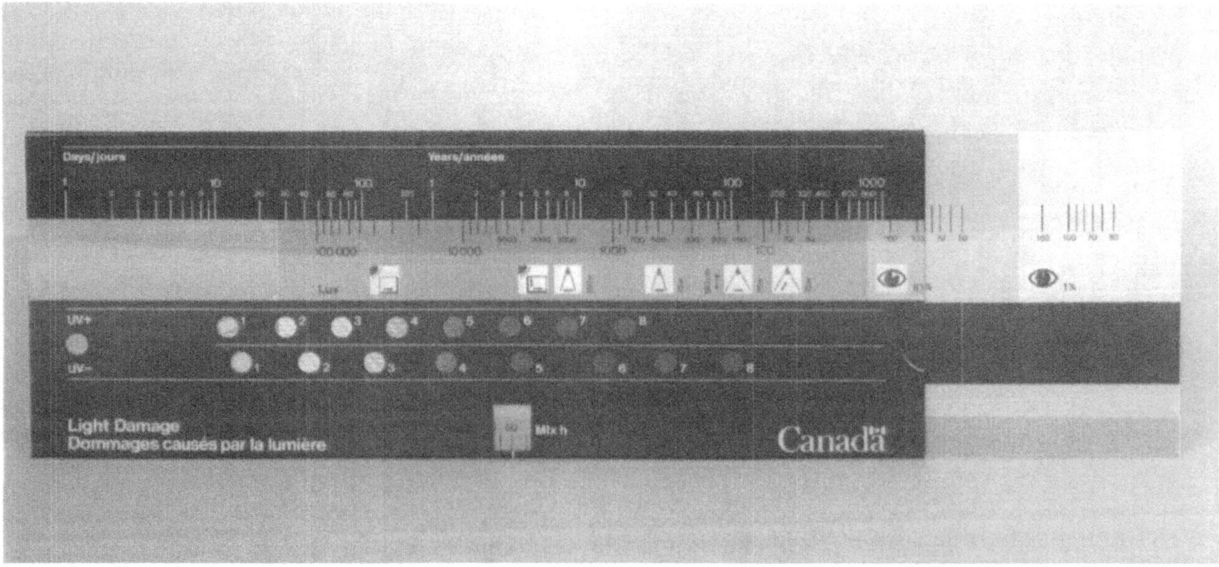

Figure 8.8 Light damage slide rule: A slide rule to determine light damage, Canadian Conservation Institute.

Figure 8.9 Drapes soften light from windows at Scotty's Castle, Death Valley National Park (Grapevine Canyon), Death Valley, California.

Figure 8.10 Visitors face windows at the entry to site.

troducing some of the traditional light control techniques into a historic house enhances preservation and achieves interpretive goals by showing visitors a little-realized aspect of life at another time. Possibly the most difficult twentieth-century notion to overcome is the idea that in order to enjoy a furnished interior, it must be bathed in light, and that light should flood into every space in the home.

When visitors enter a property, they learn about the people who occupied the home in another time and get an impression of their daily life. The visitor is often standing at one end of a room, viewing contents on display while listening to a guide. In many instances the visitor is facing a bright window, which can make it difficult to see the room's contents as anything but a series of silhouettes against the light. In order to see adequately, hot spots in a room, such as bright sunlit windows, need to be softened (figure 8.9). Our eyes are naturally drawn to such bright spots and our ability to perceive less brightly lit objects in the room is diminished. For many rooms, however, the window may be the only light source available, and once a shutter is closed or a shade is drawn to eliminate the hot spot, another source of light is needed to be able to enjoy the interior. These problems should be addressed as part of developing a lighting plan for the house.

A successful lighting strategy will gradually reduce light levels from the outside to the interior so that the visitors' eyes can adjust to the lower levels. An object faintly illuminated and placed against a dark background will appear better lit than the same object faintly lit against a bright background. By varying light levels and selectively playing them against each other and against wall and furnishing colors, a room can give the perception that its objects are more brightly lit than they actually are. A gradual increase in illumination as the tour path reaches the exit will help visitors' eyes adjust to the outdoor lighting conditions more effectively and will lessen the chance for tripping and stumbling when visitors exit the building.

Lighting Strategies

There are a wide range of lighting options that can be used effectively to light historic interiors for visibility, atmosphere, and authenticity while preserving collections on display. Planning the lighting for a historic house museum is just as important as developing a lighting plan for a museum exhibit gallery. In both instances, if displayed collections are to be seen and appreciated, they must be safely lit to proper advantage.

The goal of successful lighting should be to reduce the duration of exposure, reduce the intensity of the light, eliminate harmful portions of the light spectrum, and allow for appreciation of collections and the safety of the visitors. The lighting techniques should strive for relative historical accuracy without becoming overly dramatic. It is notable that our lighting technologies can permit features to be enhanced in ways that were not possible in past centuries. A curio cabinet used to display small collectibles in a stately home can be fitted with small spotlights using a light emitting diode (LED) or a fiber-optic system that permits the visitor to appreciate each precious article. Paintings or architectural features can also be highlighted by similar artificial means. However, highlighting too much in a room can impart a false impression to the visitor and may divert the attention from the interpretive message.

One aspect of a lighting scheme that should be considered is the amount of light needed to safely carry out curatorial and conservation functions in the space. Light levels will need to be raised to a safe level for routine cleaning and handling of artifacts to avoid damage or accidents to collections.

COMMONLY USED LIGHTING SYSTEMS

Effective lighting appears "natural" for its context. It provides good visibility without creating false impressions and without damaging collections. This can be achieved by combining natural light coming through windows with a variety of artificial systems. The selection of the type of artificial lighting system to be used should be made before the fixture is selected. The potential for heat buildup, spectrum availability, UV light components, lifespan of the lamp, access, costs, and maintenance should all be taken into account. Fixtures can then be chosen for the selected light type.

Often in practice the exact opposite occurs. Fixtures are already installed or were chosen without considering lamping restrictions. Lamps and fixtures may be chosen for their style, their placement in the room, or their ability to be hidden over or behind a door. An incandescent lamp (the ordinary household electric light) is probably the most commonly used supplemental light source in a historic house. Some interiors have period gas or oil fixtures that have been electrified. It is important to not use lamps with too high a wattage in converted light fixtures, as they can crack or damage the historic shades and fittings.

Torchiere lamps are used in many furnished interiors. These tall lamps are selected because they direct light to the ceiling, where it is diffused and bounced back down into the room. They can be hidden behind open doors and bed hangings. When skillfully used, these lamps can be a successful light source, but when high-wattage bulbs are used or the lamp is placed in the visitors' line of sight, the glare will affect appreciation of the room's contents. Torchiere lamps should be used with incandescent lightbulbs of low wattage. They can be a significant source of infrared radiation, creating unsafe temperatures within the space.

In the past, bare fluorescent tube bulb fixtures were often installed in the space above a doorway to direct light into a period room from above the visitors' head (figure 8.11). This installation was common in the 1950s and 1960s. If the visitor can stand only in the doorway, rather than entering the room, this method can provide enough ambient light for a smaller room. However, the fixture/tube must be inspected regularly so that the ballast does not fail, spreading an acrid smoke in the house. Fluorescent bulbs are generally cool, but they may have a UV component that should be eliminated through filtration. Some lamps are good for accurate color rendition but others are not. It is important to pay attention to the spectral reflectivity charts for each bulb selected to ensure adequate color rendering. Transmission curves of spectral reflectivity are available for every lamp sold and can be requested from the lighting provider or manufacturer.

Advances in lighting that include technologies such as LED and fiber-optic systems are being introduced into the historic furnished interior. These energy-efficient systems are particularly useful for exhibit cases. A well-designed lighting installation can greatly enhance the visitors' experience in a home. If the historic house museum uses exhibit cases for display, there are numerous other types of lamps and fixtures that can be used. Consult a reference on museum lighting for more information in this area (see bibliography).

SYSTEMS OF LIGHT CONTROL

It is best to begin light control where it enters the building. At the level of the windows, UV can be filtered out with polyester-based films that adhere to the glass (fig-

Figure 8.11 Fluorescent tube set over doorway of furnished room.

ure 8.12). There are many films on the market with differing purposes and performance criteria (figure 8.13). As product formulations change frequently, it is important to review product literature when deciding which film to place on windows. It is also wise to take a sample reading from the batch that you have purchased before installation on your windows to ensure that it is performing to standard. Be sure that the film filters the shorter UV wavelengths of between 325 and 400 nm, which are not blocked by the window glass. These UV-filtering films do not reduce harmful visible light unless they are also tinted. Tinted filters are available in many shades and colors or with coatings such as sputtered-titanium mirroring. Such films may not be suitable for all applications in the historic house.

There are a few relevant issues to consider about these films. It is not recommended to apply film to historic glass, because removal of old film can be difficult and has been known to damage original glass panes. They should be professionally installed to avoid the formation of bubbles between the glass and the plastic film. The manufacturer should specify special window maintenance procedures to avoid damage and scratching on the film surface. Filters should be adhered to all windows in a room (not just the south-facing windows) to adequately protect the room's contents. The films have a limited life expectancy and will eventually lose their ability to filter out UV radiation.

Figure 8.12 Solar X film installed on a window at Sagmore Hill National Historical Site. Harpers Ferry Center Division of Conservation Slide Library.

Figure 8.13 UV film samples of various tints and thicknesses.

UV-filtering acrylic and polycarbonate sheets may be used where films are not appropriate. Typically, large sheets cut to the size of the window are hung from hooks, attached using a hook and loop fastener or magnets, or screwed into replacement sashes. Individual panes of plastic can also be cut and fixed in place using small glazier's points. Sheets that are too tight in a window frame should not be installed, as expansion and contraction of the plastic sheet upon heating and cooling can damage the frame and sill. Airtight installation can lead to condensation buildup between the glass window and the plastic sheet, which will damage the surrounding surfaces. Properly installed sheets can also provide the benefit of another layer of insulation against cold or heat at the window site.

An alternative to installed plastic sheets is the use of roller shades. Both tinted and clear UV-filtering shades can be purchased and installed in a window. They must be kept pulled down at all times to provide protection against UV—wherein lies the potential for failure when using this system. There is a small amount of UV and light bleed at the edge of the shade that must be anticipated and mitigated, and these shades may not filter the wavelengths required for artifact protection. Sensitive objects should not be placed in these areas.

Visible light entering a house can also be controlled with exterior or interior shutters, canopies, awnings, shades, curtains, and blinds (figure 8.14). The system used should be appropriate to the time period of the property. Physical evidence of shutters, curtain supports, and the like can be detected under layers of paint or can be found when architectural elements are examined by a specialist. Clues are often present despite the ravages of deterioration and remodeling. Period photographs, diaries, inventories, and letters may describe or illustrate furnishings and provide information about window treatments. Sympathetic use of window coverings can eliminate windows as lighting hot spots in a room and improve the visitors' experience while reducing the risk to the collection from light exposure. A daily routine that uses such original systems can be very effective in reducing light levels while enhancing interpretation.

Figure 8.15 shows the evolution of the window treatments at Melrose Mansion (part of the Natchez National Historical Park) from the point at which the site went from being a private home to a National Park. Research revealed what window treatments were used by the original owners, and the Park faithfully reproduced them. The photos show how the shutters, blinds, and drapes all added to the elegance and comfort of the room, while controlling light and thereby providing protection for the furnishings.

The path of the sun across the room should be noted, and direct sunlight should not be allowed to fall on displayed artifacts. Shutters, shades, and other window coverings can be adjusted manually during the day. Once natural light has been controlled at its entry point, artificial light within the room should also be controlled. Bulb wattage should be as low as possible while providing a safe level of lighting. On-demand or

Figure 8.14 Lincoln Home National Historical Site, Springfield, Illinois. The site uses exterior shutters (left), interior roller shades (bottom left), and interior slat blinds (bottom right) to control light in the home. Harpers Ferry Center Historic Furnishings Slide Library.

Figure 8.15 ***Left*****: Drawing room window at Melrose Mansion, Natchez National Historical Park, Natchez, Mississippi, when site first became part of the National Park Service. Original mid-nineteenth-century silk drapes in place, with later period lace curtains. Curators closed the exterior shutters to control light at the site while researching original window treatments.** ***Right*****: Research revealed that the Melrose original owners had green wooden slat blinds with silk tapes and silk drapes on the interior windows. The exterior shutters were also original to the house.**

visitor-activated controls help limit the duration of exposure because the lights come on only when the exhibit is actively being viewed by a visitor. All unnecessary lights should be off when the museum is closed or sections are not in use.

Light can also be controlled at the object level. Light-sensitive materials should not be placed near windows or in other strong light sources. Artificial light sources should not be focused on light-sensitive objects. In the past, furnishings may have had removable slipcovers that protected the fancier "show cloth" underneath and were removed for special visitors. Permanent covers also existed over sensitive or very precious objects. The cover would be folded back or pulled to the sides to display the object. For example, a frame displaying a miniature portrait collection on a library table might be covered with a red velvet curtain that when folded back behind the frame revealed its treasures.

When a home was closed up for the season or when the owner was traveling, muslin sheets were used to cover furniture and carpets were rolled up. These are practices that sites can adopt and interpret. Covers were also placed over paintings, books, and other precious objects.

Preventive Conservation and Light Control

Adjusting shades and blinds and keeping furnishings covered were routines for the head of the household or the housekeeping staff. Today curators, docents, students, and custodial staff manage these responsibilities. Preventive conservation duties have expanded to include monitoring and recording light levels and using dosimeters to document or predict damage from light exposure. These routines are essential to keeping administrators and other caretakers informed about ongoing damage to collections, and they are instrumental to effecting change to preserve collections.

Figure 8.16 Cover placed over installed painting on the walls at Adams National Historic Site, Quincy, Massachusetts.

Lighting and Accessibility

Congress passed the American with Disabilities Act (ADA) in 1992. It is a federal civil rights law that prohibits the exclusion of people with disabilities from many activities in which non-handicapped people routinely participate, including the enjoyment of museums and historic house museums. Since 1992, museums have been learning to comply with the act and make the buildings, collections, and exhibits more accessible to all. Lighting design is an important component in this process.

Adequate lighting is needed for handicapped visitors to be able to safely navigate through spaces and for vision-impaired visitors to be able to see some of the objects and spaces in the museum. Visitor safety must be given adequate consideration, making low light levels an area of concern. Access and preservation must be balanced for the good of both the collection and the visitor. Good lighting design will, in fact, help accomplish the goal of making collections accessible. Planned use of light and color can help produce a clearly marked tour route that identifies potential obstacles, steps, or changes in floor levels. Incremental lighting can provide transition spaces where light levels become increasingly higher or lower, allowing the eye to adjust gradually to the new lighting environment. Elimination of glare and hot spots and consistent brightness throughout the tour route help to keep eyes adjusted. This technique is particularly helpful for visually impaired and elderly visitors. Objects should be sufficiently lit to accommodate visually impaired visitors, unless the light levels required will damage the artifacts.

More information about the ADA and its impact on museums and how to fund projects to make your institution more accessible can be found by contacting the American Association of Museums. Also consult the Smithsonian Institution's "Guidelines for Accessible Exhibition Design."[28]

Figure 9.1 An HVAC system.

Preventive Conservation and Environmental Control

SUITABLE CONTROL OF THE temperature and relative humidity in a museum environment is the most significant means by which a collection of objects can be preserved and their deterioration processes slowed. Improper control of the environment can also be a significant means by which a historic structure can be damaged and its deterioration accelerated. As discussed previously, written guidelines and goals should be prepared to formalize the organization's approach to environmental conditions in the historic site museum. Additionally, a clear understanding of environmental control is essential to navigate the costs and benefits needed to protect both collections and structures.

There is an excellent discussion on the preparation of an institutional environmental control policy by Bradley in the Preprints of the 11th Triennial ICOM-CC Meeting (1996) with a copy of the environmental policy developed for the British Museum.[1] The staff and administration of the British Museum decided to address environmental control issues without specifying actual numerical limits and values. They chose instead to address the concepts and rationale behind environmental control and its essential role in preserving the collections.

For the context of this book, the environment will include temperature, relative humidity, and atmospheric pollution. Temperature and relative humidity are intimately interrelated and they both affect the severity and rate of chemical interaction of atmospheric pollutants with collection and structural materials.

TEMPERATURE AND RELATIVE HUMIDITY

Temperature

When environmental control is discussed in the museum context, it is temperature that is often listed first, although the specific temperature of the environment is perhaps the least important aspect of the environment for collection preservation. Temperature is important for four reasons. The first is that elevated temperatures can increase the rate of chemical reactions, as discussed in chapter 4, "Intellectual and Physical Controls." It is estimated that for every drop in temperature of 9°F, the deterioration rate of an object is cut in half.[2] This is one reason that many repositories of photographic negatives store their collections in cold storage. It is hoped that unstable photographic materials will survive longer in reduced temperature environments.

The second reason that temperature is important is that water expands in volume when it freezes at 32°F. Water can be found in the cells of organic materials, for example, or in small cavities in stone or ceramics. The expansion associated with freezing causes damage to the cells or cavities where ice/water is located within collection objects and the materials of the structure.

The third concern regarding temperature is that some materials, like waxes and resins, become tacky and may even melt at temperatures near high ambient ranges. If the temperature is kept above freezing and below the melting point of collection objects, it will not immediately affect the physical preservation of collections. If the temperature is kept at the high end of ambient room temperature for long periods of time, creep, sagging, and deterioration reactions will accelerate.

Studies indicate that changes in temperature, under conditions of constant relative humidity, do create stresses that are strong enough to damage composite objects like paintings[3] and restrained materials like joined wood. It appears that problems may arise with changes in temperature in mixed media objects, where one material shrinks in response to cooling faster, or to a larger extent, than the surrounding materials. This differential response to temperature change creates stresses between neighboring materials that may cause damage to the object. These studies show that stressed materials eventually relax and achieve equilibrium with neighboring materials if enough time is allowed at the

When the National Park Service opened the Russian Bishop's House in Sitka, Alaska, for tours it did so during the summer months only. The furnished rooms of the house were "mothballed" and the house closed in winter. However, one part of the building is a consecrated Russian Orthodox chapel, which was kept open for services. As years passed, more tourists traveled to Alaska and wanted to be able to see the historic site. Today, the NPS keeps the building open year-round, and all mothballing traditions of an annual closure are forgotten.

new temperature level. As more research is done, the response of collection objects to changes in temperature under constant relative humidity will be better understood.

Temperature is also important because there is a trend to provide for the visitors' comfort in order to increase visitation. Houses that once closed for six months of the year have been fitted with heating systems in order to stay open during the winter months.

If the actual temperature reading of a space is not intrinsically thought to be critical to object and building preservation, why the concern about temperature levels and ranges? The fourth, and most significant, reason why temperature is important to collection and building preservation is that it affects the relative humidity.

Relative Humidity

Put most simply, relative humidity (RH) is the amount of water that air holds at a specific temperature relative to the total water the air can hold at that specific temperature. When air holds all the moisture it can hold at a specific temperature it is said to be saturated and is considered to be at 100 percent RH. Suppose one took air from the room at ambient (room) temperature and sealed it in an airtight cube, somewhat like what happens when you close a food storage container. If the sealed cube were placed in a refrigerator where the temperature was lower, condensation would form on the inside of the cube, even without the addition of extra water. If the cube were removed from the cool enclosure and allowed to return to room temperature, the condensation would evaporate back into the air within the cube. The cube is not "breathing." Moisture is condensing out of the air in the cube as the temperature is lowered, because cool air can hold less water than hot air. The appearance and disappearance of condensation in the container is a direct result of the physics of temperature and relative humidity.

This phenomenon occurs because air can only hold a fixed amount of water at a fixed temperature. If the temperature is changed, the amount of water it can hold will change. If the temperature goes up, the air can hold more water. It will absorb moisture from the surroundings until it reaches equilibrium. It will absorb the water from any source it can find (plants, earth, your skin, fibers, organic materials). If the temperature goes down, the air can hold less water and will release any extra moisture as condensation and deposit the condensate as water on the coldest surfaces nearby. This is what happens on a glass of iced tea when it is taken outside on a hot day. The warmer air outside comes into contact with the outside of the glass container that has been cooled by the ice cubes. As the air nears the glass it begins to cool or drop in temperature. When this happens, the moisture in the air that is cooling down condenses on the outside of the glass (figure 9.2). (This is the same principle that is used in dehumidification via air-conditioning; this is why the air conditioner drips.) On a microcosmic scale, this deposition and absorption of moisture by the air occurs with every minute fluctuation in temperature. The moisture is deposited and absorbed by the materials in the surrounding environment. In the case of a museum or historic house, this includes the materials that make up our objects and our historic buildings.

Think for a minute about what happens on a hot summer day in a humid town on the southeastern coast of the United States as visitors enter and leave an air-conditioned historic house. The door opens and a burst of hot, moist air and visitors enter through the front door. All of the surfaces near the door are already colder than the outside air because they have been cooled by the air-conditioning. When the moist air from the hot humid outdoors or from the visitors' moist respired air comes into contact with the paintings, porcelain, furniture, and textiles near the door, moisture will condense from the warm, moist air onto these surfaces.

In the winter when structures are heated the warmed air becomes very dry unless it is re-humidified by a humidifier. As the temperature of the air is raised, it can hold more moisture. It will seek to absorb more moisture from the surrounding materials. If no additional moisture is provided by a humidifier, the dry air will absorb moisture from wherever it can find it. In a museum or historic house, the sources of moisture will include wood furniture, wood walls, wood floors, tex-

Figure 9.2 Condensation.

tile fibers, leather, and other organic materials that naturally contain water in their chemical makeup and serve as moisture buffers.

The same problems can be found within the actual structures of a building. Condensation can be a problem on wall surfaces, ceilings, and in the wall cavities and structures of the building. Newly constructed and rehabilitated buildings have insulation and vapor barriers to help control or eliminate problems of condensation, but older structures may not. Many older buildings were not heated, humidified, or air-conditioned to the degree they are today, if at all. They were not designed or made for the conditions we prefer in buildings today. The effect of the local climate on the building is an additional complicating factor that must be considered in controlling the environment in historic structures. In locations with very cold winters, it can be difficult or impossible to maintain an interior relative humidity of 50 percent or more (long cited as a target RH for museum collections) without causing serious condensation problems (within walls and on window glass) as the humidified air comes into contact with outside air or surfaces cooled by the outside air. Additionally, residences were not built or designed for the exaggerated number of users and occupants created when they are converted into public museums. Some of the most heavily visited sites in America can receive over two thousand visitors per day. The thresholds, floors, and stairs were never expected to be able to handle this level of usage. A residential heating, ventilation, and air-conditioning (HVAC) system can handle a normal number of door and window openings and a normal number of occupants, but few are designed to operate with the doors open all day long or to handle the heat and humidity generated by two thousand visitors per day.

The Impact of Relative Humidity Levels and Fluctuations on Collections and Structures

Organic materials, like the wood in walls and the paper and textiles of our collections, contain two kinds of water, *adsorbed* and *bound*. The adsorbed water is essentially sitting in contact with the organic molecule but is not actually bound to the molecule through chemical bonds. The bound water is actually part of the molecule that comprises the material itself. It is bound in place through chemical bonds. The adsorbed water can contribute to the flexibility of an organic material by lubricating the movement of adjacent molecules or fibers against each other. The bound water is an integral and essential part of the molecules that comprise materials. When adsorbed water is lost, a material may become less flexible, but the flexibility may be restored if the material is rehydrated or rehumidified. When bound water is lost, permanent chemical and physical damage occurs that cannot be reversed. The water cannot be replaced. Embrittlement and weakening occur. Bound water loss from organic materials can generally happen at relative humidity levels below about 25 to 30 percent.[4] This phenomenon determines the lower "safe" limit for relative humidity levels for collections and building materials.

The safe upper limit level for relative humidity is determined either by the potential ability for mold to grow at high relative humidity levels or the harmful condensation of moisture within the building materials or structure. Museum pest populations also flourish in higher levels of relative humidity. Mold growth is a serious problem for collection materials, structural materials, and people who are exposed to it. Active mold growth results in the digestion of proteins and starches from organic materials, causing staining and color change from digestive processes and sometimes-serious health problems for staff and guests. It is a problem for collections, structures, and people. The problems for collections and structures and specific solutions associated with mold activity are discussed further in chapter 10, "Preventive Conservation and Integrated Pest Management."

There is some discussion among mycologists and environmental scientists as to what relative humidity levels contribute to active mold growth. Many believe that relative humidity levels above 60 to 65 percent can encourage active growth, while others disagree.[5] In some instances, different species of mold have been shown to become active under different environmental conditions. The history of the environmental conditions for the substrate on which the mold grows may also be significant. Materials that have high equilibrium moisture content or that have been in high relative humidity in the recent past may support active mold growth at a lower relative humidity than the same material from a drier environment.[6] Suffice it to say, this phenomenon is complex and not yet completely understood. Specialists investigating the relationship of relative humidity to mold-related deterioration of collections believe that a mid-level RH, between 25 and 65 percent as outside limits, will provide the best general environment for mold-free mixed collections.[7]

Special conditions can exist in historic structures that allow condensation to form within wall and floor structures of buildings. The condensation can cause a range of problems such as the movement of soluble salts, the growth of mold colonies, the dissolution of structural adhesives, and the weakening of plaster and other construction materials. These problems can also be caused by roof, gutter, and other drainage problems, which are discussed in chapter 12, "Preventive Conservation and the Historic House Structure." Uncontrolled moisture of any kind anywhere in a historic structure or museum is a serious problem that will lead to deterioration of the collection and the building.

William Rose presents an excellent discussion of the application of architectural and engineering principles to the study of in-wall condensation in a structure in his book entitled *Water in Buildings: An Architect's Guide to Moisture and Mold*.[8] Rose evaluates the use of various tools for the study and understanding of moisture differences in materials and structures to investigate the potential for condensation within the building envelope under different environmental conditions. These methods use indoor and outdoor temperatures and relative humidity levels; thermal resistance values for elements of the building structure; vapor permeabilities of materials; and the psychrometric chart to anticipate the conditions under which condensation or vapor phase differences might occur and the location or interface where it is likely. Rose discusses the pros and cons of several methods, but generally indicates that very complex computer modeling is the only accurate way to try to understand the moisture engineering of a structure. These complex methods are still evolving and show great promise for use in better understanding of historic structures in the future.

The Evolution of Environmental Standards for Collections and Historic Structures

The role that temperature and relative humidity play in the preservation of materials has been noted empirically as far back as the late 1800s.[9] Just prior to World War I, several authors noted the role that relative humidity played in the damage and deterioration of wall paintings.[10] These investigators determined that large fluctuations in RH were damaging, and that based on the average ambient humidity in the London climate, a RH between 55 and 60 percent might be helpful in reducing fluctuations. While they realized this was fairly arbitrary, they recommended this RH range for museum environments.[11]

When World War II began, these recommendations were used in deciding the environmental conditions for storage of the National Gallery's art collections, which were moved to a local slate quarry for safekeeping. While they were in storage, "normal panel damage disappeared. After the war, the National Gallery installed control systems."[12] Following the lead of the National Gallery, architects and engineers began to use these values, based on fairly circumstantial information, as standards for the museum community. "Museum users assumed that the values were scientific, based on a significant minimum in deterioration. Originators knew 50% RH emphasized mechanical phenomena and neglected chemical phenomena: they knew it was a nice round number and the specified fluctuations were not derived from artifact needs, but in the museum world at large, non-conformity became transgression."[13]

Collections in England that had been kept at consistent ambient relative humidity levels of around 60 percent with temperatures generally around 60°F–65°F were quickly dried out by new heating and cooling and dehumidification systems that raised the temperature and lowered the relative humidity. The environmental changes caused cracks and splits to appear in objects; veneer began curling and lifting; gilt decoration popped.

During the early 1980s, the staff at a large historic house museum in the Northeast became increasingly concerned about the effects of their poor environmental conditions on their important decorative arts furniture collection. The curators and conservators advocated an HVAC renovation project that would provide environmental conditions for the museum that complied with the current best practice recommendation of a relative humidity of 55% ± 2% and a temperature of 70°F ± 2°F for an optimum museum environment. The staff wrote a successful federal grant application to secure funding for the HVAC renovation and the work was completed in the middle 1980s. During the first winter, a maintenance employee noticed that the stucco exterior of the historic building seemed to be spalling and exfoliating. He noted that the damage was confined to the northwest façade of the house. At first, the building maintenance staff suspected a roof leak, but no evidence of roof problems was found.

Finally, the suggestion was made that the new relative humidity levels created in the interior of the house might be causing the problem. The spalling was closely examined and it was found that ice crystals were forming under the stucco and forcing the exterior finish off the building. The building had no vapor barrier. The higher levels of relative humidity on the interior were permitting moisture-laden air to permeate the interior of the wall materials. Upon contact with the colder outside air, the moisture condensed from the air to form water droplets that quickly froze. Because the water droplets expanded upon freezing, they forced the stucco off the exterior walls. The damage was first noticed on the shaded northwest façade, where the exterior wall remained the coldest for the longest period during the day.

The building maintenance staff tested this theory by lowering the interior relative humidity. The crystallization and spalling stopped. It was determined through experimentation that the specific climatic conditions for the region combined with the specific wall construction materials used in the structure created a situation where the relative humidity could be brought as high as 37 percent in the winter months without detrimental effect to the building itself. A compromise was required between the environmental needs of the collection in the historic house and the environmental needs of the house structure itself.

Today museum and engineering professionals are painfully aware of the need for this type of compromise. However, decisions cannot be made without exchange and discussion between the various disciplines that are stakeholders in historic site museums. The "New Orleans Charter for Joint Preservation of Historic Structures and Artifacts" of 1992 formalizes this reality, and no one today would make this same mistake.

Museums in newer buildings and those purpose built as museums were investing heavily in closely controlled HVAC systems. Historic structures were having serious problems conforming to this trend in preservation practice. Institutions in historic structures were seriously damaging their historic buildings in an effort to keep up with the standards.

Conservators that worked regularly with collections in historic structures would suggest that the collections would be compromised by keeping them in the poor environmental conditions of their uncontrolled historic structures. Historic house museums began to move toward the addition of environmental systems to provide the "standard" conditions to protect their collections. Those that couldn't were convinced to remove original pieces to other museums for safekeeping or place them into storage, leaving reproductions for display in the houses.[14]

Conservators working with historic house collections have questioned the "70°F ± 2°F and 55% ± 2% RH" guidelines. They continued to try to understand the issues and adapt the needs of the collections and structures to the everyday reality of the site.[15]

In the early 1990s a number of conservation scientists were trying to use a more theoretical approach to determine the relationship between temperature, relative humidity, and deterioration. David Erhardt and his colleagues at the Conservation and Analytical Laboratory, Museum Support Center, Smithsonian Institution, looked at the fundamental nature of the chemical reactions that contribute to material deterioration.[16] They looked at the primary deterioration mechanisms for each general class of materials found in museum collections and historic structures. They considered hydrolysis and oxidation reactions for glass and ceramics, wood, paper-based materials, textiles, and so on. They determined the parameters of heat and water input needed for each deterioration reaction to go forward and to speed up or slow down for each material. Based on their investigations, they suggested a range of temperature and relative humidity levels under which most deterioration could be moderated for the majority of materials. In general, they found that the relative humidity levels could and should be lower than those previously cited.

At the same time other scientists were looking into the role that environmental fluctuation plays in material deterioration.[17] They found that it takes longer for materials to react to a relative humidity fluctuation than had been thought. Hence short-term fluctuations in RH of a few hours' duration are less of a concern than fluctuations that last a day or longer.[18] This makes it possible to permit more short-term fluctuations, if the conditions stabilize over a longer time frame. Scientists and conservators also studied the complexity of the reaction of composite material systems to environmental fluctuation, like paintings with many different layers of materials bound together.[19] The different layers of the painting structure react differently to temperature and relative humidity changes, causing delamination and cupping as well as cracking and interlayer voids. They found that perhaps temperature fluctuations might play a larger role than suspected in the deterioration of composite and other structures, and the reaction of materials to temperature changes might be expressed much more rapidly.

At the same time, the Image Permanence Institute (IPI), a nonprofit research laboratory at the Rochester Institute of Technology, began advocating for a broad approach to environmental monitoring and created a toolkit to manage environmental monitoring and data interpretation. With support from the National Endowment for the Humanities (NEH), the Institute for Museum and Library Services (IMLS), and the Andrew W. Mellon Foundation, IPI created a data logger for environmental monitoring called the Preservation Environment Monitor (PEM) and new software for data analysis called the Climate Notebook. Together they form a comprehensive tool to monitor environment, document the capabilities of building systems, evaluate risks to collections, and analyze data, and they create a process to manage a site's environment. Once baseline environmental data are recorded and building systems are documented, the software helps analyze the preservation quality of a museum environment and create action levels for change. While inclusion in this chapter is not meant to be an endorsement of these products, their widespread acceptance and use in the profession and their unique reporting tools warrant a discussion.

IPI seeks to encourage institutions to adopt what they call a "preservation environment management process," which mirrors the holistic approach advocated in this book. Careful documentation, acquisition of data, and a team approach in which all interests are represented at the table create best practices for the management of the building and the collections. IPI's Climate Notebook software organizes and analyzes the monitoring data with this goal in mind.

The Climate Notebook includes calculators that demonstrate the effect that changes in temperature and relative humidity have on the rate of deterioration of organic materials. It calculates dew point, mold risk factor, and dimensional change due to moisture absorption or desorption.[20] It also contains the Preservation Index (PI) to express how ambient temperature and RH affect the rate at which collections experience decay.[21] Calculations are based on unchanging temperature and relative humidity conditions. To reflect the real museum environment where conditions shift seasonally or more often, the Time-Weighted Preservation Index (TWPI) was created to quantify organic decay and illustrate the effects of fluctuating conditions over a period of time.[22] This tool offers institutions the information needed to understand the effect of the environment on its particular collections and manage the environment for effective preservation.

The Evolution of Solutions for Environmental Control in Historic Buildings

The changing knowledge base in understanding environmental control and deterioration has given us more reliable guidelines for temperature and relative humidity parameters for historic site museums. Improvements in heating, cooling, and humidity control systems have also expanded the number of options available. Discussion and a willingness to find suitable compromises to protect historic structures and collections are creating a new protocol for determining environmental conditions and systems in historic house museums.[23] These new approaches include the adoption of broader environmental standards, the use of inherent ventilation and control systems designed as part of the historic building, the use of controlled ventilation for RH moderation, and the use of humidistats rather than thermostats. Rose's demonstration of the use of complex engineering for investigating potential building moisture interactions may also prove to be very useful in negotiating building and collection environmental needs. Continued improvement and innovation should be expected in this area.

Clarifying the goals for architects, engineers, conservators, and administrators in discussions about environmental control for collections and historic buildings is essential for good decision making and effective and appropriate solutions. As in many cases, cross-discipline communication can be challenging and needs the input of all of the team members.

SCIENTIFIC MEASUREMENT AND MONITORING OF TEMPERATURE AND RELATIVE HUMIDITY

Monitoring Programs

The rationale for an environmental monitoring program involves the need to know what environmental conditions the collection and structure are currently exposed to and to understand whether or not these conditions are contributing to deterioration. Baseline environmental data are generally gathered for at least one full calendar year for each area where collections are found and for each area where there are concerns for the building.

Collected data will give the institution an idea of the high and low values for the year and also give an overview of the extent that seasonal outdoor climatic variation affects the interior conditions. Looking at the highs and lows over the course of all four seasons can indicate what major control shortfalls exist. For example, in the Great Plains states, where it is very cold in the winter and relatively dry throughout the year, most institutions have problems with keeping the relative humidity high enough to prevent desiccation of materials, particularly in the winter when heating systems are used. Even in the summer months in this region, high relative humidity is rarely a problem. In other parts of the country this may not be the case. In more humid regions, high relative humidity is the issue rather than low relative humidity. The broad annual overview is essential for understanding potential problems and determining appropriate solutions. It is essential because it indicates what improvements are actually needed.

The second and equally important aspect of monitoring is the need to detect and understand isolated or cyclical "events" that may occur in the interior environment due to control shortfalls or equipment problems. With regular monitoring, it is possible to know when there are both major and minor fluctuations in the environmental conditions. Software programs exist that will display the temperature and relative humidity readings as raw data, charts, or graphs to help visualize trends. Statistics present minimum, maximum, mean, and standard deviation. Facility managers who are given target ranges can evaluate whether the system operations are satisfactory and adjust accordingly. Study of the charts and trend logs can help indicate what the problems might be, when they occur, and how long they last (i.e., whether they will adversely affect the condition of the collection or the structure). Events can also presage problems with HVAC systems and provide important information for use in planning and scheduling building system maintenance, repairs, and replacements.

Under special circumstances, sensors are placed in wall and other structural cavities in the building to monitor cavity environmental conditions. If there are suspected problems with cavity condensation or water leaks, this may be done in an effort to better understand the environmental dynamics within the structure. The monitoring of the outside air is also often included to provide information about daily outdoor conditions, which is sometimes used for control of the HVAC and other building systems. Outside air may be able to be tapped as a source for temperature or humidity moderation.

Museum monitoring can often be done in concert with the HVAC system and its internal sensing devices. Monitoring done by the museum staff with room instrumentation, like a hygrothermograph or a data logger, measures the actual room conditions, not the conditions that an HVAC system of sensors will record. HVAC system sensors are usually mounted in return air ducts or supply air ducts or even outside the structure. They do not indicate what the actual room conditions are. They control the function of the HVAC system and are not necessarily configured to provide the kinds of information that collection and site managers may need. It is possible to integrate the two monitoring programs, but this requires thought, planning, and some modification of both programs. A standard HVAC system monitoring program cannot be directly substituted for a collection/structure monitoring program because they measure different data. Often the addition of a few extra sensors to an HVAC monitoring system can provide the extra data that the collections/structure managers will need.

Tools for Monitoring Temperature and Relative Humidity

MEASURING TEMPERATURE The measurement of temperature in museums is fairly straightforward. Standard glass and mercury or glass and alcohol thermometers are often used. These instruments are based on the amount that mercury or alcohol physically expands when the temperature rises (the thermal coefficient of expansion) to indicate the current temperature. As the mercury or alcohol expands it moves up the glass thermometer tube, where calibrated demarcations indicate the temperature. Mercury measuring devices are accurate and effective but are gradually being replaced in home use due to the health risks associated with mercury. They are often still used in laboratories.

Digital thermometers are commonly used today. They operate through the use of thermocouples (small versions of the bimetallic strip in recording hygrothermographs described below), resistance coils, thermal resisters, or transformers to produce a signal that can be read on a digital display. Digital thermometers are not as accurate as mercury thermometers and require careful and regular calibration. They can be inexpensive and can be very small, making them suitable for discreet placement in the historic site setting. Mercury and digital thermometers are made under many brand names and can be found at drug stores, hardware stores, and electronics stores. Several units are made for the conservation and museum field and are sold through conservation and archival suppliers.

Small historical societies and museums often still use wound or battery-operated hygrothermographs to monitor their environmental conditions (figure 9.6). A hygrothermograph has a mechanism for a rotating paper chart on which the temperature and relative humidity are recorded in ink. This instrument contains a mechanical temperature mechanism that uses a metallic strip that is made up of two different metal alloys, each with a different coefficient of expansion, to measure the temperature. When the temperature changes, the different metal alloys on each side of the bimetallic strip expand or shrink a different amount, causing the strip to bow. The bimetallic band bows in one direction or another as the different alloys expand or contract differently. The bowing of the band controls the movement of the pen on the chart. Thus the temperature reading is recorded on the chart. This tool for measurement can be very effective and does not require expensive computers and software, as other methods do. Most can be set to read for a thirty-day cycle and will accept felt-tip pens (rather than the older purple-ink nib pens). Hygrothermographs are large and may be difficult to discreetly include in a period room or exhibition setting. Some companies sell round instruments that record on a circular graph paper rather than a rectangular paper. Several large scientific instrument manufacturers make hygrothermographs. They should also be periodically calibrated by the manufacturer.

Data loggers, small digital recording devices that require a computer and software, have become the high-tech professional standard for monitoring environmental conditions in organizations that can afford them (figure 9.3). They are small units that can be placed throughout the historic structure and in storage and exhibit locations. They can be programmed to record a variety of readings for temperature and relative humidity at different time intervals and for different periods of time. Other than the cost and the need for a computer and software, their biggest drawback is that they need to be connected to a computer or physically taken to a computer so that the data can be downloaded and analyzed before any information can be accessed. (With a recording hygrothermograph, all the data for thirty days is instantly visible in situ on the chart.) Some data loggers do digitally display current readings and minimum and maximum readings, but they cannot show a trend log (the curve on the hygrothermograph chart) without the computer interface. The units and the software needed are moderately expensive. The user must have access to a suitable computer and training to install and use the system. The operator must learn to use the software. There are number of different manufacturers and types available.

MEASURING RELATIVE HUMIDITY There are two numerical figures that are commonly used in the discussion of interior environments that represent the relationship between temperature and humidity. One is called the relative humidity. This number, expressed as a percentage, gives an idea of how much moisture is in the air at the specific temperature at that moment. The formula for relative humidity is:

$$\text{RH (\%)} = \frac{\text{the amount of water vapor in the air at a specific temperature}}{\text{the maximum amount of water vapor air could hold at that temperature}}$$

The second numerical figure is called the "dew point." This is the temperature at which air of a specific humidity content will become saturated with moisture and will deposit water droplets on nearby surfaces as "dew" or condensation. The dew point is calculated with a psychrometric chart.[24] The psychrometric chart graphically represents the relationship between a dry thermometer bulb and a wet thermometer bulb (figure 9.4). Thus, it is a measure of the evaporative abilities of the air under different temperature and humidity conditions.

Temperature, relative humidity, and dew point are related, and one needs to understand the relationship

Figure 9.3 An example of a datalogger.

to effectively control the collection environment. When temperature is a constant, RH and dew point increase and decrease in tandem. When RH is a constant, temperature and dew point increase and decrease together. But when dew point is a constant, temperature and RH go in opposite directions. As the air cools, the RH will increase until it reaches 100 percent, at which point condensation will occur.

PSYCHROMETRIC CHART The measuring tools for humidity and relative humidity are called psychrometers. The most reliable and (when properly used) the most accurate instrument is the battery-powered psychrometer (figure 9.5). This instrument contains two glass and mercury thermometers; one of which is fitted with a clean cotton sock that is saturated with distilled water. The instrument is fitted with a battery-operated fan. By operating the fan, airflow is created across the two thermometers, one dry and one wet. The airflow should continue until the temperature readings on the thermometers stabilize, usually from four to ten minutes. The relationship between the dry bulb temperature reading and the wet bulb temperature reading will be expressed as the relative humidity, read off an enclosed chart or slide rule. The temperature will be the dry bulb reading. Manually operated sling psychrometers are also available. These require the operator to sling

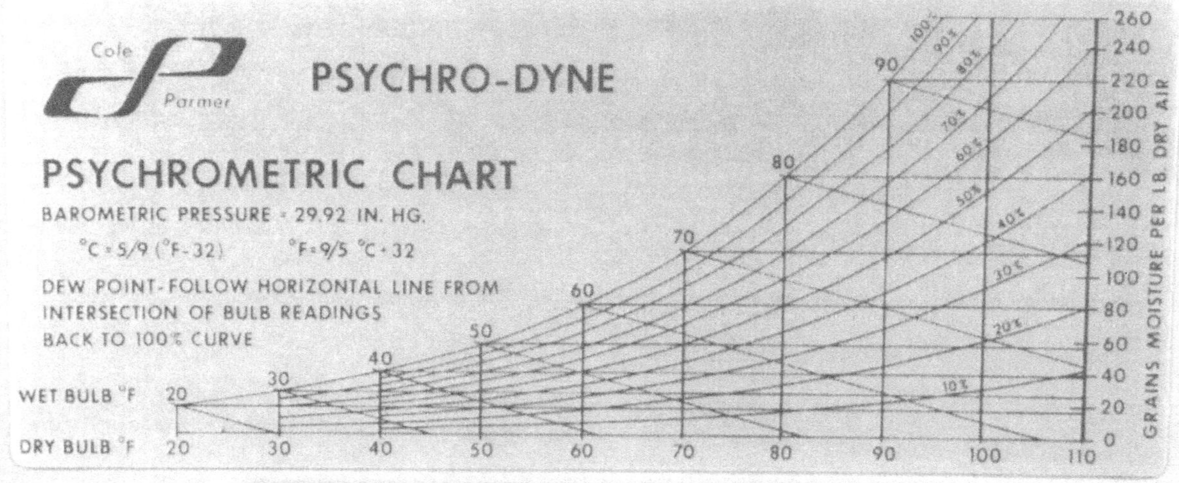

Figure 9.4 An example of a psychrometric chart.

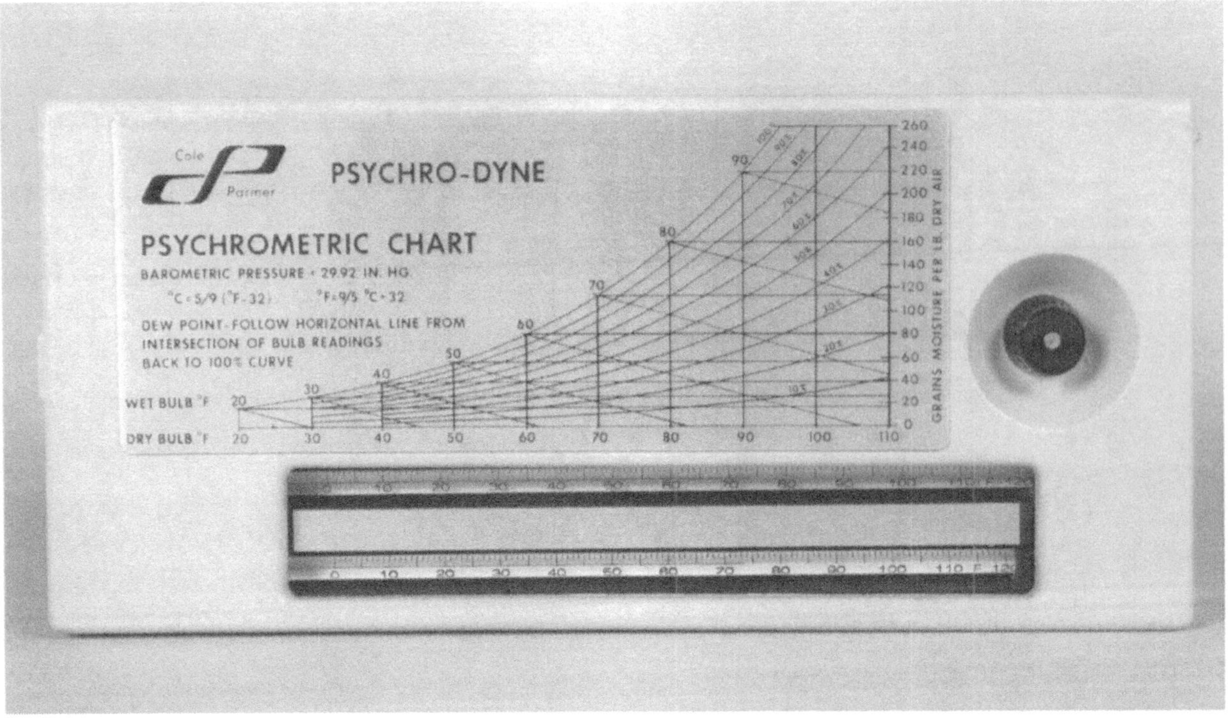

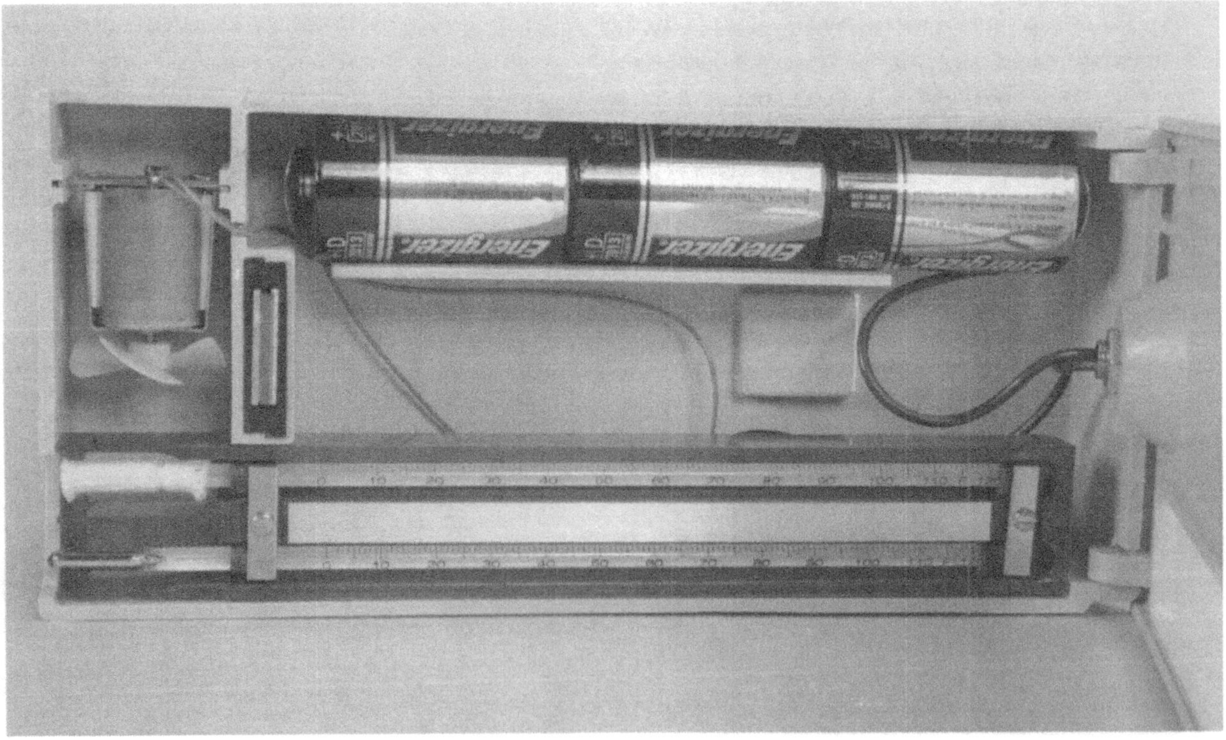

Figure 9.5 An example of a battery-powered psychrometer; exterior (top), interior (bottom).

the instrument at arm's length. Manual sling psychrometers are less accurate than the battery-powered ones, due to irregularities introduced through operator error.

Institutions still successfully use some variation of the recording hygrothermograph, which measures relative humidity directly and enters it on a paper chart recording. With a hygrothermograph, the relative humidity is measured by a bundle of hairs connected at each end with metal clips. One of the metal clips is fitted to the recording arm of the unit that records relative humidity. The special hairs are carefully selected and calibrated to shrink and swell in a consistent manner in response to changes in the relative humidity. As the hairs shrink or swell they change in length and move the arm that carries the recording pen. As one might expect, the hygrothermograph is a sensitive instrument that should be handled carefully.

Digital meters usually measure relative humidity through the use of calibrated hygrometric salts, which absorb and give off moisture to retain a specific humidity level. The humidity level, combined with the digitally determined temperature reading, is used to calculate the relative humidity.

Another common item used to measure relative humidity is the colored paper indicator card (figure 9.7). The measuring portion of the card is paper that has been impregnated with a dye that changes color as the relative humidity changes. Many of these dyes are derived from lichen and are also used in pH indicator papers. Others are cobalt salts, which are also used in indicating silica gel. (Cobalt is a potential health hazard when inhaled, so these indicators should not become wet.) The impregnated paper is lined up to a scale on the hygrometer so that the color changes coincide with relative humidity level demarcations. These measuring devices are not terribly accurate and can deteriorate over time, especially in conditions of high relative humidity. They are very inexpensive and can be used in many applications due to their small size. They are discarded after their useful lifespan.

The dial hygrometer is another common type of environmental monitoring device (figure 9.8). It is a round metal dial that indicates temperature and relative humidity by the movement of two opposing needle indicators. These meters are moderately priced and fairly small in size. They can read to a moderate level of accuracy and need to be calibrated regularly, like all of the other instruments discussed above.

It is important to note that the scientific measurement of temperature and relative humidity is not without its limitations and complications. Relative humidity can only be measured (at best and by the most sophisticated measuring devices) to within a ±2% margin of accuracy. Add to the margin of error for measuring relative humidity the margin of error for measuring temperature, which is needed to calculate the relative humidity, and one easily sees that it is not reasonable to expect an exact relative humidity reading. It is, however, critical to ensure that all of the equipment being used to monitor temperature and relative humidity is working properly, is properly calibrated, and is providing the most accurate readings possible to overcome this inherent margin of error in the data.

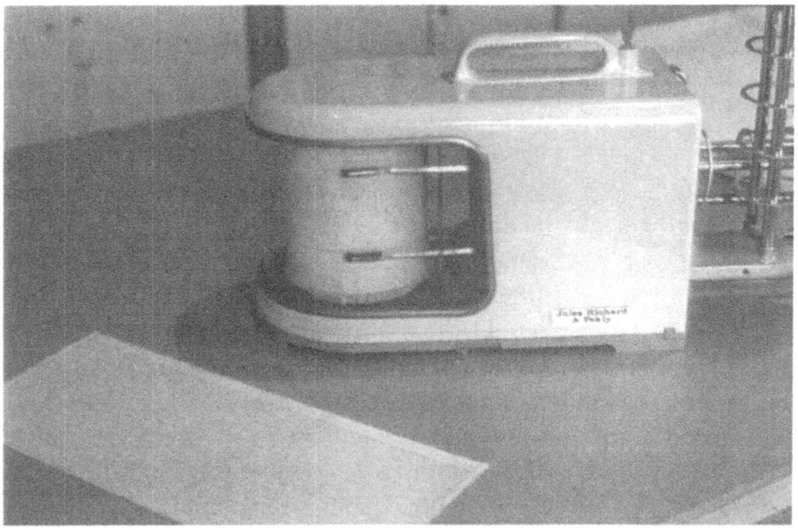

Figure 9.6 An example of a hygrothermograph.

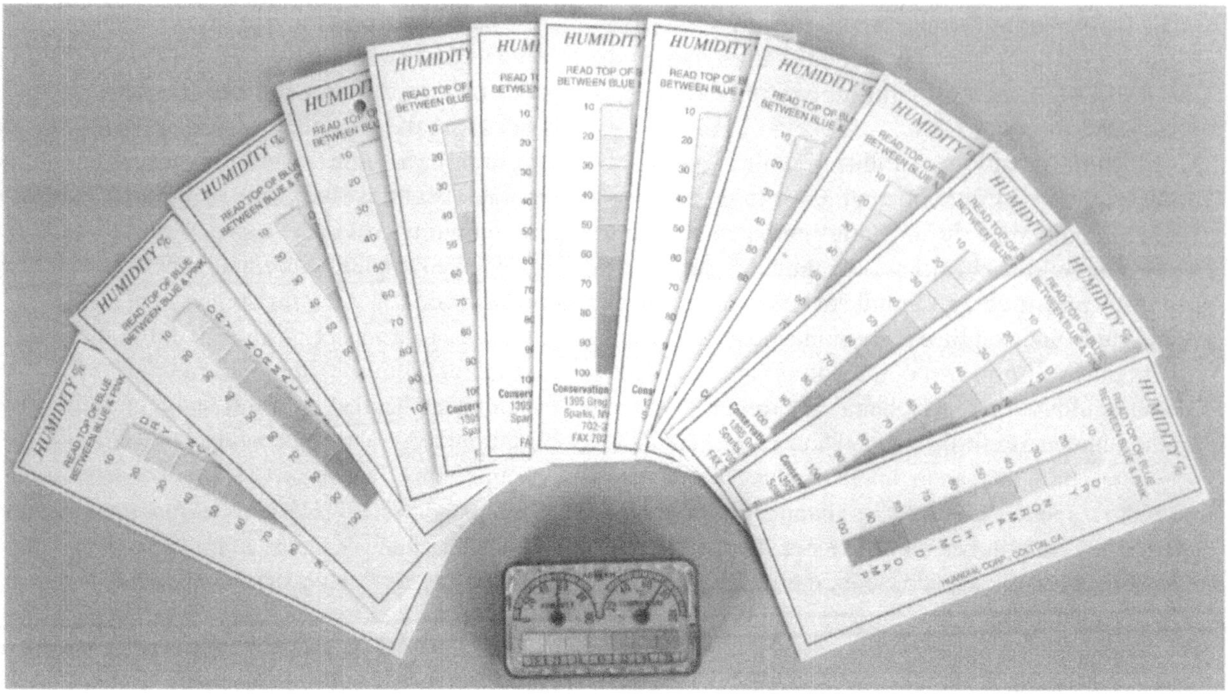

Figure 9.7 Paper RH indicator strips.

As is the case with any sensitive, expensive instrument, these monitoring devices must be handled and used carefully by trained operators. They all require regular calibration to read accurately and work properly. A brief training session with a conservator can provide the necessary expertise to set up a simple monitoring program. The measurement of temperature can be in degrees Fahrenheit or Celsius. The margin of error is determined by the measuring device and can be found in the literature that comes with each measuring unit.

Engineers and architects use these figures and instruments when designing and operating heating, cooling, and ventilation systems. Familiarization with them and their use will facilitate discussions with these professionals.

Figure 9.8 An example of a dial hygrometer.

ATMOSPHERIC PARTICULATES AND POLLUTION

Another aspect of the environment that can play a negative role in preservation of the collection and the structure is atmospheric pollution. Atmospheric pollution includes gaseous materials and particulate, or solid, materials in the air. Gaseous pollutants are classified as either indoor or outdoor, depending on where they are generated. Outdoor gaseous pollution includes gases such as ozone, sulfur dioxide, nitrogen dioxide, nitric acid vapors, and peroxyacetylnitrate. These are primarily produced by the combustion of fuels by cars and commercial enterprises. Indoor gaseous pollution includes gases such as aldehydes, organic acids, hydrogen sulfide, carbonyl sulfide, and pesticides. Particulate matter can be dust from soil, granules from rubber tires, particles from the incomplete combustion of petroleum products, pollen grains from plants, soot from fires, and plaster and other dust from construction (or destruction, as on 9/11). Particulate matter is often referred to simply as dust, but it may contain oily, waxy, and abrasive components that make removal and cleaning a problem.

The presence and amounts of outdoor atmospheric pollutants vary greatly depending on location and climate of the site. It is best to get data for each specific historic building museum location from the state or federal air quality control organization for the locality for reference. Reports are printed every year or every few years and provide all the information needed to assess the outdoor atmospheric pollutant threat for the museum's locality.

Particulate Pollutants

It is relatively easy to control particulate pollution with sound intellectual and physical controls for the museum. One can reduce outdoor pollutants in the interior environment by reducing the ventilation rate in the space and reducing the intake of outdoor air. Keeping windows closed during peak particulate seasons such as the spring tree pollen time and fall harvest time is a simple measure. Objects that are especially sensitive to dust can be protected with microenvironments such as special cases or housings. Checking for drafts of excessive airflow near items can alert the curator to areas where excess dust may accumulate. Making sure that building air leaks around windows and doors are sealed will help prevent the ingress of particulate matter. Requiring construction work areas to be carefully sealed with sheets of plastic or board will reduce the risk of construction and plaster dust. Upgrading the filtration levels for HVAC filters and vacuum cleaner filters will also help. The American Society of Heating, Refrigerating, and Air-Conditioning Engineers (ASHRAE) has set a minimum standard of filtration for habitation spaces that includes a 25 percent pre-filter, an 85 percent main filter bank, and a 45 percent post-filter of activated carbon. This is the ASHRAE 52/76 standard.[25] Many methods and tools exist for removal of particulate materials that do find their way into the interior and onto objects.

Another aspect of dust is its abrasive nature. Observant conservators and technicians working to keep vignettes and period-room settings well dusted have remarked on the wear and abrasion caused by dust on surfaces.

Gaseous Pollutants

EXTERNAL SOURCES It is much more difficult to control gaseous pollutants in museum spaces, and gaseous filtration systems are often prohibitively expensive. They work either by washing the air through a water spray or mist wash or by filtering the air through a solid material that absorbs or adsorbs the pollutant gas. Filtration units can be part of the HVAC system, or they can be portable stand-alone units for room use.

The approach often taken for control of outdoor gaseous pollutants in the museum environment is to try to eliminate pollution at the source, if possible. Outside sources include general urban or regional air pollution caused by automobiles, buses, factories, fires, and other activities. This pollution can be controlled ultimately only by those creating the pollution and is usually regulated by governmental programs and standards. Ozone levels, sulfur dioxide levels, and carbon monoxide levels are generally a problem only in large urban areas like New York City, Chicago, and Los Angeles. If the institution in question is in or near one of these areas, it might be necessary to consider a gaseous pollutant filtration capacity for the HVAC system. Burning of leaves and wood outdoors near museums

A NOTE ABOUT DUST

In a fascinating article written for *Discover* magazine in 1986, P. W. Moser describes the contents of dust bunnies taken from a variety of locations in her apartment and office.[26] She notes that over 43 million tons of dust fall on the United States each year. Most of it is soil, followed by salt, volcanic dust, and soot from forest fires. Hair, skin flakes, textile fibers, pollen grains, insect parts, dust mites, mold spores, fungi, and bacteria are all common elements in the house dust bunny. Moser writes that dust is international in its travels and even extraterrestrial. Dust from comets and meteorites contribute 10,000 tons of weight to the earth each year.

For institutions with high levels of attendance, other things may be found in dust. Analysis of dust vacuumed off of the Star-Spangled Banner at the National Museum of American History at the Smithsonian Institution showed a very high percentage of blue cotton fibers—lint from blue jeans worn by visitors.[27]

should be limited. Tour and school bus drivers should be asked to turn off bus engines while waiting for groups to return. Buses should not be permitted to idle near any historic or collection-holding structures or, more specifically, near any air intake grates or ducts.

INTERNAL SOURCES Internal sources of gaseous pollution include substances related to the HVAC system (cleaning agents or conditioning agents), smoking, cooking, fires, candles, and off-gassing from interior materials. Eliminating smoking, cooking, fire, and burning of real candles from the interior can control much internally generated pollution. Off-gassing from wood, glues, paints, carpet pads, carpeting, acidic cardboard, and other materials can be reduced or eliminated by carefully screening these materials before introducing them to the interior environment. Much research has been done and is under way to identify safe materials for use in proximity to collections.[28]

For special-collection materials that are particularly sensitive to gaseous pollutants, special measures can be taken to prevent exposure of these items to gases. For example, silver is tarnished by exposure to sulfur-containing gases and can be protected from these gases by using barriers such as clear coatings (which must be professionally applied to objects), silver cloth, and silver paper (figure 9.9). These barriers block or absorb the sulfurous gases before they can reach the silver. Metal building fixtures and hardware can be coated with protective coatings to prevent gaseous attack, as well. Sensitive works of art on paper can be housed or matted with paper products containing adsorbents like activated charcoal or zeolites, which will also serve as absorbers or barriers to gaseous pollutants.

THE MEASUREMENT OF ATMOSPHERIC POLLUTANTS There are a number of methods used to measure atmospheric pollution. One method involves taking an air sample and analyzing the contents in a chemistry and physics laboratory. Several companies sell sample-taking devices. After the sample is taken at the site, the device is mailed back to the company, where the contents in the sample will be analyzed and a report sent back to the site. Draeger tubes are one example of this type of sample-taking device method.[29] Another method involves exposing a test material (usually a

A curator from a historic house museum that exhibits a historic vignette of a late-sixteenth-century tavern room noted that all of the metal objects in the vignette seemed to be actively corroding unexpectedly after many years of stability on display. The objects were sent to a conservator for examination. The conservator noted that the corrosion was found only on one side of each metal object. Curious about the distribution of the corrosion, the conservator realized the need to visit the display area on-site. After visiting the vignette display and reviewing the exhibition layout, the conservator realized that the corrosion was directional, occurring on the same side of each object on display.

A survey of the room indicated that the direction was consistent with the flow of air from a ceiling air vent in the room. The conservator suggested that there might be residual caustic liquid from the water treatment compounds used in the humidification system. This, however, would not explain the sudden onset of the active corrosion unless the compound had recently been changed. Several calls and faxes between the HVAC engineers on the house staff and the conservator indicated that no change had been made to the water treatment methods for the humidification system. The engineers indicated that they were already aware of the potential for residual caustic effects from humidification treatments and that they had purposely selected an inert method to prevent this problem.

One afternoon after the conversation with the engineers, as the conservator sat in puzzled contemplation in the vignette area, a workman walked in with a spray can and sprayed an aerosol compound into a junction in the air duct traversing the room. The maintenance employee was using a spray cleaner to clean the copper hot water reheat coils in the duct that provides heated air to the vignette and room. He was applying the product without turning off the airflow. Over-spray was being carried through the duct and being blown into the vignette. The employee was newly hired and had instituted this practice on his own initiative "to improve the efficiency and energy savings" of the HVAC system in the building. He had not read the instructions on the can indicating that the spray should only be used when the airflow had been halted. He was not aware that time should be allotted for the spray to evaporate before turning the airflow back on. The spray turned out to contain sulfuric acid, which was responsible for the sudden, localized outbreak of active corrosion on the objects.

Figure 9.9 Tarnish on a silver teapot. Half is protected with a synthetic coating.

polished and reactive metal coupon) to the air in question and then analyzing the corrosion and oxidation that forms on the test material. Once the corrosion and oxidation products are known, the pollutants can often be deduced. Both methods are fairly expensive and require several weeks if not months to complete.

Another method that has been used in conservation has received various levels of acceptance. The Oddy Test[30] is used to test materials before they are placed in proximity to museum collections to see if they will off-gas harmful gases. A small sample of the material in question is sealed in a container with several metal test coupons and a pH indicator paper. A small amount of water is added to elevate the RH inside the container. The container is heated in an oven to accelerate deterioration and off-gassing, so that test results can be garnered in a shortened period of time. The amount and types of corrosion and oxidation formed on the test coupons is used as an indicator of whether or not the material will produce harmful gases in the collection environment. The pH indicator is used to determine whether the harmful gases are acid, neutral, or alkaline. This method is less expensive but also less scientifically rigorous. The results can be hard to evaluate and hard to reproduce. There are many sources of error and there is potential to set up the testing vials incorrectly. A few laboratories have standardized their methods and feel comfortable with their results,[31] although most of these laboratories do not provide testing services outside their parent institution.

THE HEATING, VENTILATION, AND AIR-CONDITIONING SYSTEM

An HVAC (heating, ventilation, and air-conditioning) system is comprised of a series of interconnected mechanisms that cool, heat, dry, humidify, circulate, filter, and sense the interior air of a structure. Common components include boilers, exchange coils, chillers, blowers, circulating pumps, humidifiers, dehumidifiers, valves, and dampers. It is not the intent of this book to provide detailed information about all HVAC systems, but basic descriptions of the main types will be described below.[32]

HVAC systems have evolved over the years. Early methods of controlling the interior environment relied on features built into the architecture and setting of a house. Trees were planted and placed for maximum summer shade and wind blockage. Transom windows and ventilation shafts were planned and used to circulate cooler air from lower floors to upper floors. Shades were used to block sunlight. Lines of trees served as windbreaks. Lambrequins, drapes, and other interior curtains insulated heated areas from unheated areas. Fireplaces, woodstoves, and coal stoves were used to heat spaces.

In the 1800s, steam power was harnessed in boilers that heated low-pressure hot water radiator systems, and many used gravity or convection-driven hot air systems.[33] Forced hot air systems were developed during the 1850s with the invention of power-driven fans. This period also saw the advent of the use and concept of insulation in structures.[34] Oil, gas, and electric sources of power were developed in the early 1900s, as were ducted forced air systems. By the mid-1900s, air-conditioning systems were developed and became common. Insulating and sealing the building were options developed throughout this period. The last century ended with the development of sophisticated electronic controls for complex HVAC systems.[35]

HVAC configurations in historic properties will most likely include elements from the original systems combined with elements added and modified over time. Original ventilation structures like ventilation shafts may have been modified or completely blocked. Transoms may have been filled in and painted over. Original systems may be cobbled together or even be on their last legs. Many old systems cannot be repaired because parts are no longer available, are too costly to fabricate, or do not conform to current codes/regulations.

A thorough inventory should be made of any original elements. An HVAC engineer should evaluate the existing system for potential problems and for the potential for improvements before any plans regarding the HVAC system are made. Whenever possible, passive period features such as transoms and ventilation shafts should be used. Chapter 12, "Preventive Conservation and the Historic House Structure" presents an in-depth discussion of the building and its preservation/maintenance issues.

HVAC System Elements

The parts used to make up a heating and cooling system can be classified in a number of ways. One way is to separate water-based (hydronic) systems from air-based systems. Hydronic systems use boilers and chillers to make hot and cold water, which is piped throughout the structure and used to heat or cool the air. Air-based systems use condensers, chillers, furnaces, and blowers to change the temperature of the air and to blow it around the duct system. Some systems combine the two types.[36]

HVAC systems can also be classified by heating source (oil, gas, electric, open combustion), by cooling source (direct expansion, chilled water, evaporative, night cooled), and by delivery method (forced air, gravity air, water radiant, steam radiant, electric radiant). Dehumidification can be provided by refrigeration, heat/re-cool methods, and by desiccant systems. Humidification can be provided by atomization (steam, spray, mist) or evaporation methods. The following list briefly describes each of these methods.

HEATING SOURCES/METHODS A furnace fired with fuel oil, electricity, or natural gas is used to produce hot air for circulation.

Boilers full of water heated with fuel oil, electricity, or natural gas are used to produce hot water or steam for circulation.

Radiators and floor and wall piping can be used to circulate hot water or steam and radiate heat into spaces.

Electrical resistance can be used to generate heat in filaments or fins that radiate the heat into spaces.

Cold winter air can be circulated underground and brought up to ambient underground temperatures (around 58°F) to warm it before using more conventional heating methods. This can be called geothermal heating.

Open fires using wood or coal can be used to heat air or water for circulation.

COOLING METHODS Direct expansion (DX) cooling units use the thermodynamics of the liquid/gas phase transition of a refrigerant to cool a set of copper coils that can be used to cool air for circulation. Heat transfer like this is also used in a heat pump system.

Chilled water-cooling systems circulate water that has been chilled by a set of refrigerant coils. The chilled water is circulated and used to cool the air.

Evaporative cooling uses the temperature drop associated with evaporation to cool the air. This method is successful only in very dry environments. Air is passed through a water spray or mist to be cooled.

Specialized desiccants can also be used to cool the air.

Night cooling uses a slab or underground air space that radiates heat away during the night. The air is passed over the cooled slab or through the cooled air space for cooling. This can be called geothermal cooling.

DEHUMIDIFICATION METHODS A refrigerant can be used to cool air, which causes moisture in the air to condense out of the air and drain away. The cooled, dry air is circulated or mixed with more humid air to create the desired relative humidity.

Dehumidification can also be achieved by heating the air to reduce the RH.

Desiccant systems (solid and liquid) can be used to dehumidify air. Desiccants absorb water vapor from the air, which is then circulated.

HUMIDIFICATION METHODS Steam or a water spray or mist can be used to humidify the air. Air is passed through a chamber of steam spray or mist and then circulated.

Evaporative humidification systems pass air through a sponge or lens that is wetted with water. The air, which has absorbed some of the water and reached a higher RH, is circulated.

A plenum is a large empty space, sometimes an enclosed metal box, where conditioned air is mixed before being circulated throughout or removed from a building. Many buildings with drop ceilings use the space above the ceiling as a large mixing plenum.

Many different combinations of HVAC components can be designed as isolated or packaged unit systems that are portable to condition a specific small space. Examples of isolated units that perform one of many of the functions of a HVAC system include window air-conditioning units, space heaters, and more sophisticated packaged computer-controlled systems like Liebert brand units.

Circulation and Outside Air

Some features of air circulation and air mixing should be mentioned. When air is pumped through a ducted system or any time there is a significant difference between the outdoor and indoor temperatures, pressure variations will develop between the interior and exterior of a structure. It is best to induce positive pressure in the interior of a building. This will cause air to flow from the interior to the exterior and will help maintain more constant conditions inside. However, positive pressure can also drive moist humidified air into wall cavities that are at a lower temperature, thus inducing condensation in the wall cavity. A balance should be determined for the relative air pressures. Positive internal pressure can help keep particulate matter out of the building. When air leaks or other openings like doors and windows are open, the air will flow out of instead of into the structure.

Another concept relating to airflow and HVAC systems is that of constant air volume (CAV) versus variable air volume (VAV). CAV refers to the situation where a constant volume of air is being blown throughout the system. VAV systems include a VAV box, where air is collected and parceled out in varying volumes to different zones or areas of the system as needed. In a VAV system, a small room will receive a smaller volume of air than a larger room. VAV systems offer more flexibility and ultimately more control of interior conditions.

A third aspect of airflow in an HVAC system is filtration, important for controlling the air quality in a structure. Standard particulate filtration for a residence is about 67 percent. For museums this is not sufficient. The ASHRAE recommendations of 52/76 discussed above should be the minimum standard for a museum. Filtration does, however, interfere with air flow and air pressure in a space. The level of filtration possible in a system will depend on the amount and strength of the airflow available. Extra filtration should not be used when the HVAC system cannot accommodate it safely.

Sensing and Controls

Sensing and controls for the earliest HVAC systems were manual. Self-contained sensors include mercury thermometers and mercury-controlled thermostats. Pneumatic controls, which work by using compressed air, are used to open and close valves and control dampers in systems. Electric sensors and controls use bimetallic strips to affect the conductivity of a circuit and thus to electrically control valves and dampers. Electronic circuits convert the electric reading from a sensor to produce an output signal that electronically controls a valve or damper. All of these types of sensors and controls may be found in older systems. They may also be found in combination in the systems in older structures.

The current technology used for HVAC sensing and control is called direct digital control (DDC). DDC systems work by directing signals and data from analog or digital sensors to computer microprocessors that use control logic in software programs to direct valves, operate dampers, and sense other data in the system to perform specific actions. These DDC control systems range in complexity, but in general provide excellent and efficient operation of the HVAC system. DDC systems can interface with most of the earlier control and sensor mechanisms, so they can be designed for use in hybrid or mixed systems in older buildings. They can be accessed and controlled off-site through the use of a modem or can be hard wired to a control location. It is easy to integrate the use of data loggers with a DDC system.

Looking at Systems Drawings

If it is necessary to upgrade the HVAC system or replace it, electrical, plumbing, mechanical, and structural drawings will be required. The historic site administrators must carefully review the proposal drawings before they are approved. It can be very helpful to have a historical architect, an architectural conservator, or a conservator go over these drawings before approval. This can take a few minutes to a few hours, at most, on the part of the specialist and may prevent serious and costly oversights. A conservator will look for ways to limit the potential risks to the collections and structure. He or she will look for structural changes that might impact the building itself, such as cutting new pathways for ducting or plumbing, and for placement of proposed plumbing or fire suppression lines over collection storage spaces and exhibits. He or she will investigate the basic type of system proposed and look for potential associated risks. The conservator can also prepare a written set of guidelines and concerns for the engineering firm and can explain these concerns to the engineers and others.

Drawings can be made at a variety of times in the life of the system. Original drawings can give insight into the original intent of the system designer. However, modifications will have been made over time, so the original drawings will most likely not represent the actual state of the system. Drawings showing proposed modifications may be found, but changes always occur during work that will diverge from the original plans. The wise thing to do is to request "as done," "as built," or "as is" drawings, to be produced after modifications are completed. If no drawings are available, it may be necessary to produce a set of "as is" drawings before new plans can be made. Drawings are usually divided into mechanical (HVAC), electrical (and lighting), plumbing (and sprinkler system), and structural (building structure) drawings. One needs to look back and forth between these different sets of drawings to get the overall picture of the building systems. Most drawings use standardized symbols and letter codes to denote items. There should be a legend of symbols in the set of drawings and a list of notes. Here are a few examples of some common abbreviations:

HVAC: heating, ventilation, and air-conditioning
DDC: direct digital controls
CWS: cold water supply
CWR: cold water return
HWS: hot water supply
HWR: hot water return
CAV: constant air volume
VAV: variable air volume
AHU: air handling unit
DX: direct expansion
NC: noise criteria
CFM: cubic feet per minute
FCU: fan coil unit
RA: return air
SAF: supply air fan
RAF: return air fan
HWP: hot water pump
CWP: chilled water pump
SA: supply air
RA: return air
OA: outside air
RTU: roof top unit
Btu: British thermal unit (of energy)
ATC: automatic temperature control

Inventory Your System

It is advisable to have an inventory of your HVAC system. An HVAC engineer or other HVAC maintenance professional can help draw up a description and an inventory of the parts of your system, including the sensors and controls. Information about past modifications should be gathered, as well. Any previous system drawings should be collected and archived. Consider this to be the equivalent of the catalogue and inventory records for collection objects. The description and inventory and any drawings that are found will be important tools in devising maintenance plans and in determining when and how the HVAC system may need extensive upgrades or replacement.

The Impact of Systems on the Historic Building and Collection

An HVAC system clearly has an effect on the environmental conditions within a historic structure. The system will also have a significant effect on the physical structure itself in terms of space for mechanical equipment installation and space for ductwork, plumbing, and electrical service. New system installation or the modification of an old system must be planned to induce as little negative impact on the structure as possible. An ideal system would provide careful yet flexible control of the environment, accurate long-term data collection on the ambient room conditions, minimal impact on the physical structure of the building, low-cost maintenance, and low risk of accidental mishap (leaks, blowbacks). Older modified systems often have safety features that were added after the fact such as belt covers or drip pans. These introduce risk to the safety of the staff, the collection, and the structure.

Drip pans, for example, are added under units where condensation is likely to occur or where plumbing connections may be weak. They are metal pans designed to catch water that comes from the HVAC system and direct it to a drain. They are installed directly beneath HVAC elements in ceilings and me-

Figure 9.10 An HVAC system fitted into the spaces of a historic house.

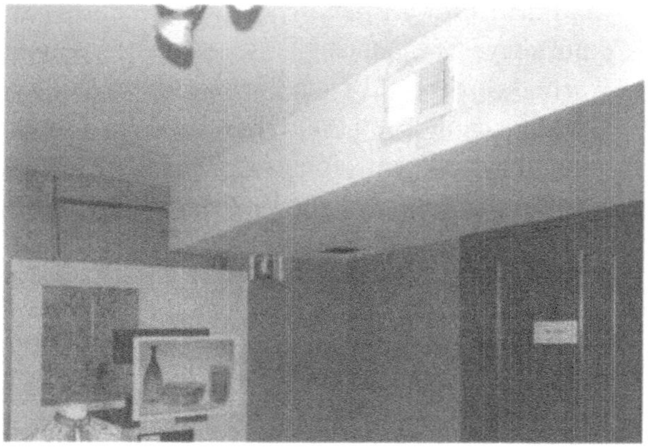

chanical spaces where the elements are located. If they are not scrupulously maintained they become a significant leak risk. Insect carcasses, dust, and debris that fall into the pans can block the drains. Drip pans with clogged drains fill with water and gradually overflow, causing slow drips that may go undetected for a long time. They can also fail catastrophically, when the HVAC element fails and dumps a volume of water all at once. If the drain is not functional, a major water leak will result. The use of these risky, after-market drip pan fixes should be avoided in redesigned systems, and system maintenance needs to be meticulous where they already exist. Dirt covering condenser coils will keep the system from operating efficiently. A dirty evaporator coil can become covered with mildew. Regular inspection and maintenance activities are fundamental to the preventive program.

Talking with HVAC Contractors and Engineers

When the need arises to talk with HVAC professionals about the special requirements of the collection and the historic structure, the museum professional must have a fundamental understanding of environmental control and a familiarity with the language of heating, cooling, and ventilation systems. If the museum professionals have no experience in HVAC systems and environmental control, they will not understand the perspective of the HVAC professionals in the discussion. Unless the HVAC professionals have personal experience in working with cultural collections and historic structures, they will have no understanding of the basic needs and concerns that the museum professionals bring to the discussion. If either party is not knowledgeable of the basic position of the other, the conversation will be less than successful. Every effort should be made to educate both parties and to bring out and discuss the potential misunderstandings and oversights that could occur between the perspectives of the two professions.

Maintenance staff from a local HVAC company, which was probably trained in-house and on the job, cannot be expected to understand the needs and goals of preventive collections and structure care in a historic building. They will have had minimal exposure and experience with older systems and may have little knowledge of museum environmental standards. They will often assume that the museum professionals have no knowledge of HVAC equipment (often rightly so) and do not really know what they are talking about.

The best solution to bridge this gap in perspective is to start discussion slowly and to carefully explain the needs of the collection and structure, to see if the HVAC representative actually understands fundamental principles like the dynamic relationship between temperature and relative humidity and the nature of an older HVAC system. If you suspect that the HVAC representative does not grasp your perspective, ask to speak to a supervisor—and certainly do not agree to any proposed measures until both parties are sure they understand the situation thoroughly. If the museum professional is hesitant in his or her understanding of HVAC principles, a historical architect, conservator, or other museum colleague should be engaged to represent the needs of the museum collection and structure in the discussions. This can sometimes be accomplished via conference call or phone conversation. As always, if in doubt, get a second opinion or find a more knowledgeable HVAC professional. Colleagues at nearby museum organizations may be able to refer contractors with whom they have had successful interactions.

Figure 9.11 What the curator says; what the HVAC engineer hears. Drawing by Tom Sain.

What to Do If the System Fails

If the HVAC system fails, there is often no reason to panic. The first thing to do is to notify the responsible maintenance person, engineer, or contractor so that he or she can arrive on-site to check out the problem as soon as possible. Often the problem will be simple and can be corrected in a few minutes. This is the case when there has been an outage, slump, or surge in power. Variances in the electrical supply can result in some portion of the system or the system controls automatically shutting down. The engineer or contractor should be able to restart the operations manually.

If the problem appears to be of potentially longer duration, the next step is to try to close down the building in an effort to retain the remnants of the conditioned air that has already been produced inside the structure. If the outside air is close to the conditions desired inside the building, this might not be necessary. If the outside air is not close to the conditions desired inside (too humid, dry, hot, or cold), every effort should be made to limit the exchange of interior and exterior air through all avenues, including the outside air intake on the HVAC system, doors and windows, flues, and exhaust fans. These outside air pathways should be shut down until the problems are solved. Some buildings can hold acceptable interior conditions for many hours without significant change. A close watch on a hygrothermograph chart, data logger display, or other instrument readings will indicate the direction that the interior conditions will drift and when they may become problematic.

If the interior conditions begin to drift into levels that are outside the selected safe values for the building, remember that the dynamic relationship between temperature and relative humidity can be manipulated. For example, if the system failure occurs on a hot, humid summer day and the building is sealed (outside air ventilation is halted), it may be possible to combat rising relative humidity levels by raising the interior temperature. (Hot air can hold more moisture than cold air.) For the reverse, if a problem occurs in a house on a cold day and the relative humidity begins to drop near the lower permissible limits, the engineers could raise the relative humidity in the house by allowing the room temperature to fall. Clear focus on the environmental goals for a building and pragmatic solutions like these can usually help limit the potential problems caused when an HVAC system fails, often allowing plenty of time for the repair work to be completed and the system brought back on line.

If the problem is more serious, it may be necessary to move collections or take measures to protect the structure. Erroneous injection of steam or soot (from a furnace blowback, for example) into the ventilation system and hence into the building interior are obviously more serious problems that cannot be pragmatically mitigated. Efforts should focus on keeping the interior building temperature above freezing, irrespective of the interior relative humidity. If heat is lost and opening the taps and permitting water to flow through the system does not keep the pipes from freezing, the collections should be removed. In preparation for emergencies of this scale, it is best to have a preselected alternate location for temporary collection storage and a predetermined method of moving the collection items to the alternate location.

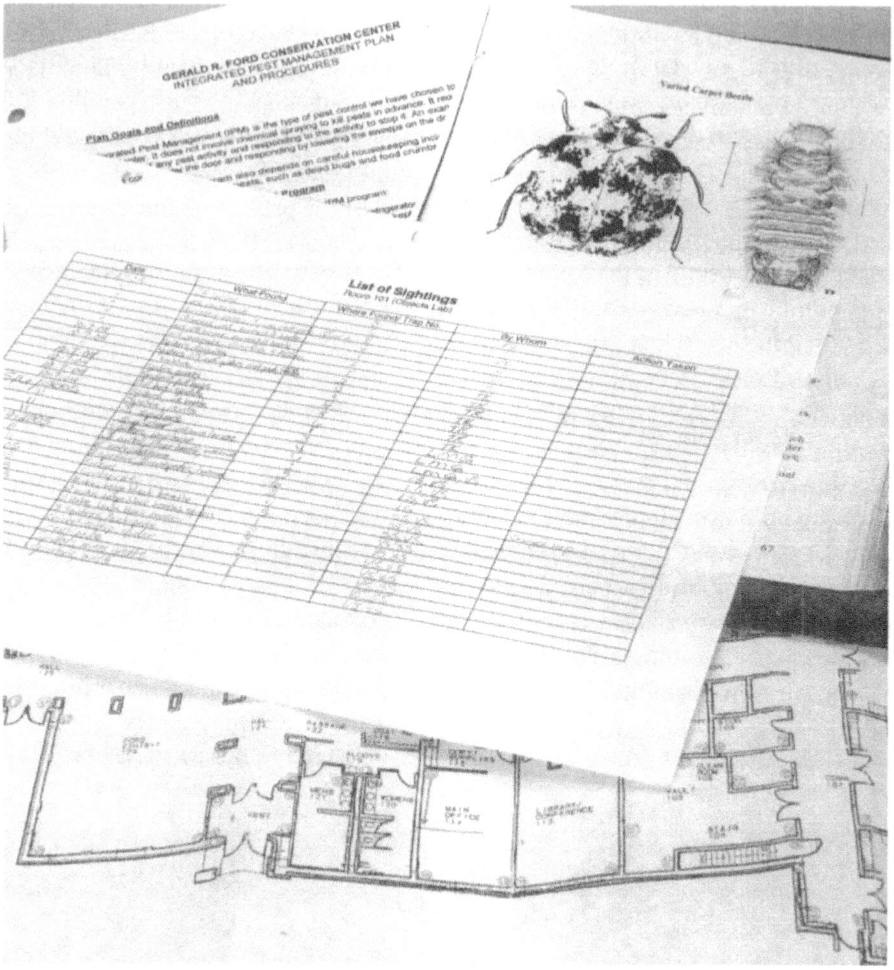

Figure 10.1 Collection of reports and monitoring documentation.

CHAPTER 10

Preventive Conservation and Integrated Pest Management

MUSEUM PESTS ARE DEFINED as those organisms that damage or destroy museum structures and collections. They include microorganisms, insects, rodents, birds, and other vertebrates that are destructive in the museum setting. When a pest infestation occurs, building structures can be weakened or objects irreversibly damaged. It is important to realize that while there are a large number of pests, few are identified as museum pests. Any pest has the potential to be problematic in the museum environment, and therefore the impact of all pests must be understood and controlled.

Integrated pest management (IPM) is the multifaceted program of pest control that is recommended. It employs ecologically based procedures that rely on multiple interventions with minimal disturbance to the ecosystem. Its focus is the long-term reduction of biodeterioration using a safe, cost-effective, and holistic approach, without depending solely on pesticides. All factors that contribute to conditions that make biodeterioration a concern are considered, beginning with the building, to human factors, to the biology of the pest itself.

Integrated Pest Management is the ideal process to keep pests under control at a historic site. It is an effective strategy that promotes the use of a variety of prevention and control techniques that relate to the topic of implementing intellectual and physical controls to manage pest problems. It is based on the principles of habitat modification in conjunction with biological and physical controls. A primary goal of IPM is to reduce pesticide use, and the application of a chemical control is generally a last resort. Every historic site should have a written IPM plan that is site specific and addresses the cultural and historical needs of the property and the surrounding ecosystem. The strengths of IPM come from the fact that it guides museum staff through a decision-making process that clarifies when and what actions to take in order to prevent and control pests. While an IPM plan is site specific, the fundamental principles of IPM apply to all museums.

BIODETERIORATION

A variety of processes collectively referred to as biodeterioration worsen the chemical or physical condition of historic sites and collections due to the actions of living organisms. The term "museum pests" includes both vertebrate and invertebrate organisms that can feed on collections and cause damage to textiles, leather, furniture, paper, libraries and archives, ethnographic items, and natural history specimens.

Microorganisms such as mold (fungi), algae, and bacteria are spore-bearing organisms that absorb nutrition and can reproduce sexually or asexually (figure 10.2). They are characterized by fuzzy growths of any color (conspicuous masses of filament, or *hyphae*) that develop from microscopic spores carried in the air or found in soils, food, and plant matter. Mold grows when nutrients and a suitable environment exists. Generally when relative humidity is above 65 percent, temperature is high, light levels are low, and there is a lack of ventilation, mold growth can occur. Both organic and inorganic materials can be damaged by mold. Microorganisms can be a human health hazard as an allergen and/or a pathogen. Staff need to take personal safety precautions to avoid exposure through inhalation, skin contact, or ingestion (figure 10.3).

Many museum pests are arthropods that have biting mouthparts, such as wood-boring beetles, dermestid beetles, silverfish, and clothes moths. They feed on collections, causing holes and weakening structures (figure 10.4). Pests may be hidden within a structure, and damage is not apparent until pest activity is acute. Organic collection materials (especially textiles, paper, wood, leather, and other animal products) serve as nutrient sources for pests and are particularly susceptible to damage or total destruction. While there are thousands of species of insects, only a few attack museum collections. However, all pests need to be controlled.

Mice, rats, and other vertebrates are often problematic in historic houses. They can weaken structures and damage collections by gnawing and by staining

Figure 10.2 Microorganism growth on a piano.

them with their excrement. Pigeons and birds that roost in attics may attract pests such as dermestid beetles that feed on feathers. Their droppings may present a health hazard.

Dead pests in attics, basements, or voids in walls can adversely affect collections if their decomposing bodies attract other pests such as dermestids. When the dead pest is consumed, they will move on to the collection. Found or trapped pests must be cleaned up and disposed of immediately (figure 10.6).

The effect of pests on collections can be devastating. Objects that are chewed, shredded, torn, or stained are difficult to interpret and may be unsuitable for display without conservation treatment. Their value for research is also diminished. Consistent preventive measures initiated at historic sites against all pest invaders will have the positive result of protecting the collection.

TRADITIONAL METHODS OF PEST CONTROL

Museums routinely used pesticides in collections. It is not uncommon to go into a storage area and still smell the strong odor of a moth repellent. Many different types of insecticides and fumigants have been used on collection materials, such as naphthalene (moth balls), para-dichlorobenzene (moth crystals), thymol, arsenic, dichlorovos (Vapona pest strips), and methyl bromide, to name but a few. These chemicals are no longer recommended for use in collections. Some of them are known or suspected carcinogens, which are harmful to those working with the collections and to the objects themselves.

Figure 10.3 Vacuuming moldy collections outdoors and in protective gear.

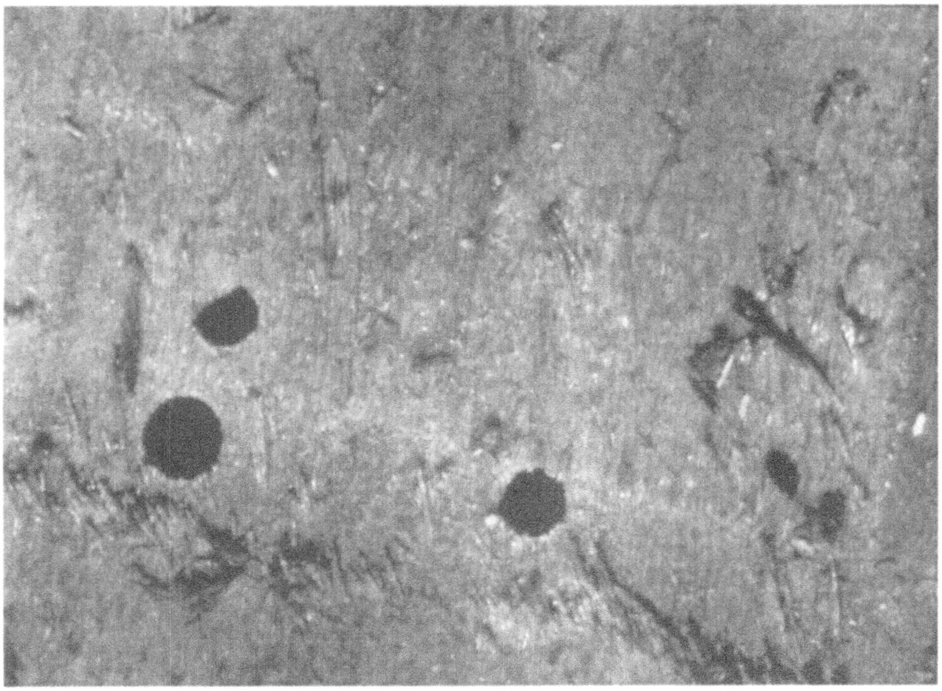

Figure 10.4 Wood-boring beetle holes. Harpers Ferry Center, Division of Conservation Slide Library.

Health Concerns from Pesticide Exposure

Pesticides can be a health hazard for all who use the collections, and a liability for the institution. It is not recommended to rely on interventions that use chemical pesticides to kill an infestation. Many less toxic and environmentally safe options exist if an infestation is detected at a site. Exposure to pesticides can cause an immediate reaction such as skin or eye irritation, nausea, and breathing difficulty. There can also be long-term problems from pesticide exposure, such as liver damage. It is not possible to know what an individual's sensitivity to these substances may be; therefore, it is reasonable to take precautions when working with collections that may have been exposed to pesticides.

Few museums maintained adequate records about pesticide use in their collection. Review any catalogue records that exist to ascertain if your collection may have been exposed to pesticides. The objects themselves may exhibit signs of pesticide or fumigant contamination, which can manifest as corrosion on metals, color change to textiles, and surface staining. To keep your pesticide exposure to a minimum, you should practice good hygiene, such as washing your hands frequently. Take simple precautions such as wearing

Figure 10.5 Mouse trap in historic house museum baited with cotton, not a food product. Rodents will still be attracted to the cotton for a nesting material.

Figure 10.6 Mummified mouse carcass that will attract more pests.

gloves and a lab coat or smock. If you suspect that your collection has been exposed to pesticides, additional precautions may be needed, such as wearing a respirator or other personal protective equipment.

RECOMMENDED METHOD OF PEST CONTROL: INTEGRATED PEST MANAGEMENT

The foundations of IPM are prevention, monitoring, detection, identification, and mitigation. Prevention includes reduction and avoidance of pest attractions, prevention of pest entry, and modification of the environment or habitat to discourage pest activity. Monitoring looks for evidence of pest activity in and around the site and on collections through routine inspections and trapping. Pests trapped and detected in the course of monitoring need to be identified accurately. Staff need to know if they have a museum pest or a "miscellaneous" pest such as an ant, so that eradication actions and treatments are appropriate.

Each pest should have an assigned action threshold, at which level steps are taken to reduce their number. One live carpet beetle found in textile storage is the action threshold for that type of pest, and immediate mitigation actions are required. One ant found in textile storage is tolerated, and monitoring and improvement to sanitation controls and exclusion are taken. The rationale behind the action threshold is that some pests can be tolerated at some low level.

Mitigation success is improved when the identified pest's life cycle is known. Pest eradication can be performed by chemical or nonchemical means, although nonchemical means are preferred. The process comes full circle to examine the human factors or conditions that permitted the infestation and to improve the site's intellectual and physical controls and the biological systems of prevention. IPM uses all available biological, environmental, and modern pest management resources to prevent unacceptable levels of damage to buildings, collections, and environment.

Successful pest management requires the participation of all staff. Its success relies heavily on prevention through successful implementation of intellectual and physical controls, good housekeeping and sanitation practices, and good building maintenance. Consistent insect trapping and monitoring is essential for the program. In order to develop an IPM strategy, site administrators should understand that all staff and visitors need to participate. Leadership from management is needed in order to build consensus to adopt successful practices. Ultimately, it will be a pest management coordinator who will be responsible for implementing the daily routines of IPM, but that person needs to know that management and staff support them in their actions to effect positive changes to control pest populations.

THE INTEGRATED PEST MANAGEMENT PLAN

A written IPM policy is necessary to record procedures and measure results. The plan should begin with a clear statement of goals. Staff and volunteer roles and responsibilities should be discussed. The document should be developed specifically for the site based on the five principles of IPM. The plan is a working reference that is revised and reviewed regularly. The thought of writing and initiating a plan can be daunting, but it will be most successful when representatives of all the staff and volunteers have input, develop the plan together, and agree to abide by the procedures and protocols that are established.

Prevention

Preventing museum pest infestations in structures and collections is the most cost-effective means for managing pests. Successful pest prevention is the result of following good housekeeping regimes and modifying pest habitats.

BUILDING EXTERIOR Acknowledging the symbiotic relationship between the building and the collections means that IPM includes actions that keep pests out of the building. Attaching sweeps on doors, removing vegetation on the building exterior, and creating a dead zone at the foundation help to keep pests from entering the building.

A "dead zone" or "hot zone" is an area about twelve inches wide that is created by placing gravel to a depth of three to four inches around the foundation. The gravel should be laid on top of a weed barrier such as a geotextile. Insects do not like to cross gravel, and the weed barrier will prevent plants from growing up between the pebbles.

Plants—especially flowers, shrubs, or trees—should not be planted close to the building. Remove moss, vines, ivy, and other climbing plants from the walls and from the roof, if not historically accurate. If wisteria or another vine is documented to have grown on the façade, porch, or another feature of the site, use trellis systems to trail vines without permitting them to grow on the building itself. The building site should be graded properly so that drainage surrounding the building is adequate and water is led away from the structure. All roof drains and downspouts should be kept clear of debris and in good working condition.

If lights are attached to the building, they can attract insects through the ultraviolet light they emit. Lamps close to a building should have low ultraviolet output. Lights on the property that are away from the building should have a high ultraviolet output to draw flying pests away from the structure.

All garbage and trash should be disposed of as soon as possible and kept in vermin-proof containers away from the building. Do not permit wood, debris, and

Figure 10.8 Flowers growing too close to building.

Figure 10.7 Dead zone at a site.

construction materials to pile up or be stored too close to the building, as they provide a good home to rodents who may move inside. Remove bird and insect nests from eaves and doorways and debris from ledges and gutters.

Seal all unnecessary holes in the building, and seal and caulk around holes for electrical cables, water pipes, telephone connections, and waste pipes. Doors and windows should be tight fitting and kept closed at all times. Door sweeps should be attached to the bottom of doors to close gaps. Insect screening (small mesh size) should cover windows, if appropriate for the interpretive period of the site.

Building maintenance needs to be performed to a high standard. Roof, window, building leaks, and plumbing or sewer leaks must be repaired promptly. Water and moisture sources for pests need to be eliminated. The National Park Service publishes an excellent resource on finding and eliminating moisture in buildings.[1]

BUILDING INTERIOR The interior environment and its control is usually a balance between human comfort and object preservation. Lowering the temperature and relative humidity and increasing air circulation is related to reducing the level of pest activity inside. The environmental conditions at the site need to be within accepted parameters for museum collections. Pests are promoted by environments with too-high levels of relative humidity, without good air circulation, and with areas that are dark and left undisturbed for long periods of time. Indoor humidity and temperature should be kept as cool and dry (generally between 50 percent RH and not higher than 65 percent RH) as practical. (See chapter 9, "Preventive Conservation and Environmental Control.") Insect activities such as feeding and reproduction will slow as temperatures fall.

Modify the habitat of pests by eliminating food and water sources. Food preparation and consumption areas should be far away from the collections, preferably in another building. Restrict eating and food to designated areas, which should be kept spotlessly clean. Daily trash disposal and removal from the building is very important, particularly if curatorial storage areas are located in buildings that support lunchrooms, offices, and other administrative functions. Food consumption or storage should not be permitted in the museum and curatorial storage spaces. Provide trash receptacles specifically designated for food-related garbage and empty them at the end of the day.

Visitors should not be permitted to carry food or drink into the site, nor should they be permitted to chew gum inside. Trash receptacles should be at the entry to the site, and tour guides should request that visitors dispose of their food there. Receptions and events that serve food and drink should not be held in a collection area. When a site does host such receptions, the caterer needs to be given written instructions on where food preparation and distribution is permitted and how to manage trash disposal.

The building interior should be well maintained and kept clean. Routine vacuuming prevents the accumulation of dirt and dust that provide nutrients for insects and is critical to the control of pests. It is important to clean throughout the building but particularly under furniture that is rarely moved; along baseboards and cracks in floorboards; inside and behind heaters, vents, and ducts; and in dark closets. Vacuum in corners and in places that are usually left undisturbed. The contents of the vacuum bag can contain insects that may escape. Dispose of the used bag by removing it from the vacuum cleaner outside the building, not inside a furnished room or storeroom. Wrap it in a plastic bag and dispose of it in a covered trash bin located outside the premises.

Designate a room for inspecting all incoming items. Isolate any incoming loans, new acquisitions, or exhibit props and thoroughly inspect them to ensure that items are pest-free before placing them in collection spaces. When incoming materials seem to have some form of insect damage, they should be sealed in polyethylene and monitored by sealing a sticky trap in the package (but do not let the sticky substance touch the object). Monitor the piece for a period of time (a month or more) to ensure that any pests have had time to incubate and you are sure it is pest-free. Any material containing evidence of an active infestation must be treated by appropriate means as delineated in the IPM plan. Nonchemical means such as freezing or placement in an anoxic environment is appropriate for most collection materials. A dedicated space for holding suspect materials is necessary, and this area needs to be carefully monitored to ensure infestations do not spread. Be sure that shipping crates and ordered supplies are also inspected before entering a collection area.

When a piece on display or in storage shows signs of an active pest infestation, it should be removed from display/storage and isolated immediately. A bag or box should be brought to the object for wrapping. Do not carry an infested object through collection spaces. After removal and isolation, clean the surrounding area by vacuuming. Monitor this area frequently, perhaps through the placement of extra pest traps.

Moisture attracts pests, so bring as little water as possible into the house. The HVAC system and appliances such as a dehumidifier produce a condensate that needs to be monitored and/or emptied frequently. Insulate pipes to prevent condensation and repair pipes that leak.

Live flowers, logs, food, and organic soils harbor insect pests and should be discouraged in the site. Use artificial food and flowers in the exhibits. At some sites live flowers are intrinsic to the room and its interpretation. In these instances, establish protocols such as inspection to reduce the threat of pests and place the flowers in refrigeration the day before introducing them into the house.

Good sanitation practices are vital to pest prevention. A general site cleanup and implementing good sanitation routines reduces food, water, and harborage available to pests. While it is impossible to eliminate all pest food sources, a site can decrease the number of food sources, which in turn will reduce pests and make early detection easier.

Complete eradication of all pests is not feasible. Establishing an action threshold when management of each species is initiated is vital. When a carpet beetle is found on a wool coverlet, it is at an action level. The coverlet and surrounding area are inspected for additional pests and the coverlet itself is treated by vacuuming, freezing, or another method that is delineated in the IPM plan. Not all pests will elicit such action, but a museum pest will.

Figure 10.9 Artificial flowers on mantel at Melrose Mansion, Natchez National Historical Park, Natchez, Mississippi. The flowers are changed to reflect the seasons.

Monitoring and Detection

Monitoring is the ongoing process of inspection, trapping, and documenting pests and environments to determine if populations are increasing, decreasing, or remaining stable. Interpretation of the information will result in maintaining current work practices or taking different or additional actions for positive change. Monitoring will help to signal that the action threshold level for populations of pests has been reached and that management actions are required. Monitoring will help signal a museum pest infestation as early as possible.

Inspect the furnished rooms, storage, and collections regularly. There are numerous signs of museum pest infestations to look for during an inspection. Dermestids cast their larval skins, moths leave feeding debris or frass on and around their food, powder post beetles leave exit holes on wood, hair may fall from fur or pelts, and gnaw marks may edge paper. Look for evidence of live or dead insects on window ledges or on damaged organic objects; be aware of flyspecks; the darkening of ceiling light fixtures; evidence of rodents, including droppings, odor, and sounds; and pest debris found in vacuum bags. Report and track any incident. A pest activity report should be filled out, noting any damage or pest evidence on an artifact or the building fabric. Some collection materials such as wool, feathers, leather, and so on are at a higher risk for pest infestations. These pieces need to be inspected frequently to assess the effectiveness of exclusion and pest management strategies.

Setting out sticky traps, pheromone traps, and glue boards is a critical element in the monitoring program (figures 10.5 and 10.11). They are reliable indicators of the type and volume of pests at a site. Various types of traps are commercially available and some are simple to make. You need to be thoughtful about trap placement. Ventilation ducts, window areas, places where debris and dust collects, rarely disturbed areas, and dark areas are all appropriate locations. Use a floor plan of the building to note all obvious points of entry for a pest. Initially use a grid pattern over the entire area to be monitored by traps (figure 10.1). Traps should be placed at various heights: floors, on shelves, false ceilings. Record the location of the traps and their

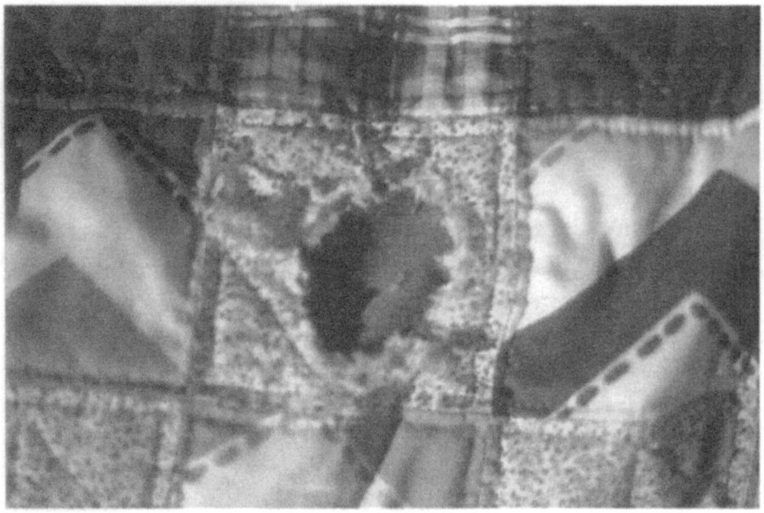

Figure 10.10 Rodent damage to a quilt.

date of placement. Regularly (weekly or monthly) check the traps and identify the trapped pests. Record all findings to begin to develop a journal of pest activity at your site. A good description of the process of using sticky traps is Nancy Odegaard's *Insect Monitoring in Museums.*[2]

Replace the sticky traps regularly. The glue will eventually harden and become ineffective. Also the glue is not toxic to the live insects on the traps, who may pass into another phase of their life cycle and escape the trap. Do not let so many insects accumulate on the traps that they will attract other pests.

Pest Identification

Pests need to be identified accurately for an IPM program to be successful. This includes all insects that are captured in traps. Pests have different life cycles, food preferences, eating habits, and social behaviors, so they should be identified as specifically as possible by genus and species. A pocket field guide to insects is an excellent illustrated resource to aid in the process. A magnifying glass or a microscope is useful. When pests cannot be identified by staff, the IPM coordinator should send an example of the pest to a specialist for proper identification. Most states have cooperative extension offices that can provide this assistance.

A reference collection of dead insect specimens that have been found during the inspection process is an excellent learning and training tool for site staff. All staff should participate in collecting specimens, which helps to increase their awareness of IPM issues. Each department should have a supply of small plastic bags, resealable bags, or small vials; tweezers; and labels to use to collect specimens and note the location, date, and time collected. All pests found on-site should be in the specimen collection, not just museum pests.

Once pests are detected and identified, a pest tracking system (often a computer program) is very helpful to understand the scope of the problem. The IPM plan will need to include procedures to follow when pests are found in collections, whom to contact, and what actions or treatments to perform. An incident report keeps all relevant information in one document including control actions, follow-up monitoring, and post treatment evaluation. The report is a simple system for documenting actions and archiving the record.

A computer database such as Microsoft Access is particularly useful for tracking data acquired from reviewing the sticky traps. All pest activity should be entered into this database to perform the analysis. When data are entered consistently, the analysis will reveal problematic locations and seasonal pest activity. This documentary evidence of pest problems can be used to obtain support or additional resources for the IPM program.

Mitigation

The purpose of monitoring is to initiate nonchemical means of control when museum pests are detected or when nonmuseum pests are detected at an action threshold level. Seek the source of the infestation, review suspected pest entry points, requirements for food and water, and safe harborages for reproduction, and modify the environment appropriately. Reestablish

Figure 10.11 Sticky trap set out in a room.

prevention routines in the form of exclusion, sanitation, and improved housekeeping, which will generally control most pest problems by diminishing or eliminating populations.

When a museum pest is detected, step up inspection routines, wrap and isolate any affected objects, and proceed with one of the several nonchemical eradication methods. Object materials and condition, pest, and site resources will help determine which eradication technique to pursue.

A simple system of vacuuming an infested object, sealing it in polyethylene, and monitoring and periodic vacuuming (if necessary) is a practical solution for a pest problem that is not very advanced (figure 10.12).

Some collection materials such as textiles can be placed in a very low temperature environment (such as –20°C), which can kill insects if the temperature drop is rapid and the objects stay at this temperature for at least a week (figure 10.13). Not all materials can be subjected to this treatment, so discuss problematic materials with a conservator. Freezing does not pose any health risks nor does it require a lot of expensive equipment. The treatment success rate is increased the lower the temperature drops and the longer the object is exposed to it. The objects must be protected from condensation that could form as a result of the rapid temperature change.

Artifacts can also be placed in an environment deficient in oxygen to kill pests. The agricultural and food industries use modified atmospheres extensively for pest control. For the smaller museum, the simplest system seals the infested object in a low-permeability plastic bag with an oxygen scavenger that will reduce the levels of oxygen in the package until the insects can no longer breathe and die. Another method modifies the atmosphere by replacing the oxygen with carbon dioxide, argon, or nitrogen to kill the pests. It is recommended to work with a conservator in developing which eradication techniques are appropriate for your collection.

When miscellaneous pests reach the action threshold and nonchemical means of pest management fail to produce acceptable results, chemical alternatives may be considered. Select the most effective pesticide and least toxic possible, and the one with the lowest risk. Ideally it should have a long contact time with the pest—for example, a powder that clings to the pest. To maximize its effectiveness, use the chemical during the pest's most vulnerable stage of development. The pesticide should pose little hazard to persons, resources, or the environment. Document all actions.

The IPM plan should contain supporting documentation such as safety requirements, applicable Material Safety Data Sheets (MSDSs), and a bibliography. Include external references such as the names, addresses, and telephone numbers of local resources like the county extension representative, pest control suppliers and what they supply, and any other site-specific IPM information.

Some sites may have governmental policies or regulations that affect pests and pesticide usage. This is true of any federal or state site. Governmental policies that may affect any site could include National Environmental Protection Act (NEPA) regulations. It is important that these policies are reviewed and adhered to as the IPM plan is developed.

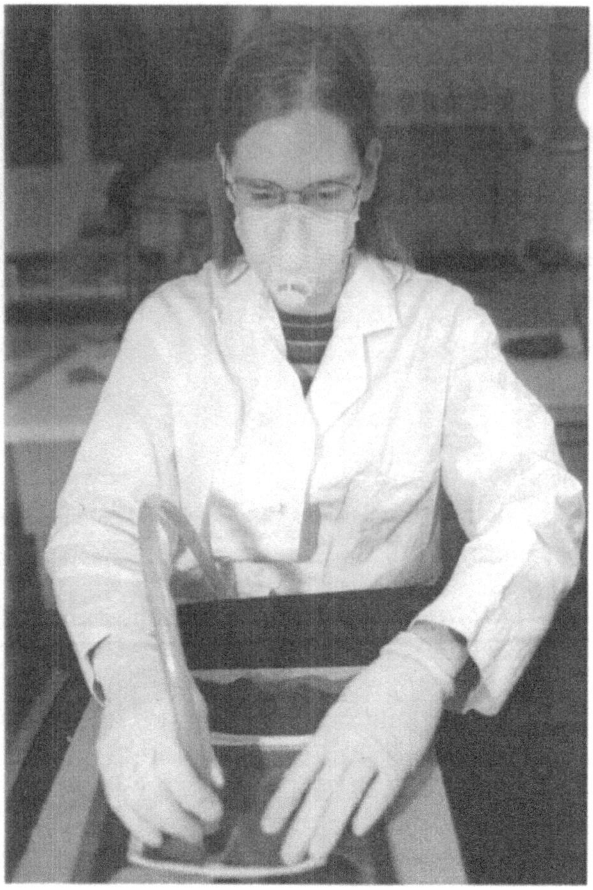

Figure 10.12 Vacuuming artifacts.

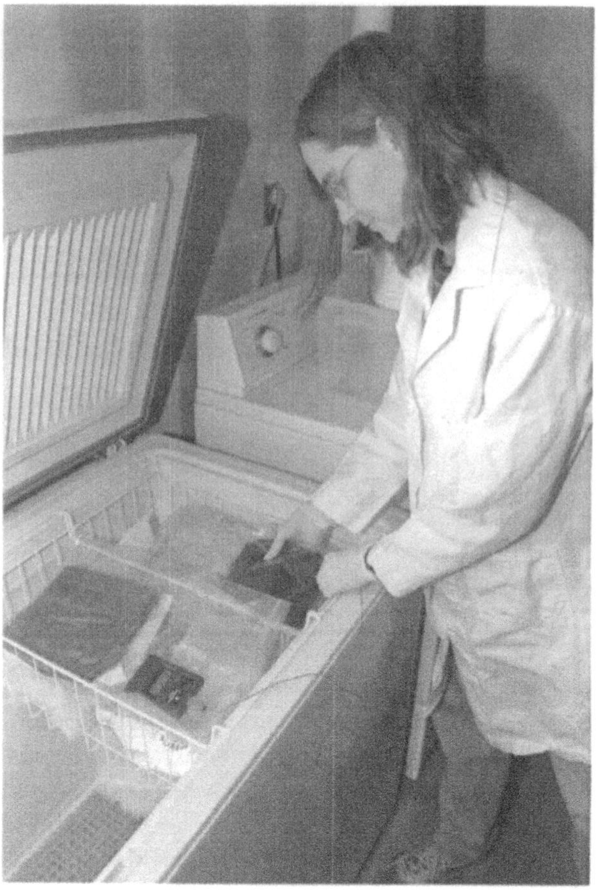

Figure 10.13 Freezing artifacts.

CONTRACTING OUT PEST CONTROL Many institutions find it convenient to have an agreement with a local pest control company that visits the site regularly to take care of pest problems. This practice may be the only pest control system the museum uses. Too often the firm comes in and sprays a chemical where pests may or may not exist. The museum administrator may not know what chemical is being used or where and rely on the expertise of the firm to take care of them. Rarely do these firms understand the special needs of a museum. If your pest control is provided by a contractor, a staff member should be assigned to monitor the process closely. The staff member needs to accompany the person who performs the treatments, review reports, keep and update product literature, MSDSs, and documentation on the contract in one file. While most commercial firms will supply monthly chemical eradication to the majority of their clients, many firms will specialize their services and work with a historic house site to apply IPM procedures. If your museum uses a contractor for your IPM program, significant staff time and involvement is still required to improve site conditions and to make the environment inhospitable to pests. The process does not end with a routine visit from a pest control company. IPM is a continuous process of assessment and evaluation, and one that results in long-term benefits for the institution and the environment.

COMMON MUSEUM PESTS

The following listing is not meant to include all of the pests that you will encounter in the museum environment. The pests included here are those that are primarily problematic for collections in that they discolor, weaken, or destroy artifacts. A good insect reference guide is a must for the museum library. In addition, there are excellent Web resources that offer magnified color images of pests.[3]

As noted previously, pest identification is one of the foundation elements of IPM. Pest identification is achieved through visual identification, knowledge of pest biology, and recognition of physical evidence. All pests caught in a trap should be identified by genus and species. Damage or secondary evidence will assist to identify a problem when no pest is trapped or found. Pests can leave behind cast larval skins, eggs, and droppings. An alert inspector will recognize such evidence and look for the pest and determine the threat it poses. Pests also inflict characteristic damage on a structure or object. A threadbare section of a woolen coat may be evidence of a clothes moth problem. Recognizing the type of damage a pest causes is another tool that can help signal when a problem may be present and action is required.

Microorganisms

Microorganisms include fungi, algae, yeasts, and bacteria that can cause the deterioration of both organic and inorganic materials. Mold and mildew are terms used to describe a variety of fungi. They are spore-bearing organisms with absorptive nutrition and no chlorophyll that reproduce sexually or asexually. They are characterized by fuzzy growths of any color (conspicuous masses of filament, or *hyphae*) and develop from microscopic spores carried in the air. Although it is virtually impossible to kill the spores, which are omnipresent, microorganism growth can be inhibited by environmental control. See chapter 9, "Preventive Conservation and Environmental Control." For the spores to become active, they must have a food source and an appropriate environment. This environment is different for each type of fungi; however, as a generalization, they exist in moist conditions in which the RH is 65 percent or higher. Textiles and leather are particularly susceptible to fungal attack, because fibers and soils found on fabrics and surfaces contain necessary nutrients.

Before fungal damage is apparent to the eye, there is often a characteristic musty odor present. Detection may be possible under an ultraviolet light, as the growths will fluoresce (figure 10.14). Close examination will generally reveal stains with clearly visible pigmentation. Identification under a microscope is possible, or growths may be cultured for identification. Cellulose fibers are most susceptible to fungal growth.

Figure 10.14 Examining a paper artifact for microorganism growth using a UV lamp.

Insects

Directly or indirectly, insects pose the greatest biological threat to a collection. They feed on organic materials, causing damage such as holes and stains, and leave frass (insect debris) behind. Some species merely burrow through materials such as textiles in search of other food sources; others make holes with their mouth parts. Each species of insect has its own traits and characteristics, and thus causes different types of damage to collections. As a result, a varied approach to prevention and treatment is necessary to stop infestation. The vulnerability of a material is related to its chemical makeup and the required nutritional needs of the pest.

CLOTHES MOTHS The very common webbing clothes moth (*Tineola bisselliella*) and the less common case-bearing or case-making clothes moth (*Tinea pellionella*) are two species of moths that are well known for damaging textiles. There are general characteristics shared by both species. The small and mobile larvae feed on fibers and cause damage. Larvae are 10–12 mm long, with a white to translucent body and a brownish head. They feed on proteins, such as wool, hair, feathers, and fur. Contaminants in fabric such as food deposits, drink, sweat, and urine stains provide essential nutrients for growth. Larvae digest keratin and chitin (the exoskeleton of insects) and they will chew through other materials such as plant materials and synthetic fibers while looking for a food source. The latter are consumed and excreted unaltered. In general, excrement is the same color as the food source, so if they feed on a red woolen coat, the debris will be red. The larvae may travel from the food source to pupate in floor and wall crevices.

Adult moths are approximately 12 mm long with a wingspan of 12–14 mm. Their wings are ringed or spotted and they have long legs. Adults are tan or light gray with a satiny sheen. They avoid light, which distinguishes them from other moths that enter buildings and often fly toward light sources.

Adults lay between thirty and two hundred eggs, which are approximately 1 mm in size. Eggs are laid throughout the year when conditions are favorable. If the environment is about 75°F (24°C) and 75 percent RH, a new generation can be produced in one month; in less favorable conditions this period can extend to years. Eggs are often laid among the threads of a fabric and are fastened by gelatinous material so that they do not shake off readily.

The webbing clothes moth (*Tineola bisselliella*) is the most common type of moth museum pest in the United States. Adults live fifteen to thirty days. Larvae sometimes spin a silken tube or mat under which to feed. The larval stage lasts from one month to more than two years, depending on conditions. A caste pupal skin or cocoon is left behind.

The case-bearing or case-making clothes moth (*Tinea pellionella*) is found more commonly in the southern United States. Adults are tan or light gray, often with three distinct dark spots on each wing. They live four to six days. These moths produce only one or two generations per year. Larvae are 6–9 mm long and always makes a case that is carried as it feeds. This stage lasts two to three months.

Damage. Moths pose a serious threat to textiles, feathers, and other proteinaceous materials. Damage includes holes that have sharp, distinct edges, distinguishing them from tears or fraying. Holes may be concentrated in soiled areas. Damage may also appear as grazing patterns on the surface, especially on wool nap and pile fabrics. Trails may be noted following the weave structure, such as along the weft of a carpet. Cocoons and webbing may be found in seams or folds or other dark and difficult-to-see areas of a textile. Frass and debris fall off the object.

DERMESTID BEETLES Dermestidae are a large family of insects, including larder beetles, hide beetles, and carpet beetles. Damage is caused by the larval stage, which feeds on proteinaceous materials such as hides, fur, feathers, wool, silk, leather, and insect exoskeletons. They also eat carbohydrates and will eat through cellulose, plastics, and synthetics to get at a food source. Dermestidae coleoptera, or carpet beetles, are the most common dermestid beetle to create problems in museum collections. There are three varieties: black, common, and varied, which look slightly different and are very damaging to proteinaceous materials. Larvae are hairy and bristly, with the hairs arranged in neat rows along the body length. The larvae molt many times; larval cast skins have long hairs and can be mistaken for the larvae themselves. They feed in dark, undisturbed locations and leave cast skins and frass near damaged areas. Frass is powdery and found around the food source. Larvae can wander far from that source to pupate, to be encountered on materials they do not eat. The larval stage may last from two or three hundred to six hundred days, depending on species.

Adult carpet beetles are round, with cranial antenna. Beetle length and color vary depending on species, but generally they are 3–11 mm in length, and yellow to brown in color. Coloration varies depending on the species. Adults do not shun light and can be found on windowsills. They are often brought indoors on fresh-cut flowers and are particularly attracted to white flowers. Eggs are pearly white, very difficult to see, and easily damaged. They are deposited on or near a food source.

The common carpet beetle (*Anthrenus scrophulariae*) adults are black speckled with white, with a longitudinal band of orange-red scales. Mature larvae are 5 mm long and golden brown or yellowish with long hairs at the tail end.

The varied carpet beetle (*Anthrenus verbasci*) adults are black with orange or yellow patterns. Mature larvae are 5 mm long and brown, with long hairs at the tail end.

The black carpet beetle (*Attagenus megatoma*) adults are dark brown or black. Mature larvae are 7–8 mm long at maturity, with an elongated body with a long tail of hairs. Larvae vary from light to dark brown.

Damage. Dermestid larvae are a serious threat to proteinaceous materials, especially textiles, feathers, and taxidermy specimens. They are apt to destroy a large area on one portion of an object such as a garment or carpet. Feeding patterns are discriminating, which means that there may be a greater loss to one area over another. They create holes that have distinct edges. They also create damage through grazing, evident in rather wandering paths. On pile carpets, the pile will generally be consumed first. Carpet beetles feed away from light in folds, seams, or on surfaces that are against an exhibit deck or at the bottom of a storage drawer. Cast larval skins are often scattered throughout the damaged area.

SILVERFISH AND FIREBRATS Silverfish (*Lepisma saccharina* and *Ctenolepisma longicaudata*) and firebrat

(*Thermobia domestica*) are primarily attracted to starch-based materials and will feed on both cellulose and protein materials. Silverfish are extremely resistant to starvation and have cellulose-digesting bacteria in their digestive system. Firebrats have starch-, fat-, and protein-digesting enzymes in their digestive system. Unlike the previous insects discussed, there is no larval stage.

For both species, immature insects or nymphs hatch two weeks after eggs are laid. Looking like small adults, they are attracted to starches and some cellulose materials, but in the absence of preferred food sources, they will chew on almost anything. They continue to molt throughout this cycle and shed skin is left behind. The insects prefer elevated temperatures, high relative humidity, and excessive dampness, and their presence may be a warning of a damp microenvironment that needs correction.

Silverfish (*Lepisma saccharina*) range between 12 and 18 mm and are carrot shaped. They possess two long segmented antennae that protrude from the head and three filaments that protrude from the tail. Their bodies are covered with silver scales.

Firebrats (*Thermobia domestica*) are wingless, nocturnal, fast-moving creatures with a flattened carrot shape. Their bodies have a banded appearance with light and dark stripes. There are two antennae at the head and three long filaments attached to the tapered (posterior) end. Firebrats and silverfish leave small holes on paper and textiles and yellowish stains on the material they have been eating. Their grazing patterns appear on surface finishes.

CRICKETS There are several distinct groups of crickets, but it is the house (*Acheta domesticus*) and field (*Gryllus spp.*) cricket that cause damage to museum collections, particularly textiles. Depending on environmental conditions, adults lay between one hundred and seven hundred eggs, which hatch after eight to twelve weeks. Adult crickets are 13–30 mm long. House crickets are lighter and less robust than field crickets. They enter buildings in cooler weather. Adults typically feed on plants but will eat silk, wool, cotton, and linen—especially if stained. Synthetics, plastics, and rubbers may also be damaged.

ROACHES Roaches are one of the most common insect pests in buildings. They are found near warm areas and a water source; they are nocturnal. Eggs are laid in capsules. Nymphs begin to feed as soon as they hatch. They molt six or seven times before reaching maturity in about two months. General characteristics shared by roaches include adults that are brown in color, some with two stripes on the thorax. They range in size from 11 mm for the German cockroach to 40 mm for the American cockroach, and they live about six months.

Five types of roaches are commonly found in the United States:

American cockroach (*Periplaneta americana*) (Linneas)
Smokey brown cockroach (*Periplaneta fuliginosa*) (Serville)

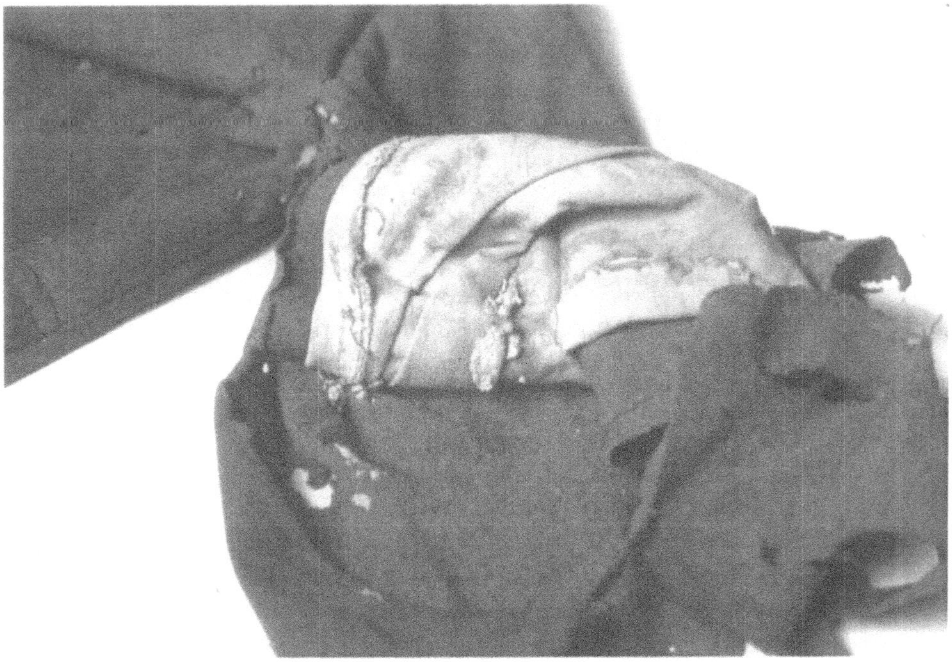

Figure 10.15 Dermestid beetle damage to a textile.

Oriental cockroach (*Blatta orientalis*) (Linneas)
Brown banded cockroach (*Supella longipalpa*) (Serville)
German cockroach (*Blatelle germanica*) (Linneas)

Damage. Roaches chew holes in silk and cotton fabrics, presumably where food has been spilled. They are attracted to materials that are starched and sweat stained. They eat carbohydrates and proteins, and they look for human foods. They are a hazard to applied labels and book bindings because they eat glue and starch. Roaches may leave stains on collections from vomit, secreted abdominal fluids, and feces.

OTHER INSECTS Two other types of insects bear mentioning here. Houseflies and related flies such as the black and cluster flies can be a problem at historic house sites. They are distributed worldwide and can carry serious diseases. Good sanitation and debris management in and around the site is essential for their control. The Asian lady beetle, *Harmonia axyridis*, is relatively new to the United States but is rapidly becoming a problem in structures. They look similar to our native lady beetle (ladybug), which is usually considered a beneficial insect and stays outside and feeds on other insects. The Asian lady beetle is tan to yellow to red in color and can have black spots on the wing covers. They come into a building in the fall looking to winter over inside. They crawl on windows, on walls, and in attics, and they emit a noxious odor and yellowish staining fluid before they die. Vacuuming up those pests found inside the museum is essential, and sealing their means of entry into the building will help to control populations.

Small Animals

RODENTS Rodents such as mice and rats are generally nocturnal and secretive and are rarely sighted unless an infestation is advanced. They learn from experience and will alter their pattern of behavior to changed conditions. The sound of gnawing, running, and scratching may be heard inside walls and false ceilings. Droppings may be the key to species identification and a clue to the extent of the infestation. Mouse droppings are very small with pointed ends. They should not be confused with cockroach droppings, which look similar but have blunt ends and may be ridged.

Rodents prefer limited areas and repeatedly use the same pathways, leaving tracks, rub marks and signs of gnawing, and a urine trail that will fluoresce under ultraviolet light. In heavy rat or mouse infestations a peculiar musty odor may be present, especially in poorly ventilated areas. Mice and rats and other small animals usually damage collection materials by chewing and incorporating them into their nests (figures 10.10 and 10.16). Their droppings and urine will stain materials.

Rodents can carry diseases such as hantavirus, a serious pulmonary disease. For information, see the Centers for Disease Control and Prevention website.[4]

BATS Bats may roost in the roof areas of historic houses. They should be eliminated through exclusion techniques.

BIRDS Several birds will nest in and around houses, developing high populations and seriously impacting the building and collections. The pigeon is probably the most common pest, but sparrows and starlings can also be a problem. All prefer the protection of ledges, eaves, or attic vents for shelter and nest building. Their droppings are unsightly, acidic and therefore damaging to stone, and most seriously can carry disease such as the lung disease histoplasmosis.[5]

Remove food sources to prevent establishment of bird populations. Seal up vents with fine wire mesh, seal holes and crevices, and eliminate landing sites. When dealing with some of these infestations, it is important that you use the appropriate personal protective equipment and follow good sanitation and cleanup practices.

TREATING INFESTED ARTIFACTS

The decision to treat an infested artifact depends on whether the infestation is active or inactive. Active infestations require immediate treatment, which begins with isolating it from all other materials. Inactive infestation can be dealt with by removing debris from the object, then isolation, and monitoring over a prescribed period of time. Preventive treatments are used as a precaution when new materials come into the collection environment. Many treatments can begin with vacuuming, some with freezing. No matter what the treatment, the life cycle of the pest should be considered in the treatment decision. Sometimes it is necessary to keep the piece bagged and monitor it over a long period of time. Some of the treatments listed have consequences that are deleterious to the object and humans, and require careful consideration.

General Treatments: Mechanical Removal

The mechanical removal of microorganism growth, pests, and surface soil from leather, textiles, furs, and natural history specimens through vacuuming is a routine preservation activity. Vacuuming removes pests, food sources, frass, castings, and webbing, and it is the

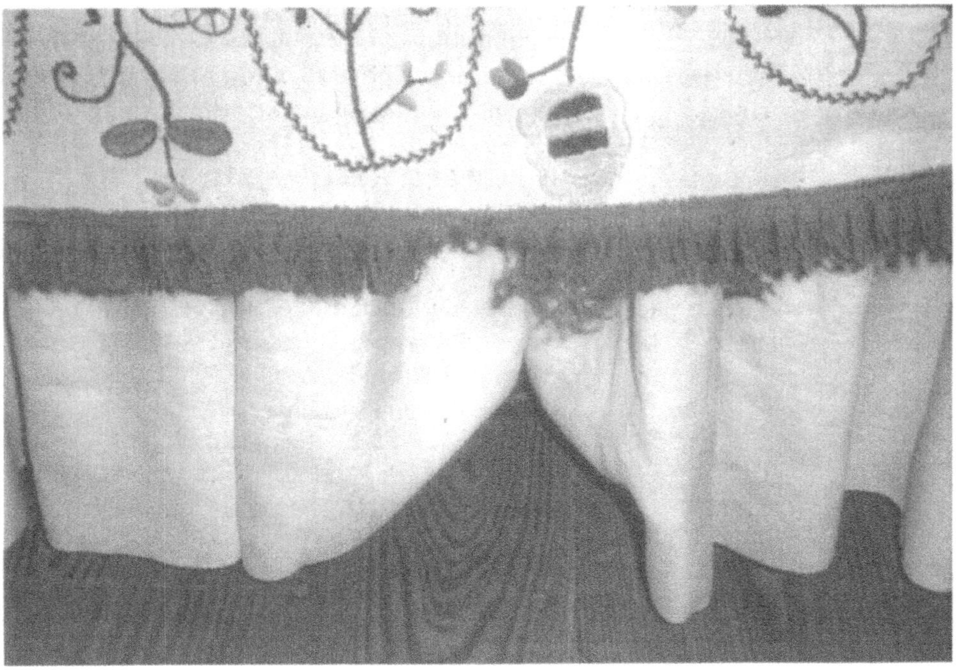

Figure 10.16 Chewed woolen fringe on a bed-covering.

most commonly used procedure in museum pest control. Vacuuming is used in prevention and also in dealing with active or inactive infestations.

A good vacuum cleaner is an essential tool in reducing damage from insects. It should have a variable suction, a variety of attachments, and high filtration properties created by a high-efficiency particulate air (HEPA) filter. Microorganisms and insects are trapped within the levels of filtration and are not exhausted back out into the room. The accumulated debris gathered by the vacuuming must be disposed of outside the building so that the live insects and insect eggs do not have the opportunity to reinfest the building. Brushes and hoses should be thoroughly cleaned after use.

Cleaning Treatments: Solvent Cleaning

Dry-cleaning solvents will eradicate insect infestations and kill fungi but may not be an appropriate treatment for many types of artifacts. They are most commonly used on textiles but may not be appropriate for fragile textiles. The solvents can have a deleterious effect on plastic beads and trimming, pigment paints, leather, suede, and fur.

Wet cleaning is commonly used on textiles and can remove live insects, frass, and eggs by floating them away. It is also used for paper-based materials that have issues with microorganism growth. It may not be appropriate for fragile materials.

Low-Temperature Pest Management

Freezing insects by rapid temperature change can be an effective process for eradication on certain artifacts such as feathers, leather, and textiles. When proper procedures are followed, no damage to the artifacts is observed.[6] Objects with paint, certain adhesives, glass beads, and gelatin sequins should not be frozen.

Heating

Elevated temperatures will kill insects, but it is essential to ensure that the required temperature of 50°C and more does not harm the artifact. Procedures in which the RH around the object is maintained throughout the heating process have been used successfully in Europe.[7]

Modified Atmosphere Treatments

Anoxic conditions in which oxygen is depleted and replaced by suffocant atmospheres such as carbon dioxide, nitrogen, and argon are effective alternatives to fumigation. Objects are sealed in a high-oxygen barrier film or placed in a fumigation chamber for the procedure. These gases have proven to be effective, and they have replaced the fumigant gases such as Vikane (sulfuryl fluoride), ethylene oxide, and methyl bromide for most museum applications.

Chemical Eradication

Chemical fumigation is a health and safety concern and may damage collections and the environment.

Figure 10.17 Person wearing personal protective equipment to work in a building with a rodent infestation.

Your museum collections may have been exposed to a number of common chemicals.

Para-dichlorobenzene (PDB) is a volatile crystal that sublimes at ordinary temperatures and has a characteristic penetrating odor. It is a commonly used treatment in the home and consequently finds its way into museums. PDB vapors can cause irritation to the skin, throat, and eyes as well as produce narcotic symptoms such as dizziness, nausea, and headache. Chronic health effects include dermatitis, liver, and kidney damage. The carcinogenic effects are under investigation.

Naphthalene (moth balls) is a repellent commonly used in museums because it can be purchased in the local supermarket or hardware store.

Insecticides are pesticides designed to kill insects, but they may also affect other small animals by the disruption of vital processes through chemical action. Few are suitable for collections.

HEALTH AND SAFETY

Toxicity

Many types of fungi are pathogenic. In the absence of identification, take reasonable safety precautions. Wear appropriate personal protective equipment, which may include a respirator and gloves, when handling a contaminated object or working in a biological fume extractor. Mechanically remove spores and growth by using a HEPA filter vacuum. Spores should not be exhausted back into the room.

Exposure to pesticides can cause a variety of health problems—some acute, others resulting in a chronic illness. Concerns vary according to the type of pesticide and the amount and duration of exposure.

Exposure to the pest can also be a health hazard. Microorganisms and fecal matter can carry disease.

Safety

All personnel involved in rodent trapping or inspections and who are brought into close contact with rodent debris need to wear approved personal protective equipment (figure 10.17) and follow federal Centers for Disease Control and Prevention (CDC) guidelines. At a minimum, personal protective equipment will include rubber or latex gloves and a particulate mask capable of screening particles as small as 0.3μ in size (i.e., a HEPA filter). Snap traps are recommended for rodent control, not glue boards and live traps. The snap trap protects staff from bites and limits the spread of disease. Use only HEPA filter vacuums for spore removal and the removal of animal droppings. MSDSs should be read and understood before handling any chemical fumigant.

CHAPTER 11

Preventive Conservation and the Historic House Landscape

LUCY LAWLISS, ASLA, SUPERINTENDENT,
GEORGE WASHINGTON BIRTHPLACE NATIONAL MONUMENT

THE INTEGRATED APPROACH to preservation of the historic house museum considers the site and all of its features—house, landscape, furnishings, and collections. Therefore, the care of the landscape setting should be comparable to the care given the contents of the house and the house itself. The mission statement for the historic house museum should include the site in its entirety with all of its features, so that no one aspect of the property unnecessarily dominates another. The challenge for house museum managers is to use the landscape to give the house and its significant builder and/or owner a setting and environmental context, as well as to prompt visitors to what they can expect to find inside the house. An integrated and balanced approach to the landscape, the house, and its contents will provide the richest possible visitor experience.

At the same time, one must recognize that the historic setting of the house may have to satisfy the contemporary needs of a public museum by providing access to the site; parking for cars, buses, and associated vehicles; accessible on-site pedestrian circulation to various points in the landscape; and new facilities for storage and maintenance. Given that burden, it is imperative that the landscape history and existing conditions be documented along with the history and condition of the structures (main and supporting), the furnishings, and other collections. Only with a complete historical picture is it possible for managers to decide treatment approaches that weigh the benefits and impacts of management decisions on the various resources under their care.

LANDSCAPE OR GARDEN RESEARCH AND STEWARDSHIP

Anyone who maintains a yard—from a simple grass plot to a complex landscape of gardens, lawns, and mature trees—understands that without regular care, and sometimes in spite of care, landscapes evolve and change over time. Young trees grow large and shade out flower beds. Invasive ground covers, left unmanaged, take over adjacent woodlands, and woodlands expand and occupy historic lawns. Many bulbs and perennials, if undivided, diminish over time. Therefore, rehabilitating or restoring a historic landscape to any particular period is a challenge and should be undertaken with a full understanding of the historic conditions and what is involved in recapturing and maintaining that condition within the current budget and staffing.

Related to these issues is the desire of many stewards of historic properties to portray period gardens that are in keeping with the architectural style and construction date of the house. This is where historical documentation of the property is critical. First, can research confirm that gardens—functional or aesthetic—were a part of the historic house setting? This may require archaeological investigation, depending on the age of the house and the environmental conditions of the region. Second, if the house museum is significant for its owner or occupant, was that person or the family contemporary to the architecture of the house, and was that person a gardener or did he or she have the means to employ one? Without research and site investigation, one cannot assume that the period of significance for the landscape matches the construction date of the house. Even if the historic owner developed the house, work on the landscape often lagged behind construction of the house and its interior. Because the landscape features can more easily be updated, along with the fact that plants die and need to be replaced, the style and period of the landscape may postdate the style and construction date of the house.

Another thing to keep in mind as one undertakes site research is that historically very few people had the

Figure 11.1 Frederick Law Olmsted National Historic Site, Brookline, Massachusetts. Contemporary (above) and historic (right) images of the Fairsted and Olmsted Elm.

means or inclination to sustain ornamental gardens. Until the mid-twentieth century, most American yards consisted of functional spaces. The front yard was the public face of the household and its maintenance and appearance was probably different (and better) than the back or side yards. In many cases the nonpublic spaces were places of work, and if there was a garden at all, it was a utilitarian space to supplement the family's need for herbs and vegetables. Therefore, unless there is documentation to support the owner's interest in and ability to maintain an ornamental garden, one should not impose a "sentimental" or "popular" aesthetic on the historic setting of the house. The facts associated with the development and maintenance of an owner's private landscape will always be more interesting than a fictional landscape.

Finally, the successful conservation of the historic house and all of its resources is the result of a well-conceived and well-executed stewardship plan. To that end, it is important to keep in mind that the degree of control the museum manager can impose on the building, its interior, and associated collections is greater than what can be imposed in the "natural" world of the landscape, and management plans should reflect this fact. The professional skills and disciplines associated with these areas of the house museum are also distinct and different. Despite this fact, the extent to which these diverse professionals communicate and support one another's goals and the methods to achieve them will determine the successful implementation of an integrated conservation approach.

The National Park Service's Park Cultural Landscapes Program along with the Olmsted Center for Landscape Preservation have formalized the research and evaluation process necessary to determine both the overall preservation approach and treatment for individual features of a historic landscape. The *Guide to Cultural Landscape Reports: Contents, Process, and Techniques* (1998, rev. 2005) presents a successful methodology to guide site managers to create or contract for a Cultural Landscape Report.[1]

UNDERSTANDING AND CARING FOR THE ARCHAEOLOGY OF THE HOUSE MUSEUM SITE

The layers of history associated with the historic landscape of a house are not always visible, but to the eye trained in reading the landscape, features lost to time and natural processes can be "seen" and recovered. Thorough research of the historic, and if applicable, the prehistoric record may indicate where archaeological

Figure 11.2 Restoration of the parterre at Hampton National Historic Site, Towson, Maryland.

THE CULTURAL LANDSCAPE REPORT

A Cultural Landscape Report (CLR) documents the history and significance and proposes treatments of a cultural landscape. The report evaluates the history and integrity of the landscape, including any changes to its geographical context, features, materials, and use.[2]

Historical research is an important component of the CLR. A site should include a cultural landscape study as part of its overall planning process, but more often than not the studies are undertaken when a major change to the site is proposed. A CLR is essential if any site-disturbing work such as a new visitor center or parking area is being considered. The report should supply management with the information needed to prevent the loss of the landscape's character-defining features.

As with the Historic Structure Report, the creation of a CLR is often a team effort involving specialists with expertise in landscape architecture, archaeology, history, and—depending on the need—forestry, agriculture, and horticulture, among others.

Contents

Since the landscape is a continually changing resource, no one report structure fits all sites. But the essential information in a report should include:

Table of Contents
Acknowledgments (if appropriate)
Administration (Report Summary)
History of the Cultural Landscape
Treatment Proposals
¶Illustrations
Appendixes
Bibliography

There are many Web resources that can guide site managers in developing project goals and in developing a contract for a CLR. The National Register of Historic Places has several bulletins based on landscape type that will be of interest.[3] *The Secretary of the Interior's Standards for the Treatment of Historic Properties* provides the broad guidance and policy for treatment and the NPS Technical Preservation Services has many online publications that are invaluable.[4]

A Cultural Landscape Report has become the standard tool for determining preservation treatment in a framework of historical research, existing conditions documentation, and treatment recordation. Once the historical research is complete, another important resource for guiding the selection of appropriate landscape treatment is *The Secretary of Interior's Standards for the Treatment of Historic Properties with Guidelines of the Treatment of Cultural Landscapes* (1996).[5] Both of these resources should be consulted as managers undertake research, treatment, and long-term management of their historic settings and landscapes.

remains are likely to be found. For instance, historic maps that only show the location of primary structures and outbuildings suggest where walks might be located by the layout and orientation of the buildings and site. Indications of fence lines or even property boundaries, if the use of the property is known, suggest lines along which fence posts or wall foundations can be located. Overgrown lines of vegetation often contain the remains of fences, and woody vegetation that was consistently pruned records this treatment along its bark at woody nodes. Slumped ground can indicate the final stages of a rotting stump, the age and species of which may be determined. Undergrowth areas or "crop marks" may indicate zones where archaeological remains like pavement, foundations, formal planting beds, or trash areas may be inhibiting growth. Disturbed areas that have utility lines, drains, or footpaths also tend to discourage growth because topsoil ended up below the less-fertile subsoil in the construction process. Conversely, lush green or overgrown areas may indicate locations that are highly fertile as a result of former associations with food storage or wastes, or with excess water associated with old fountains, pumps, springs, and the like.

Areas indicated as garden plots or agricultural fields on maps can be located accurately on-site because of the different soil composition and areas of compaction associated with cultivated ground. Sometimes historic field and yard patterns, otherwise indistinguishable from a human perspective, can be read from aerial photographs, where larger land-use patterns become evident and lines lost on the house museum property can be traced outside the boundary if the land-use setting has remained consistent. Plow scars in the subsoil can indicate the direction of plow furrows. The regular patterns of fruit trees and vine plantings can be located by the root stains in the subsoil for accurate restoration of orchards and vineyards. Even species of plants have been determined successfully by recovery and analysis of seed and pollen samples that can be located in and around the root-ball pattern left in the soil just below the surface.

The application and success of various techniques for analyzing site features is often related to the natural environment of the site. Dryer, cooler sites where vegetative growth cycles are seasonal may retain archaeological records longer than warm, moist sites where vegetative growth is continuous year-round. Therefore, it is always a good idea before proceeding with site-disturbing activities that an archaeologist knowledgeable of the period of significance and of the physical context of the historic home review the landscape documentation to assist with the identification of sensitive areas. Even if a budget does not allow immediate excavation of an area of potential interest, an archaeological record that is left undisturbed is available for future analysis. One that has been disturbed is lost to everyone. Despite the high cost associated with landscape and garden archaeology, it is of growing professional interest to archaeologists, garden historians, and historical landscape architects for whom other sources of documentation often do not exist. For many landscapes, the archaeological record, if protected, is a most valuable resource for the site because it retains the history of what actually happened in the landscape and not what one thought or wished to have happened.

UNDERSTANDING THE PHYSICAL CONTEXT OF THE HISTORIC HOUSE SITE—YARDS, LANDSCAPES, AND ENVIRONS

The spatial organization and makeup of a historic house setting may be an important aspect of the life and life ways of the people associated with the landscape. Understanding the layout and hierarchy of spaces on a site can reveal how they were used and by whom. It is not surprising that oral histories with house servants or agricultural labor—free or enslaved—reveal radically different perspectives of the site than the same records from the perspectives of the owner and the owner's family and friends. The landscape of work and the landscape of leisure may overlap in the same space, but they may be widely separated temporally, seasonally, or even socially. An example of this often occurs around the name of the property—the informal name of the house and property used by laborers and tenants may be different from the formal name used by the family and the community.

From the earliest records describing American settlement, there has always been a great importance placed on presenting the house to the public—street or waterway—or more accurately stated, to the community, as a means of establishing the family's moral standards and place in society. Andrew Jackson Downing, the mid-nineteenth-century horticulturalist, landscape designer, and tastemaker, codified much of this thinking in his widely read *Landscape Gardening, a Treatise on the Theory and Practice of Landscape Gardening, Adapted to North America* (1841).[6] Downing was not the first and certainly not the last arbiter of how Americans should present themselves through the design and care of their home grounds. A presentable and tasteful front yard was equated with a family's social standing, and if ornamental plants were included in the landscape at all, they were likely to have occupied a place in the front yard.

What happened beyond the front yard is very much associated with the period of significance, the economic and the geographic setting of the house. The State of Georgia, Historic Preservation Section, sponsored *Georgia's Living Places: Historic Houses in Their Landscaped Settings*[7] through the research efforts of Catherine Howett, professor emeritus of landscape architecture and historic preservation, University of Georgia. Professor Howett established residential landscaping types that survive in Georgia. The earliest example, and one common across the United States and sustained through the centuries here and abroad, is described as the landscape of work. As an extension of the dwelling or house, in climates conducive to working outdoors, areas of the residential yard were used for specific work tasks or were marked with circulation routes between house and barns, outbuildings, and outlying agricultural areas. This type of landscape is most often associated with a self-supporting agrarian lifestyle. Small kitchen gardens may have been cultivated in side or rear yards, with agricultural fields, woodlots, and orchards located outside the immediate house grounds. Enclosing—or excluding—fences, paths, and sight lines were important components of this landscape. Today these yards can look ornamental to our modern eye, and some examples did follow an "ornamental farm" approach, a style that gained popularity among the literate elite during the eighteenth century.

Moving forward into the nineteenth century, the growing middle class had the ability to obtain and maintain an ornamental yard as an aspect of their residential setting. This pattern is documented in small towns and more urban settings, and was guided by a growing availability of periodicals, books, and horticultural societies. These resources flourished in the post–Civil War era and were accentuated by a growing national interest in both European garden and park precedents as well as in American native plants. While wealthy homeowners developed ever more eclectic, elaborate, and complex landscapes with the help of the nascent profession of landscape architects (the American Society of Landscape Architecture was founded in 1899), even home owners of modest means had sources for plants and related materials with which to create an ornamental landscape or garden.

By the mid-twentieth century, when the yard was no longer needed as a place to accomplish daily work tasks, the backyard was everywhere evolving into a landscape of leisure. The use and look most Americans associate with the backyard is a post–World War II phenomenon that was popularized by publications such as *Sunset* magazine. While the front yard continued to play a largely public role, with the advent of air-conditioning and television, the front porch lost its prominence as a social space and associated plantings and furnishings began to disappear inside the house or to the backyard.

These were and continue to be sources for design ideas, appropriate plants for various uses and setting, and small-scale furnishings. This trend continued well into the twentieth century, with a resurgence of interest in the late twentieth century that continues today. For anyone interested in gardening or ornamental landscapes—at any income level—there has been a plethora of information available on beautifying and enjoying one's home grounds, and regionally available sources should be consulted.

DOCUMENTING AND CARING FOR THE LIVING LANDSCAPE OF THE HOUSE MUSEUM

The constructed features of the landscape, which includes fences, walks, outbuildings, and site furnishings relate closely to the care and conservation of the house exterior, and are more adequately covered in chapter 12, "Preventive Conservation and the Historic House Structure," which focuses on the structural elements of the house. This section will focus on the living, or biotic, elements in the landscape. Conservation of the living resources—trees, shrubs, and ground covers, as well as in some cases the historic animal species associated with the house museum—may be as important as the conservation of the contents and archives associated with the house and its significant occupants. Depending on the age, significance, and physical environs of the historic house museum—which includes its surviving vegetation—there may be important information that suggests what the predevelopment condition of the landscape was like, as well as information about what was planted to create the historic house setting. Large trees were often noted as boundary markings on historic plats, and their genus and species may say something about the forest cover at the time of development. Long-lived trees in particular may represent surviving artifacts from the period of significance or before. Because of the changing styles and tastes in garden design and plants, remnant vegetation may represent species, varieties, or cultivars no longer available in the modern nursery trade, and therefore may be candidates for propagation when developing treatment plans.

The Olmsted Center for Landscape Preservation (OCLP), a National Park Service center that focuses on the research, planning, and stewardship of historic landscapes, recommends a multistep process to develop a preservation—or conservation—maintenance plan. This approach is detailed in the *Guide to Developing a Preservation Maintenance Plan for a Historic Landscape*[8] and used the Frederick Law Olmsted National Historic Site, a historic house museum in Brookline, Massachusetts, as a laboratory. The OCLP makes the point that preservation maintenance is a distinct type of maintenance because of the interest in perpetuating the historic character of the landscape. Therefore, a rose is *not* a rose is *not* a rose is *not* a rose. To give an example, a sprawling multiple-bloom multiflora rose cannot be substituted for an upright single blooming hybrid tea rose with the hope of achieving the same effect or character. It is essential to understand a plant's habit of growth and the importance, timing, and duration of the bloom period and its importance to the overall composition. More importantly, it is essential to understand how it was to combine with other plants to provide a particular landscape character. In many cases, it is the overall character and not the importance of individual plants that is significant.

The following section summarizes the procedures for creating a historic landscape preservation maintenance plan, adapted from the OCLP *Guide to Developing a Preservation Maintenance Plan for a Historic Landscape.*

Define Objectives

At the start of any planning effort, it is essential to outline the issues associated with making a preservation maintenance plan work within the existing maintenance program's budget and personnel. This is the opportunity to have a designated leader engage all the relevant professionals with the landscape maintenance staff or landscape contractor, and in some cases outside expertise, to address common or overlapping concerns in the landscape. For example, this is the opportunity to address the issue of granite fines from gravel walks being tracked into the house entry hall or the noise of using contemporary garden equipment in a historic setting when the house museum is open to visitors. Assemble all relevant information in a way that it can be utilized by all the interested participants and in a place where it can be easily accessed and added to throughout the planning effort. It is perhaps worth noting that in the absence of a CLR—the fundamental landscape research and treatment document—the preservation maintenance goals should focus on maintaining the status quo with the goal of not removing or damaging any potentially significant landscape feature.

Organize Areas and Categories of Landscape Features

Subdivide the landscape into management zones or character areas that help organize preservation maintenance. To be of most use, the subdivisions should be illustrated on a map that not only delineates the areas along logical and identifiable areas or lines in the landscape but also locates and names the principal features within each zone. The date and source of the map is helpful to record and, depending on the complexity of the landscape, a naming or numbering system could be developed to establish consistent references. (Agreeing on "feature names" and formalizing the names with specific locations in the planning process are essential to sharing a common language when treating and maintaining the landscape.) It should also be noted in the inventory whether the management zones relate to historic zones or historic uses or are purely based on current practices. Either approach is valid, but it is important to note for future managers.

Inventory Landscape Features

Inventory all the landscape features that are being managed and include their name, origin, age, and size.

Initial Field Inspection and Summary of Work Needed

Conduct field inspections for historic and nonhistoric landscape features to establish their existing condition, their desired condition (removal may be appropriate in the case of nonhistoric features), and whatever work is needed to improve/change the condition. If it is not reasonable to collect information for all the landscape features or all management zones, target the most significant or most visited. Ideally this should be determined through the landscape research process. Do not forget to include elements that detract from the landscape and over time need to be controlled or eliminated. An obvious example of a detractor is an invasive, nonnative plant. If the information is available either as a description or image, the historic condition of the feature or character area should be included with the inventory record.

Feature Data and Record Keeping

Decide on and use a consistent record-keeping format that includes text and photographs to capture feature data, including its historical significance, associated preservation practices, potential pest or disease problems, and helpful references. It may include notes on propagation, replacement, damage, or other major changes to the landscape. This can be as simple as a three-ring binder of information or as complex as using a computer-based geographic information system (GIS).

Create Seasonal Calendar

Compile preservation practices into an annual calendar that describes the optimum time to look for specific problems, as well as the way to carry out work when a problem is identified. Annual or seasonal events at the house museum should be included on this calendar, with the corresponding information on how to mitigate the impacts of large groups.

Periodic Field Inspection and Review of Work

Once a baseline is established through a feature inventory, a schedule of periodic field inspections can be determined for the character-defining features as well as for those features that need to be controlled or eliminated over time. The intent of this field inspection is to highlight damage, deterioration, or potential problems as they appear because it will be easier and more affordable to address problems as they arise than to wait until they become serious or widespread. Therefore, time of year and frequency of inspection is important. For example, if the spread of a certain flowering plant is desirable, it would be essential to do an inspection during the flowering period. However, if walk or driveway potholes occur after a cold winter, a late winter or early spring inspection should be scheduled to understand the extent of that winter's damage and to assess the amount of work involved in getting the walk or drive ready for spring traffic. It may be important to schedule inspections of certain features after big events such as wedding receptions or seasonal visitation surges (e.g., spring garden week) to understand the effect of these uses on the historic landscape. With accumulated documentation it may be possible to find a way to mitigate effects or find ways to include the additional costs of treatment in rental or event fees.

Recognize that the effectiveness of inspections will depend on the ability and knowledge of the person(s) doing the inspection, so use trained people. Also, create records that include the name of the person doing the inspection and date so that subsequent inspections, recognizing the potential for personnel turnover, will have that information. Inspections are valuable and take time and therefore must be scheduled in light of the overall maintenance workload.

The other side of the field inspection process is a summary of the work needed to correct an identified condition. It is very helpful if the inspection forms document both work needed and the best time to accomplish it, which would logically feed into a seasonal maintenance work calendar. Once the identified task is completed, record when the work was done and the amount of time and the number of staff needed to complete the work. With this information systematized, maintenance staff should get better at predicting work as well as its costs in time, labor, and materials. This follow-through documentation will allow for a more accurate landscape maintenance calendar and budget to be developed over time.

Record Keeping

Maintain an ongoing record of overall and feature-level preservation plans and accomplishments in a format that works for your site. If possible, there are many advantages of collecting the information in a computer database. Records are easily created and updated by one person and if available, shared digitally through a network, e-mail, or website. However, a low-technology paper system that is kept in an easily accessed notebook may be just as useful and something non–computer users will be able to access. Seasonal calendars that reflect when inspections and work are to be done should also be kept as part of the digital file or in the maintenance notebook for easy reference.

Take the time to organize and develop a landscape preservation maintenance plan. It has the potential of becoming a useful repository of landscape information that often is lost or goes unrecorded but may be invaluable for landscape decision making when problems arise. In the absence of a CLR, a historic home can at least ensure that there is no deterioration of the existing condition. If features are lost, the preservation maintenance plan becomes a record of change to inform future landscape research. Documenting the existing landscape and monitoring for change is a first, and important, step to an ongoing conservation effort.

THE VISITOR AND THE HISTORIC HOUSE LANDSCAPE

Opening a historic house to the public requires that a certain level of change must occur to the site, building, and interior in order to accommodate visitor access and new uses. On-site changes almost inevitably mean the addition of parking areas—sometimes large enough to allow for bus parking and turn-around space—walks, and access points to the house that are fully accessible. That any or all of these changes and additions will impact the historic landscape goes without question, so the challenge is to have the least amount of impact possible. When dealing with a small property, parking should be sought off-site at a nearby location. If the historic landscape is an estate or agricultural setting, historic research will be critical to assist managers in determining areas where visitor services (circulation, parking, visitor center, or restrooms) will have the least impact on the significant features. It is important to document and plan for historic and contemporary views to and from the main house grounds when making this evaluation. Even when accommodations for these contemporary uses need to be on-site, recognize that they are happening within the historic landscape and treat them as part of that setting as opposed to new landscape elements with their own vocabulary of design, scale, and materials.

MONITORING THE CONDITIONS OF THE HISTORIC HOUSE LANDSCAPE

Even though monitoring is mentioned as part of the preservation planning process, the value of this effort is worth repeating. In the same way that monitoring the conditions of the internal house environment is critical to ensuring adequate care of its furnishings and contents, only monitoring the landscape will tell managers if they are achieving their conservation goals. Without established monitoring protocols, managers cannot be sure that, for instance, selected vegetation to be controlled or eradicated is actually diminishing with seasonal treatment, or that vegetation to be encouraged are increasing in numbers as a response to maintenance. With good information, maintenance can be adjusted to achieve the desired results.

Therefore, it is essential to establish baseline conditions for the management zones, especially before new work begins, so that desired outcomes can be measured and documented. Unlike interior monitoring, which monitors the atmospheric conditions in order to sustain the same environment throughout the year, external monitoring is about the level of impacts within a changing environment—growth, light, temperature, and moisture—as well as the effect of one's own maintenance practices. Natural and cultural activities will maintain or change the condition of the landscape over time. With a baseline established, stewards can measure change and adjust practices to respond to an ever-evolving environment. This is essential if the overall historic character of a house museum property is to survive with its significant features intact.

Figure 11.3 Façade of Hampton Mansion with wisteria vines, Hampton National Historic Site, Towson, Maryland.

CHAPTER 12

Preventive Conservation and the Historic House Structure

REBECCA L. STEVENS, ARCHITECT, AIA, NCARB

THE HISTORIC HOUSE MUSEUM must address the preservation needs of the collections as well as those of the historic structure, for together they interpret and make tangible our cultural heritage. In the ideal partnership, a preservation architect and a collections conservator collaborate as part of the team that formulates and guides the site's preservation strategies. Successful preventive conservation programs require the commitment of all those engaged in any aspect of the house museum, from docents to director to board members. Representatives from all levels of the organization must be involved in developing the preventive conservation program from its inception through regular evaluations.

DEFINING PRESERVATION

Preservation is the process of applying measures necessary to sustain the existing form, integrity, and materials of a historic property.[1] In general, preservation focuses primarily on ongoing maintenance and secondarily on repair of historic materials and features of a property. However, it may include improvements to mechanical, plumbing, and electrical systems.

It is important to be familiar with the terms *preservation maintenance* and *treatment.* Preservation maintenance is defined as action to mitigate wear and deterioration of a historic property without altering its historic character. Work includes protecting the structure's condition, making repairs when its condition warrants (with the least degree of intervention, including limited replacement in-kind), replacing an entire feature in-kind when the level of deterioration or damage of materials precludes repair, and stabilization to protect damaged materials or features from additional damage. *Treatment* is defined as work carried out to achieve a particular historic preservation goal. It may be the deliberate alteration of the chemical and/or physical aspects of cultural property, aimed primarily at prolonging its existence. Treatment may consist of stabilization and/or restoration. These words are used routinely in discussions regarding collections, but they mean something different to a preservation architect or facility manager from what they mean to a conservator. Preservation maintenance principles, practices, and techniques are based, in some measure, on international charters; on specific laws in some countries and municipalities; on *The Secretary of the Interior's Standards for the Treatment of Historic Properties*; and on professional guidelines and practices.

THE VALUE OF THE HOUSE MUSEUM'S BUILDING

The building is frequently the reason the museum was founded, and in the eyes of the public, the museum and the building are one and the same. In fact, often a house museum's building is the one irreplaceable artifact. It is part of the collection and, usually, the largest object within the collection (see figure 12.1). The building serves as the icon for the museum and also has cultural value as an object.[2] Like other older buildings, a house museum is a tangible link to the past, enriching our day-to-day lives by illuminating the times and people that created it.

However, the structure is also a functional space: It supports staff and visitor activities, serves as a gathering space for public tours and events, and provides office and storage space. With those activities comes wear and tear on the building's fabric. Preventive maintenance is important for the safe and comfortable operation of the house for staff and visitors and for the preservation of the structure—because, once lost, the house and the record of the culture that created it are gone forever. A preventive maintenance plan within the overall preventive conservation program is crucial to prolonging the existence of the authentic building.

Figure 12.1 The 1732 log Presbyterian Session House near the Hershey factory. In 1929 chocolate manufacturer M. S. Hershey erected this glass enclosure to protect it, which created a display case for the log structure "as artifact." The two structures were listed on the National Register of Historic Places in 2006.

One fact remains inescapable: "No maintenance, no building"[3] (see figures 12.2–12.5).

The structure is usually a museum's biggest asset, and large capital investments were likely made to purchase and restore it. Even after restoration, the building uses a large part of the museum's annual operating budget. Over time the cumulative costs of maintaining the building along with its utilities and systems can more than double the cost of the original structure.[4] Of course, the monetary and cultural value of the property is greatly reduced if the building falls into disrepair or is altered through indiscriminate modern repairs.[5]

THE HISTORIC HOUSE AS AN EXHIBIT CASE

The house museum structure serves as an exhibit case for the rest of the collection, protecting it from the outdoor environment, vandalism, theft, and natural disasters. Rain, wind, pollution, extreme temperatures, light, pests, and vegetation continuously assault roofs, walls, and foundations. The building's envelope (its roof, walls, basement, windows, and doors) is subjected to additional stress caused by the differences between the indoor and outdoor environments. Slowing the rate of deterioration and protecting the structure from premature loss through preventive maintenance is good for the entire collection.

Deferring maintenance, on the other hand, can have unintended consequences, both big and small. For example, a leaf-filled, overflowing roof gutter gives the impression that the museum is not valued by those who manage the site. If left too long, the overflowing water can cause wood deterioration and mortar joint erosion (see figure 12.6). The water can migrate through the roof and walls, saturating the house's structure and finishes. This can damage plaster, paint, floors, furnishings, and wall hangings. If water infiltration is excessive, the moisture can raise the interior

Figure 12.2 In 1769–1770, Francis Lightfoot Lee built Menokin, a plantation manor house in the northern neck of the Virginia colony's Tidewater region. In 1940 the Historic American Building Survey documented Menokin. The photograph shows a greatly worn but still inhabited house that had remained nearly unaltered from its original construction.

Figure 12.3 Within thirty years of documentation, Menokin had collapsed into ruin because a tree had fallen into the roof and the hole had remained unpatched. The house had been as close to maintenance-free as a building can be—solid masonry with a timber and slate roof and no modern utilities. It had survived intact for more than two hundred years, but lack of timely repair resulted in the loss of the rare colonial plantation house.

Figure 12.4 In the late 1990s the Menokin Foundation launched "Rubble with a Cause," a program to restore the historic house and grounds. Before building, forensics, or archaeology began in earnest, a protective shelter was erected over the ruin, which slowed the rate of deterioration, provided access for researchers, and allowed visitors to view the ruin safely during guided tours.

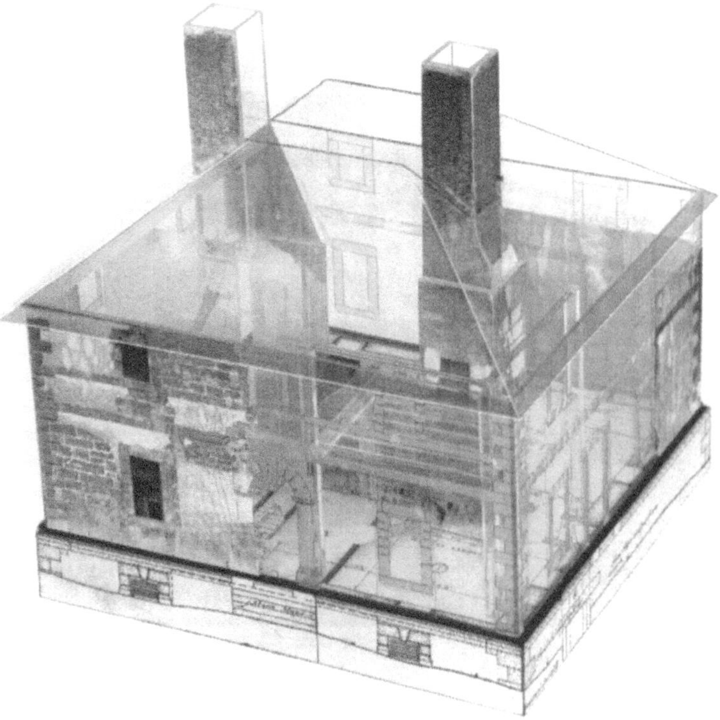

Figure 12.5 The Menokin Foundation envisions a cutting-edge restoration for Menokin. Salvaged and conserved fragments of the building walls will be reset. Structural glass blocks and sheets will infill lost masonry and roof elements. LCD glass may serve to display information about the building.

Figure 12.6 Saplings growing from debris in the gutter, unpainted sheet metal, chipped paint, and rotted wood are symptoms of the years of neglect of this 1890s house. Wood rafters in the roof are probably deteriorated as well.

humidity to unacceptable levels and allow mold to form on surfaces. This one example shows the unintended consequences of failing to develop a preventive conservation/maintenance program. Such a program is vitally important to the successful protection and preservation of the collection.

MAINTENANCE VERSUS REPLACEMENT

Maintenance of a house museum requires annual expenditures, but lack of steady funding can cause the building to be neglected, ultimately resulting in even greater costs to correct greater deterioration. In the long run, it may become prohibitively expensive to accurately restore or replace deteriorated materials. Preventive maintenance performed on a planned schedule slows deterioration and postpones or obviates the need for replacement (see figure 12.7). Regular or cyclic maintenance is always more economical because it reduces operating costs and the need for recurring major capital improvements.

Administrators invest a great deal of time in raising funds to restore and rehabilitate their historic buildings with up-to-date technology while providing for contemporary functional uses.[6] Those donating or lending funds for capital improvements do so, in part, because they believe it to be a good investment and therefore sound philanthropy. They expect their investment in the museum building to be long lasting. Implementing a preventive conservation/maintenance program and carrying out simple, regular preventive maintenance and treatments is one way to demonstrate commitment to the protection of the structure and the maximizing of that investment. In fact, such a plan is critical to the long-term financial health of the museum (see figure 12.8).

ORGANIZATIONAL POLICIES

The portion of the Long-Range Institutional Plan that deals with the structure mirrors the part of the plan that deals with the movable collection. Both emphasize the intellectual controls that form the foundation for the stewardship of the historic site—namely, inventory,[7] documentation,[8] assessment, planning, and treatment. Because the professionals involved in the stewardship of the site come from different (though allied) disciplines, it is important to remember that the

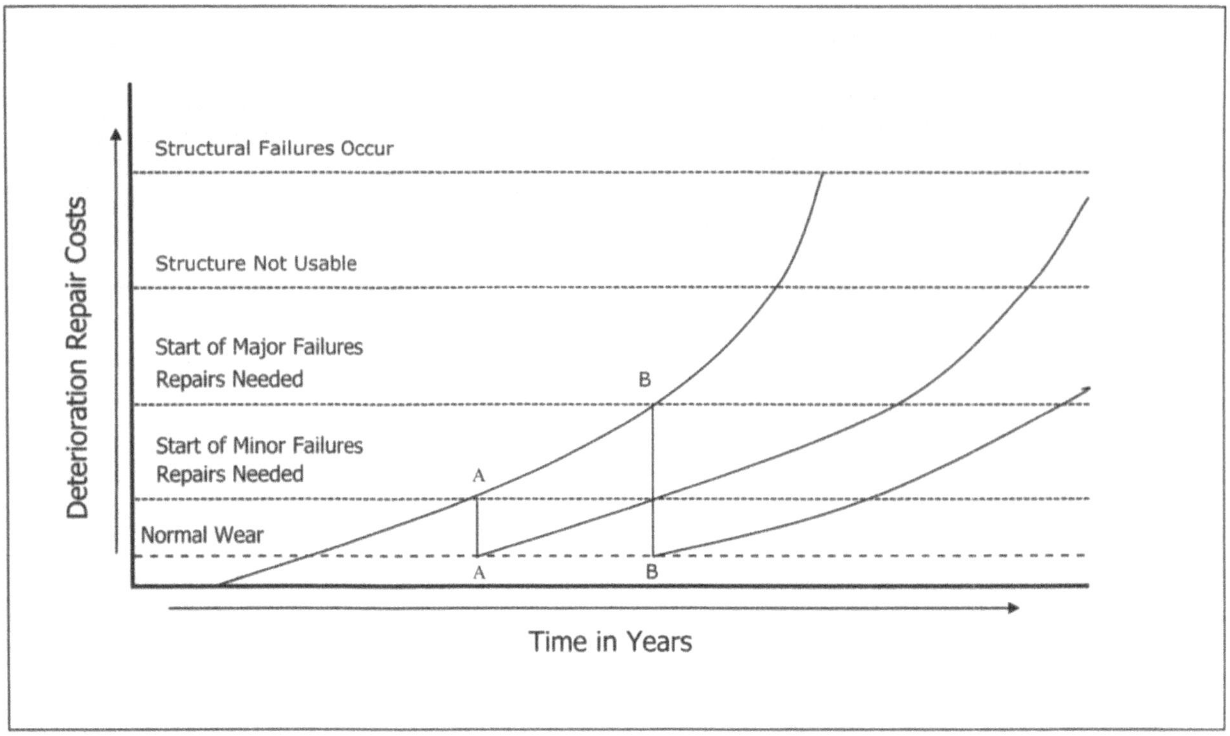

Figure 12.7 Graph depicting the cost of neglecting a building over time.

terms *preservation, treatment, maintenance,* and *restoration* will have different meanings for different team members.

INTELLECTUAL CONTROLS

The buildings and the site, as well as the movable collection, must have intellectual controls upon which the Preservation Master Plan is based. The work of developing the intellectual controls (inventorying, recording, documenting, and assessing condition) is both a *process* and a *product.* The process helps the team learn about the historic property and the product helps the team manage the property. Intellectual controls are important, for they will define the organization and its mission over decades (see figures 12.9 and 12.10).

The organization uses its written mission statement, statement of philosophy, or legislated purpose to guide the preservation process. Setting goals and objectives helps focus the preservation approach to meet the museum's mission. This process determines why the house museum is valuable and what service the house is expected to perform for the organization.[9] For example, the value of the museum building may be its architecture, so extending the life of character-defining architectural materials, features, and spaces through a preservation approach is a key part of the work plan.[10] A highly decorative porch on a building valued for its architecture will receive frequent painting, vegetation removal, pest control, and gutter cleaning. Elements of the porch that finally require more than routine maintenance will be either conserved in place, partially replaced, or selectively replaced-in-kind in order to retain as much of the original fabric as possible (see figures 12.11 and 12.12).

The management approach could be more flexible in regard to the repair or replacement of materials for a museum in a historic structure with no outstanding architecture or architectural fabric from the building's period of significance or no significant ties to an important historic person or event (see figure 12.13). In this case, the building's value lies in its function as a safe shelter for humans and for the collections within, and in its ability to evoke a particular period of time. The preservation of extant materials and building features may not be as important in the maintenance plan as ensuring the overall performance of the building envelope and systems. Replacing deteriorated features with appropriate substitute materials would be acceptable.[11, 12]

The preventive conservation process starts with a comprehensive inventory of assets (collection, building, landscape, etc.), documentation, and assessment of current condition. Then a preventive maintenance

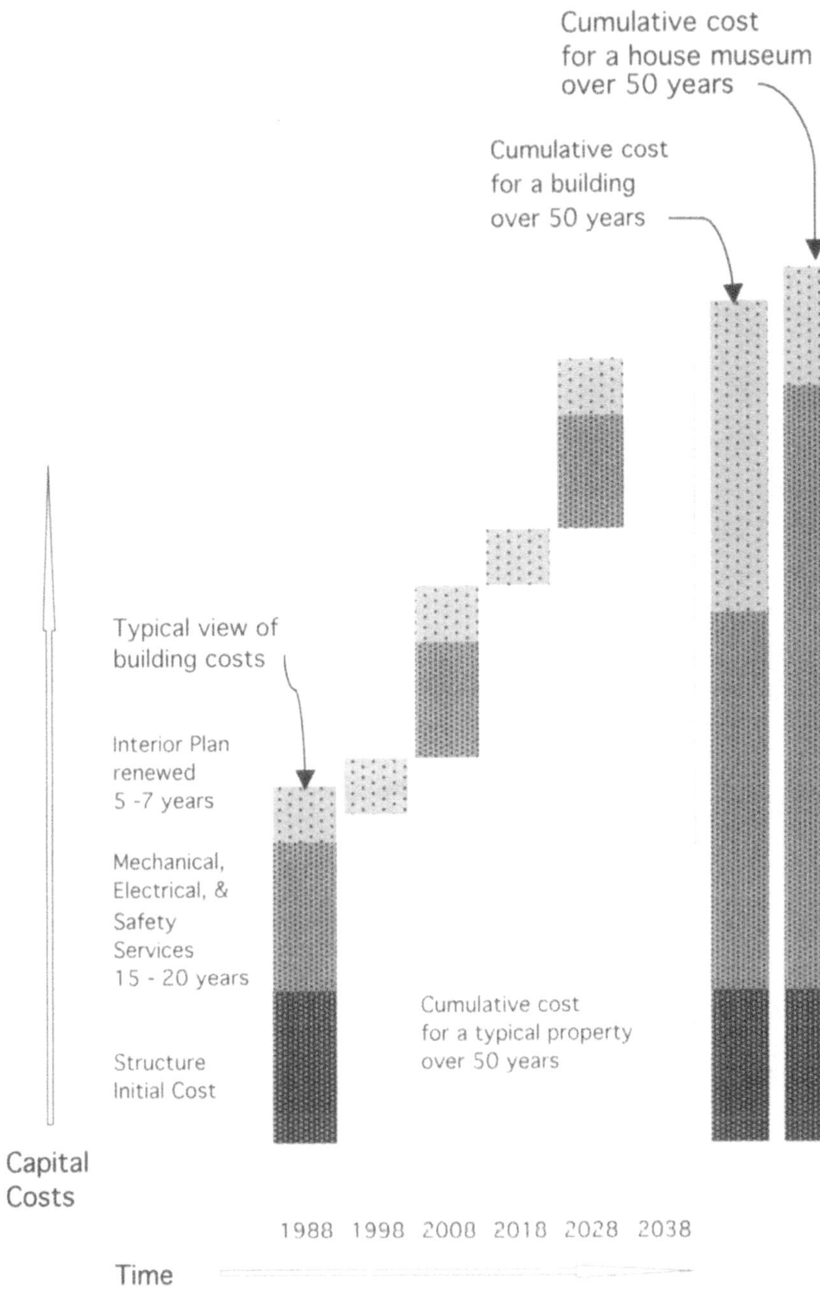

Figure 12.8 Where does the money go during the life of a building? Over fifty years of a building's life, changes can cost more than three times the initial building cost. As shown, very little goes to the initial construction when compared with the renewal costs over time. The cumulative costs of replacing obsolete utility systems and updating interiors far exceed the cost of the construction. Adapted from *How Buildings Learn* by Stewart Brand, p.13. Brand's book credited the chart to DEGW from Francis Duffy and Alex Henney, *The Changing City* (London: Bullstrode, 1989), p. 61.

plan for the structure can be prepared. Goals for the overall plan are established and then broken down into specific work objectives. Information is updated on a regular basis through routine inspections and condition assessment (evaluations). The plan is updated to reflect new information and changes in condition. The process then repeats itself: routine inspections; planning and scheduling routine work, repairs, or upgrades to treatments; completing the specified work; documenting the work; and finally, evaluating the results.

OVERVIEW OF RECORDATION AND DOCUMENTATION: "THE BUILDING CATALOGUE"

A thorough understanding of the house museum's resources (collections and buildings) is prerequisite to an effective preservation program. That understanding begins with *recordation*—the creation of accurate drawings and photographs of the interior and exterior of the site. Recordation is the minimum documentation done for a structure, and it "can be done at any time during the building's use as a museum. Ideally, however, the built environment of the property is

Figure 12.9 The Florence Griswold Museum, Old Lyme, Connecticut, is the home of American Impressionism. Its collection of art is the primary focus of this house museum, so it is acceptable that the property is maintained in better condition than during its historic period. However, a building can be over-groomed. Finding the right level of maintenance can be especially difficult for museums that must balance an accurate depiction of the past with an appealing appearance. A museum's intellectual controls should help to determine the appropriate appearance of the buildings.

Figure 12.10 During the first two decades of the twentieth century, Florence Griswold's boardinghouse served as a gathering place for Impressionist artists of the Old Lyme Colony. Photographs helped determine the general condition of the building during its historic period. This early-twentieth-century image shows artists relaxing on the front porch of the Griswold house.

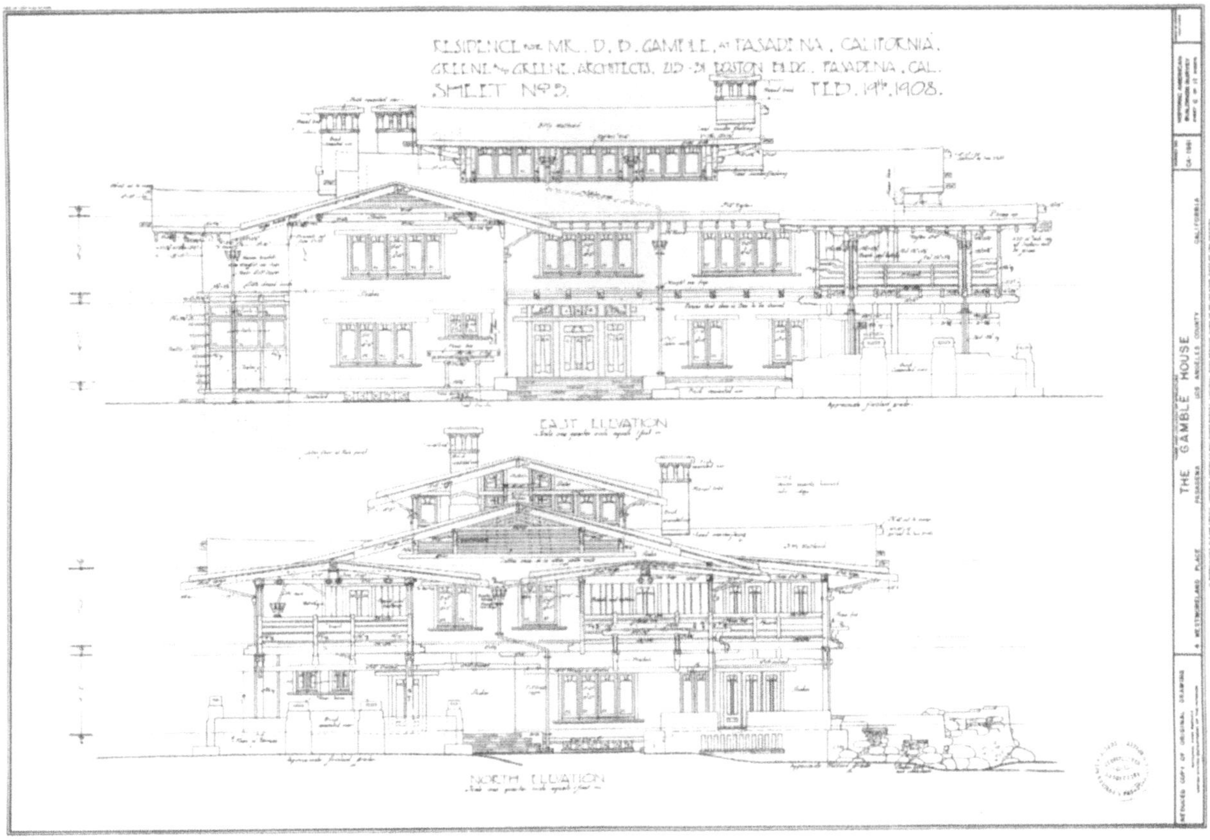

Figure 12.11 The Gamble House in Pasadena, California, is a masterpiece of American Arts and Crafts–style architecture. Charles and Henry Greene designed the house and furnishings in 1908 for David and Mary Gamble of the Procter & Gamble Company. Now operated as a house museum by the University of Southern California, the house requires careful and timely maintenance aimed at extending the useful life of the materials, joinery, and details and of the structure as a whole.

recorded when it becomes a museum and before any changes are made."[13] Recordation is the simplest form of documentation, yet it should be in-depth, thorough, and accurate enough to be useful to the long-term stewardship of the site.

Combining the recordation (graphic documentation) with other evaluation information yields a document referred to as a Historic Structure Report. If a property has been used as a museum for any length of time, then historical research on the building and information about modifications and condition of the building should be available to those managing the building.

A complete Historic Structure Report includes a detailed assessment of current condition and may include an analysis of the building's compliance with life and safety codes and universal access guidelines. It may contain repair and treatment recommendations. It typically contains information on the period(s) of the building's significance; a chronology of changes to the building; an identification of the most significant features, spaces, and materials (called character-defining features); a list of building components and their condition; and the fundamental causes of the building's deterioration. Graphic and photographic recordation, combined with documentary research, physical investigations, and an evaluation of the findings, reveal much about a property. The better the historic house is understood and appreciated as an individual structure with its own characteristics and quirks, the more likely it is to receive sympathetic stewardship and appropriate treatment. Recording, documenting, and analyzing the structure help us understand and appreciate it.[14]

DOCUMENTATION: THE HISTORIC STRUCTURE REPORT

A Historic Structure Report for a building:

- Chronicles the physical development of the house from its original construction through its latest changes (for example, the evolution of a one-room cabin to a multiroom wood-sided house)

Figure 12.12 Most house museums with significant architecture have interiors that are as important as their exteriors. These images (top and left) of the Gamble House show that preventive conservation/maintenance of a building does not stop at the outside walls. Conservation of a house museum's architectural integrity requires the coordinated efforts of everyone involved in its care, including the housekeeping staff, conservators, and facility workers.

Figure 12.13 The goal of conservation maintenance for older or historic buildings is the same as for those with architectural significance: preserving the integrity of character-defining features and extending the life of the historic materials. For the Maria Mitchell Natural Science Museum in Nantucket, Massachusetts, and for other historic buildings that house museum collections, more leeway can be taken in meeting the goal. For example, it is acceptable when repairing such a property to replace deteriorated features with appropriate substitute materials as long as character-defining features are retained.

- Develops a rationale for the period or periods of significance based on research about
  - historical events that occurred at the property (for example, a peace treaty was signed here or it was the home of the city's first settler)
  - the building's architecture (for example, the building is an outstanding work in an architectural style, it is an exemplary vernacular building within a region, or it is constructed solely from unusual materials)
  - famous individuals associated with the building (for example, the property was the birthplace of a president)[15]
- Identifies the character-defining features of the house that exist now and existed during the period(s) of significance[16]
- Documents the building's architecture and architectural features as well as its structural, electrical, and mechanical systems and landscaping through photographs and measured drawings[17]
- Analyzes and evaluates the existing building and determines which features, fabric, materials, systems, and elements have integrity in terms of the period(s) of significance[18]
- Analyzes and evaluates the property and systems to determine their compliance with building life/safety and health codes and universal access guidelines[19]
- Recommends work or operational changes required to correct code deficiencies and deteriorated features and to protect, preserve, and repair the property and systems
- Evaluates the effects that current and proposed uses will have on the integrity of the building and its fabric and/or suggests alternate methods or operations to achieve the desired uses while preserving and protecting the integrity of the property's significant fabric and systems[20]

STANDARDS FOR HISTORIC STRUCTURE REPORTS

In the United States, professional organizations and government agencies have their own guidelines for the production of Historic Structure Reports. Published guidelines are available from the following national organizations: the American Society for Testing and Materials (ASTM), the American Institute of Architects (AIA), and the National Park Service (NPS). Each organization's guide varies slightly in terms of the level of historical, architectural, engineering, code, material, and scientific information to be included in a report. Some guidelines suggest schematic designs for the building's treatment as a part of the standard report. Some treat the report itself as an ongoing process and require that all treatment work be recorded as an integral part of the document. (Each treatment record is added as an appendix or update to the original report.) The format and ordering of the information also vary from guide to guide.

There is no single, widely used standard format for producing Historic Structure Reports and comprehensive conditions assessment reports.[21] The depth of research and investigation is determined on a case-by-case basis. For those doing a Historic Structure Report for the purpose of developing a Preservation Master Plan, basic documentation and evaluation of the condition

There are many practical reasons to document the museum property:

Evidence. Documentation is a record of a property's existence at one point in time or over an extended period of time. Documentation is a fundamental responsibility of those who are the guardians of a property.

Mitigation. Documentation can be used to record historic structures that cannot be saved or are too large for curation in museums. Structures are destroyed for many reasons; documentation can provide future generations with the only available information on structures that have vanished.

Insurance. Documentation can provide an accurate record of a structure and serve as a form of insurance, so that in case of catastrophic loss, the structure could be reconstructed.

Communication. Graphic documentation often provides a more easily understood representation of the building than written narrative alone.

Academic Study. Documentation can provide a way to investigate artifacts from the past that may otherwise be too scattered or too difficult to visit.

Education. Documentation is used to help future generations understand and appreciate the property's cultural value. Drawings and photographs are visual tools that interpretive staff can use to instruct the public.

Definition of Treatment Areas. Documentation in the form of measured building drawings can help define areas of deterioration and treatment. They can be used when contracting for repair work on the museum; for service contracts; for installation of new building systems or utility work; and for inspections to note areas of deterioration and dam-

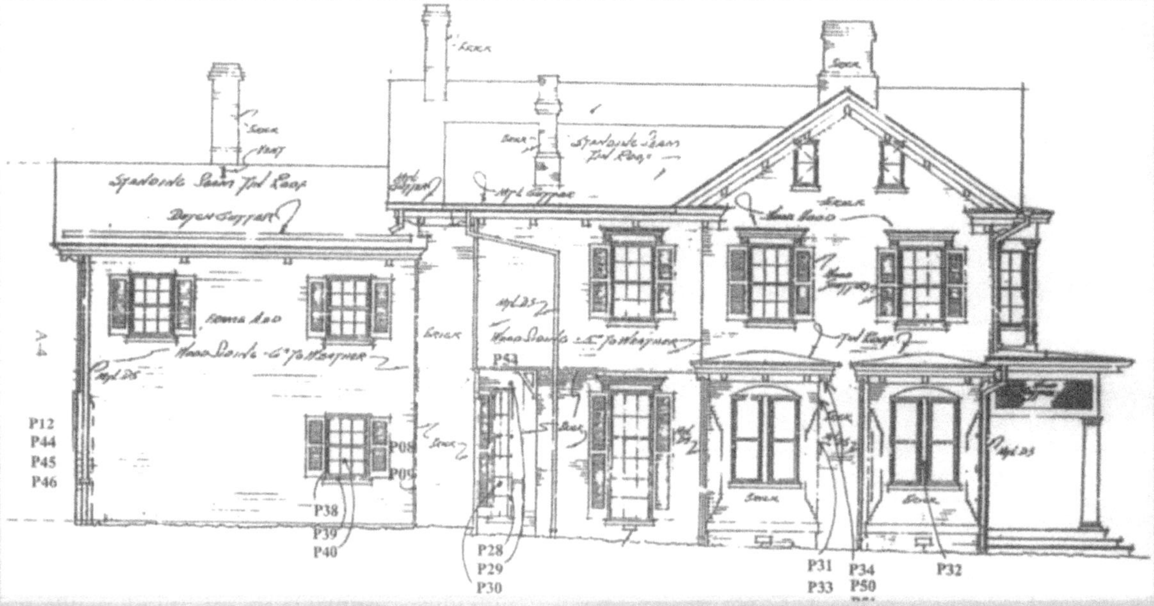

Figure 12.14 Architectural drawings of the museum are effective tools for documenting conditions, planning upcoming work, and recording conservation and preventive repairs. This 1970s architectural elevation drawing of the Frederick Douglass House was used in 2003 to record the location of paint samples taken for analysis to determine historic exterior colors. The house's historic colors were restored in the mid-2000s based on the findings of the analysis. *Source:* Original drawing modified by Barbara A. Yocum, architectural conservator, Historic Architecture Program, Northeast Region, National Park Service.

of the building's envelope, structure, utility systems, and life/safety systems are recommended.

To determine the scope, format, and level of detail that are right for a particular house museum, compare reports from house museum buildings similar to yours. Copies can be obtained through, lent by, or reviewed at

- state historic preservation offices
- the National Trust for Historic Preservation Library, University of Maryland, College Park, Maryland
- the U.S. Department of the Interior, National Park Service, Denver Service Center, Technical Information Center, Denver, Colorado

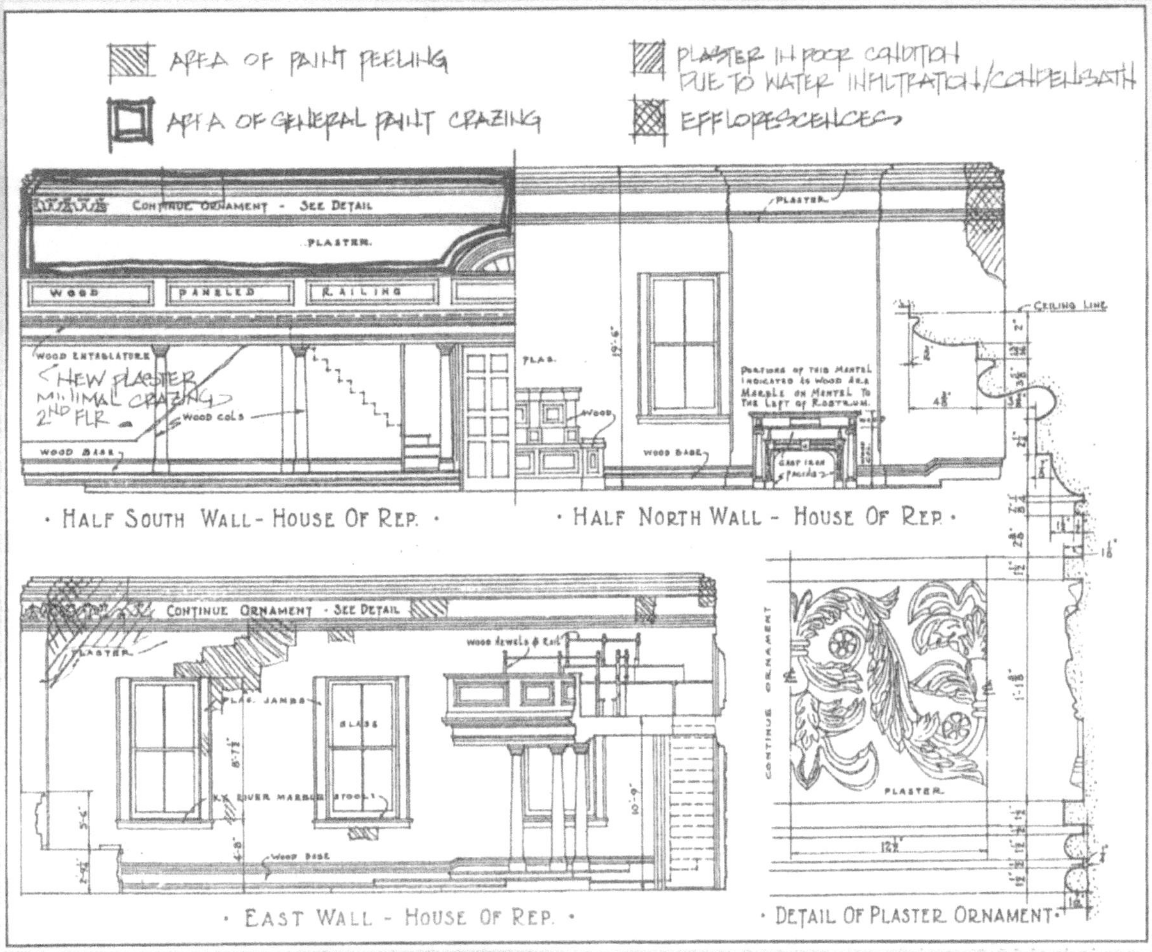

Figure 12.15 Because of their simplicity, HABS/HAER drawings are particularly useful for recording conditions and documenting work. HABS documents served as the base drawings to record plaster deterioration on the interior of Kentucky's Old State House. *Source:* Library of Congress, HABS, KY-20-1 sheet 16, modified by Rebecca L. Stevens

age, manage routine preventive treatments, and record work accomplished.

Safekeeping. Once completed, building documentation is often saved at more than one location. If recordation drawings and photographs meet Historic American Buildings Survey/Historical American Engineering Record/Historical American Landscapes Survey (HABS/HAER/HALS) standards,[22] the documentation is archived in a special collection at the Library of Congress. Documentation in the HABS/HAER/HALS collection adds prestige to the building and makes it accessible to a wider audience than records stored only at the house museum. The use of archival processes to produce and store the drawings and photographs ensures the longevity of the records.

Day-to-Day Management. Documentation provides tools for making short- and long-term decisions about the site, planning events, and recording observations of conditions and work.

- the American Institute of Architects, Historic Preservation Committee, Washington, D.C.
- the American Institute of Architects local chapters
- local historic societies and archives

THOROUGH INVESTIGATION OF THE STRUCTURE

The Historic Structure Report must thoroughly document the structure, but the level of physical investigation depends on the importance of the building, the general condition of the structure, and the complexity of the construction and systems.[23] A description of the building's history and architectural character generally precedes the technical information. An understanding of the physical performance of the building and its systems is gained through close observations, detailed inspections, and nondestructive testing such as monitoring cracks or testing paint for lead content. Some inspections may involve small amounts of selective demolition, or removal of exterior or interior building material, in order to expose things that otherwise might be hidden from view. Removing several floorboards to examine wood joist construction and condition is an example of selective disassembly that may be done as part of a full structural inspection.

UPDATING THE HISTORIC STRUCTURE REPORT

If a Historic Structure Report has been completed within the last decade, then an update to the report (an amendment) may be all that is required for use in a preventive conservation/maintenance program. The

An example of a limited destructive investigation technique is *the historic nail survey and analysis.* This technique was used to help date and determine the sequence of construction of a house situated in the middle of a Civil War battlefield. Military accounts mentioned a farmhouse used as a defensive shield. The house was strategically located at the center of action and cannonballs actually cut through the building. However, the written military account and historic battle maps failed to describe the house and the extent of damage. War claim records were not available for this property because the federal government did not pay compensation to Southern sympathizers (the landowner and tenant farmers living in the house supported the South). Early county property records to the 1860s were destroyed in the war.

Despite exhaustive searches over the last twenty years, the earliest known photograph of the house dates to 1983. The archaeological evidence found to date is inconclusive about the size and exact configuration of the Civil War–era house. Because the mission of the battlefield park is to present the land and buildings as they appeared at the time of the battle, it was vital to know if any portion of the existing building was the one standing during the battle.

A historical metallurgist was employed to help find the answer. This is a specialist in the history of construction fasteners (usually nails and screws) and the technologies and materials used in their various manufacturing processes. It was hoped that specific information about the types and ages of the nails found would help determine the chronology of various portions of the building. Nails were removed from selected locations throughout the house as directed by the preservation architect and based on previous study of the building.

Based on the types of nails found, the engineer and architect concluded that a one-story timber-framed building dating to ca. 1790 formed the core of the existing house. While the historic timber-framed building was resting on a portion of the Civil War–era house foundation, that part of the structure was now part of a larger house. Neither part was present at the Civil War engagement (1862). Nor was it deemed likely that the current house was made from timber salvaged from the Civil War–era house. The one-story timber-framed building had no evidence of war damage or reuse of timbers.

The 1790 timber structure within the larger house has great integrity of material and craftsmanship to its period of construction. The historical architect's theory of the building's development, now supported by the nail analysis, is that some time after the 1862 battle the landowner moved an undamaged pre–Civil War building to the farm to provide shelter for the tenant farmers. The moved structure was positioned on the foundation of the earlier destroyed farmhouse after its remains were cleared away.

A bonus discovery made during the physical investigation of the house, and confirmed by the nail analysis, is that the ca. 1800 original hand-planed tongue-and-groove floors were intact! These floors were found throughout the first floor and the loft (now the second floor) of the complete timber-framed section of the pre–Civil War house. Two-hundred-year-old wood floors that have not been overlaid or otherwise damaged—and still boasting their original handmade clincher sprig-headed nails—are an extremely rare treasure. The physical investigation and material analysis of the building provided information about the building that could have been gained by no other means. The Historic Structure Report is now the repository of that knowledge.

amendment assesses the current condition of the architectural features/fabric and the engineering systems, and determines whether the building is in compliance with life/safety and fire protection codes and accessibility guidelines. Anticipate nondestructive investigations for this evaluation unless conditions have changed greatly.

By comparing current conditions to those noted in the Historic Structure Report, the team can determine the rates of deterioration of the building fabric. A comparison between the former and current findings can also help evaluate the effectiveness of the museum's current conservation/maintenance program.

IMPLEMENTING A PREVENTIVE MAINTENANCE PLAN FOR THE BUILDING

The preventive conservation/maintenance plan is a dynamic program that directs the day-to-day care of the building. It is most effective if it is based on the knowledge provided in the intellectual control documents. However, the lack of complete records need not keep management and staff from implementing a preventive maintenance program. Simple tasks like the scheduled seasonal cleaning of gutters and servicing of the heating system can be the beginning of a preventive maintenance plan.

THE TEAM APPROACH

Professionals in the fields of architecture, architectural history, landscape architecture, and structural, mechanical, civil, and electrical engineering are typically on the consultation team for the initial inventory, documentation, and subsequent evaluation of a structure. A preservation architect should lead the team to update the existing inventory, investigations, and evaluations of the building. An architectural historian should do the research on the building's history, if this is the first time a physical history of an older structure has been documented, or to confirm and update research information that is more than twenty years old. The selection of other experts for participation on the team depends on a range of factors specific to the site and the nature of the structures involved. These factors include the history, style, significance, and general condition of the building and its equipment and systems, and any proposed changes in the use of the site. All the professionals chosen must have experience analyzing and evaluating heritage properties.[24] It is advisable to include a consulting curator, an objects conservator, and an archaeologist on the team, but this is not yet a common practice for most small house museums.

The museum staff and volunteers, including the curator, maintenance person, housekeeper, administrator, and docents, are adjunct participants in the inventory/evaluation because of their intimate knowledge of the building's history, significance, eccentricities, and functional performance, including its daily and seasonal functioning patterns. The on-site staff is aware of daily practices that may affect the collection and buildings.

COMPREHENSIVE CONDITION ASSESSMENT

The intellectual controls state the goals for the property and indicate what is important to save. A comprehensive condition assessment, whether part of the Historic Structure Report or a stand-alone document, is the baseline from which routine building maintenance treatments are judged for effectiveness.

The condition assessment evaluates current conditions for the purpose of planning short- and long-term treatments to the structure. Once a condition is assigned to all elements, hazards recorded, and safety risks identified, treatment priorities can be established.

Short-term treatments are initiated based upon the findings of the condition assessment and the severity or immediacy of the threat. Both influence the timing of work. The threat may be loss of fabric from use, infestation, or the environment. It may be predictable or result from an emergency. The assessment guides routine maintenance practices so the long-term goals and the museum's mission are met.

Integrating the expertise of architects, engineers, curators, conservators, architectural historians, maintenance personnel, docents, managers, and the visiting public is important because of the interdependent relationship among the house museum's components.[25]

ORGANIZING AND PREPARING A PREVENTIVE CONSERVATION/MAINTENANCE PROGRAM

Intellectual controls form the foundation for an effective preventive preservation program for a house museum. Ideally, supporting documents pertaining to technical history will also be consulted before planning starts. These supporting documents may include

- previous maintenance logs
- museum construction contract documents
- original drawings and remodeling drawings
- photographs of previous work
- guarantees from recently performed work
- manufacturers' data for materials, products, equipment, and systems installed during contemporary work campaigns

The Old State House in Frankfort, Kentucky, provides an example of how the on-site staff can help with conservation because of their familiarity with a historic building (see figure 12.16). The building houses exhibits and historical society offices and is used for docent-run tours. The heating and cooling system was not effectively controlling the interior environment. No staff working at the site was there when the system was first installed in 1976, so no one knew how the system was designed to operate. But the staff did know how the building was used day-to-day and throughout the year. The Old State House's first-floor exhibit rooms were too cold, while the second-floor legislative chambers seemed to get no air circulation at all. Condensation was a recurring problem within the building's finest architectural space—a central two-story circular staircase topped by an open domed lantern. The sun fills the stairwell and adjoining chamber entrances with natural light. Over a ten-year period, several mechanical contractors and a general engineering firm had been hired to address the problem, but the problem had persisted. The state historic preservation officer hired a preservation team to investigate the problem and make recommendations.

The team included a preservation architect, an architect apprentice, a controls and mechanical equipment engineer who specialized in historic buildings, and a preservation carpenter/wood craftsman. The team members investigated the building's systems and interviewed staff. In less than two days the team determined the cause of the problem and corrected it at virtually no cost to the state. The poor air circulation was caused by holiday decorations that were stored in closets under the balcony steps—closets that the HVAC system used as air return plenums. The return grills in the door and floor were completely covered by boxes and bags. Once the closets were cleared of stored items, air could circulate through the air systems.

The position of the legislative chamber entry doors was also contributing to the temperature and air-circulation problems (see figure 12.17). The

Figure 12.16 Kentucky's Old State House. Today it looks exactly as it did in this 1934 image. *Source:* Library of Congress, HABS, KY, 37-FRAFO, 1-17.

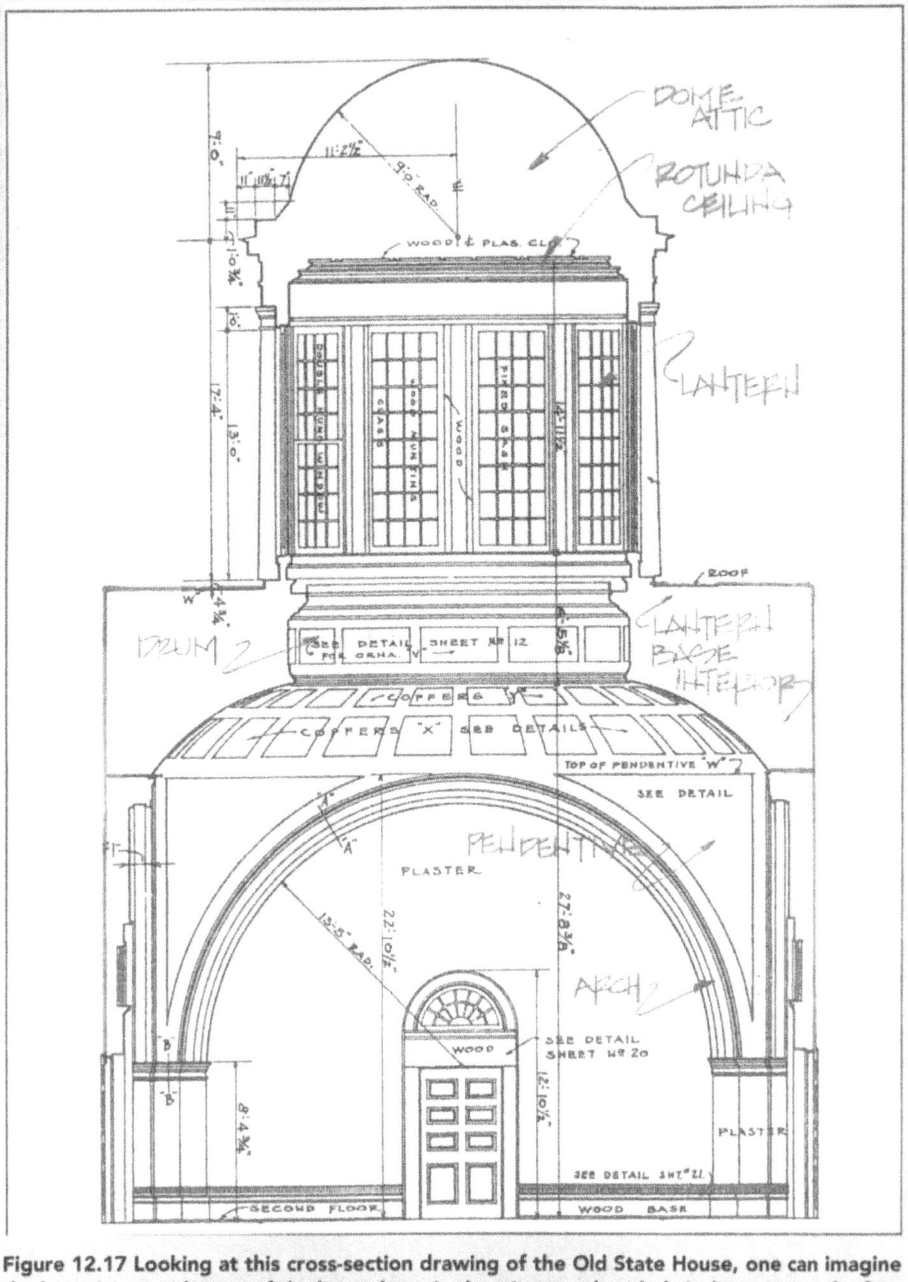

Figure 12.17 Looking at this cross-section drawing of the Old State House, one can imagine the heat rising to the top of the large dome in the winter and cooled air dropping to the first floor in the summer. The 1970s mechanical system was designed to compensate for the natural airflow in the rotunda and dome, but it was intended to work with the chamber doors closed. Keeping the chamber doors open led to serious temperature and air-circulation problems. *Source:* Library of Congress, HABS, KY-20-1 drawing 11.

team members realized that the HVAC system was designed to work with the entry doors closed. Docents were keeping the entry doors open to the light-filled stairwell day and night, but this was defeating both the system zoning and air-circulation designs. In the winter the equipment could not keep up with the heating demand on the building, since all heat produced was going up the dome, and in the summer all the cold air sank directly down the stairwell to the first-floor rooms. Everyone's knowledge was needed—and used—to solve the HVAC problem.

- operation manuals and service records for heating/cooling equipment and systems, detection and suppression systems, and so on

With supporting documents in hand, the preservation planning team can begin its work to

- set objectives to ensure that the museum buildings, both contemporary and historic, receive individual attention
- target efforts to prolong the life of the most significant or vulnerable historic/architectural features and fabric
- research and develop effective methods and procedures to ensure the protection of the significant features and fabric
- estimate the remaining service life of modern utility systems and critical building components so replacement can be budgeted into the museum's long-term plans rather than handled on an emergency or reactionary basis[26]
- develop an inspection form customized to the property's particulars
- coordinate with other proposed museum activities, rehabilitation, or repair work
- better predict whether treatments and procedures proposed in the program will have the intended effect (One question to ask is: Will improvement in the condition of one part of the collection be at the expense of another? For example, will an optimal climate for the movable collection cause moisture problems for the building?)

TOOLS FOR MANAGING THE PRESERVATION ACTIVITIES

There is a seemingly endless supply of facility management programs to assist those in charge of facility management. They are described in technical books and popular magazines, and many are available as software applications. Engineering companies, institutions, government agencies, and property managers use these tools to assist in the cost-effective management of assets. The programs range from simple paper-based inspection and scheduling forms to complex computerized scheduling, record keeping, and costing systems.

For the house museum, the important thing is to have a written overall preventive conservation/maintenance plan and put it into action. Keep it simple. The simpler and the more accessible the plan is to all the museum's caretakers, the more likely it is to be used (see figure 12.18). For small to mid-size house museums, a paper-based management system should be sufficient. Computerized programs that involve tedious data collection, exhaustive inspections, work costing, and scheduling are generally too demanding, except for larger institutions and well-staffed museums.

Most facility maintenance programs call for a cyclical process of inspecting, planning, scheduling and implementing, documenting, and evaluating. The same cycle of activities is necessary for a successful preventive conservation program. Large museum institutions with many buildings will go through the process annually. A small museum with a single house may go through the complete cycle every four years. Whether the cycle is annual or extends over a longer period of time, the program must be directed at preventive conservation/maintenance work and have continuity over an extended period of time to be effective.

As with the preparation of intellectual controls, representatives from all aspects of the organization need to be involved in developing and executing the preventive conservation/maintenance program.

ORGANIZE ROUTINE INSPECTIONS

Routine inspections of the property and collections are the linchpin of the preventive conservation/maintenance process. Intellectual controls, the Historic Struc-

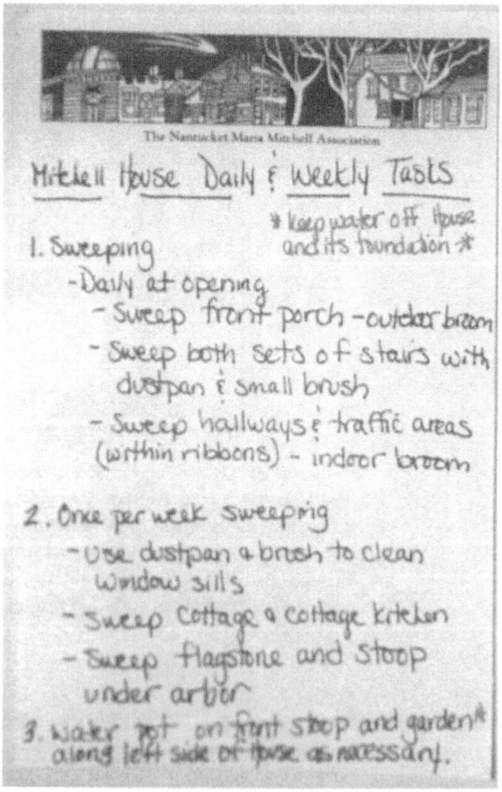

Figure 12.18 This plan for routine housekeeping (maintenance) was taped to the staff refrigerator at the Maria Mitchell House. It is simple and understandable, though not comprehensive. *Source:* Rebecca L. Stevens.

ture Report, and the supplemental building records provide guidance on what to inspect, what to look for, and how frequently to inspect. The frequency and thoroughness of the inspection and its components will be based on the team's knowledge of the building's significant features and materials, their condition, the degree to which weather and other physical forces impact the materials, rates of deterioration, functional history, and the long-term goals for the property (see figure 12.19).

Approaching routine inspections in a systematic way and using a customized inspection form ensures that important aspects of the property are checked. The form itself serves as a record of the inspection, a checklist for routine maintenance, and a monitor of condition over time. For large institutions, the inspection process and form are often customized by a team of architects or engineers who have been hired to initiate a maintenance program and develop a unique inspection form. But the inspection process and form can also be taken from a standard, "off-the-shelf" facility management program. Wherever the form originates, it should be tailored to the museum building. Remember that the inspection may not be done by the same person from year to year because of staff turnover. The form should be as simple as possible and does not have to be part of a computerized program, although many are. The house museum staff alone or with the preventive conservation/maintenance planning team can develop inspection forms for the property.

The same terms should be used each time a survey is done to ensure accurate monitoring. For example, inspections of windows would be compromised if one year conditions are noted as "good," "fair," or "poor"; the next year they are recorded as "acceptable," "serious," or "critical"; and the next year they are documented as "okay" and "bad." Uniformity in recordation makes it easier to plan treatments and accurately monitor conditions. It guides treatments and provides continuity of information. This is why a customized inspection form that is standard for a particular museum building is the most useful.

Figure 12.19 Maintenance cycle steps 1–5.

PLAN THE PREVENTIVE CONSERVATION/ MAINTENANCE WORK

Before embarking on any specific preventive conservation measures for the structure, it is important to do your homework: Research or develop effective methods, choose the right materials, and select the best practitioners to ensure that the conservation of significant features and fabric conforms to current best practices. Consultants and contractors may be needed. There is much written information on how to specify needs, solicit bids, and select contractors for building rehabilitation and repair projects.

As information is gathered about each preventive treatment, record it on standardized work sheets. In facility management programs, these are called *work procedures, project work,* or *work orders.* Keep the work request sheets in a filing system. The information on the sheets can be used to order supplies and as a reference to ensure that the right materials, tools, and equipment are available when the work is scheduled. The sheets will change over time to reflect the particulars of the house museum and improvements in means and methods. Be sure to document all work as it is done and list all materials actually used. When the work is finished, suggested materials, changes in procedures, or other information can also be noted on the forms.

SCHEDULE THE PREVENTIVE CONSERVATION/MAINTENANCE WORK

Work performed on time ensures that treatments and procedures proposed in the preventive conservation/ maintenance program will have the intended effect. A schedule that outlines a year's worth of work is the best way to make sure the work is accomplished. Use the inspection information gathered earlier to list any work items that are needed. Include new corrective projects, ongoing project work, and routine preventive conservation/maintenance work in the list. Note on the list whether the work is a preventive (proactive) or corrective (reactive) action. Over time, the annual preventive conservation/maintenance program will emerge: The schedule will contain more and more proactive items and less and less corrective or emergency work. Think

ARLINGTON HOUSE ROUTINE INSPECTION CHECKLIST
EXTERIOR

Inspected by:__________________________ **Date of Inspection:**__________

ROOF

Slate:
- ☐ Broken Slate
- ☐ Missing Slate
- ☐ Slate flaking apart
- ☐ Nails letting go
- ☐ Slate particles in valley flashing

Metal:
- ☐ Rust or corrosion spots
- ☐ Signs of previous patch jobs
- ☐ Punctures in metal
- ☐ Joints and seams broken

Clay: ☐ Broken tiles ☐ Missing tiles ☐ Nails popping up ☐ Mold or moss forming on tile

ROOFING ELEMENTS

Projections:
- ☐ Proper flashing around projections
- ☐ Weathering of mortar joints at chimneys
- ☐ Loose mortar joints that admit water
- ☐ Chimney leans
- ☐ Loose and wobbly antennae
- ☐ Loose lightning rods
- ☐ Loose and wobbly weather vane

Cornice:
- ☐ Moisture causing paint to peel at cornice
- ☐ Broken or missing cornice
- ☐ Cracks and other damages

Underside of Roof:
- ☐ Water stains on soffit boards
- ☐ Damaged soffit boards
- ☐ Damaged fascia boards

Flashing:
- ☐ Loose, corroded, or broken flashing
- ☐ Missing and uncaulked openings at the tops of flashing
- ☐ Daubs of roof cement on flashing
- ☐ Base flashing and counterflashing of vertical joints

Gutters and Leaders:
- ☐ Gutters clogged with debris or ice
- ☐ Gutters that are rusty or corroded
- ☐ Gutters that are loose, tilted, or missing
- ☐ Broken seams in metal linings of built-in gutters
- ☐ Birds nests and roosting places

EXTERIOR WALL MATERIAL

Masonry and Mortar:
- ☐ Cracks
- ☐ Loose or missing mortar joints
- ☐ Stains, wet spots, bulges, spalling, missing pieces, or efflorescence of brick
- ☐ Stains, wet spots, bulges, spalling, missing pieces, or efflorescence of stone

Siding and Sheathing:
- ☐ Cracked, loose, or broken boards
- ☐ Rotted and missing members
- ☐ Signs of veins of dirt (termite tunnels)

Stucco/ Plaster:
- ☐ Cracks, staining, loose stucco, soft spots, blisters, bulges, falling stucco

EXTERIOR FINISHES

Painting: ☐ Peeling ☐ Cracking ☐ Alligatoring ☐ Good condition ☐ Fair condition ☐ Poor condition

Figure 12.20 Arlington House routine inspection checklist: Exterior.

FENESTRATION

Windows:

- ☐ Sash not operating properly
- ☐ Hardware not operating properly
- ☐ Loose, cracked, or missing glazing putty
- ☐ Weatherstripping unsound
- ☐ Lintels cracked/damaged
- ☐ Rot and/or deterioration of wood framing

Doors:

- ☐ Out of alignment
- ☐ Deterioration of door
- ☐ Deterioration of weatherstripping
- ☐ Deterioration of frame

EXTERIOR CEILINGS AND DECKS

Wooden Supports:

- ☐ Mold and fungus present
- ☐ Wood rot
- ☐ Termite infestation
- ☐ Failure of deck seal at foundation
- ☐ Corrosion of iron fittings on members

Infestation:

- ☐ Termites present
- ☐ Damage and rot on wooden members
- ☐ Treatment needed for ants and other wood destroying insects

Porch:

- ☐ Peeling paint and water stains on the ceiling
- ☐ Rotted and warped boards in the deck
- ☐ Damaged and/or loose steps and handrails
- ☐ Rotted boards and other damages to ceiling
- ☐ Cracks and other damages on a concrete flo
- ☐ Spalling, cracks, loose and/or missing mortar joints on brick or stone

GROUNDS

Driveways and Sidewalks:

- ☐ Heaves, depressions, and other safety hazards
- ☐ Cracked or deteriorated paving material
- ☐ Damage to curb clearances
- ☐ Oil stains and/or pools of water
- ☐ Improper drainage

Landscape:

- ☐ Diseased or dead parts present in trees and bushes
- ☐ Trees overhang or touch building causing damage or trash build-up
- ☐ Creepers and vines causing damage
- ☐ Plants holding water against structure
- ☐ Tree roots damaging structure
- ☐ Bare spots show in lawn
- ☐ Shrubs need pruning

Foundation:

- ☐ Leaves and debris collecting at edge of foundation
- ☐ Improper drainage
- ☐ Cracks and spalling from subflorescence and freezing
- ☐ Leaning and bulges
- ☐ Mortar joints loose, crumbling, and/or missing

NOTES

Figure 12.20 Exterior checklist, continued.

ARLINGTON HOUSE ROUTINE INSPECTION CHECKLIST
INTERIOR

Inspected by:______________________________ **Date of Inspection:**__________

BASEMENT AND CRAWLSPACE

Load Bearing Masonry Walls:
- ☐ Leaning and bulges
- ☐ Cracks caused by structural movement or material shrinkage
- ☐ Loose/damp mortar joints and spalling
- ☐ Wet spots, stains, and water penetration
- ☐ Insect/termite infestation on wood members
- ☐ Decay on wood members

Wood Floor:
- ☐ Fungus present
- ☐ Insect/termite damage
- ☐ Cracked and badly damaged boards
- ☐ Twisted boards
- ☐ Squeaking
- ☐ Floor boards need refinishing

Interior Wall Finishes:
- ☐ Looseness detected when wall surface pushed
- ☐ Signs of dampness and/or mildew
- ☐ Loose, cracked, or bulging plaster
- ☐ Peeling and blistering evident

Wood Joists and Beams:
- ☐ Sagging at the center of span
- ☐ Springiness or vibration
- ☐ Pronounced slope in one direction
- ☐ Split at bottom of joists or beams
- ☐ Floor squeaking
- ☐ Insect infestation/decay
- ☐ Bearing on masonry
- ☐ Bulging or sagging plaster ceiling
- ☐ Overloading of joists and beams

Carpet:
- ☐ Frayed edges
- ☐ Damaged and worn out portions
- ☐ Stains

Ceiling Finishes:
- ☐ Signs of damp plaster on ceilings
- ☐ Loose, cracking, or bulging plaster
- ☐ Peeling and blistering evident

Fireplace:
- ☐ Proper connection with flues
- ☐ Damper inoperable

NOTES

Figure 12.21 Arlington House routine inspection checklist: Interior.

carefully about work priorities. For example, when gutter cleaning is left off the list of seasonal work or a roof leak remains active, is repair of an unsightly plaster ceiling the best use of time and money?

Be sure to schedule the work in a short-enough cycle to meet the conservation needs and goals of the museum. Projects can also be organized and prioritized by who will complete the work. Work that can be done by on-site staff can be separated from work that will require outside contractors, consultants, or service contracts.

KEEP CAREFUL RECORDS

While work is progressing, keep careful records of activities. Photographs of ongoing work can prove invaluable in case questions arise or anything goes wrong. Record the names of the people performing the work and keep in close contact with those overseeing it. All information should be kept in the filing system so it can be accessed by those who need it.

EVALUATE RESULTS

Periodic review of completed preventive maintenance activities is the last step in a preventive conservation/maintenance program before the cycle begins again. This is usually done on an annual basis, but it can be done with more or less frequency depending on the schedule developed for the museum.

Compare the actual cost of the work to the estimated costs. Consider staff, equipment, and supply costs for work performed by the institution's employees.

Review service contracts during the evaluation to ensure that the institution has received the services for which it contracted and that the value of those services was worth the cost. The evaluation step is the time to recommend adjustments in service contracts. For example, a service contract for lawn mowing may need to be changed to specify only hand clipping of grass along the base of a historic barn because the annual inspections have noted cut lines in the foundation stones caused by power string trimmers ("weed whackers").

The person in charge of the preventive conservation/maintenance program and others directly responsible for the plan should meet to evaluate the most recently completed round of treatment work. Current conditions can be compared to those noted in the Historic Structure Report and comprehensive condition assessments, and this comparison can help evaluate the effectiveness of the museum's current preventive conservation/maintenance program. Improvements can be implemented for the next cycle by considering factors such as costs, results, timing, materials, and observations by those who performed the work.

The evaluation records should be stored in the same location and manner as the other documentation for the preventive plan. The records can be used immediately to improve and adjust maintenance practices and to set realistic budgets for the next round of work. As the program becomes a routine part of the museum's operations, the evaluation records can be used to

- track costs over time
- determine which products and practices are the most successful for preserving the historic fabric
- demonstrate the benefits of preventive care in terms of reduced emergency work and building operation costs, and preservation of historic fabric
- predict and plan for systems replacement and one-time complex building fabric conservation treatments
- assist in fund-raising (because an organization that can show it uses its money wisely and can document its expenditures is more likely to attract grants and donors)
- justify the need for staff with certain conservation skills
- keep those involved with the museum informed about their accomplishments relative to preserving the building

It may take years for the benefits of a preventive conservation/maintenance plan to become readily apparent, even though the museum benefits from the program from its inception. It requires patience to sustain a preventive plan through the years it may take to see results. But once the program is established, its payoffs are great.

There are several ways to use the evaluation records to demonstrate the value of the program. For example, the climate control or roof drainage system may be a cause of constant problems. Use the evaluation data to demonstrate that fewer problems have occurred as a result of proactive work. Or select a system or component such as metal flashing that will fail within a given period of time if not maintained. Target a date beyond the predicted failure date and demonstrate that painting it—i.e., engaging in preventive conservation/maintenance—will prolong the life of the flashing.[27]

Finally, keep in mind that the house museum's most visible assets are its buildings. The main house is often the ambassador for the museum—the image used in advertising, on letterheads, and in brochures. Museum buildings in good repair—both outside and inside—make a favorable impression on the public and contribute to positive staff morale. An effective preventive conservation/maintenance program can help the museum earn—and keep—the respect of the public, visitors, and staff (see figure 12.22).

Figure 12.22 The Maria Mitchell House on Nantucket. Library of Congress, HABS National Park Service MASS-901, Mass, 10-NANT, 5-1, photograph by Cortlant V. D. Hubbard.

★ T H E ★ N A N T U C K E T ★

Maria Mitchell Association

ASTRONOMICAL OBSERVATORIES ★ NATURAL SCIENCE MUSEUM ★ SCIENCE LIBRARY ★ MITCHELL HOUSE ★ AQUARIUM

Figure 12.23 Organizations tend to use graphic images of their structures as their "corporate" logos. The Maria Mitchell Association on Nantucket Island uses a stylized graphic rendering of its historic buildings to create the striking logo seen here.

CHAPTER 13

Preventive Conservation and Emergencies, Safety, and Security

ACCIDENTS, FIRES, BREAK-INS, and natural disasters happen with little warning and often at the most inconvenient times. A fire starts at night and smolders, a break-in occurs during a power outage and the security system is off-line because the back-up battery power has not been checked in years and is dead, or roads are closed because of flooding and responders cannot get to your site. We can all conjure up nightmare scenarios that are not far-fetched or may have happened to a colleague. How well an institution is prepared to handle hundreds of potential disasters and emergencies is a critical part of long-term planning and the routines of preventive care.

The topic "emergencies, safety, and security" is vast and has its own areas of specialization and professionals. There are many excellent publications and Web resources to help a site adequately prepare and manage their needs in these areas. As in other areas discussed in this book, a historic house museum should seek the input of knowledgeable professionals to assist with identifying hazards, assessing risks, and proposing solutions for mitigation.

PREPAREDNESS

Emergencies can have a significant long-term impact on the life of a museum. That impact can be negative or positive, depending on how the emergency is handled. For example, a historic house museum in the Northeast was permanently closed and mothballed after a serious fire. The collections that the house held prior to the fire were salvaged and placed in permanent storage. They did not receive treatment after the fire or before they were placed in storage. In contrast, a small historical society housed in an old library building in the rural Midwest was destroyed by a winter plumbing leak. The local community rallied to save the collection. All of the salvageable collection items were cleaned and/or restored. A local businessman donated a new space on the main street of the downtown business district for the historical society to use. Today, it is a vibrant part of the active town center. These examples illustrate the extremes of how an organization can react to and eventually emerge from a serious disaster. Neither institution was prepared for an emergency nor did it have a written emergency plan, but the act of preparing and writing a plan alone will make it more likely that an institution will emerge from emergencies with a positive result.

Many different plans and policies for managing aspects of museum functions have been discussed thus far. The plan that is the easiest to ignore because it makes us so uncomfortable but is by far the most critical plan to have in place is the emergency preparedness and response plan. Much work has been done within the museum profession to develop and disseminate information about emergency preparedness and planning. There are many excellent references and sample emergency plans available on-line and in published and unpublished form. Three institutions in particular provide significant support and resources for cultural institutions. The American Institute for Conservation has a twenty-four-hour assistance line where you can talk to a conservator and a team is ready to provide an assessment.[1] Heritage Preservation's website lists practical advice and disaster resources.[2] The National Park Service and the National Center for Preservation Technology and Training websites post curatorial safety messages, disaster and emergency information, a fire prevention video, a disaster-planning portal that includes "dPlan," and much more.[3]

Generally, institutions are happy to share their internal plans and emergency materials upon request. If you do not have a plan or if you feel your plan could be improved, contact neighboring historic homes and other museums and ask them to share their plans and advice concerning emergency planning for your region.

Emergencies come in many forms: small and large, fast and slow, predicted and spontaneous. The emergency planning process prepares staff and museums to react appropriately to any and all potential events by

Figure 13.1 Gulf Islands National Seashore, Florida, after Hurricane Hugo. Photograph by Pam West.

raising hazard awareness, recognizing vulnerabilities, and taking actions to stop preventable emergencies and diminish the effects of a disaster. The objective of emergency planning is to prevent or minimize the loss of life (staff and visitors), property (house, collections, equipment), and operations (visitors, income, programming) for the organization. The emergency planning process is complex, time consuming, and needs to involve all levels of staff and all divisions or areas of activity at your museum. Planning for historic house emergencies will logically focus on the structure and the collection, but offices, maintenance shop, gift shop, and other noncollection areas must also be included. Public institutions have great responsibility for the safety and protection of their visitors, and many have separate life safety plans to protect visitors and staff.

The emergency planning process is best done by a team with different expertise and perspectives. Usually one function of an organization is tasked to lead the effort. At some museums the security department will be delegated this responsibility, in other institutions the administrative staff, and in some cases the curatorial and collections staff will lead it. Regardless of which department provides the impetus, an emergency plan is necessary; it should involve representatives of all functions of the museum, as it will affect the entire organization.

The emergency planning process has several stages. Hazards and vulnerabilities need to be identified. Museums are typically affected by power outages, fire, water incursion, floods, storms, theft and vandalism, accidents and medical emergencies, and depending on location, earthquakes or volcanoes. However, a bomb threat, terrorist attack, and riot are potential events and need to be considered in a plan. Part of the planning is to identify hazards for the structures and collections and the vulnerabilities of the collections to each type of hazard.

Begin by gathering information about the regional geographic and climatic conditions that may pose a threat, potential vulnerabilities arising from the site (perhaps trains on a nearby line transport chemicals and could derail), and unique aspects of the historic site (only the original one-lane unpaved road leads to the house) and collection (it includes a large collection of biological specimens stored in formaldehyde). A hazard/vulnerability assessment details potential risks and contributing factors that might make the effects of an emergency worse. For example, a hazard assessment of your site might reveal that the grading around your structure is poor and that water actually drains toward the foundation rather than away from the building. In the event of minor flooding, the effects will be much worse if the water flows into the foundation and basement rather than away from it. Properly regrading the landscape around the structure might mitigate the potential risks of a minor flood. Improved grading could

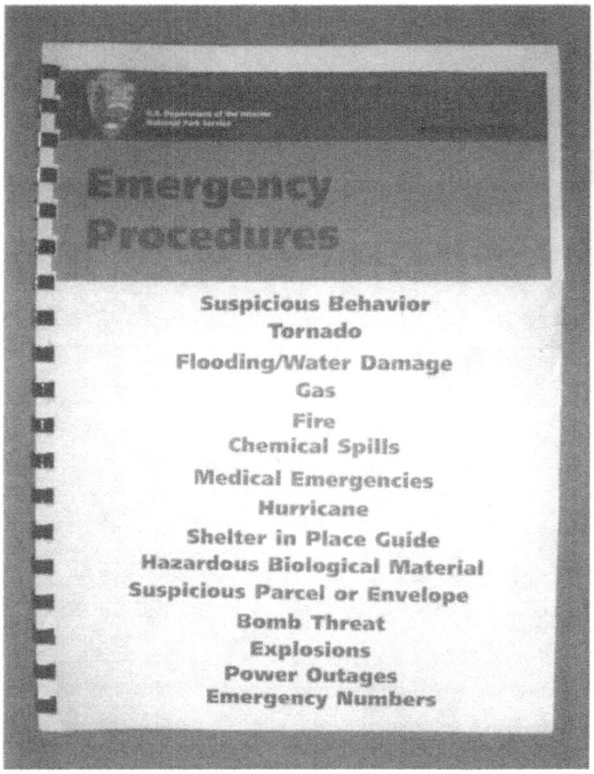

Figure 13.2 Example of a ready reference for emergencies.

carry all of the floodwaters away from the structure, leaving the house unaffected when the floodwaters abate rather than sodden and full of wet or damp collection and structural materials. Or consider a historic house that has exterior wooden shutters. If the shutters can be made functional, they can then be used to protect the house and contents from flying debris during a heavy windstorm, hurricane, or tornado (the shutters can also be used to help control lighting in the interior). The recommendations that result from the hazard mitigation assessment could include the suggestion to keep the shutters functional and to require that they be closed as part of the preparation for an approaching windstorm, hurricane, or tornado.

Hazard assessment should also involve researching the potential threats for your locale from different weather phenomena, earthquakes, flooding, hazardous cargo spills, and other accidents. Information and compiled data about these threats are available from local, state, and federal agencies and emergency management offices. Most emergency planners suggest you focus planning on those disasters that are most likely to occur in your region and thus affect your institution. For example, in Nebraska earthquakes are rare and minor when they do occur, but tornadoes are very common and often cause severe damage there. Nebraska institutions should not focus heavily on preparation to mitigate earthquakes in their emergency planning. They should expend more resources planning and preparing for tornadoes, which are much more likely to occur. The reverse is obviously true for institutions in California. Low-probability threats should not be ignored, but the level of effort and attention should be relative to the likelihood of the event.

After the hazard assessment is completed, analyze risks to determine mitigation measures and begin their implementation. Storage in the basement of a site with the original water pipe running overhead is at a high risk for damage should the pipe burst. Some measures will involve immediate alterations or improvements to the site; others may require longer-term planning and fund-raising. Record the details of all measures and recommendations in the completed response plan. The list may include repair and maintenance activities such as gutter cleaning and repair, installation of a new roof, or improvement of drainage at the site. It may include recommendations to purchase equipment like cell phones, high humidity alarms, a water detector, a public alert radio, and a ready bag or emergency response cart. Changes in procedures and routines will be proposed. For example, a leak inspection may be included in the daily security rounds or specific employees may be requested to carry a pager. The list will include precautionary steps to be added to emergency response plans, such as having personnel unplug all electronic equipment each night when they leave rather than simply turning the equipment off. The hazard assessment and recommendations are the starting point for developing the written emergency plan.

Another very important part of the hazard/risk assessment involves an inventory of all structures, collections, equipment, and other physical assets. The inventory should include enough information about each item to satisfy the insurance company and to assist in the return of stolen property, if needed. Photographs, sketches, and floor plans are an important part of this inventory. The floor plans will be used for many applications throughout the emergency planning process. Assets listed in the inventory can be ranked so that staff knows which items should be protected and/or salvaged first and which should be left until higher-priority items have been protected.

Employees, volunteers, and other human resources should also be inventoried and their skills and expertise documented. This step will be used to assign roles and responsibilities in the event of an emergency. In

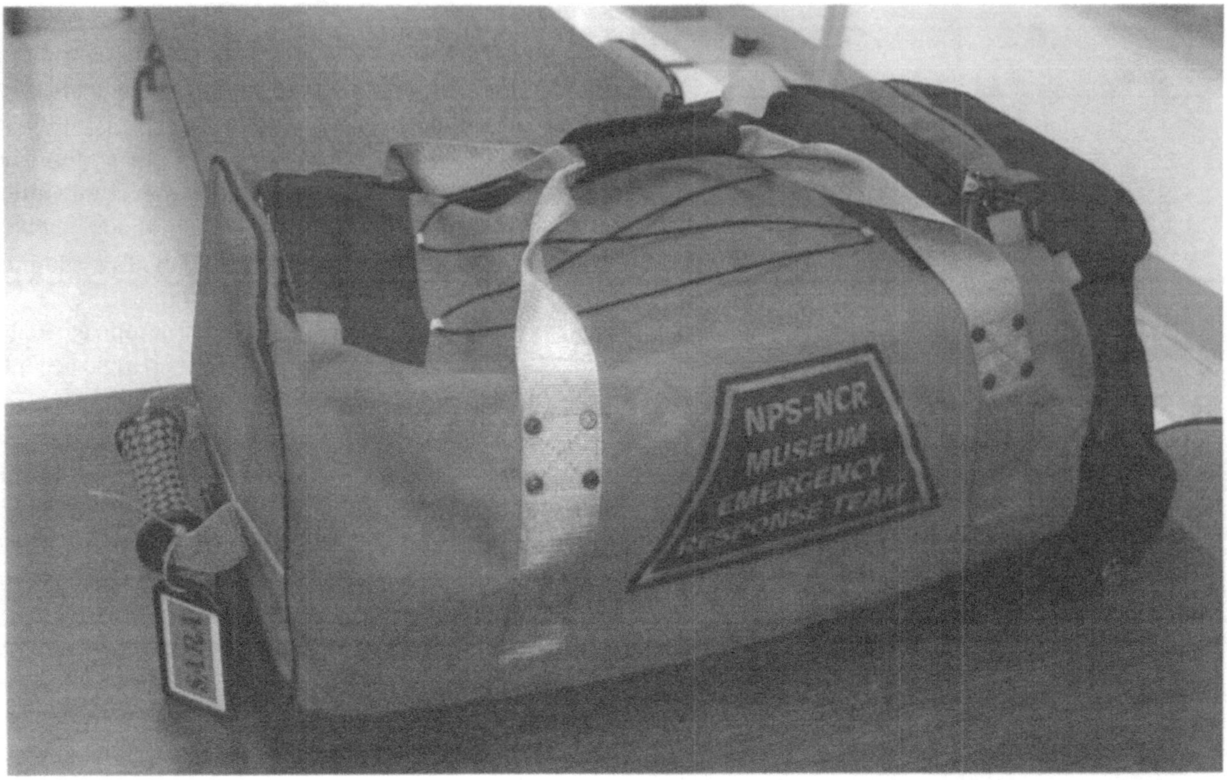

Figure 13.3 A ready bag (top) and its contents (right). Photographs by Pam West.

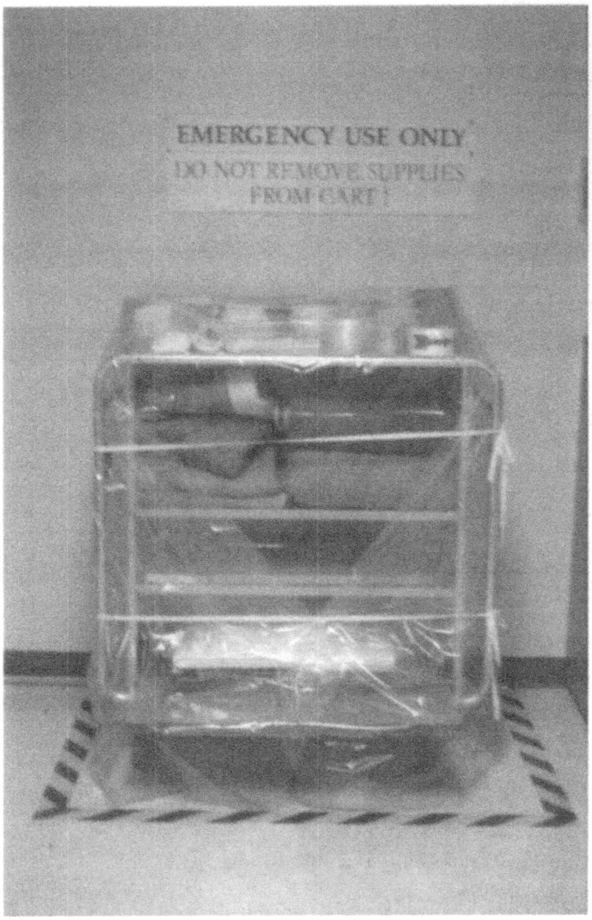

Figure 13.4 An emergency supply cart.

very small historic house settings, it is prudent to involve area museum professionals, neighbors, members of the local fire department (especially if you have a volunteer department), police, the local reporter, and other community members in the planning and response processes. For example, the local reporter may make an effective media liaison in the event that outside press arrives to cover the emergency. They will have a camera, know how to use it, and know how to communicate with other reporters, and they will be familiar with your museum, staff, and collections if they have been part of your emergency planning team.

BEFORE AN EMERGENCY EVENT

The first portion of the actual written emergency plan should focus on preparedness or what should happen before an emergency event occurs. This portion of the plan will focus on events where there is prior warning, such as hurricanes and other serious weather. For example, write instructions for how to prepare for a severe storm or blizzard. Note steps to follow when you lose power and/or water. Create lists of needed supplies and equipment for each preparation step. These instructions and lists will serve as the beginning of the actual emergency response plan. An exhaustive discussion of identification of hazards and understanding risks is found in the National Park Service's *Museum Handbook*, part 1, chapter 10, "Emergency Planning." While much of the information is for Park collections, sections A and B give an excellent description of types of hazards and what to expect.[4]

In addition to delineating hazards, this section of the plan should also describe how emergencies are detected and how people are notified when a problem occurs. When disaster strikes a historic house in the evening or on a day when the property is unattended, the emergency may be detected by a neighbor or by a passerby. Would these people know whom to call? If someone were driving by and noticed smoke, would they know? Is the name of the site and phone number of a contact clearly visible at the entrance or otherwise available? Do the neighbors know the phone numbers of key staff at home? Obviously, the observer could call 911 or the fire department, but would the 911 dispatcher or the fire department know whom to call?

Many believe that the bulk of the emergency plan is the delineation of tasks and the development of a phone tree. These are undoubtedly very important parts of a plan. However, as experience has shown, during a serious event telephone service can be cut off or overloaded, most cell phone service is disrupted or overloaded, and few of the employees assigned specific roles will actually be on-site. The plans should also include personal telephone numbers and name the staff who are on call. When such information is in a plan, distribution must be limited to protect staff privacy.

ASSESSMENT

The next part of the plan should focus on assessment of the emergency. The purpose of this quick assessment phase is to determine what kind and level of response is warranted by the event. A small leak in a hallway should not elicit the same response as a major flood affecting the collections. Several key players in the emergency plan should assess the damage or potential for damage, assess the extent and seriousness of the event, and select/enact an appropriate response. This can be as simple as blotting up the water from a small leak and calling a roof repair company to locate and fix the source of the leak. Response may also mean that the organizational emergency plan is activated and all resources are called in to deal with the disaster.

Figure 13.5 Gulf Islands National Seashore, Florida, after Hurricane Hugo. Photograph by Pam West.

RESPONSE

The next part of the plan should address the various response activities needed to deal with the most commonly occurring emergency situations and is often called the response plan. Perhaps the collections will have to be recovered, packed up, and moved off-site. Packing materials need to be on hand and a storage location held in reserve or access to refrigerated trucks to accommodate the collections has to be arranged. There are many response and recovery procedure guidelines available in the published literature. These "boilerplate" procedures should be tailored to your location and institution. The best approach might be to have a local conservator go over proposed procedures and adjust them to each specific set of variables unique to your structures and collection. Review your plan with a local conservator. This will develop a close relationship and make the conservator a better informed adjunct to the response process should he or she be called in to help.

RESTORATION OF DAMAGE

The next section of the plan should address the long-term restoration of damages to the structure and/or the collections and the restoration of operational activity at the historic structure. This can include lengthy dis-

Figure 13.6 National Park Service Museum Emergency Response Team (MERT) rinsing collections. Photograph by Pam West.

cussions with insurance representatives, surveys of damaged collection items, repairs to the structure, conservation treatment of collections, and temporary accommodation of visitors and tour groups.

REPORT AND DEBRIEF

The last portion of the plan must address the preparation of a final report about each emergency that occurs and the debriefing of staff and others involved in any response to the emergency. Training for staff, acquisition or replenishing of supplies and equipment, and the regular improvement and updating of the plan are also essential elements of a good emergency plan. As with other plans discussed in this book, there are many resources online to assist with developing a plan for your site, but remember that your plan must be specific to your site. Several Web resources are cited in the notes.[5]

SAFETY

Every aspect of museum work has a safety element that must be considered, from care in handling collection objects to designing a safe and well-lit parking lot. Many safety precautions are dictated by local, state, and federal laws, guidelines, and building codes. Most states have special guidelines for historic properties that take into account their unique features. Some safety issues are fairly unique to the museum profession, collection-holding institutions, and/or historic house museums. This chapter will not cover every important safety issue relevant to work in historic house settings in detail, but will focus on the more pervasive ones and the ones specific to preservation activities.

Physical Hazards

The most common physical hazards found in historic structures and on historic sites are the result of "human factors." The lack of resources, the need to save and reuse materials, coupled with little room, create dangerous conditions. These situations are avoidable by following good preventive care practices.

There are often walking hazards from uneven surfaces such as uneven wood flooring or uneven sidewalks

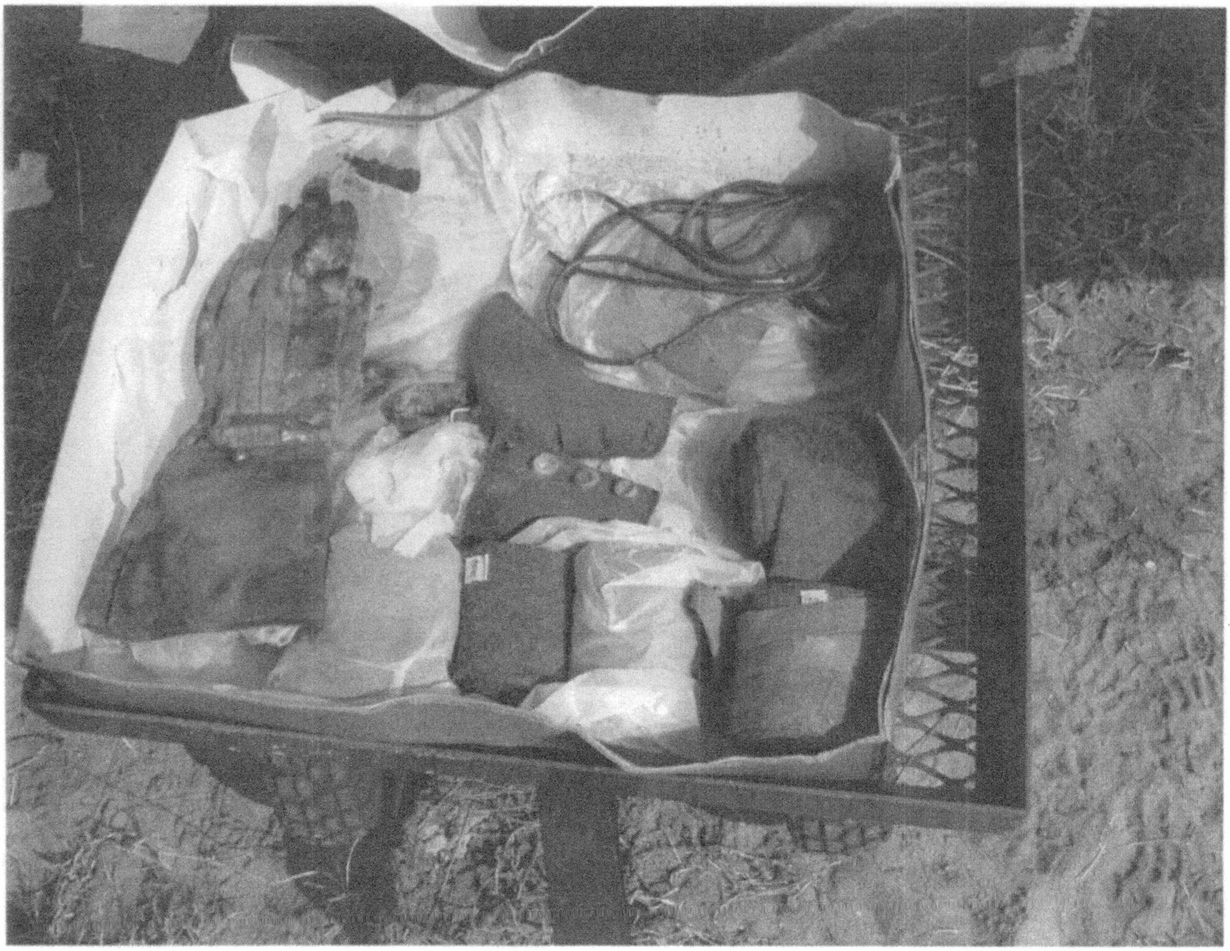

Figure 13.7 Collections packed for removal off-site. Photograph by Pam West.

Figure 13.8 Collections moved to a recovery area. Photograph by Pam West.

Figure 13.9 Photographs suspended on a line to dry after a fire.

and nonstandard-size stair treads. These problems are often unavoidable but can be mitigated with careful warning devices like signs, colored markings, and verbal notices from guides. If possible, it may be best to divert visitors to an alternate walkway. The staff themselves must remain aware of these hazards, particularly when handling and moving collection items. Other physical hazards may include doors, gates, and railings that can pinch or catch appendages or clothing, and low overhead space in doorways and stairwells. A common problem is an electrical extension cord strung across an area through which people also pass.

Chemical Hazards

Powder, liquid, mists, and vapors from chemicals used in cleaning, facility maintenance activities, building construction, collection care, conservation, landscape maintenance, and renovation projects present chemical hazards. Powders found on-site may include cleansers, fertilizers, pesticides, and dusts. Liquids may include cleansers, fertilizers, drain cleaners, solvents, paint thinner, and pesticides. Vapors and mists can be formed through evaporation, sublimation, and mechanical actions such as spraying. Many powders, liquids, mists, and vapors are flammable in addition to the other health hazards they present for ingestion, contact, inhalation, and injection. Flammable materials need a dedicated cabinet for their storage. Exposure to hazardous materials can be acute (one very large dose), chronic (many small doses over time), cumulative (doses continue to build up in the body to toxic levels), and synergistic (two or more materials that interact to make the dose of each more hazardous).

Chemical hazards common in the historic house museum setting include lead-based paint and building ma-

Figure 13.10 Good safety signage.

Figure 13.11 Poor storage and housekeeping practices at a site.

terials and hazardous compounds used in early pest control campaigns. The presence of lead-based construction materials in historic properties is well known. There is much literature available that describes methods to reduce exposure to lead from these sources. For example, the National Park Service has prepared a Preservation Brief on this topic at www.nps.gov/history/hps/tps/briefs/brief37.htm (accessed 2 June 2009).

Historic properties and collections may also have air-quality hazards from heating and cooling systems that permit mold, fungal, and bacterial growth (Legionnaire's disease). See www.nps.gov/history/hps/TPS/briefs/brief24.htm (accessed 3 June 2009) for a start. Storage areas that are infested with rodents and birds can transmit communicable illnesses (e.g., hantavirus). See www.nps.gov/history/museum/publications/conserveogram/02-08.pdf (accessed 2 June 2009) and www.co.multnomah.or.us/health/vector/posters_faqs/hantavirus.pdf (accessed 2 June 2009).

Material Safety Data Sheets

All staff should be familiar with the Material Safety Data Sheet, or MSDS, which is required by federal law under the Hazard Communication Standard for hazardous chemicals and any product used in the workplace that contains a hazardous material. The manufacturer is required to develop an informational sheet that lists the hazardous chemicals found in a product in quantities of 1 percent or greater (0.1 percent or greater if the chemical is a carcinogen). The sheet should be shipped out with the product and kept on-site at the museum. If sheets are not sent or if you have hazardous materials on-site for which there is no MSDS, contact the manufacturer and request the MSDS. You can also access thousands of MSDS records online; however, they may not be for the formulation of the product you have, so it is best to contact the manufacturer. Employers are required to keep an MSDS on-site for each hazardous material. The MSDS provides information about the identity, physical nature, chemical nature, hazards, route of entry, exposure limits, handling precautions, use precautions, spill procedures, and emergency/first aid procedures for the material. This critical information is to be used by supervisors and employees in protecting themselves, the historic structure, and the collection from hazards.

Fire Hazards, Detection, and Suppression

Historic structures also have a number of fire hazards from features such as old electrical wiring that does not meet code, electrified gas and candlelight fixtures, poorly installed or maintained fireplaces, and use of open flames (such as during a cooking demonstration). The protection of the institution from fire hazards is the responsibility of all the staff. Exits and walkways must be kept clear, sources of ignition must be controlled, smoking must be prohibited except in designated areas away from structures, and electrical equipment must be well maintained and circuits not overloaded (often a problem for older sites). Too of-

Figure 13.12 Systems and monitoring panels.

ten fire detection and suppression systems in historic structures are absent or outdated. It is difficult and costly to install updated systems in older structures. Aesthetic concerns and the need to protect original building features and materials complicate the process of selecting and installing fire detection and suppression systems. Despite the difficulties, the installation of one or more types of detection and suppression system is essential to the prudent occupation and management of any property that is to be preserved. It is irresponsible to store and exhibit collections in a structure without fire detection and suppression capabilities.

The basic types of fire detectors—photoelectric and ionization—have different costs and applications. It is best to discuss detection systems with a knowledgeable individual, perhaps your fire department personnel. Detectors must be inspected, tested, cleaned, and maintained. The only way that the fire detection system is effective, however, is when there is also a fire suppression system in place. Fire extinguishers, firefighters knowledgeable about the site and its contents, hydrants (standpipe), and automatic sprinkler systems are all part of suppression. The suppression systems need to be inspected, tested, and maintained, and personnel need training.

A fire extinguisher is the most commonly found form of suppression at sites. Multipurpose dry ABC-type extinguishers and CO_2 extinguishers are both suitable in the museum setting. Staff who discover a fire can be instrumental in controlling the emergency if they first evacuate the house, notify the fire department, and then assess the risk to themselves if they stay and use a fire extinguisher. There is also a trend away from placing fire extinguishers in public spaces and toward merely telling everyone to leave the building. Remember that human life is to be saved first and collections after all danger to life has passed. If fire extinguishers are used as part of a suppression program, staff must be trained in their proper use.

It is very important that a historic house work with the fire department to prepare for a fire emergency.

The responders should be familiar with the site, its importance, the type of collections, where hazardous materials are located, and so on. Schedule an annual tour of the site for the responders. You may want to them to have a copy of your emergency plan.

Sprinkler systems are a very effective system of fire suppression. The basic types on the market are wet pipe and mist or fog type, dry pipe, cycling, and preaction. Each system has different features that need to be matched to site conditions and be reviewed carefully when selecting a type to install. A fire safety consultant who understands historic structures, environmental requirements of such structures, and museum collections should be involved in your system planning.

It is estimated that 45 percent of the fires in libraries and museums in Canada occur between seven o'clock in the evening and five o'clock in the morning. Most are due to arson and secondly to electrical sources.[6] Defective wiring, the use of extension cords, heat-generating devices (coffeepots, irons, hair dryers, etc.), and open flames (fireplaces, candles, soldering irons, torches, and lanterns) all present preventable sources of fires. The following are common methods used to reduce the risk of damage associated with fire:

- Install automatic shutdown switches to turn off the HVAC system during a fire or fire alarm.
- Monitor construction workers and projects for potential risk and unsafe work practices.
- Require all contractors using open flames to have a staff observer.
- Keep hallways and aisles clear of materials and debris.
- Use noncombustible construction and storage materials.
- Keep all flammable materials properly labeled in closed safety cabinets.
- Install and close fire doors and barriers.
- Unplug all heat-generating devices when not in use.
- Install and maintain a fire suppression system.
- Place collection and archival materials in freezers, metal cabinetry, and fireproof safes where appropriate.

A number of professional fire safety consultants have specialized in the protection of historic buildings and museum collections. Relevant information can be located by visiting the National Fire Protection Association website, particularly the section that lists the codes established for museums under "NFPA 909: Code for the Protection of Cultural Resources Properties—Museums, Libraries, and Places of Worship" at www.nfpa.org/aboutthecodes/AboutTheCodes.asp?DocNum=909 (accessed 3 June 2009).

Historic structures can have safety problems related to access and egress in the event of fire or other disasters, such as narrow, curving stairwells; poorly illuminated halls and passages; and limited number of doors or windows. All of these safety hazards can be mitigated or eliminated by instituting operational and physical safety practices. A walk-through by a safety consultant can indicate areas of potential concern and possible methods to reduce associated risks.

Hazardous Collection Materials

We don't necessarily think that our collection materials may be a safety concern. Yet collections contain hazards from radioactive geological specimens, medical kits and drugs, nitrate-based films, unexploded munitions, and organic materials such as leather, fur, feathers, natural history specimens, basketry, and textiles that have been treated with pesticides. From the early 1800s to the mid-1900s some organic materials were treated with a range of toxic chemicals to prevent pest infestation. These chemicals included arsenic, strychnine, hydrogen cyanide, and DDT, among others. Residues from these treatments present health hazards to those who handle the collections. Warning labels should be applied to storage cabinets holding hazardous collection materials.

MUSEUM SECURITY AND PROTECTION

The preventive conservation practices that we have discussed thus far help to protect the structures and collections from environmental factors that contribute to deterioration and the process of aging. The security and protection systems and protocols established to control access around the site and collections will afford protection of the museum and personnel from unexpected, criminal, and nuisance actions such as theft, vandalism, arson, trespassing, and personal infringements. A successful security program begins with an assessment of risks, knowing the likelihood of an occurrence, understanding the severity of the incident and its impact on the institution, and mitigation. Security protection has component parts that support one another and in descending levels of protection from the site boundaries to the collections. It uses sophisticated electronic devices, and equally important, the observation and diligence of human beings. Neither high-tech equipment nor persistent human presence alone can provide prudent security for a historic site.

Elements outside the traditional realm of "security" also contribute to a crime-free environment. Orderliness in all spaces helps to make changes or intrusions more apparent. Well-trained and aware staff in every department can note abnormal activity. Proper inventory, documentation, and registration of collection items and other resources like cameras and computers will make tracking and identification of stolen items possible. Routine inspections of the site, structures, and collections will allow staff to observe potential criminal activity early and thus help prevent or detect crimes sooner.

One way to look at security is to start at the outer physical boundary or perimeter of the site and work inward to individual collection items. The outermost perimeter would be the property line, which might be bounded by a fence, gate, or natural feature. This is the first line of defense in the protection of the site. A wall or fence may deter potential criminals from entering the property. Detection and alarm systems that monitor the outer perimeter will deter trespassing. Install lighting designed for staff safety and site security while not contributing to light pollution. Once the property is entered, it is the intellectual and physical controls that the site has developed and put into practice that will now form the foundation of the security program. Delegation of authority, access rules, staffing assignments, and safety, emergency, and security plans will ensure that the "who, what, when, where, and why" of a sanctioned access is recorded and unsanctioned access is discovered promptly.

The next line of defense is the perimeter of the building or structure with its walls, roofs, windows, doors, and other entrances. Human presence, locks, barriers, and electronic monitoring at each entrance will control who and what enters and leaves the structure and when. Keys need to be controlled and not all staff need keys to all areas of the site. Staff who never open or close the museum and are not principal members of the emergency response team may not need to have a key to the front door. Key control and written opening and closing procedures are necessary for staff safety and site security.

It is also essential to have a clearly defined line between the public spaces in a building and those restricted to staff. The clearer and more controlled this boundary is within the building, the more secure all staff and property will be behind the perimeter. Visible signage, locked doors, key code entry, and security personnel at this perimeter help deter and prevent crime.

Installed deterrent and detection systems are also essential. Intrusion detection systems (which often call a monitoring company or the state or local police), alarms, sirens, motion detectors, glass-break detectors, recording devices such as a closed-circuit TV, film reinforcement for windows (nonhistoric glass), water detection/alarm, fire detection, fire suppression, and fire extinguishers are among the tools that should be in place to protect the site. The fire detection system is often part of an overarching security system.

It should not be forgotten that the exhibits themselves and the systems of storage are part of collection security. The open display plan of the historic house museum complicates protection issues, but a vulnerable object must be secured, have a customized security mount, be alarmed, and/or a staff person must accompany visitors in the furnished rooms. Exhibit cases need to have tamperproof fastenings.

Controlled access to areas where collections are stored and kept is necessary. This boundary is controlled by policy (who can have access) and by security devices (locks, codes, cards). Within these "secure" areas, collections can be locked in cabinets or drawers or kept in a vault that requires additional access permission and keys, codes, and cards. Objects temporarily outside of the inner perimeter must be protected by the use of auxiliary methods such as secure cases, security mounts, additional alarms, or additional staff.

Each perimeter discussed above can be controlled to a lesser or greater extent by the quality of the policies and procedures in place, by the equipment chosen, and by the diligence of the staff assigned to monitor access. Policies that provide a more secure environment include limiting access where possible to only those employees that need access for their work, during the times that they need to have access, monitoring the times and people who access a space, and monitoring work that goes on in a secure location. Limiting keys, limiting badges, using sign in and out logs, signing out keys from a lock box, searching bags and packages, and supervising or escorting personnel and visitors are all effective measures to increase security in a museum.

Mechanical and electronic security devices hamper intruders and alert others of their presence but these devices are most often used when the institution is closed. They do not necessarily prevent or stop criminal activity, especially during opening hours when a human being will be required to stop a crime. A well-trained staff that is alert and versed in the proper response procedures can be an invaluable asset in the protection of the museum. Several of the more high-profile museum theft attempts in the last decade were foiled by observant and diligent housekeepers and cleaning staff who reported suspicious activities.

It is essential to test and review systems and policies for currency and effectiveness. The frequency will depend on the institution's size and complexity of programs, and staff turnover. However, some actions cannot wait for a review. For example, the monitoring company for the intrusion detection alarm needs to know on the very day of a staff change that there is a new emergency contact. Procrastination or complacency can make your site vulnerable. It is recommended that the historic house museum use all of the possible community resources, from the police and fire departments to neighboring museums and universities, to help make assessments, review hazards, write plans, and design systems. Organizations may pool resources to help one another in an emergency. The safety and security of visitors and staff, structures and collections needs to be planned and trained for. Do not hesitate to use the experience of others to help your site perform this essential function.[7]

CHAPTER 14

Pulling It All Together

The Preservation Master Plan

THE MUSEUM, CONSERVATION, and architectural communities have recommended a number of "plans" that document, investigate, and develop policies and practices for historic house museums. Architectural professionals recommend Historic Structure Reports for historic buildings. When a structure is proposed for local or federal landmark status, a nomination document is completed for the property. The museum profession has developed the Museum Assessment Program, which includes four assessments, two of which relate to collection and site preservation: the MAP I, which addresses institutional management and operations, and the MAP II, which addresses collections management issues. These are not to be confused with the Conservation Assessment Program, which administers assessments that are similar to the MAP II assessment except that they are done by conservators and architectural professionals and focus on the preservation of the collection and the structure. In the National Park Service, sites are required to develop a Collections Management Plan, which is much like Conservation and MAP assessments and is specifically tailored to National Park Service systems and processes.

Institutions are recommended to have housekeeping plans, integrated pest management plans, furnishing plans, interpretive plans, emergency preparedness and response plans, collecting plans, and last but far from least, Collections Management Manuals. How do all of these divergent plans relate to one another? How is a historic house to use each specific "plan" to promote preservation and preventive care? Which plans are more important than others? Which plan should be completed first?

Fundamentally, each specific plan is one part of the larger holistic scheme designed to preserve the assets of the institution so that it can continue to function and meet its mission. Each smaller, more focused plan is part of a larger effort of the institution for self-preservation, which can be assembled into a Preservation Master Plan. Using the word *preservation* in its broadest meaning ("to maintain in safety from injury, peril, or harm; protect . . . to keep in perfect or unaltered condition"),[1] the Preservation Master Plan should serve as the guidepost to protect the institution, its structures, its landscape, and its collections from harm. The Preservation Master Plan should integrate and prioritize all of the other "plans" that address aspects of institutional preservation. Specific plans can be used directly to complete portions of the Master Plan. Clearly, many different professionals and many different mechanisms are used to produce parts of the Preservation Master Plan.

THE PRESERVATION MASTER PLAN

The Preservation Master Plan for an institution is the framework within which all preventive conservation methods and practices are organized. The plan ties together the different spheres of activity in the historic house that can be used as tools to preserve the historic properties and collections of the organization.

Elements covered in the Preservation Master Plan include intellectual controls that protect the structure(s) and collection(s). These would include all of the parts of the Collections Management Manual, such as loan, research, copyright, insurance, and other related institutional policies. Intellectual controls consist of the body of policies that define the purpose, scope, and priorities of the institution.

The Master Plan also includes all of the physical controls that correct, minimize, and prevent damage to the structure(s), site, and collection(s). Physical controls consist of the procedures that define and delineate the everyday function of the structure and the collections within, including environmental procedures, collection management procedures (like collection handling procedures, use, and repair), and maintenance procedures.

The Preservation Master Plan should begin with a summary or introduction that describes the institution, its evolution, and its character. This section should include a discussion of the purpose of the institution and its mission. It should detail the evolution of the site and the collections. The introduction should discuss the site, buildings, grounds, and landscape and their uses, and include the documentation of the site. It should describe and quantify the collections, their uses, and documentation. It should summarize the interpretive goals of the site and the interpretive uses to which the site and collection are subject. This section should also discuss the staffing and governance of the historic house museum.

The second portion of the plan should include the policies that have been written to protect the structures, landscape, and collections as discussed in chapter 4, "Intellectual and Physical Controls," and include the documentation completed for the site, structures, and collections.

The third portion of the plan should detail the physical methods and controls that are needed to prevent damage to the structures and collections, such as methods for pest control; exhibition of objects; routine building and collection maintenance programs; and the tools, methods, and materials for use in maintaining the site. This portion should also include details of inspection schedules and reporting requirements.

A team consisting of both staff and consultants should write the Preservation Master Plan. It can be written section by section and assembled over a period of years. It can start with any parts that have already been written. Portions may be assembled from other sources, such as a Historic Structure Report, a previous grant application, or a Conservation Assessment. Federal funding is available for assessments that will generate these reports, and there may be other types of outside funding as well. Much of the introductory material may already be available in other documents on hand.

The following outline delineates the recommended organization of the Preservation Master Plan for a historic site museum. It can be used as a guide for completing and assembling a Preservation Master Plan.

THE PRESERVATION MASTER PLAN: OUTLINE

A. Introduction to the Preservation Master Plan: The Organization
   1. Purpose of Site/Museum: Mission Statement, Governance
   2. Synopsis/Evolution of the Site and Collection
   3. Institutional Strategic/Long Range Plan
   4. Staff (Number, Type, Supervision, Credentials, Training)
   5. The Site, Building Structure, Grounds (HSR, Nomination Documents, CLR)
      a. Grading, Landscape, Gardens
      b. Historic Structure(s): Construction Type, Mechanical Systems
      c. Spaces within Interior Layout: Number/Types of Rooms
   6. The Collection
      a. Historic Interiors (Furnishing Plans)
      b. Types of Objects
      c. Size of Collection(s)
   7. Interpretive and Other Uses of the Site
      a. Interpretation
      b. Special Events and Other Uses
      c. Scheduling and Frequency

B. Intellectual Controls
   1. Staff Responsibilities and Access
   2. Documentation of the Structure and Site
   3. Documentation of the Collections
   4. Facilities Management Manual
   5. Collections Management Manual
   6. Environmental Control Standards and Policies
   7. Lighting Policies
   8. Pest Management Policies
   9 Interpretation and Use Policies
   10. Exhibits Policies
   11. Storage Policies
   12. Emergency, Safety, and Security Policies

C. Physical Controls
   1. Staff Reporting Structure
   2. Facilities Procedures (from Facilities Management Manual)
   3. Collections Procedures (from Collections Management Manual)
   4. Environmental Control Procedures
   5. Lighting Procedures
   6. Pest Management Procedures
   7. Interpretation and Use Procedures
   8. Exhibits Procedures
   9. Storage Procedures
   10. Emergency, Safety, and Security Procedures
   11. Routine Maintenance
      a. The Site—Landscape Design Maintenance
      b. The Building—Routine Maintenance Plan
      c. The Collections—Housekeeping and Conservation
      d. Long-Range Planning for Maintenance and Conservation
   12. Tools and Materials
   13. Scheduling, Inspection, and Reporting

MEETINGS AND INSPECTIONS

There should be regularly scheduled inspections of all the landscapes and structures and all the interior spaces, both interpreted and not, that are part of the institution's holdings, whether historic or not. These inspections can be scheduled at a frequency that makes sense to the institution. At very large sites with many structures, the inspections may cover groups of structures on a rotating timetable. At smaller institutions the entire site can be inspected several times a year. A team of participants should be organized for the inspection process and should include those responsible for the maintenance of the structures, administrators, curators, docents or interpreters, board members (if appropriate), and any needed outside specialists like engineers or architects. Someone should be assigned to take photos and someone should take notes. The recommendations from these inspections will inform needed changes and/or improvements to the Preservation Master Plan or its parts.

Another function that can be of immeasurable value in coordinating all preservation efforts is a regularly scheduled meeting of staff, volunteers, and invited guests that includes people from all areas of museum services. These meetings can be quarterly or even monthly for large active sites. Interpreters, facilities staff, administrators, curators, invited community members, and other specialists can be apprised of forthcoming activities that affect all of these areas, such as major interpretive changes, upcoming repair or construction work, or community activities that may impact the institution or vice versa. These coordinating meetings can be invaluable and can save everyone much work and expense.

STAFF TRAINING

The Preservation Master Plan can also be a tool to indicate and coordinate any needed staff training. For example, training on collection-handling techniques can be integrated into emergency response training, or briefings on important landscape features can be integrated into docent training. Landscape staff can learn about the types of hazards presented by pest infestations in the collections. Integrated training will create an informed and cross-trained staff that can better contribute to all aspects of institutional function.

ADMINISTRATION AND THE PRESERVATION MASTER PLAN

Perhaps most importantly, the Preservation Master Plan is a critical tool for the administration of an institution. The plan or its parts can be used for grant writing and development. Sections can be copied directly into grant applications, and individual and overall plans can be used to justify the need for or importance of projects of all types. The component plans will demonstrate the institution's responsible management and will indicate the rationale for chosen priorities.

The same tools can be used to justify and prioritize fund-raising activities. Foundations and donors truly want to know that their dollars are being spent in the best and most effective ways possible. The Preservation Master Plan and its parts can do this and demonstrate the thoughtful and professional administration of the site and its cultural and social assets.

The plan is also a needed tool for budgeting and strategic planning. The plan can indicate diverse institutional needs and their relative priorities. Because it integrates all of the functional areas of the institution, it will prevent planners and budget officers from overlooking critically important but perhaps low-profile needs. The plan and its parts can also help elucidate hidden costs for projects and can be used to document these costs when creating estimates for new programs or initiatives.

The Preservation Master Plan must be regularly evaluated and updated to add new needs or issues, but also very importantly to document and recognize achievements of all kinds, large and small, in attaining the goals set forth in all the various parts of the Plan. Reports on progress are important to share with board members, funders, donors, and the local community. These reports show that the institution is responsibly safeguarding its diverse assets for the future.

CONCLUSION

The recommendations made throughout this book condense the body of knowledge of many professions. The intention is to gather in one place the basic preservation needs of historic house museums operated by small staffs and/or volunteers. In the United States today, our historic sites tend to be underfunded, understaffed, and have high staff turnover rates—but they also have dedicated volunteers and community supporters and many eager visitors. It is essential to understand that every tiny accomplishment, no matter how small, on the part of the staff is a measurable step toward the end goal of sound professional institutional management. Every part of the Preservation Master Plan that is put in place provides a foundation for another part. Even seemingly unrelated steps build foundations for other achievements. As the Preservation Master Plan comes together over time, its value and power becomes more evident and its use for the institution becomes invaluable.

Notes

CHAPTER 1

1. American Institute for Conservation of Historic and Artistic Works, "Commentary 20: Preventive Conservation," in Directory (Washington, D.C.: American Institute for Conservation, 2007), 47. See Core Documents at www.conservation-us.org.
2. Suzanne W. Hull, *Chaste, Silent, and Obedient: English Books for Women, 1475–1640* (San Marino, Calif.: Huntington Library, Kingsport Press, 1982).
3. H. Glass, *The Servants Directory, Improved; or House-Keepers Companion,* 4th ed. (Dublin, printed by J. Potts, at Swift's Head in Dame-Street, 1762), 15–16.

CHAPTER 2

1. Laurence Vail Coleman, *Historic House Museums* (Washington, D.C.: American Association of Museums, 1933), 3.
2. Coleman, *Historic House Museums,* 99.
3. Patricia West, *Domesticating History: The Political Origins of America's House Museums* (Washington, D.C.: Smithsonian Institution Press, 1999), xii.

CHAPTER 3

1. Chapter 4, "Intellectual and Physical Controls," discusses intellectual controls for the collection and structure in greater detail, listing websites where examples of policies and procedures used by historic house museums and other organizations can be viewed.
2. American Institute for Conservation (AIC), *Code of Ethics and Guidelines for Practice,* www.conservation-us.org/index.cfm?fuseaction=page.viewPage&pageID=858&nodeID=1 and www.conservation-us.org (accessed 29 May 2009).
3. Sara Wolf Green, ed., *The Conservation Assessment: A Tool for Planning, Implementing, and Fund-Raising,* 2nd ed. (Washington, D.C.: Getty Conservation Institute and Heritage Preservation [formerly National Institute for the Conservation of Cultural Property], 1991), 2.
4. Institute for Museum and Library Services (IMLS), www.imls.gov.
5. Heritage Preservation, (202) 233-0800, www.heritagepreservation.org.
6. S. Michalski, *A Systematic Approach to the Conservation (Care) of Museum Collections* (Ottawa, Ont.: Canadian Conservation Institute, 1992); S. Michalski, "A Systematic Approach to Preservation: Description and Integration of Other Museum Activities," in *Preventive Conservation: Practice, Theory, and Research. Preprints to the Ottawa Conference, 12–16 September* (London: International Institute for Conservation, 1994), 8–11; R. Waller, "Conservation Risk Assessment: A Strategy for Managing Resources for Preventive Conservation," in *Preventive Conservation: Practice, Theory, and Research. Preprints to the Ottawa Conference, 12–16 September* (London: International Institute for Conservation, 1994), 12–17; and J. Ashley-Smith, *Risk Assessment for Object Conservation* (Oxford, UK: Butterworth-Heinemann, 1999), 7.

CHAPTER 4

1. It is not the intent of this discussion to replace the many invaluable references that comprise the body of professional knowledge of museum practice. The reader is directed to standard references such as R. A. Buck and J. A. Gilmore, eds., *The New Museum Registration Methods* (Washington, D.C.: American Association of Museums, 1998) for more discussion of collections management policy and practice.
2. Native American Graves Protection and Repatriation Act, Endangered Species Act, International Institute for the Unification of Private Law Convention on Stolen or Illegal Exported Cultural Objects.
3. James R. Blackaby, Patricia Greeno, and the Nomenclature Committee, *The Revised Nomenclature for Museum Cataloging: A Revised and Expanded Edition of Robert G. Chenhall's System for Classifying Man-Made Objects* (Walnut Creek, Calif.: AltaMira Press, 1995).
4. Canadian Conservation Institute *Notes* offer practical advice about the care, handling, and storage of cultural objects. Currently more than one hundred *Notes* exist and are available to order online at www.cci-icc.gc.ca/bookstore/index-e.cfm.
5. The NPS *Exhibit Conservation Guidelines* are available from the Harpers Ferry Historical Association, PO Box 197, Harpers Ferry, WV 25425; (304) 535-6881.

CHAPTER 5

1. For more information about interpretation, see the websites of the American Association of Museums, www.aam-us.org, and the National Association for Interpretation, www.interpnet.com.
2. Susanna Whatman, *The Housekeeping Book of Susanna Whatman, 1776–1800* (London: National Trust Classics, 2000).

3. *The National Trust Manual of Housekeeping: The Care of Collections in Historic Houses Open to the Public* (Oxford, UK: Elsevier, 2006), 21.

CHAPTER 7

1. For basic information on the care of nitrate-based films, see Tony Knapp and Diane Voigt O'Conner, *Care of Cellulose Nitrate Film*, National Park Service, Conserve O Gram series 18/04 at www.nps.gov/history/museum/publications/conserveogram/14-08.pdf (accessed 7 January 2009).
2. National Park Service, *Museum Handbook, Part 1* (Washington, D.C.: National Park Service, 1999), 7:1. www.nps.gov/history/museum/publications/handbook.html (accessed 6 March 2009).
3. National Park Service, *Museum Handbook*, 7:1.
4. National Park Service, *Museum Handbook*, 7:5.
5. National Park Service, Conserve O Gram series COG 4/7, 4/8 at www.nps.gov/history/museum/publications/conserveogram/conserv.html (accessed 6 March 2009).
6. National Park Service, *Museum Handbook*, 7:5.
7. National Park Service, *Museum Handbook*, 7:20.
8. Carolyn L. Rose and Amparo R. de Torres, eds., *Storage of Natural History Collections: Ideas and Practical Solutions* (Pittsburgh, Pa.: Society for the Preservation of Natural History Collections, 1992), 255–56.
9. American Institute for Conservation, "Current Conservation Treatment and Practices, Storage VIII," in *The Textile Specialty Group Catalogue* (Washington, D.C.: AIC, 1998).
10. Rose and de Torres, eds., *Storage of Natural History Collections.*
11. National Park Service, Conserve O Gram series COG 4/4 at www.nps.gov/history/museum/publications/conserveogram/conserv.html (accessed 6 March 2009).
12. William K. Hollinger, "Microchamber Papers Used as a Preventive Conservation Material," in *Preventive Conservation Practice, Theory and Research, Preprints of the Contribution to the Ottawa Congress, 12–16 September 1994*, 212–16.
13. Hollinger, "Microchamber Papers," 213.

CHAPTER 8

1. Thomas Brill, *Light* (New York: Plenum Press, 1980), 3.
2. Brill, *Light*, 64.
3. Brill, *Light*, 65.
4. Stefan Michalski, "The Lighting Decision," in *Fabric of an Exhibition, Preprints of Textile Symposium '97* (Ottawa, Ont.: Canadian Conservation Institute, 1997), 97.
5. Michalski, "The Lighting Decision," 97. Cited in Garry Thomson, *The Museum Environment*, 2nd ed. (Oxford, UK: Butterworth-Heinemann, 1986).
6. David Layman, "Lighting Design Terminology: A Mini-Lesson," *Exhibitionist* 13, no. 1 (Spring 1994): 46–47.
7. National Institute of Standards and Technology, Special Publication 330 (SP 330), *The International System of Units (SI)* (Gaithersburg, Md.: National Institute of Standards and Technology, 2008).
8. Terry T. Schaeffer, *Research in Conservation: Effects of Light on Materials in Collections; Data on Photoflash and Related Sources* (Los Angeles, Calif.: Getty Publications, 2001).
9. See the Environmental Protection Agency website, www.epa.gov/mercury/spills/index.htm#fluorescent (accessed 19 December 2008).
10. Thomson, *The Museum Environment*, 19–20.
11. Linda Bullock and David Saunders, "Measurement of Cumulative Exposure Using Blue Wool Standards," in *ICOM Committee for Conservation, 12th Triennial Meeting, Lyon, 29 August–September 1999, Preprints*, Vol. 1 (London: James & James, 1999), 26.
12. Blue Wool Standard, British Standards Institute, 1992.
13. Robert Feller, "Studies on Photochemical Deterioration," paper presented at the International Council of Museums, Fourth or Fifth Triennial Meeting, Venice, 13–18 October 1975.
14. Feller, "Studies."
15. S. Gerlach et al., *Accelerated Ageing of Light Dosimeters*, paper presented at the CEEES meeting in Nuremberg (Germany), 15 May 2003, db.re.fh-koeln.de/networkExchange/lido/ceees_300303.doc.
16. Mauro Bacci et al., "Indoor Environmental Monitoring of Colour Changes of Tempera-Painted Dosimeters," in *ICOM Committee for Conservation, 12th Triennial Meeting, Lyon, 29 August–3 September, Preprints*, Vol. 1 (London: James & James, 1999), 3–7; Marianne Odlyha, "Microclimate Indoor Monitoring in Cultural Heritage Preservation," Birkbeck University of London, School of Biological and Chemical Sciences. www.bbk.ac.uk/bcs/staff/odlyha_eu_mimic.html (accessed 29 May 2009).
17. Bacci et al., "Indoor Environmental Monitoring," 4.
18. Bertrand Lavédrine, "The Preservation of France's Cultural Heritage: Preventing Deterioration due to Exposure to Light," *CNRS INFO, Science and Colors*, March 2001, no. 391. www.cnrs.fr/cw/en/pres/n391couleng/html/n391coula04.htm.
19. Bertrand Lavédrine, "The Blue Pink Scale: A New Dosimeter for the Exhibition of Photographs and Sensitive Artifacts," in *Care of Photographic Moving Image and Sound Collections. Conference Papers, July 20–24, 1998*, edited by S. Clark (Leigh, UK: Institute of Paper Conservation), 121–28.
20. LiDo, "A Light Dosimeter for Monitoring Cultural Heritage: Development, Testing and Transfer to Market." www.lido.fraunhofer.de/index.html (accessed 7 August 2003).
21. LiDo, "Recent Results." www.lido.fraunhofer.de/index.html (accessed 7 August 2003).

22. LiDo, "Recent Results."
23. Gerlach et al., "Accelerated Ageing of Light Dosimeters."
24. Ivan Petkov and Jean-Michel Nunzi, "New Two-Functional UVR Sunscreen Protector and Dosimeter," www.photobiology.com/photobiology2000/petkov (accessed 30 July 2003).
25. Gerlach et al., "Accelerated Ageing of Light Dosimeters."
26. Canadian Conservation Institute, *A Light Damage Slide Rule*, CCI Note 2/6 (Ottawa, Ont.: Canadian Conservation Institute, 1988).
27. www.apti.org/resources/charters2.cfm (accessed 9 February 2009).
28. Smithsonian Institution, Smithsonian Accessibility Program, Office of the Provost, www.si.edu/opa/accessibility/exdesign (accessed 3 March 09).

CHAPTER 9

1. S. Bradley, "Development of an Environmental Policy for the British Museum," in *Preprints of the 11th Triennial ICOM-CC Meeting, Edinburgh, 1–6 September*, Vol. 1 (London: James & James, 1996).
2. S. Michalski, "Relative Humidity in Museums, Galleries, and Archives: Specification and Control," in *Bugs, Mold, and Rot II*, 51–62 (Washington, D.C.: National Institute of Building Sciences, 1993).
3. M. Mecklenburg and C. Tomosa, "Mechanical Behavior of Paintings Subjected to Changes in Temperature and Relative Humidity," in *Art in Transit: Studies in the Transport of Paintings*, edited by M. Mecklenburg, 173–216 (Washington, D.C.: National Gallery of Art, 1991).
4. D. Erhardt and M. Mecklenburg, "Relative Humidity Re-examined," in *Preventive Conservation Practice, Theory, and Research, Preprint of the Contributions to the Ottawa Congress, 12–16 September*, 32–38 (London: International Institute for Conservation, 1994).
5. G. Scott, "Moisture, Ventilation, and Mould Growth," in *Preventive Conservation Practice, Theory, and Research, Preprints of the Contributions to the Ottawa Congress, 12–16 September*, 149–53 (London: International Institute for Conservation, 1994).
6. Scott, "Moisture."
7. Michalski, "Relative Humidity in Museums."
8. W. Rose, *Water in Buildings: An Architect's Guide to Moisture and Mold* (Hoboken, N.J.: Wiley, 2005).
9. S. Michalski, "Relative Humidity: A Discussion of Correct/Incorrect Values," *Preprints of the ICOM Committee for Conservation, 10th Triennial Meeting, Working Group 17, Lighting and Climate Control* (Washington, D.C.: ICOM-CC, 1993), 624.
10. Michalski, "Relative Humidity: A Discussion," 624.
11. Michalski, "Relative Humidity: A Discussion," 624.
12. Michalski, "Relative Humidity: A Discussion," 624.
13. Michalski, "Relative Humidity: A Discussion," 624.
14. Barbara Heller, personal communication.
15. R. L. Kerschner, "A Practical Approach to Environmental Requirements for Collections in Historic Buildings," *Journal of the American Institute for Conservation* 31 (1992): 65–76.
16. Erhardt and Mecklenburg, "Relative Humidity Re-examined," 32–38.
17. Michalski, "Relative Humidity in Museums," 51–62.
18. Michalski, "Relative Humidity in Museums," 51–62.
19. Michalski, "Relative Humidity in Museums," 51–62.
20. Image Permanence Institute, *Step by Step Workbook: Achieving a Preservation Environment for Collections* (Rochester, N.Y.: Rochester Institute of Technology, 2005), 22.
21. Image Permanence Institute, *Step by Step Workbook*, 17.
22. Image Permanence Institute, *Step by Step Workbook*, 18.
23. R. Kerschner, "Implementation of Practical Climate Control Strategies at the Shelburne Museum," in *Conservation of Heritage Interiors, Preprints of a Conference Symposium 2000, Ottawa, Canada, May 17–20* (Ottawa, Ont.: Canadian Conservation Institute and the Association for Preservation Technology, 2000); R. Nylander and N. Carlisle, "The Codman House: A Case Study in Preserving and Interpreting Context," in *Conservation in Context: Finding a Balance for the Historic House Museum, Proceedings from the Symposium, March 7–8*, edited by W. C. Jessup (Washington, D.C.: Andrew Mellon Trust and National Trust for Historic Preservation, 1994), 1002.
24. Garry Thomson, *The Museum Environment*, 2nd ed. (Oxford, UK: Butterworth-Heinemann, 1986).
25. ASHRAE 52, www.ashrae.org.
26. P. Ward Moser, "All the Real Dirt on Dust," *Discover* (November 1986): 106–15.
27. R. Androsko, Curator of Textiles, "Memorandum: Internal Report on the Star Spangled Banner Conservation Project," National Museum of American History, Smithsonian Institution, December 1981.
28. P. Hatchfield, *Formaldehyde: How Great Is the Danger to Museum Collections?* (Cambridge, Mass.: Center for Conservation and Technical Studies, Harvard University Art Museums, 1987); T. Padfield, D. Erhardt, and W. Hopwood, "Trouble in Store," in *Science and Technology in the Service of Conservation, Preprints of the Washington D.C. Congress of the International Institute for Conservation*, edited by N. S. Brommelle and Garry Thomson (Washington, D.C.: ICOM-CC, 1982), 24–27; C. E. Miles, "Wood Coatings for Display and Storage Cases," *Studies in Conservation* 31, no. 3 (1986): 114–24; and Philadelphia Museum of Art, "What Effect Does Exposure to Indoor Air Pollutants Have on a Museum's Collections?" www.philamuseum.org/collections/22-393-209.html?page=4.
29. www.buydraegertubes.com/draegertubes.aspx.

30. J. A. Bamberger, E. G. Howe, and G. Wheeler, "A Variant Oddy Test Procedure for Evaluating Materials Used in Storage and Display Cases," *Studies in Conservation* 44, no. 2 (1999): 86–90; Art Conservation Research Center, "Oddy Test," www.cmu.edu/acrc/oddy_test.htm; and Joseph Bamberger, "The Oddy Test Improved," Metropolitan Museum of Art, www.metmuseum.org/Works_of_Art/objects_conservation/spring_2003/oddy.asp.
31. www.orionanalytical.com.
32. An excellent in-depth discussion of the topic can be found in Sharon C. Park, *Heating, Ventilating and Cooling Historic Buildings*, National Park Service Preservation Briefs 24, www.nps.gov/history/hps/TPS/briefs/brief24.htm (accessed May 19, 2009).
33. The Old House Web, "Heating, Ventilating, and Cooling Historic Buildings: Problems and Recommended Approaches, History of Mechanical Systems," www.oldhouseweb.com/how-to-advice/historical-mechanical-systems.shtml.
34. The Old House Web, "Heating, Ventilating, and Cooling Historic Buildings."
35. The Old House Web, "Heating, Ventilating, and Cooling Historic Buildings."
36. T. E. Mull, *HVAC Principles and Applications Manual* (New York: McGraw-Hill, 1998), 10.1–10.25.

CHAPTER 10

1. Sharon C. Park, "Holding the Line: Controlling Unwanted Moisture in Historic Buildings," NPS Preservation Brief 39, www.nps.gov/history/hps/tps/briefs/brief39.htm (accessed 4 July 2009).
2. 206.180.235.135/waac/wn/wn13/wn13-1/wn13-107.html (accessed 29 August 2009).
3. National Park Service, "Integrated Pest Management: Museum Pests," at www.nps.gov/phso/ipm/museum.htm (accessed 4 July 2009), has numerous links including applicable Conserve O Grams on pests. Several universities and government agencies contribute information and images to The Bugwood Network, www.insectimages.org (accessed 4 July 2009). Insects Limited has a tab for museum pests at www.insectslimited.com (accessed 4 July 2009). Museum professionals can network on IPM issues at www.museumpests.net/newpage/default.html (accessed 4 July 2009).
4. The Centers for Disease Control and Prevention have excellent information about symptoms at cdc.gov/ncidod/diseases/hanta/hps and procedures on rodent control at www.cdc.gov/rodents (accessed 4 July 2009).
5. See www.cdc.gov/nczved/dfbmd/disease_listing/histoplasmosis_gi.html (accessed 4 July 2009).
6. Ellen M. Carrlee, "Summary of Potential Artifact Damage from Low Temperature Pest Management," *Postprints of the Textile Conservation Group of the American Institute for Conservation, Joint Session with the Objects Specialty Group, Miami*, Vol. 12 (Washington, D.C.: American Institute for Conservation, 2001), 75–83.
7. David Pinninger, Annette Townsend, and Adrian Meyer, *Pest Management in Museums, Archives, and Historic Houses* (London: Archetype, 2001).

CHAPTER 11

1. Robert R. Page, Cathy A. Gilbert, and Susan A. Dolan, *A Guide to Cultural Landscape Reports: Contents, Process, and Techniques*, rev. ed. (Washington, D.C.: National Park Service, 2005).
2. Charles A. Birnbaum, "Protecting Cultural Landscapes: Planning, Treatment, and Management of Historic Landscapes," www.nps.gov/hps/tps/briefs/brief36.htm (accessed 29 October 2008).
3. National Register publications and guidelines can be found at www.nps.gov/history/nr/publications/bulletins.htm (accessed 29 October 2008).
4. www.nps.gov/history/hps/tps/publications.htm (accessed 25 May 2009).
5. Charles A. Birnbaum and Christine Capella Peters, eds., *The Secretary of the Interior's Standards for the Treatment of Historic Properties with Guidelines for the Treatment of Cultural Landscapes* (Washington, D.C.: National Park Service, 1996); also available at www.nps.gov/history/hps/hli/landscape_guidelines/using.htm (accessed 29 October 2008).
6. Alexander Jackson Downing, *A Treatise on the Theory and Practice of Landscape Gardening as Adapted to North America*, 6th ed. (1841; New York: A. O. Moore, 1859).
7. Catherine Howett, *Georgia's Living Places: Historic Houses in Their Landscaped Settings* (Atlanta: Historic Preservation Section, Division of Parks, Recreation, and Historic Sites, Georgia Department of Natural Resources, 1991).
8. Margaret Coffin and Regina M. Bellavia, *Guide to Developing a Preservation Maintenance Plan for a Historic Landscape* (Boston: Olmsted Center for Landscape Preservation, National Park Service, 1995).

CHAPTER 12

1. Kay D. Weeks and Anne E. Grimmer, *The Secretary of the Interior's Standards for the Treatment of Historic Properties with Guidelines for Preserving, Rehabilitating, Restoring, and Reconstructing Historic Buildings* (Washington, D.C.: U.S. Department of the Interior, National Park Service, Cultural Resources Stewardship and Partnerships, Heritage Preservation Services, 1995).
2. The Sixth International Congress of Architects, Madrid, articulated the first internationally recognized conservation principles in 1904, with "The Preservation and Restoration of Architectural Monuments." In 1932 member countries in the Assembly of the League of Nations signed the Athens Charter for the Restoration of

Historic Monuments. Development and adoption of common guides continued in 1964 by UNESCO with the Venice Charter, arguably the most widely known and followed charter. As refined over the last forty-five years by ICOMOS (International Council on Monuments and Sites), the principles have consistently recognized that cultural properties are of outstanding universal value from the point of view of history, art, science, ethnology, and anthropology. Since the UNESCO Convention of 1970, a more extensive definition of movable cultural property has been adopted to prohibit and prevent the illicit import, export, and transfer of cultural properties. For this reason the UNESCO and ICOMOS general definitions of cultural properties now differentiate those that are movable from those that are immovable.

3. Stewart Brand, *How Buildings Learn: What Happens after They're Built* (New York: Viking Penguin, 1994), 110.
4. Brand, *How Buildings Learn*, 2–13.
5. Brand, *How Buildings Learn*, 12–13.
6. Refer to *The Secretary of the Interior's Standards for the Treatment of Historic Properties* (United States) and the ICOMOS charters of Burra, New Zealand, and Appleton for the definitions of *preservation*, *rehabilitation*, and *restoration* used in this chapter. The AIC (American Institute for the Conservation of Historic and Artistic Works) definition for *preservation* is similar to the U.S. and international definitions. The process of rehabilitation is not defined by the AIC, perhaps because modification of archaeological artifacts, artistic works, statuary, and monuments and objects to provide a contemporary function is not common. As defined in the Burra and New Zealand charters, *restoration* means "returning the existing fabric of a place to a known earlier state by removing accretions or by reassembling existing components without the introduction of new materials." The U.S. Secretary of the Interior's standards allow for the construction of missing elements using new materials, if the replacement of missing features from the restoration period is not conjectural and they are substantiated by documentation and physical evidence. The Secretary of the Interior's restoration standards permit limited and sensitive upgrading of mechanical, electrical, and plumbing systems and other code-required work to make a property functional. AIC defines *restoration* as a "procedure intended to return cultural property to a known or assumed state, often through the addition of non-original material."
7. To inventory the collections means to produce a comprehensive list of objects. To inventory the structures means to produce a comprehensive list of immovable assets owned or managed by the museum, if there is more than one structure. For a museum with a single asset, inventorying the structure can be the identification of rooms, spaces, parts, and character-defining features of the building.
8. Documentation for the structures is analogous to cataloguing for the movable collection. Documentation includes drawings such as those produced in conformity with Historic American Building Survey standards and the Historic Structure Report.
9. The form used to nominate buildings to the National Register of Historic Places has a section that discusses the historical significance of a structure. The form can help in understanding the value of the building.
10. Preservation Brief 17, *Architectural Character: Identifying the Visual Aspects of Historic Buildings as an Aid to Preserving Their Character*, by Lee H. Nelson, FAIA, discusses building authenticity and architectural features. The brief is one of a series of guides developed by the U.S. Department of the Interior, National Park Service, Heritage Preservation Services Division to provide assistance to property owners. Available digitally through the National Park Service, Heritage Preservation Services, or as a hard copy through the U.S. Government Printing Office, Washington, D.C. 20402.
11. Preservation Brief 16, *The Use of Substitute Materials on Historic Building Exteriors*, by Sharon C. Park, AIA, provides guidance on the use of replacement materials.
12. For understanding the philosophical difference between preservation and rehabilitation and how that affects treatment practices, see *The Secretary of the Interior's Standards for the Treatment of Historic Properties with Guidelines for Preserving, Rehabilitating, Restoring and Reconstructing Historic Buildings*. The standards with guidelines are available as a book through the U.S. Government Printing Office and in digital format through the National Park Service website at www.nps.gov/history/hps/tps/standguide (accessed 29 August 2009). There are four treatments recognized by the Secretary of the Interior: preservation, rehabilitation, restoration, and reconstruction.
13. International charters starting with the 1979 Burra Charter, the 1993 Code of Ethics, and the 1996 Sophia Principles recommend that conservation work start with the physical features of a site being fully recorded and placed in a public archive before any intervention proceeds.
14. The Historic American Buildings Survey, the Historic American Engineering Record, and the Historic American Landscape Survey (HABS/HAER/HALS) are all programs of the U.S. Department of the Interior, National Park Service. Standards were developed for documentation as part of the 1980 revisions to the National Historic Preservation Act. The Secretary of the Interior was directed to develop "a uniform process and standards for documenting historic properties by public agencies and private parties for purposes of incorporation into, or complementing, the national historical architectural and engineering records within the Library of Congress." These standards derived from existing HABS and HAER standards. *The Secretary of the Inte-*

rior's Standards and Guidelines for Architectural and Engineering Documentation (hereafter referred to as HABS/HAER standards) were published in 1983 as part of "Archeology and Historic Preservation; Secretary of the Interior's Standards and Guidelines" (*Federal Register*, 29 September 1983). See also Charles Peterson, foreword from *Recording Historic Structures: Historic American Buildings Survey/Historic American Engineering Records*, ed. John A. Burns and the staff of HABS/HAER, 2nd ed. (Washington, D.C.: National Park Service, U.S. Department of the Interior, 2004), or the National Park Service at www.nps.gov/history/hdp (accessed 26 May 2009).

15. The significance is based on U.S. National Register of Historic Places criteria. Not all house museums are listed on the National Register of Historic Places, nor do they need to be for the property to be an important heritage property. Criteria from the National Register are used as the example because it is acknowledged as the standard upon which to judge the relative importance of a property. A period of significance is developed if the owner has not previously determined what period in the building's history is important or if legislation has not prescribed the date of importance. Periodically it is worthwhile to reevaluate a building's period of significance because of new research findings or because the physical fabric of a building has integrity to a period other than the original construction or other than the owner's currently designated period of significance.
16. The National Park Service produces a series of technical documents on preservation of older buildings. Preservation Brief 17 describes how to determine the character-defining features of a structure, www.nps.gov/history/hps/tps/briefs/brief17.htm.
17. Typical HABS documentation is an accurate record of what can be seen on the surface of a structure, as it existed at the time the building was measured. Research on the structure's history can be part of the document. However, HABS documentation excludes investigation within walls and floors, forensics of a building's construction and materials, inspections with analysis and evaluation of conditions, and research into the physical changes that have occurred to a building over time. Historic Structure Reports and comprehensive condition assessments are documents that contain in-depth information.
18. Because treatment plans and interpretation of a house museum usually are based on a single period of time, it is important to have a clear understanding of what the building's period of significance is and what integrity the building and its setting retain from that period, if any. International charters for the preservation and protection of heritage sites emphasize the retention of the evolved site (building) rather than removal or reconstruction of building parts to recreate a place as it appeared during a single time in history. At the time of this writing, the typical historic house museum in the United States is restored and managed to represent one period in the life of the building.
19. Knowing which code to follow can be confusing. It is the responsibility of the licensed architects and engineers to be familiar with the codes that apply to a particular building. The life/safety, health, and zoning codes to which a house museum must adhere are dependent on the code adopted by the government having jurisdiction over that property. States within the United States tend to adopt one of several model building codes; then the state, county, or city may modify these model codes to fit the conditions within their area. In 2001 the International Code Council released a model code, the International Building Code (IBC). It has been adopted by most states. The IBC, which has clauses that address existing buildings, has superseded most building codes oriented specifically to historic structures. Local zoning regulations and historic district overlays can affect work on historic house museums. Not associated with the other building code groups, the National Fire Protection Association (NFPA) develops and maintains more than three hundred codes and standards to provide safety to life and protection of property. Government, insurance, and industry officials throughout the world use NFPA codes. NFPA code 909 addresses cultural resources, and code 914 covers fire protection of historic structures.
20. Some information in a Historic Structure Report has a longer "shelf life" than other data. Information about a building's history, its significance, and its character-defining features does not become dated as quickly as information about conditions. Recommendations to correct code deficiencies and deteriorated conditions are usable for a short time period—one to five years. This is because of the dynamic nature of buildings and also because of changes to building codes. Sometimes only the engineering systems, architectural fabric conditions, and building code analysis need to be updated to provide the information to implement a conservation program.
21. The Institute of Museum and Library Services, Heritage Preservation, has established standards for building assessments funded through its grant program.
22. Preservation Brief 35, *Understanding Old Buildings: The Process of Architectural Investigation*, by Travis C. McDonald Jr., is a useful reference when beginning a Historic Structure Report or condition assessment.
23. Not all buildings require an expensive and exhaustive investigation, but all historic house museum buildings deserve some evaluation by building professionals along with documentation of their findings.
24. Reference *The Secretary of the Interior's Standards for Professionals and International Charters.*
25. Integrated conservation is a concept emphasized in all the international (ICOMOS) charters and declarations. The charters' emphasis on this is summarized in

D. Bell's *Technical Advice Note 8: The Historic Scotland Guild to International Conservation Charters* (Edinburgh: Historic Scotland, 1997): "No part of a building can be usefully considered in isolation from the rest of the fabric, no building can be evaluated without including its use and its inhabitants and no site is unaffected by the sometimes contradictory demands of society. All Charters underline the need of those involved in work on protected sites not only to have sufficient expertise and experience of their own discipline but to be able to appreciate problems and to ask for and accept the expertise of others."

26. Raymond C. Matulionis and Joan C. Freitag, eds., *Preventive Maintenance of Buildings* (New York: Van Nostrand Reinhold, 1991), 29.
27. Matulionis and Freitag, *Preventive Maintenance*, 29.

CHAPTER 13

1. American Institute for Conservation (AIC-CERT), www.conservation-us.org/index.cfm?fuseaction=Page.viewPage&pageId=593&parentID=472 (accessed 30 June 2009).
2. Heritage Preservation: Heritage Emergency National Task Force, www.heritagepreservation.org/programs/taskfer.htm (accessed 13 February 2009). Heritage Preservation also has an excellent reference *Field Guide to Emergency Response* which includes an instructional DVD. They have downloadable forms at their website, such as a disaster supply shopping list that will help an institution create its plan: www.heritagepreservation.org/pubs/fgforms.htm (accessed 29 May 2009).
3. National Park Service *Primer for Disaster Preparedness, Management and Response,* www.nps.gov/history/museum/publications/primer/primintro.html, and "Curatorial Safety Messages," www.nps.gov/history/museum/safety/index.htm (accessed 13 February 2009). See also "Cultural Shock: Fire Protection for Historic and Cultural Property 1995-01," www.ncptt.nps.gov/index.php/culture-shock-fire-protection-for-historic-and-cultural-property-1995-01 (accessed 13 February 2009); "Development of a Prototypical Fire Risk Index to Evaluate Fire Safety in Historic Buildings," www.ncptt.nps.gov/development-of-a-prototypical-historic-fire-risk-index-to-evaluate-fire-safety-in-historic-buildings-1998-08; and "dPlan," at www.ncptt.nps.gov/category/disaster-recovery (accessed 29 August 2009).
4. National Park Service, *Museum Handbook, Part 1,* "Emergency Planning," www.nps.gov/history/museum/publications/mhi/chap10a-b.pdf and www.nps.gov/history/museum/publications/mhi/chap10c-f.pdf (accessed 29 May 2009).
5. Getty Art Museum, getty.art.museum/conservation/publications/pdf_publications/emergency_plan.pdf; Northeast Document Center, www.dplan.org (accessed 29 May 2009); and list of museum disaster plans at 206.180.235.135/bytopic/disasters (accessed 29 August 2009).
6. Paul Baril, "Fire Prevention Programs for Museums," Technical Bulletin No. 18 (Ottawa, Ont.: Canadian Conservation Institute, Department of Canadian Heritage, 1997).
7. American Society for Industrial Security (ASIS) is an organization for security professionals and has a Museum, Library, and Archive Security Council. Visit their website at www.asisonline.org. In 2002 ASIS and the AAM jointly adopted "Suggested Guidelines in Museum Security." See www.stevekeller.com/Steve_Keller_&_Associates_Website/Articles_and_Downloads_files/GuidelinesRev2002.pdf (accessed 2 June 2009).

CHAPTER 14

1. *The American Heritage College Dictionary*, 3rd ed. (Boston: Houghton Mifflin, 1993).

Bibliography

40 Code of Federal Regulations (CFR) 260-267. Hazardous Waste Management Regulations. Washington, D.C.: U.S. Government Printing Office, 2006.

Adams, Stuart, Peter Brimblecombe, and Young Hun Yoon. "Comparison of Two Methods for Measuring the Deposition of Indoor Dust." *Conservator* 25 (2001): 90–94.

Adams, Stuart, Katherine Eremin, and James Tate. "Monitoring of Deposited Particle Levels within the Royal Museum of Scotland: Distribution Patterns and the Effects of Nearby Construction Work." *Conservation Science 2002, Papers from the Conference held in Edinburgh, Scotland, 22–24 May.* London: Archetype, 2002.

Alaska State Museum. "Basic Techniques for Making and Mounting Exhibit Labels." April 27, 2007. www.museums.state.ak.us/Bulletin/makinglabels.html (accessed 29 May 2009).

American Association for State and Local History. "Housekeeping" (slide/tape program). Nashville, Tenn.: American Association for State and Local History, n.d.

American Institute for Conservation of Historic and Artistic Works (AIC). *Code of Ethics and Guidelines for Practice.* www.conservation-us.org/index.cfm?fuseaction=page.viewPage&pageID=858&nodeID=1 and www.conservation-us.org (accessed 29 May 2009).

———. "Current Conservation Treatment and Practices, Storage VIII." In *The Textile Specialty Group Catalogue* (Washington, D.C.: AIC, 1998).

———. *Directory.* Washington, D.C.: American Institute for Conservation, 2007.

American Society for Industrial Security (ASIS). "Suggested Guidelines in Museum Security." www.stevekeller.com/Steve_Keller_&_Associates_Website/Articles_and_Downloads_files/GuidelinesRev2002.pdf (accessed 2 June 2009).

American Society of Heating, Refrigerating, and Air-Conditioning Engineers (ASHRAE). *Handbook of Fundamentals.* Atlanta, Ga.: ASHRAE, 1989.

Anderson Notter Associates. *The Salem Handbook: A Renovation Guide for Homeowners.* Salem, Mass.: Historic Salem, 1977.

Androsko, Rita. Memorandum: Internal Report on the Star Spangled Banner Conservation Project. National Museum of American History: Smithsonian Institution, December 1981.

Appelbaum, Barbara. *Guide to Environmental Protection of Collections.* Madison, Conn.: Sound View Press, 1991.

Art Conservation Research Center. "Oddy Test." www.cmu.edu/acrc/oddy_test.htm.

Ashley-Smith, J. *Risk Assessment for Object Conservation.* Oxford, UK: Butterworth-Heinemann, 1999.

Ashurst, John, and Nicola Ashurst. *Practical Building Conservation.* Hants, UK: Gower Tower Press, 1988.

Ashurst, Nicola. *Cleaning Historic Buildings.* 2 vols. London: Donhead, 1994.

Babin, A., and M. McCann. *Waste Management and Disposal for Artists and Schools.* New York: Center for Safety in the Arts, 1992.

Bacci, Mauro, et al. "Indoor Environmental Monitoring of Colour Changes of Tempera-Painted Dosimeters." In *ICOM Committee for Conservation, 12th Triennial Meeting, Lyon, 29 August–3 September, Preprints.* Vol. 1. London: James & James, 1999.

Bachmann, Konstanze, ed. *Conservation Concerns: A Guide for Collectors and Curators.* Washington, D.C.: Smithsonian Institution Press, 1992.

———. *Conservation Concerns: A Guide to Collections Care.* Washington, D.C.: Smithsonian Institution Press, 2001.

Baker, Rex O., Gerald R. Bodman, and Robert M. Timm. "Rodent-Proof Construction and Exclusion Methods." In *Prevention and Control of Wildlife Damage,* edited by Scott E. Hygnstrom, Robert M. Timm, and Gary E. Larson. Lincoln: University of Nebraska Coop Extension, 1994.

Ball, Stephen, and Peter Winsor, eds. *Larger and Working Objects: A Guide to Their Preservation.* London: Museum and Galleries Commission, 1997.

———. *Standards in the Museum Care of Larger and Working Objects.* London: Museum and Galleries Commission, 1994.

Bamberger, Joseph. "The Oddy Test Improved." Metropolitan Museum of Art, www.metmuseum.org/Works_of_Art/objects_conservation/spring_2003/oddy.asp.

Bamberger, J. A., E. G. Howe, and G. Wheeler. "A Variant Oddy Test Procedure for Evaluating Materials Used in Storage and Display Cases." *Studies in Conservation* 44, no. 2 (1999): 86–90.

Baril, Paul. "Fire Prevention Programs for Museums." Technical Bulletin No. 18. Ottawa, Ont.: Canadian Conservation Institute, 1997.

———. "Fire Protection Issues for Historic Buildings." Ottawa, Ont.: Canadian Conservation Institute, 1998.

Beard, Geoffrey. *Upholsterers and Interior Furnishing in England, 1530–1840.* New Haven, Conn.: Yale University Press, 1997.

Bell, D. *The Historic Scotland Guide to International Conservation Charters.* Edinburgh: Historic Scotland, 1997.

Bendix, Caroline, and Chris Calnan. "Dust Monitoring in National Trust Libraries." *Paper Conservation News* 102 (2002): 14–15.

Bennett, Gary W., John M. Owens, and Robert M. Corrigan. *Truman's Scientific Guide to Pest Control Operations.* Duluth, Minn.: Edgell Communications, 1988.

Bertalan, S. "Mold: How It Grows and Causes Damage to Archival Collections." *American Archivist,* Special Preservation Issue (1991): 58–62.

Best Manufacturing. "Disposable Nitrile Glove Is Accelerator Free." 14 July 2003. www.techniglove.com/nitrile.html (accessed 29 May 2009).

Birnbaum, Charles A. "Protecting Cultural Landscapes: Planning, Treatment, and Management of Historic Landscapes." www.nps.gov/hps/tps/briefs/brief36.htm (accessed 29 October 2008).

Birnbaum, Charles A., and Robin Karson, eds. *Pioneers of American Landscape Design.* New York: McGraw-Hill. 2000.

Birnbaum, Charles A., and Christine Capella Peters, eds. *Making Educated Decisions: A Landscape Preservation Bibliography.* Washington, D.C.: National Park Service, 1995.

———. *The Secretary of the Interior's Standards for the Treatment of Historic Properties with Guidelines for the Treatment of Cultural Landscapes.* Washington, D. C.: National Park Service, 1996.

Bishop Museum. "Care of Silver." 1996. www.bishopmuseum.org/research/pdf/cnsv-silver.pdf (accessed 29 May 2009).

Blackaby, James R., Patricia Greeno, and the Nomenclature Committee. *The Revised Nomenclature for Museum Cataloging: A Revised and Expanded Edition of Robert G. Chenhall's System for Classifying Man-Made Objects.* Walnut Creek, Calif.: AltaMira Press, 1995.

Blumenthal, Sara K., comp. *Federal Historic Preservation Laws.* Washington, D.C.: U.S. Department of the Interior, National Park Service, Cultural Resources Programs, 1993.

Bock, Gordon. "Composition Shingles of the 1920s and 1930s." *Old House Journal* 18, no. 3 (May–June 1990): 28–31.

———. "Making Sense of Metal Roofs." *Old House Journal* 20, no. 4 (July–August 1992): 30–33.

———. "Wood-Shingle Roof Care." *Old House Journal* 18, no. 3 (May–June 1990): 36–38.

Borror, Donald J., and Richard E. White. *A Field Guide to Insects: America North of Mexico.* 2nd ed. Boston: Houghton Mifflin, 1998.

Bowman, Janet Gilliland, and Barbara M. Reagan. "Filtered and Unfiltered Lights and Their Effects on Selected Dyed Textiles." *Studies in Conservation* 28 (1983): 35–44.

Bradley, S. "Development of an Environmental Policy for the British Museum." In *Preprints of the 11th Triennial Meeting, Edinburg, 1–6 September,* Vol. 1, ICOM-CC. London: James and James, 1996.

Brand, Stewart. *How Buildings Learn: What Happens after They're Built.* New York: Viking Penguin, 1994.

Brereton, Christopher. *The Repair of Historic Buildings.* London: English Heritage, 1995.

Brill, Thomas. *Light.* New York: Plenum Press, 1980.

Bromelle, N. S., Garry Thomson, and Perry Smith, eds. *Conservation within Historic Buildings.* London: International Institute for Conservation of Historic and Artistic Works, 1980.

Brown, Dennis B. "Using Natural Ventilation and Other Passive Techniques to Influence Temperature and Humidity in Historic Buildings." *Museums in Historic Buildings Symposium, 23–25 September, New Orleans.* AIC/APT, 1991.

Brown, Robert Wade. *Residential Foundations.* New York: Van Nostrand Reinhold, 1984.

Bruckle, Irene. *North American Graduate Programs in the Conservation of Cultural Properties.* Buffalo, N.Y.: ANAGPIC, 2000.

Bryne, Richard. "On the Roof: How to Inspect and Maintain It." *Canadian Heritage* (February 1982): 38–40.

Buck, R. A., and J. A. Gilmore, eds. *The New Museum Registration Methods.* Washington, D.C.: American Association of Museums, 1998.

Buck, R. D. "Inspecting and Describing the Condition of Art Objects." *Museum News* 56 (May–June 1978): 29–33.

Building Research Council, National Research Council. "Committing to the Cost of Ownership: Maintenance and Repair of Public Buildings." American Public Works Association, Special Report 60. Washington, D.C.: National Academies Press, 1990.

Bullock, Linda, and David Saunders. "Measurement of Cumulative Exposure Using Blue Wool Standards," *ICOM Committee for Conservation, 12th Triennial Meeting, Lyon, 29 August–3 September, Preprints.* Vol. 1. London: James & James, 1999.

Burns, John A., ed. *Recording Historic Structures: Historic American Buildings Survey/Historic American Engineering Record.* Washington, D.C.: National Park Service, 2004.

Burt, S. H., ed. *What Every One Should Know: A Cyclopedia of Practical Information.* New York: A. L. Burt, 1888.

Butcher-Younghans, Sherry. *Historic House Museums: A Practical Handbook for Their Care, Preservation, and Management.* New York: Oxford University Press, 1993.

Butcher-Younghans, Sherry, and Gretchen E. Anderson. "Technical Leaflet #171: A Holistic Approach to Museum Pest Management." *History News* 45, no. 3 (May–June 1990).

Buys, Susan, and Victoria Oakley. *The Conservation and Restoration of Ceramics.* Oxford, UK: Butterworth-Heinemann, 1993.

Calnan, C., and B. Haines, eds. *Leather: Its Composition and Changes with Time.* Northampton, UK: Leather Conservation Centre, 1991.

Canadian Conservation Institute (CCI). *Dealing with the Fungal Problem in Museums.* Ottawa, Ont.: Canadian Conservation Institute.

———. *Dealing with the Insect Problem in Museums: Prevention, Identification, and Non-Chemical Control.* Ottawa, Ont.: Canadian Conservation Institute.

———. *Examining for Insect Infestations.* Ottawa, Ont.: Canadian Conservation Institute, 1996.

———. *A Guide to the Preservation of Archival Materials.* Ottawa, Ont.: Canadian Conservation Institute, 1977.

———. *A Light Damage Slide Rule.* Ottawa, Ont.: Canadian Conservation Institute, 1988.

———. *Mount-Making for Museum Objects.* Ottawa, Ont.: Canadian Conservation Institute, 1998.

———. *Slide Rule to Determine Light Damage.* Special Publication. Ottawa, Ont.: Canadian Conservation Institute, 1994.

———. *Ultraviolet Filters.* Ottawa, Ont.: Canadian Conservation Institute, 1994.

———. *Using a Camera to Measure Light Levels.* Ottawa, Ont.: Canadian Conservation Institute, 1989.

Carrlee, Ellen M. "Summary of Potential Artifact Damage from Low Temperature Pest Management." *Postprints of the Textile Group of the American Institute for Conservation, Joint Session with the Objects Specialty Group, Miami,* Vol. 12, 75–83. Washington, D.C.: American Institute for Conservation, 2001.

Cedar Mesa Project. "Antiquities Laws and Regulations." Cedar Mesa Project. bcn.boulder.co.us/environment/cacv/cacvregs.htm (accessed 29 May 2009).

Chambers, J. Henry. *Cyclical Maintenance for Historic Buildings.* Washington, D.C.: U.S. Department of the Interior, National Park Service, 1976.

Chicago Conservation Center. "Rug Identification Notes." chicagoconservation.com/pages/rug_id.htm (accessed 21 May 2009).

Child, Robert E., ed. *Electronic Environmental Monitoring in Museums.* London: Archetype, 1993.

———. "Insect Damage as a Function of Climate." In *Museum Microclimates,* edited by Tim Padfield and Karen Borchersen. Copenhagen: National Museum of Denmark, 2007.

Chimney Safety Institute of America. "Chimney Liners." July 17, 2003. www.csia.org/HomeownerResources/ChimneySafetyInfo/AboutChimneyLiners/tabid/117/Default.aspx (accessed 29 May 2009).

Christiansen, Monty L. *Vandalism Control Management for Parks and Recreation Areas.* State College, Pa: Venture Publishing, 1983.

Clapp, Anne F. *Curatorial Care of Works of Art on Paper.* New York: Lyons & Burford, 1987.

Clean Air Delivery Rate (CADR). "About Air Cleaners." www.cadr.org/consumer-aircleaners.htm (accessed 29 May 2009).

Coffin, Margaret, and Regina M. Bellavia. *Guide to Developing a Preservation Maintenance Plan for a Historic Landscape.* Boston: Olmsted Center for Landscape Preservation, 1995.

Coleman, Laurence Vail. *Historic House Museums.* Washington, D.C.: American Association of Museums, 1933.

Collings, Janet. *Old House Care and Repair.* London: Donhead, 2002.

Commoner, L. A. "Warning Signs: When Textiles Need Conservation." In *Conservation Concerns: A Guide for Collectors and Curators,* edited by K. Bachmann, 85–90. Washington, D.C.: Smithsonian Institution Press, 1992.

Craddock, Ann Brooke. "Control of Temperature and Humidity in Small Institutions." Bulletin no. 7. New York: Cooper-Hewitt Museum/New York State Conservation Consultancy, 1985.

Crews, Patricia Cox. "A Comparison of Clear Versus Yellow Ultraviolet Filters in Reducing Fading of Selected Dyes." *Studies in Conservation* 33 (1988): 87–93.

———. "A Comparison of Selected UV-Filtering Materials for the Reduction of Fading." *Journal of the American Institute for Conservation* 28 (1989): 117–25.

Cuthbertson, B. "The Federal Hazardous Waste Regulations for Household Hazardous Waste Collection Programs." Proceedings of the Fifth National Conference on Household Hazardous Waste Management, November 5–7, 1990, San Francisco.

Cutkomp, L. K., and Mark Ascerno. *Silverfish and Firebrats and Their Control.* Minneapolis: University of Minnesota Agricultural Extension Service, 1981.

———. *Woodborers, Bark Beetles, Seed Insects in Houses.* Minneapolis: University of Minnesota Agricultural Extension Service, 1985.

Cuttle, C. "A Proposal to Reduce the Exposure to Light of Museum Objects without Reducing Illuminance or the Level of Visual Satisfaction of Museum Visitors." *Journal of the American Institute for Conservation* 39 (2000): 229–44.

Cuttle, K. "Exhibit Lighting and Conservation." In *Museum Exhibit Lighting: Beyond Edison: Lighting for the Next Century,* presented by National Park Service and Washington Conservation Guild, May 6–8, 1996. Washington, D.C.: National Park Service, 1996.

Dann, Nigel, and Timothy Cantell. "Maintenance: From Philosophy to Practice." *Journal of Architectural Conservation* 1, March 2005.

Darling, P. W. "A Local Preservation Program: Where to Start." *Library Journal* 2343 (1976): 234–38.

Davey, Andy, ed. *The Care and Conservation of Georgian Houses: A Maintenance Manual for Edinburgh New Town.* 4th ed. Oxford, UK: Architectural Press, 1995.

David, Jonathan. "Lighting: Conservation, Preferences, and Practicalities." *Museum Journal* 87 (1987): 141–54.

Davidson, Caroline. *Women's Worlds: The Art and Life of Mary Ellen Best, 1809–1891.* New York: Crown, 1985.

Davis, Gerald, ed. *Building Performance: Function, Preservation, and Rehabilitation.* West Conshohocken, Pa.: American Society for Testing and Materials, 1986.

Davis, Nancy. *Handle with Care: Preserving Your Heirlooms.* Rochester, N.Y.: Rochester Museum and Science Center, 1991.

Davison, Sandra. *Conservation and Restoration of Glass.* 2nd ed. Oxford, UK: Butterworth-Heinemann, 2003.

Denslagen, Wim. *Architectural Restoration in Western Europe: Controversy and Continuity.* Amsterdam: Architectura and Natura Press, 1994.

Derrick, Michele R., et al. "Sulfuryl Fluoride (Vikane): A Review of Its Use as a Fumigant." *Journal of the American Institute for Conservation* 29, no. 1 (1990): 77–90.

Dexter-Lord, G., and B. Lord, eds. *The Manual of Museum Planning,* 2nd ed. London: Altamira Press, 1999.

Dorge, Valerie, and Sharon L. Jones. *Building an Emergency Plan: A Guide for Museums and Other Cultural Institutions.* Los Angeles, Calif.: Getty Conservation Institute, 1999.

Downing, Alexander Jackson. *A Treatise on the Theory and Practice of Landscape Gardening as Adapted to North America.* 6th ed. New York: A. O. Moore, 1859.

dPlan: The Online Disaster-Planning Tool for Cultural and Civic Institutions, www.dplan.org.

Duckworth, W. D., et al. *Preserving Natural Science Collections: Chronicle of Our Environmental Heritage.* Washington, D.C.: National Institute for Conservation, 1993.

Earl, John. *Building Conservation Philosophy.* London: Donhead, 2003.

Eastman Kodak Company. "Conservation of Photographs." Kodak Special Guides, F-40. Rochester, N.Y.: Eastman Kodak Company, 1986.

Eaton, Linda. "Let There Be Light: Winterthur's Lighting Project." In *Textiles Revealed: Object Lessons in Historic Textile and Costume Research,* edited by Mary M. Brooks, 93–98. London: Archetype, 2000.

Edwards, Stephen, et al. *Pest Control in Museums: A Status Report.* Lawrence, Kans.: Association of Systematic Collections, 1988.

Ellis, Margaret Holben. *The Care of Prints and Drawings.* Nashville, Tenn.: American Association for State and Local History, 1987.

Emergency Response and Salvage Wheel. Washington, D.C.: National Institute for Conservation, 2005.

Emerton, Gerald. *The Pattern of Scottish Roofing.* Edinburgh, Scotland: Historic Scotland, Technical Research and Education Division, 2000.

———. *Scottish Conservation Handbook: A Guide to the Conservation and Restoration of Historic Artifacts and Cultural Property.* Edinburgh, Scotland: Historic Scotland, Technical Research and Education Division, 2002.

Environmental Protection Agency (EPA). *Identifying Your Waste: The Starting Point.* EPA Publication No. EPA530-F07-029. Washington, D.C.: Environmental Protection Agency, 1997.

Eremin, Katherine, et al. "Monitoring of Deposited Particle Levels within the Museum of Scotland: During and after Construction." *Conservator* 24 (2002).

Erhardt, David, and Marion Mecklenburg. "Relative Humidity Re-examined." In *Preventive Conservation Practice, Theory, and Research, Preprint of the Contributions to the Ottawa Congress, 12–16 September,* 32–38. London: International Institute for Conservation, 1994.

Erhardt, David, Charles Tumosa, and Marion Mecklenburg. "Applying Science to the Question of Museum Climate." In *Museum Microclimates,* edited by Tim Padfield and Karen Borchersen. Copenhagen: National Museum of Denmark, 2007.

Esposito, William. "IAP 2001, Presentation 21: Field Determination of Particle Filtration Efficiency." iaq.dk/iap/iap2001/2001_21.htm (accessed 26 October 2003).

Fawcett, Jane. *Historic Floors: Their History and Conservation.* Woburn, Mass.: Butterworth-Heinemann, 1998.

Federal Emergency Management Agency (FEMA). "Wind Zones in the United States." www.fema.gov/graphics/library/wmap.gif (accessed 29 May 2009).

Feilden, Bernard M. *Conservation of Historic Buildings.* 3rd ed. Oxford, UK: Architectural Press, 2003.

Feller, Robert L. "Control of Deteriorating Effects of Light upon Museum Objects." In *Contributions to Conservation Science: A Collection of Robert Feller's Published Studies on Artists' Paints, Paper, and Varnishes.* Pittsburgh, Pa.: Carnegie Mellon University Press, 2002.

Fikioris, Margaret A. "Textile Cleaning and Storage." *Museum News* 55, no. 2 (September–October 1976): 13–18.

Fine Art Care and Treatment Standards (FACTS). "500 Years of Art on Paper," 2005. Fine Art Care and Treatment Standards. artfacts.org/artinfo/presentations/500_Years_of_Art/Index.html (accessed 29 May 2009).

Fitch, James Marston. *Historic Preservation: Curatorial Management of the Built World.* Charlottesville: University Press of Virginia, Fourth Dimension of Preservation, 1990.

Florian, Mary-Lou. *Control of Biodeteriorations: Methodology Used in Insect Pest Surveys in Museum Buildings: A Case History.* Rome: International Council of Museums—Committee for Conservation, 1987.

———. *The Effect on Artifact Materials of the Fumigant Ethylene Oxide and Freezing Used in Insect Control.* Rome: International Council of Museums—Committee for Conservation, 1987.

———. "The Freezing Process: Effects on Insects and Artifact Materials." *Leather Conservation News* 3, no. 1 (1986).

———. *Heritage Eaters; Insects and Fungi in Heritage Collections.* London: James & James, 1997.

Florian, Mary-Lou, D. P. Kronkright, and R. E. Norton. *The Conservation of Artifacts Made from Plant Materials.* Los Angeles, Calif.: Getty Conservation Institute, 1990.

Fram, Mark. *Well-Preserved: The Ontario Heritage Foundation's Manual of Principles and Practices for Architectural Conservation.* Erin, Ont.: Boston Mills Press, 1988.

Franklin, Benjamin. *Poor Richard's Almanac.* Philadelphia, Pa.: Benjamin Franklin, 1758.

Friedman, Donald. *The Investigation of Buildings: A Guide for Architects, Engineers, and Owners.* New York: Norton, 2000.

Furr, A. K. *CRC Handbook of Laboratory Safety.* 5th ed. Boca Raton, Fla.: CRC Press, 2000.

Ganiaris, H., and D. Sully. "Showcase Construction: Materials and Methods Used at the Museum of London." *Conservator* 22 (1998): 57–67.

Garrison, James W., and Elizabeth F. Ruffner. "Adobe: Practical and Technical Aspects of Adobe Conservation." Paper presented at a conference held by Heritage Foundation of Arizona, Tucson, Arizona, March 26–28, 1983.

Garskof, Josh. "Wood Shingle Report." *Old House Journal* 22, no. 6 (September–October 1994): 50–51.

Gayle, Margot, David W. Look, and John G. Waite. *Metals in America's Historic Buildings: Use and Preservation Treatments.* Rev. ed. Washington, D.C.: National Park Service, Technical Preservation Services, 1992.

Gerlach, S., et al. "Accelerated Ageing of Light Dosimeters." Paper presented at the CEEES meeting, Nuremberg, Germany, 15 May 2003. db.re.fh-koeln.de/networkExchange/lido/ceees_300303.doc (accessed May 2003).

Getty Conservation Center: "The Conservation Assessment: A Proposed Model for Evaluating Museum Environmental Management Needs." September 1999. www.getty.edu/conservation/publications/pdf_publications/assessmodeleng.pdf (accessed 29 May 2009).

Gilbert, Christopher. *The Life and Work of Thomas Chippendale.* New York: Macmillan, 1978.

Gilliam, Jan Kirsten, and Betty Crowe Leviner. *Furnishing Williamsburg's Historic Buildings.* Williamsburg, Va.: Colonial Williamsburg Foundation, 1991.

Girouard, Mark. *Life in the English Country House.* New Haven, Conn.: Yale University Press, 1978.

Glass, H. *The Servants Directory, Improved; or House-Keepers Companion.* 4th ed. Dublin, printed by J. Potts, at Swift's Head in Dame-Street, 1762.

Goldberg, L., and S. Weintraub. "Health and Safety News." *AIC News* 26, no. 1 (January 2002).

Goodall, Harrison. *Preventive Maintenance for Historic Buildings.* Pueblo West, Colo.: Harrison Goodall, 2001. (Compact disc.)

Grann, David. "A Man out of Time." *New York Times Magazine,* 29 December 2002.

Green, Sara Wolf, ed. *The Conservation Assessment: A Tool for Planning, Implementing, and Fund-Raising,* 2nd ed. Washington, D.C.: Getty Conservation Institute and Heritage Preservation, 1991.

Greenberg, Ronald M., ed. "Creative Teaching with Historic Places." *Cultural Resource Management* 23, no. 8 (2000): 3–52.

———, ed. "*Using* Museum Collections." *Cultural Resource Management* 18, no. 10 (1995): 3–68.

Greenfield, J. *Building a Better Case.* Denver, Colo.: University of Denver, Rocky Mountain Conservation Center, 1992.

Grimmer, Anne E. *Keeping It Clean: Removing Exterior Dirt, Paint, Stains, and Graffiti from Historic Masonry Buildings.* Washington, D.C.: U.S. Department of the Interior, National Park Service, Preservation Assistance Division, 1988.

Grimstad, Kirsten, ed. *Adobe 90 Preprints 6th International Conference on Conservation of Earthen Architecture, Las Cruces, New Mexico, October 14-19, 1990.* Los Angeles, Calif.: Getty Conservation Institute, 1990.

Griswold, Mac, and Eleanor Weller. *The Golden Age of American Gardens.* New York: Abrams, 1991.

Grzywacz, C. M. "Air Quality Monitoring." In *Storage of Natural History Collections: A Preventive Conservation Approach,* edited by C. L. Rose, C. A. Hawks, and H. H. Genoways, 135–46. Iowa City: Society for the Preservation of Natural History Collections, 1995.

Hanson, Shirley, and Nancy Hubby. *Preserving and Maintaining the Older House.* New York: McGraw-Hill, 1983.

Hardiman, Alan. *Tried and Tested (Advice for Owners of Old Buildings in Bath).* Bath, UK: Beacon Books, 1997.

Hardyment, Christina. *Behind the Scenes: Domestic Arrangements in Historic Houses.* New York: Abrams, 1997.

Harris, Samuel Y. *Building Pathology, Deterioration, Diagnostics, and Intervention.* New York: Wiley, 2001.

Hatchfield, Pamela B. *Formaldehyde: How Great Is the Danger to Museum Collections?* Cambridge, Mass.: Center for Conservation and Technical Studies, Harvard University Art Museums, 1987.

———. *Pollutants in the Museum Environment: Practical Strategies for Problem Solving, Exhibition and Storage.* London: Archetype, 2002.

———. "Wood and Wood Products." In *Storage of Natural History Collections: A Preventive Conservation Approach,* edited by C. L. Rose, C. A. Hawks, and H. H. Genoways, 283–90. Iowa City: Society for the Preservation of Natural History Collections, 1995.

Heaver, Melissa M. *Housekeeping for Historic Homes and House Museums.* Washington, D.C.: National Trust for Historic Preservation, 2000.

Hedges, Stoy A. *Field Guide for the Management of Structure Infesting Ants.* Cleveland, Ohio: Franzak & Foster, 1993.

———. *Field Guide for the Management of Structure Infesting Beetles.* Cleveland, Ohio: Franzak & Foster, 1996.

———. *Field Guide for the Management of Structure Infesting Flies.* Cleveland, Ohio: Franzak & Foster, 1994.

Hedges, Stoy A., and Mark S. Lacey. *Field Guide for the Management of Urban Spiders.* Cleveland, Ohio: Franzak & Foster, 1995.

"HEPA-Zone." www.air-zone.com/orderhepazone.asp (accessed 29 May 2009).

Heritage Preservation and National Park Service. *Caring for Your Historic House.* New York: Abrams, 1998.

Historic Preservation Maintenance Procedures. Technical Manual TM5-801-2. Washington, D.C.: Department of the Army, 1977.

Hodges, H. *Artifacts: An Introduction to Early Materials and Technology.* London: Duckworth, 1989.

Hollinger, William K. "Microchamber Papers Used as a Preventive Conservation Material." In *Preventive Conservation: Practice, Theory and Research, Preprints of the Contribution to the Ottawa Congress, 12–16 September 1994,* 212–16.

Holmstrom, Ingmar, and Christina Sandstrom. *Maintenance of Old Buildings: Preservation from the Technical and Antiquarian Standpoint.* Stockholm, Sweden: Central Office of National Antiquities and the National Swedish Institute for Building Research, 1972.

Homes, Hannah. *The Secret Life of Dust: From the Cosmos to the Kitchen Counter; The Big Consequences of Little Things.* New York: Wiley, 2001.

Horie, C. V. "Solar Control Films for Reducing Light Levels in Buildings with Daylight." In *Conservation within Historic Buildings. Preprints of the Contributions to the Vienna Congress, International Institute for Conservation of Historic and Artistic Works, 7–13 September 1980,* 49–54. London: International Institute for Conservation, 1980.

Howell, David, et al. "Monitoring Dust in Historic Houses." *Conservation Science 2002,* Papers from the Conference held in Edinburgh, Scotland, 22–24 May 2002. London: Archetype, 2002.

Howett, Catherine. *Georgia's Living Places: Historic Houses in Their Landscaped Settings.* Atlanta: Georgia Department of Natural Resource, Division of Parks, Recreation, and Historic Sites, Historic Preservation Section, 1991.

Hoy, Suellen. *Chasing Dirt: The American Pursuit of Cleanliness.* Oxford, UK: Oxford University Press, 1995.

Hughes, John, and Jan Valek. *Mortars in Historic Buildings: A Review of the Conservation Technical and Scientific Literature.* Edinburgh: Historic Scotland, 2003.

Hull, Suzanne W. *Chaste, Silent, and Obedient: English Books for Women, 1475–1640.* San Marino, Calif.: Huntington Library, Kingsport Press, 1982.

Image Permanence Institute. *Step by Step Workbook: Achieving a Preservation Environment for Collections.* Rochester, N.Y.: Rochester Institute of Technology, 2005.

International Institute for Conservation of Historic and Artistic Works. *Conservation within Historic Buildings, Vienna Congress.* London: International Institute for Conservation of Historic and Artistic Works, 1980.

International Property Maintenance Code. Country Club Hills, Ill.: International Code Council, 2003.

Iowa, Jerome. *Ageless Adobe: History and Preservation in Southwestern Architecture.* Santa Fe, N.M.: Sunstone Press, 1985.

Jacques, David, ed. "The Techniques and Uses of Garden Archaeology." *Journal of Garden History* 17, no. 1 (1997).

Jenkins, Joseph. *The Slate Roof Bible: Everything You Wanted to Know about Slate Roofs, Including How to Keep Them Alive for Centuries.* Grove City, Pa.: Jenkins, 1997.

Jester, Thomas C., ed. *Twentieth-Century Building Materials: History and Conservation.* New York: McGraw-Hill, 1995.

Jester, Thomas C., and Sharon C. Park. *Making Historic Properties Accessible.* Preservation Brief 32. Washington, D.C.: National Park Service, Preservation Assistance Division, 2003.

Johnson, LeRoy, Jr., ed. *Handbook of Maintenance Techniques for Building Conservation in the Strand Historic District, Galveston, Texas.* Rev. ed. Austin: Texas Historical Commission, 1984.

Judd, Henry A. *Before Restoration Begins: Keeping Your Historic House Intact.* American Association for State and Local History, Technical Leaflet 67. *History News* 28, no. 10 (October 1973).

Keck, Caroline K. *A Handbook on the Care of Paintings.* Nashville, Tenn.: American Association for State and Local History, 1970.

Keller, J. Timothy, and Genevieve P. Keller. *How to Evaluate and Nominate Designed Historic Landscapes.* National Register Bulletin 18. Washington, D.C.: U.S. Department of the Interior, National Park Service, 1994.

Keller, Steven R., and Darrell R. Willson. "Security Systems." In *Storage of Natural History Collections: A Preventive Conservation Approach,* edited by C. L. Rose, C. A. Hawks, and H. H. Genoways, 51–56. Iowa City: Society for the Preservation of Natural History Collections, 1995.

Kerschner, Richard L. "Implementation of Practical Climate Control Strategies at the Shelburne Museum." In *Conservation of Heritage Interiors, Preprints of a Conference Symposium 2000, Ottawa, Canada, May 17–20.* Ottawa, Ont.: Canadian Conservation Institute and the Association for Preservation Technology, 2000.

———. "A Practical Approach to Environmental Requirements for Collections in Historic Buildings." *Journal of the American Institute for Conservation* 31 (1992): 65–76.

Kitchen, Judith L. *Caring for Your Old House.* Washington, D.C.: Preservation Press, 1991.

Knight, Barry. "Measuring Particulates in Historic Buildings: A Comparison of Methodologies." In *Indoor Air Pollution Copenhagen 2001,* Presentation 18, 57–67. iaq.dk/iap/iap2001/2001_18.htm (accessed 29 May 2009).

Knight, Barry, and David Thickett. "Determination of Response Rates of Wooden Objects to Fluctuating Relative Humidity in Historic Properties." In *Museum Microclimates,* edited by Tim Padfield and Karen Borchersen. Copenhagen: National Museum of Denmark, 2007.

Knight, John, ed. *Learning from Our Building: A State of the Practice Summary of Post-Occupancy Evaluations.* Federal Facilities Council Technical Report No. 145. Washington, D.C.: National Academies Press, 2001.

———. *The Repair of Historic Buildings in Scotland: Advice on Principles and Methods.* 3rd ed. Edinburgh: Historic Scotland and English Heritage, 1995.

Lafontaine, R. H., and K. J. Macleod. "A Statistical Survey of Lighting Conditions and the Use of Ultraviolet Filters in Canadian Museums, Archives, and Galleries." *Journal of the Canadian Conservation Institute* 1 (1976): 41–44.

Lavédrine, Bertrand. "The Blue Pink Scale: A New Dosimeter for the Exhibition of Photographs and Sensitive Artifacts." In *Care of Photographic Moving Image and Sound Collections. Conference Papers, July 20–24, 1998*, edited by S. Clark, 121–28. Leigh, UK: Institute of Paper Conservation, 1999.

———. "Mise au point d'un actinometre pour le controle de l'exposition des photographies et des objects sensibles a la lumiere." *ICOM Committee for Conservation, 12th Triennial Meeting, Lyon, 29 August–3 September 1999, Preprints.* Vol. 1. London: James & James, 1999.

———. "The Preservation of France's Cultural Heritage: Preventing Deterioration due to Exposure to Light." *CNRS INFO, Science and Color* 391 (March 2001).

Layman, D. "Lighting Design Terminology: A Mini-Lesson." *Exhibitionist* 13, no. 1 (Spring 1994): 46–47.

Leek, John. "Managing Maintenance," "Exterior Woodwork Details," "Epoxy Repairs for Exterior Wood," "Exterior Wood Columns," and "Wood Gutters." *Practical Restoration Reports.* Portland, Me.: Historic Homeworks, 1994–2007.

Lein, H. L. "Protecting Museums from Threat of Fire." In *Care of Collections*, edited by Simon Knell, 276–79. New York: Routledge, 1994.

Linn, Bjorn. *Conservation of Old Buildings.* Document D6:1975. Stockholm: National Swedish Building Research, 1975.

Lithgow, Katy, Helen Lloyd, Peter Brimblecombe, Y. H. Yoon, and David Thickett. "Managing Dust in Historic Houses: A Visitor/Conservator Interface." In *Preprints, ICOM Committee for Conservation, Fourteenth Triennial Meeting, The Hague, 12–16 September 2005.* London: James & James, 2005, 662–69.

Lively, John, ed. *Fine Homebuilding Questions and Answers about Building.* 2nd ed. Newtown, Conn.: Taunton, 1990.

Lloyd, Helen. "Strategies for Visitor Management at National Trust Properties." In *Fourth European Commission Conference on Research for Protection, Conservation and Enhancement of Cultural Heritage: Opportunities for European Enterprises, Strasbourg 22–24 November 2000*, 165–171. Luxembourg: European Commission, 2002.

Lloyd, Helen, Caroline Bendix, Peter Brimblecombe, and David Thickett. "Dust in Historic Libraries." In *Museum Microclimates*, edited by Tim Padfield and Karen Borchersen. Copenhagen: National Museum of Denmark, 2007.

Lloyd, Helen, Katy Lithgow, Peter Brimblecombe, Young Hun Yoon, Kate Frame, and Barry Knight. "The Effects of Visitor Activity on Dust in Historic Collections." *The Conservator* 26 (2002): 72–84.

London, Mark. *Looking After Your Sash and Case Windows.* Edinburgh: Historic Scotland, Technical Research and Education Division, 2002.

———. *Masonry: How to Care for Old and Historic Brick and Stone.* Washington, D.C.: Preservation Press, 1988.

Long, Jane S., and Richard W. Long. *Caring for Your Family Treasures.* New York: Abrams, 2000.

MacLeish, A. Bruce. *The Care of Antiques and Historical Collections.* Nashville, Tenn.: AltaMira, 1985.

Maekawa, Shin, Burt Ankersmit, Edgar Neuhaus, Henk Schellen, Vincent Beltran, and Foekje Boersma. "Investigation into Impacts of Large Numbers of Visitors on the Collection Environment at Our Lord in the Attic." In *Museum Microclimates*, edited by Tim Padfield and Karen Borchersen. Copenhagen: National Museum of Denmark, 2007.

Magaziner, Henry Jonas, and Robert D. Golding. *The Golden Age of Ironwork.* Ocean Pines, Md.: Skipjack Press, 2000.

Mailand, Harold, and Dorothy Stites Alig. *Preserving Textiles. A Guide for the Non-Specialist.* Indianapolis, Ind.: Indianapolis Museum of Art, 1999.

Mallis, Arnold. *Handbook of Pest Control.* Cleveland, Ohio: Franzak & Foster, 1990.

Marko, Ksynia. *Textiles in Trust.* London: Archetype, 1997.

Matulionis, Raymond C., and Joan C. Freitag, eds. *Preventive Maintenance of Buildings.* New York: Van Nostrand Reinhold, 1991.

McClelland, Linda Flint, Timothy J. Keller, and Genevieve P. Keller. *Guidelines for Evaluating and Documenting Rural Historic Landscapes.* Washington, D.C.: National Park Service, 1990.

McDonald, Maureen A. "Evaluation of UV Glazing Materials." *Environment and Deterioration Research Report No 1012.* Ottawa, Ont.: Canadian Conservation Institute, 1985.

McGiffin, Robert F. *Furniture Care and Conservation.* Nashville, Tenn.: American Association for State and Local History, 1989.

McKean, James N. *Strings Magazine Guide to Common Sense Instrument Care.* San Anselmo, Calif.: Strings Magazine, 1990.

Mecklenburg, M., and C. Tomosa. "Mechanical Behavior of Paintings Subjected to Changes in Temperature and Relative Humidity." In *Art in Transit: Studies in the Transport of Paintings*, edited by M. Mecklenburg, 173–216. Washington, D.C.: National Gallery of Art, 1991.

Melville, Ian, and Ian Gordon. *The Repair and Maintenance of Houses.* London: Estates Gazette, 1979.

Metropolitan Museum of Art. "Biodeterioration in Museum Collections." www.metmuseum.org (accessed 29 May 2009).

Mibach, Lisa. "Collections Care: What to Do When You Can't Afford to Do Anything." *History News.* Technical Leaflet. Nashville, Tenn.: American Association for State and Local History, 2000.

Michalski, Stefan. "The Lighting Decision." In *Fabric of an Exhibition, Preprints of Textile Symposium '97.* Ottawa, Ont.: Canadian Conservation Institute, 1997.

———. "Relative Humidity: A Discussion of Correct/Incorrect Values." *Preprints of the ICOM Committee for Conservation, 10th Triennial Meeting, Working Group 17,*

Lighting and Climate Control (Washington, D.C.: ICOM-CC, 1993).

———. "Relative Humidity in Museums, Galleries, and Archives: Specification and Control." In *Bugs, Mold, and Rot II*, 51–62. Washington, D.C.: National Institute of Building Sciences, 1993.

———. "A Systematic Approach to Preservation: Description and Integration of Other Museum Activities." In *Preventive Conservation: Practice, Theory, and Research. Preprints to the Ottawa Conference, 12–16 September*, 8–11. London: International Institute for Conservation, 1994.

———. *A Systematic Approach to the Conservation (Care) of Museum Collections.* Ottawa, Ont.: Canadian Conservation Institute, 1992.

Miles, C. E. "Wood Coatings for Display and Storage Cases." *Studies in Conservation* 31, no. 3 (1986): 114–24.

Miller, Naomi F., and Kathryn L. Gleason, eds. *The Archeology of Garden and Field.* Philadelphia: University of Pennsylvania Press, 1994.

Mills, Edward, ed. *Building Maintenance and Preservation: A Guide to Design and Management.* Oxford, UK: Architectural Press, 1994.

Milne, Lorus, and Margery Milne. *National Audubon Society Field Guide to North American Insects and Spiders.* New York: Knopf, 1980.

Moore, B. P., and S. L. Williams. "Storage Equipment." In *Storage of Natural History Collections: A Preventive Conservation Approach*, edited by C. L. Rose, C. A. Hawks, and H. H. Genoways, 255–67. Iowa City: Society for the Preservation of Natural History Collections, 1995.

Morgan, J. *Conservation of Plastics.* London: Conservation Unit, Museums and Galleries Commission, 1991.

Mortimer, Martin. *The English Chandelier.* Suffolk, UK: Antique Collectors' Club, 2000.

Morton, W. Brown, III, et al. *The Secretary of the Interior's Standards for Rehabilitation and Illustrated Guidelines for Rehabilitating Historic Buildings.* Washington, D.C.: U.S. Department of the Interior, National Park Service, Cultural Resources, Preservation Assistance Division, 1992.

Moser, Penny Ward. "All the Real Dirt on Dust." *Discover*, November 1986.

Moss, Roger W. *Lighting for Historic Buildings: A Guide to Selecting Reproductions.* Washington, D.C.: Preservation Press, 1988.

Mostafavi, Mohsen, and David Leatherbarrow. *On Weathering: The Life of Buildings in Time.* Cambridge, Mass.: MIT Press, 1993.

Mull, Thomas E. *HVAC Principles and Applications Manual.* New York: McGraw-Hill, 1998.

Murtagh, William J. "Janus Never Sleeps." In *Past Meets Future: Saving America's Historic Environments*, edited by Antoinette J. Lee. Washington, D.C.: Preservation Press, 1992.

"Museum Exhibit Lighting. An Interdisciplinary Approach: Conservation, Design, and Technology." *Preprints from a special pre-session of the AIC 25th Annual Meeting, San Diego, California, 1997*, presented by the National Park Service and the American Institute for Conservation of Historic and Artistic Works.

Museums and Galleries Commission. *An Illustrated Guide to the Care of Costume and Textile Collections.* London: Museums and Galleries Commission, 2000.

———. "Museum and Gallery Security." In *Collections Management*, edited by Anne Fahey, 239–43. London: Routledge, 1995.

———. "Security Is Everybody's Business." In *Collections Management*, edited by Anne Fahey, 235–38. London: Routledge, 1995.

Museums Australia Victoria. "The Effects of Storage and Display Materials on Museum Objects." Info Sheet #7. www.mavic.asn.au/services/resources (accessed 29 May 2009).

National Committee to Save America's Cultural Collections. *Caring for Your Collections.* New York: Abrams, 1992.

National Fire Protection Association. *NFPA 909 Code for the Protection of Cultural Resource Properties—Museums, Libraries, and Places of Worship.* Quincy, Mass.: National Fire Protection Association, 2005.

National Institute of Standards and Technology. *The International System of Units (SI).* Special Publication 330 (SP 330). Gaithersburg, Md.: National Institute of Standards and Technology, 2008.

National Park Service (NPS). *Conserve O Gram* series. NPS Curatorial Services Division: 1979–2009. Available through Superintendent of Documents, U.S. Government Printing Office, Washington, DC 20402 and at www.nps.gov/history/museum/publications/conserveogram/cons_toc.html (accessed 31 August 2009).

———. "Cultural Shock: Fire Protection for Historic and Cultural Property 1995-01." www.ncptt.nps.gov/index.php/culture-shock-fire-protection-for-historic-and-cultural-property-1995-01 (accessed 13 February 2009).

———. "Curatorial Safety Messages." www.nps.gov/history/museum/safety/index.htm (accessed 13 February 2009).

———. "Development of a Prototypical Fire Risk Index to Evaluate Fire Safety in Historic Buildings." www.ncptt.nps.gov/development-of-a-prototypical-historic-fire-risk-index-to-evaluate-fire-safety-in-historic-buildings-1998-08.

———. "Director's Order #77-7: Integrated Pest Management (IPM)." *Pest Management Manual.* Washington, D.C.: National Park Service, 2000.

———. *Exhibit Conservation Guidelines: Incorporating Conservation into Exhibit Planning, Design, and Fabrication.* Harper's Ferry, W.V.: National Park Service, 1999. Compact disc produced by the Division of Conservation.

———. *Housekeeping for Historic Sites.* National Park Service; New York State Office of Parks, Recreation, and Historic Preservation; and Society for the Preservation of New

England Antiquities, 1996. Video produced by Fred Woods Productions.

———. *Museum Handbook, Part I: Museum Collections.* Washington, D.C.: National Park Service, Museum Management Program, 2006.

———. *Preservation Briefs 1–43.* Washington, D.C.: National Park Service, Heritage Preservation Services, 1975–2009.

———. *Primer for Disaster Preparedness, Management and Response,* www.nps.gov/history/museum/publications/primer/primintro.html.

The National Trust Manual of Housekeeping: The Care of Collections in Historic Houses Open to the Public. Oxford, UK: Elsevier, 2006.

Nazaroff, William W., et al. *Airborne Particles in Museums.* Research in Conservation 6. Marina del Rey, Calif.: J. Paul Getty Trust, 1993.

Nazaroff, William W., Lynn G. Salmon, and Glen R. Cass. "Concentration and Fate of Airborne Particles in Museums." *Environmental Science and Technology* 24, no. 1 (1990).

Nebraska State Historical Society: "Are You Prepared?" www.nebraskahistory.org/disaster/Emergency_Planning_Guide.pdf (accessed 29 May 2009).

Noetzel, D. M., and Mark Ascerno. *Carpet Beetles and Clothes Moths.* Minneapolis: University of Minnesota Agricultural Extension Service, 1981.

Norris, D. H. "Historic and Contemporary Photographic Prints." In *Storage of Natural History Collections: A Preventive Conservation Approach,* edited by C. L. Rose, C. A. Hawks, and H. H. Genoways. Iowa City: Society for the Preservation of Natural History Collections, 1995.

Nylander, R., and N. Carlisle. "The Codman House: A Case Study in Preserving and Interpreting Context." In *Conservation in Context: Finding a Balance for the Historic House Museum, Proceedings from the Symposium, March 7–8,* edited by W. C. Jessup. Washington, D.C.: Andrew Mellon Trust and National Trust for Historic Preservation, 1994.

Odegaard, N. *A Guide to Handling Anthropological Museum Collections.* Tucson, Ariz.: The Western Association for Art Conservation, 1992.

Odlyha, Marianne. "Microclimate Indoor Monitoring in Cultural Heritage Preservation." Birkbeck University of London, School of Biological and Chemical Sciences. www.bbk.ac.uk/bcs/staff/odlyha/research (accessed 29 May 2009).

Ogden, S. *Preservation Planning: Guidelines for Writing a Long-Range Plan.,* chaps. 1–2. Washington, D.C.: American Association of Museums, 1997.

———, ed. "Storage and Handling." In *Preservation of Library and Archives Materials: A Manual.* Andover, Mass.: Northeast Document, 1999.

Olkowski, William, Sheila Daar, and Helga Olkowski. "Pests of Fabric, Feathers, and Paper." In *Common Sense Pest Control.* Newtown, Conn.: Taunton Press, 1991.

Orme, Alan Dan. *Reviving Old Houses: Over 500 Low-Cost Tips and Techniques.* Pownal, Vt.: Garden Way Publishing, 1990.

Owen Myers, Nancy. *Implementing Integrated Pest Management at National Historic Sites in the Mid-Atlantic Region of the National Park Service.* Washington, D.C.: Center for Urban Ecology, National Park Service, 1992.

Oxley, Richard. *Survey and Repair of Traditional Buildings: A Sustainable Approach.* London: Donhead, 2003.

Padfield, T., D. Erhardt, and W. Hopwood. "Trouble in Store." In *Science and Technology in the Service of Conservation, Preprints of the Washington D.C. Congress of the International Institute for Conservation,* edited by N. S. Brommelle and Garry Thomson. Washington, D.C.: ICOM-CC, 1982.

Page, Robert, Cathy A. Gilbert, and Susan A. Dolan. *A Guide to Cultural Landscapes Reports: Contents, Process, and Techniques.* Rev. ed. Washington, D.C.: National Park Service, 2005.

Paine, Shelley Reisman. "How to Control Environmental Conditions in Historical Agencies and Museums." AASLH Technical Report 3. Nashville, Tenn.: American Association for State and Local History, 1985.

Palfreyman, John, and Gordon Low. *Studies of the Domestic Dry Rot Fungus* Serpula lacrymans *with Relevance to the Management of Decay in Buildings.* Edinburgh: Historic Scotland, 2002.

Parker, Thomas A. *Study on Integrated Pest Management for Libraries and Archives.* Paris: UNESCO, 1988.

Pearlstein, Ellen. "Pollutant Sources, Material Effects, Measurement Terminology, and Standards." Lecture for first year WUDPAC students, Winterthur, Delaware, May 13, 2003.

Peltz, Perri, and Monona Rossol. *Safe Pest Control Procedures for Museum Collections.* New York: Center for Occupational Hazards, 1983.

Perkins, R. "Comparison of Temperature and Relative Humidity Dataloggers for Museum Monitoring." *AIC News* 26, no.1 (2001): 16–19.

Petkov, Ivan, and Jean-Michel Nunzi. "New Two-Functional UVR Sunscreen Protector and Dosimeter." www.photobiology.com/photobiology2000/petkov (accessed 30 July 2003).

Phifer, R. W., and W. R. McTique Jr. *Handbook of Hazardous Waste Management for Small-Quantity Generators.* Chelsea, Mich.: Lewis Publishers, 1988.

Philadelphia Museum of Art. "What Effect Does Exposure to Indoor Air Pollutants Have on a Museum's Collections?" www.philamuseum.org/collections/22-393-209.html?page=4.

Pinninger, David, Annette Townsend, and Adrian Meyer. *Pest Management in Museums, Archives, and Historic Houses.* London: Archetype, 2001.

Poore, Patricia, ed. The Old House Journal *Guide to Restoration.* Dutton, New York: Dutton, 1992.

Preservation Directorate. "Guide to Preservation Matting and Framing." Washington, D.C.: Library of Congress. www.loc.gov/preserv/care/mat.html

———. "Preserving Works on Paper: Manuscripts, Drawings, Prints, Posters, Maps, Documents." Washington, D.C.: Library of Congress. www.loc.gov/preserv/care/paper.html (accessed 29 May 2009).

Provincial Museum of Alberta. *Housekeeping Our Heritage: Practical Advice for Alberta Collections.* Edmonton: Provincial Museum of Alberta, 1984.

Pyne Press, comp. *Lamps and Other Lighting Devices, 1850–1906.* Princeton, N.J.: Pyne Press, 1972.

Rabun, J. Stanley. *Structural Analysis of Historic Buildings: Restoration, Preservation, and Adaptive Reuse Applications for Architects and Engineers.* New York: Wiley, 2000.

Racine, Laurel. "On the Inside Looking Out: Guidelines for the Treatment of Historic Furnished Interiors." *CRM: Journal of Heritage Stewardship* 7 (2001).

Ransom, W. H. *Building Failures: Diagnosis and Avoidance.* 2nd ed. London: Spon, 1996.

Reilly, James. *Care and Identification of 19th-Century Photographic Prints.* Rochester, N.Y.: Eastman Kodak Company, 1986.

Reilly, Julie. "Celluloid Objects: Their Chemistry and Preservation." *JAIC* 30, no. 2 (Fall 1991): 145–62.

———. "Writing Your Emergency Plan." In *Are You Prepared? A Guide to Emergency Planning,* 21–40. Lincoln: Nebraska State Historical Society for the Nebraska Museum Association, 1997.

Reilly, Julie A., and Martin Mortimer. "The Care and Conservation of Glass Chandeliers." *Journal of the American Institute for Conservation* 37, no. 2 (Summer 1998).

Rempel, Siegfried. *The Care of Photographs.* New York: Lyons & Burford, 1987.

Revere Copper Products. *Copper and Common Sense: Sheet Copper Design Principles and Construction Techniques.* 8th ed. Rome, N.Y.: Revere Copper Products, 2005.

Richardson, Barry. *Remedial Treatment of Buildings.* 2nd ed. Oxford, UK: Butterworth-Heinemann, 1995.

Ritzenthaler, Mary Lynn. *Archives and Manuscripts: Conservation, a Manual on Physical Care and Management.* Chicago: Society of American Archivists, 1983.

Rivers, R. "Handling Guidelines for Paper-Based Collections in Archives and Libraries." Available at the Gerald R. Ford Conservation Center, Omaha, Nebraska, 1998.

Roberts, Barbara O. "Emergency Preparedness." In *Storage of Natural History Collections: A Preventive Conservation Approach,* edited by C. L. Rose, C. A. Hawks, and H. H. Genoways, 81–99. Iowa City: Society for the Preservation of Natural History Collections, 1995.

Robson, Patrick. *Structural Repair of Traditional Buildings.* London: Donhead, 1999.

Roff, W. J., J. R. Scott, and J. Pacitti. *Fibres, Films, Plastics, and Rubbers.* London: Butterworth, 1971.

Rose, Carolyn L., and Amparo R. de Torres, eds. *Storage of Natural History Collections: Ideas and Practical Solutions.* Pittsburgh, Pa.: Society for the Preservation of Natural History Collections, 1992.

Rose, C. L., and C. Hawks. "A Preventive Conservation Approach to the Storage of Collections." In *Storage of Natural History Collections: A Preventive Conservation Approach,* edited by C. L. Rose, C. A. Hawks, and H. H. Genoways, 1–20. Iowa City: Society for the Preservation of Natural History Collections, 1995.

Rose, C. L., C. A. Hawks, and H. H. Genoways, eds. *Storage of Natural History Collections: A Preventive Conservation Approach.* Iowa City: Society for the Preservation of Natural History Collections, 1995.

Rose, William. "Effects of Climate Control on the Museum Building Envelope." *Journal of the American Institute of Conservation* 33, no. 2 (1994): 199–210.

———. *Water in Buildings: An Architect's Guide to Moisture and Mold.* Hoboken, N.J.: Wiley, 2005.

Royal Netherlands Academy of Arts and Sciences and European Commission on Preservation and Access. "A Virtual Exhibition of the Ravages of Soot, Water, Moulds, Fungi, Bookworms, and Other Pests." www.knaw.nl/ecpa/expo.htm (accessed 29 May 2009).

Rushlight Club, comp. *Early Lighting: A Pictorial Guide.* Boston: Rushlight Club, 1972.

Ruskin, John. *The Seven Lamps of Architecture.* Mineola, N.Y.: Dover, 1990.

Ryan, V. M. *Integrated Pest Management.* Denver, Colo.: University of Denver, Rocky Mountain Conservation Center, 1996.

Rybcznski, Witold. *One Good Turn: A Natural History of the Screwdriver and the Screw.* New York: Scribner, 2000.

Sandwith, Hermione, and Sheila Stainton. *The National Trust Manual of Housekeeping.* London: Penguin Books in association with The National Trust, 1991.

Saunders, David. "Pollution and the National Gallery." National Gallery Technical Bulletin, Vol. 21. London: National Gallery, 2000.

Schaeffer, Terry T. *Research in Conservation: Effects of Light on Materials in Collections; Data on Photoflash and Related Sources.* Los Angeles, Calif.: Getty Publications, 2001.

Schmidt, Anne Lisbeth, Pernille Bronée, Kåre Kemp, and Jes Fenger. "Airborne Dust in a Museum Environment." IAP 2001, Presentation 20. iaq.dk/iap/iap2001/2001_20.htm (accessed 26 October 2003).

Schultz, Arthur W., ed. *Caring for Your Collections: Preserving and Protecting Your Art and Other Collectibles.* New York: Abrams, 1992.

Scott, G. "Moisture, Ventilation, and Mould Growth." In *Preventive Conservation Practice, Theory, and Research, Preprint of the Contributions to the Ottawa Congress, 12–16 September,* 149–53. London: International Institute for Conservation, 1994.

Scott, Jude. *Museum and Archival Supplies Handbook.* Toronto: Ontario Museum Association, Toronto Area Archivists Group, and the Getty Conservation Institute, 1985.

Seale, William. *Recreating the Historic House Interior.* Nashville, Tenn.: American Association for State and Local History, 1979.

Seaquist, E. O. *Diagnosing and Repairing House Structure Problems.* New York: McGraw-Hill, 1980.

Sebor, A. J. "Heating, Ventilating, and Air-Conditioning Systems." In *Storage of Natural History Collections: A Preventive Conservation Approach*, edited by C. L. Rose, C. A. Hawks, and H. H. Genoways, 135–46. Iowa City: Society for the Preservation of Natural History Collections, 1995.

Self, Robert L. "Window Films." *Conservation DistList* message distributed September 27, 2002.

Selwitz, C., and S. Maekawa. *Inert Gases in the Control of Museum Insect Pests.* Los Angeles, Calif.: Getty Conservation Institute, 1998.

Shelley, M. *The Care and Handling of Art Objects.* New York: Metropolitan Museum of Art, 1987.

———. "Warning Signs: When Works on Paper Require Conservation." In *Conservation Concerns: A Guide for Collectors and Curators*, edited by K. Bachmann, 35–38. Washington, D.C.: Smithsonian Institution Press, 1992.

Simpson & Brown Architects. *Conservation of Plasterwork.* Rev. ed. Edinburgh: Scottish Lime Center, 2002.

Smith, Eric H., and Richard C. Whitman. *NPCA Field Guide to Structural Pests.* Dunn Loring, Va.: National Pest Control Association, 1992; Supplement 1, 1995.

Spafford-Ricci, Sarah, and Fiona Graham. "The Fire at the Royal Saskatchewan Museum, Part 2: Removal of Soot from Artifacts and Recovery of the Building." *Journal of the American Institute of Conservation* 39, no. 1 (2000): 37–56.

Spennemann, Dirk H. R., and David W. Look, eds. *Disaster Management Programs for Historic Sites.* Albury, NSW, Australia: Association for Preservation Technology, U.S. National Park Service, and The Charles Stuart University, 1998.

Sprigg, June. *Domestick Beings.* New York: Knopf, 1984.

Staehli, Alfred. "Historic Structures Maintenance Guide for Mount Rainier National Park." Seattle, Wash.: National Park Service, Pacific Northeast Region, Cultural Resources Division, 1983.

Stahl, Frederick A. *A Guide to the Maintenance, Repair, and Alteration of Historic Buildings.* New York: Van Nostrand Reinhold, 1984.

Stearns, Brian, Alan Stearns, and John Meyer. *The Slate Book: How to Design, Specify, Install, and Repair a Slate Roof.* Morrisville, Vt.: Vermont Slate and Copper Services, 1998.

Sticky Pad Reader. www.hanby.co.uk/Sticky%20Pad%20Reader.htm (accessed 29 May 2009).

Stoner, Joyce Hill. "Documenting Ourselves: The History of 20th-Century Conservation." *IIC Bulletin* (1998).

Story, Keith O. *Approaches to Pest Management in Museums.* Suitland, Md.: Conservation Analytical Laboratory, Smithsonian Institution, 1985.

Stout, George L. *The Care of Pictures.* New York: Dover, 1975.

Strang, Tom. *Museum Pest Management.* Ottawa, Ont.: Canadian Conservation Institute, 1992.

———. "Principles of Heat Disinfestation." *Integrated Pest Management for Collections, Proceedings of 2001: A Pest Odyssey*, edited by H. Kingsley, D. Pinniger, A. Xavier-Rowe, and P. Windsor. London: James & James, 2001.

Sullivan, Charles, and Eileen Woodford. *Maintaining Your Old House in Cambridge.* Cambridge, Mass.: Cambridge Historical Commission, 1988.

TechniGlove International. "Technically Advanced Nitrile Gloves." www.techniglove.com/nitrile.html (accessed 29 May 2009).

Tennent, Norman H., and Joyce H. Townsend. "Light Dosimeters for Museums, Galleries and Historic Houses." *Lighting, a Conference on Lighting in Museums, Galleries and Historic Houses. Bristol, 9–10 April 1987.*

Thickett, D. "Sealing of MDF to Prevent Corrosive Emissions." *Conservator* 22 (1998): 49–56.

Thomson, Garry. *The Museum Environment.* 2nd ed. Oxford, UK: Butterworth-Heinemann, 1986.

Truman, Lee C., Gary W. Bennett, and William L. Butts. *Scientific Guide to Pest Control Operations.* Orlando, Fla.: Harcourt Brace Jovanovich, 1982.

Tufnell, Richard N. *Building and Repairing Kentucky Rock Fences.* Lexington, Ky.: Dry Stone Masonry Institute of North America, 1995.

Tyler, Norman. "Early History of the Preservation Movement." In *Issues of Historic Preservation.* New York: Norton, 2000.

———. *Historic Preservation: An Introduction to Its History, Principles, and Practice.* New York: Norton, 2000.

U.S. Department of Health, Education, and Welfare. *Pictorial Keys to Arthropods, Reptiles, Birds, and Mammals of Public Health Significance.* Washington, D.C.: U.S. Department of Health, Education, and Welfare, 1967.

Van der Reyden, D. "Paper Documents." In *Storage of Natural History Collections: A Preventive Conservation Approach*, edited by C. L. Rose, C. A. Hawks, and H. H. Genoways. Iowa City: Society for the Preservation of Natural History Collections, 1995.

Veloz, Nicolas F. *An Ounce of Prevention: The Preservation Maintenance of Outdoor Sculpture and Monuments.* Alexandria, Va.: Private printing, 1983.

Verrall, A. F., and T. Amburgey. *Prevention and Control of Decay of Homes.* Washington, D.C.: U.S. Government Printing Office, 1975.

Victoria and Albert Museum: "Museums and Their Interaction with Museum Objects." www.vam.ac.uk/res_cons/conservation/journal/number_44/materials-museum-objects/index.html (accessed 29 May 2009).

Virginia Association of Museums. *Conservation Awareness Technical Assistance Leaflet.* Richmond, Va.: Virginia Association of Museums, 1987.

Waller, R. R. "Conservation Risk Assessment: A Strategy for Managing Resources for Preventive Conservation." In *Preventive Conservation: Practice, Theory, and Research. Preprints to the Ottawa Conference, 12–16 September,* 12–17. London: International Institute for Conservation, 1994.

———. "Risk Management Applied to Preventive Conservation." In *Storage of Natural History Collections: A Preventive Conservation Approach,* edited by C. L. Rose, C. A. Hawks, and H. H. Genoways, 21–27. Iowa City: Society for the Preservation of Natural History Collections, 1995.

Watt, David, and Belinda Colston, eds. *Conservation of Historic Buildings and Their Contents: Addressing the Conflicts.* London: Donhead, 2003.

Watt, David, and Peter Swallows. *Surveying Historic Buildings.* London: Donhead, 1996.

Weaver, Martin E. *Conserving Buildings: A Guide to Techniques and Material.* New York: Wiley, 1993.

Webster, T., and Mrs. Parkes. *The American Family Encyclopedia of Useful Knowledge.* New York: Derby & Jackson, 1858.

Weeks, Kay D., and Anne E. Grimmer. *The Secretary of the Interior's Standards for the Treatment of Historic Properties with Guidelines for Preserving, Rehabilitating, Restoring, and Reconstructing Historic Buildings.* Washington, D.C.: U. S. Department of the Interior, National Park Service, Cultural Resources Stewardship and Partnerships, Heritage Preservation Services, 1995.

Weintraub, Steven, and Gordon Anson. "Technics: Natural Light in Museums: An Asset or a Threat?" *Progressive Architecture,* May 1990, 49–54.

Weintraub, S., and S. Wolf. "Macro- and Microenvironments." In *Storage of Natural History Collections: A Preventive Conservation Approach,* edited by C. L. Rose, C. A. Hawks, and H. H. Genoways, 123–34. Iowa City: Society for the Preservation of Natural History Collections, 1995.

Wellheiser, Johanna G. *Nonchemical Treatment Processes for Disinfestation of Insects and Fungi in Library Collections.* The Hague, Netherlands: International Federation of Library Associations and Institutions, 1992.

West, Patricia. *Domesticating History: The Political Origins of America's House Museums.* Washington, D.C.: Smithsonian Institution Press, 1999.

Whatman, S. *The Housekeeping Book of Susanna Whatman 1776–1800.* London: National Trust Classics, 2000.

Whelchel, Harriet, ed. *Caring for Your Historic House.* Heritage Preservations and National Park Service. New York: Abrams, 1998.

White, Richard E. *A Field Guide to the Beetles of North America.* Boston: Houghton Mifflin, 1983.

Whitford, M. J. *Getting Rid of Graffiti: A Practical Guide to Graffiti Removal and Anti-Graffiti Protection.* London: Van Nostrand Reinhold, 1992.

Wilcox, U. V. "Facility Management." In *Storage of Natural History Collections: A Preventive Conservation Approach,* edited by C. L. Rose, C. A. Hawks, and H. H. Genoways. Iowa City: Society for the Preservation of Natural History Collections, 1995.

Williams, Marc A. *Keeping It All Together: The Preservation and Care of Historic Furniture.* Worthington: Ohio Antique Review, 1990.

Williams, R. Sam, Mark T. Knaebe, and William Feist. *Finishes for Exterior Wood.* Madison, Wisc.: Forest Products Society, 1996.

Wilson, J. Andrew. "Fire Protection." In *Storage of Natural History Collections: A Preventive Conservation Approach,* edited by C. L. Rose, C. A. Hawks, and H. H. Genoways, 57–80. Iowa City: Society for the Preservation of Natural History Collections, 1995.

Wolf Green, Sara, ed. *The Conservation Assessment: A Tool for Planning, Implementing, and Fund-Raising.* Washington, D.C.: Getty Conservation Institute and Heritage Preservation, 1998.

"Wood Burning Fireplace Maintenance." homebuying.about.com/library/weekly/aa1_13000a.htm (accessed 29 May 2009).

Yapp, Bob, and Rich Binsacca. *About Your House (with Bob Yapp).* San Francisco: Bay Books, 1997.

Yoon, Young Hun, and Peter Brimblecombe. "Contribution of Dust at Floor Level to Particle Deposit within the Sainsbury Centre for Visual Arts." *Studies in Conservation* 45, no. 2 (2000).

———. "Soiling by Coarse Particles in the Museum Environment." *IAQ 2000,* Presentation 15. iaq.dk/iap/iaq2000/2000_15.htm (accessed 15 Oct 2003).

Zycherman, Lynda A., and John Richard Schrock, eds. *A Guide to Museum Pest Control.* Washington, D.C.: Foundation of AIC and Association of Systematic Collections, 1988.

Supplier Resources

Archivart
40 Eisenhower Drive
Paramus, NJ 07652
Tel.: 800-804-8428
Fax: 888-273-4824
www.archivart.com

Art Preservation Services
315 East 89th Street
New York, NY 10128
Tel.: 212-722-6300
Fax: 212-427-6726
http://aspnyc.com

Benchmark
PO Box 214
Rosemont, NJ 08556
Tel.: 609-397-1131
Fax: 609-397-1159
www.benchmarkcatalog.com

Conservation Resources International
5532 Port Royal Road
Springfield, VA 22151
Toll-free: 800-634-6932
Tel.: 703-321-7730
Fax: 703-321-0629
www.conservationresources.com

Conservation Support System
PO Box 91746
Santa Barbara, CA 93190
Tel.: 805-682-9843
Fax: 805-682-2064
www.silcom.com/~css

Dick Blick Art Materials
PO Box 1267
Galesburg, IL 61402-1267
Toll-free: 800-723-2787
Fax: 800-621-8293
www.dickblick.com

Fisher Scientific
9999 Veterans Memorial Drive
Houston, TX 77038-2499
Toll-free: 800-766-7000
Tel.: 281-820-9898
Fax: 800-926-1166
www.fishersci.com

Gaylord Brothers
PO Box 4901
Syracuse, NY 13221-4901
Toll-free: 800-962-9580
Toll-free fax: 800-272-3412
E-mail: customerservice@gaylord.com
www.gaylord.com

Grainger
11200E 210 Hwy
Kansas City, MO 64161-9370
Tel.: 800-323-0620
www.grainger.com

Hollinger Corporation
9401 Northeast Drive
PO Box 8360
Fredricksburg, VA 22404
Toll-free: 800-634-0491
Toll-free fax: 800-947-8814
E-mail: hollingercorp@intersurf.net
www.hollingercorp.com

Image Permanence Institute Climate Notebook
Rochester Institute of Technology/IPI
70 Lomb Memorial Drive
Rochester, NY 14623-5604
Tel.: 585-475-5199
Fax: 585-475-7230
www.imagepermanenceinstitute.org/index.shtml

Lab Safety Supply
PO Box 1368
Janesville, WI 53547-1368
Toll-free: 800-356-0783
Toll-free fax: 800-543-9910
www.labsafety.com

Light Impressions
PO Box 2100
Santa Fe Springs, CA 90670
Toll-free: 800-828-6216
Fax: 800-828-5539
www.lightimpressionsdirect.com

Metal Edge, Inc.
6340 Bandini Boulevard
Commerce, CA 90040
Toll-free: 800-862-2228
Toll-free fax: 888-822-6937
www.metaledgeinc.com

Northeast Document Conservation Center
100 Brickstone Square
Andover, MA 01810-1494
Tel.: 978-470-1010
Fax: 978-475-6021
www.nedcc.org/resources/suppliers.php

Preservation Products Unlimited
6929 Seward Avenue
PO Box 29109
Lincoln, NE 68529
Tel.: 402-467-2948
Toll-free: 800-648-7329

Rio Grande
7500 Blue Water Road, NW
Albuquerque, NM 87121
Toll-free: 800-545-6566
Fax: 800-965-2329
www.riogrande.com

The Southeastern Library Network
1438 West Peachtree Street, NW
Suite 200
Atlanta, GA 30309
Tel.: 800-999-8558
Fax: 404-892-7879
E-mail: helpdesk@solinet.net

Talas
330 Morgan Avenue
Brooklyn, NY 11211
Tel.: 212-219-0770
Fax: 212-219-0735
www.talasonline.com

TestFabrics, Inc.
415 Delaware Avenue
PO Box 26
West Pittston, PA 18643
Tel.: 570-603- 0432
Fax: 570-603-0433
www.testfabrics.com/index.html

University Products
517 Main Street
PO Box 101
Holyoke, MA 01041
Toll-free: 800-628-1912
Tel.: 413-532-3372
Toll-free fax: 800-532-9281
Fax: 413-432-9281
E-mail: info@universityproducts.com
www.universityproducts.com

American Association for State and Local History (AASLH)
1717 Church Street
Nashville, TN 37203-2991
615-320-3203
www.aaslh.org

American Association of Museums (AAM)
1575 Eye Street NW, Suite 400
Washington, DC 20005
202-289-1818
www.aam-us.org

American Institute for Conservation of Historic and Artistic Works (AIC)
1156 15th Street NW, Suite 320
Washington, DC 20005
202-452-9545
www.conservation-us.org

The American Institute for Conservation of Historic and Artistic Works (AIC) is the national membership organization of conservation professionals dedicated to preserving the art and historic artifacts of our cultural heritage for future generations.

Providing a forum for the exchange of ideas on conservation, AIC advances the practice and promotes the importance of the preservation of cultural property by coordinating the exchange of knowledge, research, and publications. AIC's *Code of Ethics and Guidelines for Practice* defines appropriate conduct for the field.

AIC conservation professionals combine unique skills in the arts and sciences gained through study and training in art history, chemistry, studio art, and related disciplines. They are experts in the conservation of paintings, paper, books, photographs, textiles, decorative arts, sculpture, and wooden artifacts as well as architectural, archaeological, natural science, and ethnographic materials.

AIC members are practicing conservators, conservation scientists, educators, administrators, collections care professionals, technicians, and students; archivists, curators, and other museum and library professionals; and architects and art historians. AIC also welcomes members from other disciplines who are interested in conservation.

American Institute of Architects (AIA)
Historic Preservation Committee
1735 New York Avenue NW
Washington, DC 20006
800-AIA-3837
www.aia.org

American Society of Civil Engineers (ASCE)
1801 Alexander Bell Drive
Reston, VA 20191
800-548-2723
www.asce.org

American Society of Landscape Architects (ASLA)
636 Eye Street NW
Washington, DC 20001-3736
202-898-2444
www.asla.org

American Society of Mechanical Engineers
3 Park Avenue
New York, NY 10016-5990
800-843-2763
www.asme.org

American Society for Testing and Materials (ASTM International)
100 Barr Harbor Drive
PO Box C700
West Conshohocken, PA 19428-2959
610-832-9500
www.astm.org

Association for Preservation Technology International (APTI)
(*APT Bulletin: Journal of Preservation Technology*)
4513 Lincoln Avenue, Suite 213
Lisle, IL 60532-1290
630-968-6400
www.apti.org

APT currently has active chapters in eleven regions: Australia, Delaware Valley (Philadelphia), Northeast, Northwest, Ohio River Valley, Ottawa Valley, Rocky Mountain, Southeast, Texas, Washington (D.C.), Western.

Each of these chapters carry APT's mission as a multidisciplinary organization dedicated to advancing the application of technology to the conservation of the built environment. Most chapters have been formed to allow APT members within a geographic region to continue the international aims and objectives of APT at a local level. Like APT, the chapters aim to encourage, promote, and advance research, training, and the dissemination of information relating to preservation technology and the historic preservation of buildings, sites, and objects.

The mission of the Association for Preservation Technology International is:

- To provide a useful forum for the promotion of the continued development of preservation technology
- To contribute to the research, collection, and publication of information on all aspects of preservation technology
- To encourage and participate in education and training in the knowledge, techniques, and skills of preservation technology
- To stimulate the establishment of national and local collections of reference data and artifacts for the study of preservation technology
- To maintain and disseminate an information data bank including listing of members and sources of materials, supplies, and services related to preservation technology

Campbell Center for Historic Preservation Studies
203 East Seminary
Mount Carroll, IL 61053
815-244-1173
www.campbellcenter.org

The Campbell Center offers continuing education in historic preservation, museum studies, preventive collections care, and conservation. The center offers the participant a scholarship-supported program of certification in preventive collections care for the beginning, mid-career, and senior-level heritage professional. All course offerings are "material-based." Each course focuses on the inherent chemical and/or physical properties and limitations of the artifact material(s), the role environmental factors play in material(s) degradation, and conservation/preventive conservation strategies, which mitigate and/or slow degradation.

Heritage Preservation
National Institute for Conservation
1012 14th Street NW
Washington, DC 20005
202-233-0800
888-388-6789
www.heritagepreservation.org
www.heritagepreservation.org/CAP/about.html

The Conservation Assessment Program (CAP) is available to eligible museums. In 2006, the administration of CAP changed from a federal grant to a technical assistance program supported through a cooperative agreement with the Institute of Museum and Library Services. Despite the change in administration, the program itself is essentially the same.

CAP provides a general conservation assessment of your museum's collection, environmental conditions, and site. Conservation priorities are identified by professional conservators who spend two days on-site and three days writing a report. The report can help your museum develop strategies for improved collections care and provide a tool for long-range planning and fund-raising.

CAP offers a maximum of two assessors per institution. Most museums are provided a conservator to assess the museum's collections. If your institution has living collections (zoos, aquariums, nature centers, botanical gardens, and arboreta), you can be provided a zoologist, botanist, or horticulturalist as the collections assessor. If you have a historic structure (a building more than fifty years old), you may also get an architectural assessor.

Historic American Building Survey/Historic American Engineering Record/Historic American Landscape Survey Collection (HABS/HAER/HALS Collections)
Prints and Photographs Division
Library of Congress
101 Independence Avenue SE
Washington, DC 20540
202-707-6394
www.memory.loc.gov/ammen/hhhtm/hhhome.html

Historic Preservation Learning Portal
National Park Service
www.historicpreservation.gov

This search engine was developed by the Federal Preservation Institute for historic preservation practitioners and researchers interested in preservation information from reliable sources.

Institute of Electrical and Electronic Engineers
3 Park Avenue, 17th Floor
New York, NY 10016-5997
212-419-7900
www.ieee.org

International Preservation Trades Workshop
c/o Preservation Trades Network (see below)
www.iptw.org

The International Preservation Trades Workshop is the only such annual event in North America. Along with the International Trades Education Symposium, it provides a unique opportunity for tradespeople, educators, preservationists, students, and others from the United States and abroad to exchange experiences, learn skills, and find common ground in the application of the skilled trades to conservation of the built environment.

National Center for Preservation Technology and Training (NCPTT)
National Park Service
645 College Avenue
Natchitoches, LA 71457
www.ncptt.nps.gov

Mission: NCPTT advances the use of science and technology in historic preservation. Working in the fields of archeology, architecture, landscape architecture, and materials conservation, the Center accomplishes its mission through training, education, research, technology transfer, and partnerships.

Background: NCPTT is an important part of our nation's preservation and conservation community—which, in turn, is a vital part of our nation's cultural life. NCPTT serves the community that fostered its creation—and, in turn, serves the nation and the world.

Efforts to establish a national preservation center within the National Park Service have been evolving for nearly two decades. The national need for an initiative that could promote and enhance national preservation efforts was highlighted in a 1988 report to Congress prepared by the Office of Technology Assessment (OTA).

In response to the clearly stated need for a national preservation initiative, Congress passed the Historic Preservation Act Amendments of 1992, creating NCPTT, NCPTT's advisory board and NCPTT's grants program. NCPTT fulfills the OTA report's recommendations to develop and distribute skills and technologies that enhance the preservation, conservation, and interpretation of prehistoric and historic resources throughout the United States.

NCPTT Research Priorities:

- Protect cultural resources against vandalism, looting, terrorism, and natural disasters
- Conserve architectural materials of the "recent past"
- Develop appropriate technologies to preserve houses of worship and cemeteries
- Monitor and evaluate preservation treatments
- Study environmental effects of pollution on cultural resources
- Document and preserve threatened cultural landscapes

National Conference of State Historic Preservation Officers
444 North Capital Street NW, Suite 342
Washington, DC 20001-1512
www.ncshpo.org

The National Conference of State Historic Preservation Officers (NCSHPO) is the professional association of the state government officials who carry out the national historic preservation program as delegates of the Secretary of the Interior pursuant to the National Historic Preservation Act of 1966. It is the point of contact for the State Historic Preservation Officers (SHPOs).

National Trust for Historic Preservation
1785 Massachusetts Avenue NW
Washington, DC 20036-2117
800-944-6847
www.preservationnation.org

The National Trust for Historic Preservation is a nonprofit membership organization bringing people together to protect, enhance, and enjoy the places that matter to them. By saving the places where great moments from history—and the important moments of everyday life—took place, the National Trust for Historic Preservation helps revitalize neighborhoods and communities, spark economic development, and promote environmental sustainability. With headquarters in Washington, D.C., six regional and field offices, twenty-nine historic sites, and partner organizations in all fifty states, the National Trust for Historic Preservation provides leadership, education, advocacy, and resources to a national network of people, organizations, and local communities committed to saving places, connecting us to our history, and collectively shaping the future of America's stories.

Preservation Trades Network (PTN)
PO Box 249
Amherst, NH 03031-0249
866-853-9335
www.ptn.org

PTN was conceived in 1995 at an Association for Preservation Technology (APT) conference roundtable strategy session in Washington, D.C. At the time, representatives of the preservation trades felt it important for the preservation trades to be recognized as a valued member of preservation project teams. To do this, the preservation trades took action to build a community of like-minded individuals who share knowledge of the process of historic preservation as it occurs in the field. PTN was formed to provide a focus on and support of the sharing of the preservation trade's knowledge of the physical process of preservation, of how to shape and work historic materials. From this beginning PTN became a Task Force of APT.

PTN believes that the preservation trades can make a difference by sharing information about their crafts among peers. Learning to share enhances the relationships of trades working with trades, and improves the effectiveness of the preservation trades within the overall preservation project team. Accordingly, PTN has set itself to building a community of preservationists who share in a hands-on approach.

The International Preservation Trades Workshop (see above) is the primary event organized and sponsored on an annual basis by PTN.

Society of Architectural Historians
1365 North Astor Street
Chicago, IL 60610
312-573-1365
www.sia-web.org

Society for the Preservation of New England Antiquities (SPNEA)
141 Cambridge Street
Boston, MA 02114
617-227-3956
www.historicnewengland.org

Technical Preservation Services
National Park Service
1849 C Street, NW, 2255
Washington, DC 20240
www.nps.gov/history/hps/tps

Technical Preservation Services is the nation's leading provider of information and guidance on the care of historic buildings. Technical Preservation Services provides the tools and information necessary to take effective measures to protect and preserve historic buildings, ranging from historic masonry and window repairs to lead paint abatement to accessibility for people with disabilities.

Preservation Tech Notes are case study examples of how to sensitively preserve and repair historic materials and features in a range of categories from masonry to glass. They provide traditional and innovative solutions to specific problems in preserving heritage resources for architects, contractors, and maintenance personnel.

Preservation Briefs and Tech Notes may be purchased in hard copy from the Government Printing Office (GPO). The online TPS Catalog provides the complete Preservation Briefs listing, stock numbers, prices, and a mail-in order GPO form. The PBS may be ordered *directly* from GPO using a major credit card by calling 866-512-1800. Also order Preservation Briefs from the U.S. Government Printing Office Online Bookstore using a secure order form. Browse a topic, "Buildings, Landmarks, and Historic Sites," and scroll down to "Preservation Methods."

Whole Building Design Guide
National Institute of Building Sciences (NIBS)
1090 Vermont Avenue NW, Suite 700
Washington, DC 20005
202-289-7800
www.wbdg.org

Web Resources

American Association for Information and Image Management (AIIM): www.aiim.org
American Association for State and Local History (AASLH): www.aaslh.org
American Association of Museums (AAM): www.aam-us.org
American Institute for Conservation of Historic and Artistic Works (AIC): www.conservation-us.org
American Institute of Architects (AIA): www.aia.org
American Library Association (ALA): www.ala.org
American Museum of Photography: www.photographymuseum.com/archival.htm
American Society for Industrial Security (ASIS): www.asisonline.org.
American Society for Testing and Materials (ASTM): www.astm.org
American Society of Appraisers: www.appraisers.org
American Society of Civil Engineers (ASCE): www.asce.org
American Society of Landscape Architects (ASLA): www.asla.org
American Society of Mechanical Engineers: www.asme.org
Amigos Library Services: www.amigos.org
Appraisers Association of America: www.appraisersassoc.org
Association for Living History Farm and Agricultural Museums (ALHFAM): www.alhfam.org
Association for Preservation Technology International (APTI): www.apti.org
Association of Midwest Museums: www.midwestmuseums.org
Association of Moving Image Archivists (AMIA): www.amianet.org
Association of Research Libraries: www.arl.org
Balboa Art Conservation Center (BACC): www.bacc.org
Bonhams: www.bonhams.com
Book Arts: www.philobiblon.com
Bugwood Network: www.insectimages.org
Campbell Center for Historic Preservation Studies: www.campbellcenter.org
Canadian Conservation Institute (CCI): www.preservation.gc.ca/index_e.asp
Canadian Heritage Information Network (CHIN): www.chin.gc.ca/English/index.html
Canadian Museums Associations: www.museums.ca
Cellulose Acetate: Annotated Bibliography: www.nla.gov.au/anica/annib.html
Centers for Disease Control and Prevention: www.cdc.gov
Centre de Conservation du Quebec: Preserv'Art Database: http://preservart.ccq.mcc.gouv.qc.ca/index.aspx?langue=e
Chicago Conservation Center: http://chicagoconservation.com
Chicora Foundation: www.chicora.org/index.html
Chimney Safety Institute of America: www.csia.org/home/liners.html
Christie's: www.christies.com/home_page/home_page.asp
Conservation Center for Art and Historic Artifacts (CCAHA): www.ccaha.org
Conservation Register: www.conservationregister.com
Council on Library and Information Resources (CLIR): www.clir.org
Cylinder, Disc, and Tape Care in a Nutshell: Library of Congress: www.loc.gov/preserv/care/record.html
Daguerreian Society: www.daguerre.org
dPlan: www.dplan.org
Environmental Protection Agency: www.epa.gov
Fisher Scientific: www.fishersci.com
Gateway for Resources and Information on Preservation (GRIP): www.knaw.nl/ecpa/grip
Getty Conservation Center: www.getty.edu/conservation
Green Seal (environmental evaluations): www.greenseal.org/resources/reports.cfm
Hearthstone Historic House Museum: www.focol.org/hearthstone
Heritage Areas Bulletin Board: National Park Service: www.historicpreservation.gov
Heritage Health Index: www.heritagepreservation.org/HHI/index.html
Heritage Preservation: www.heritagepreservation.org
Historic American Building Survey/Historic American Engineering Record/Historic American Landscape Survey Collection (HABS /HAER/HALS Collections), Library of Congress: www.memory.loc.gov/ammen/hhhtm/hhhome.html
Historic Scotland: www.historic-scotland.gov.uk
H-Museum: www.h-net.org/~museum/index.html
How Stuff Works: www.howstuffworks.com
How to Get Rid of Things (pest control information): www.getridofthings.com/get-rid-of-bugs.htm

Illinois Heritage Association (IHA): www.prairienet.org
Image Permanence Institute: www.imagepermanence institute.org
Insects Limited: www.insectslimited.com
Institute of Museum and Library Services (IMLS), Conservation Assessment Program (CAP): www.imls.gov
Insurance Information Institute: www.iii.org
Intermuseum Conservation Association (ICA): www.ica-artconservation.org
International Centre for the Study of the Preservation and Restoration of Cultural Property (ICCROM): www.iccrom.org
International Council of Museums (ICOM): http://icom.museum
International Institute for the Unification of Private Law (UNIDROIT): www.unidroit.org
Iron Bridge Museum—UK: www.ironbridge.org.uk/collections/mystery_objects
Kilgarlin Center for Preservation of the Cultural Record: www.ischool.utexas.edu/kilgarlin/about.php
Kodak: Storage and Handling Film: www.kodak.com/US/en/motion/support/storage.jhtml
Library of Congress Preservation Directorate: www.loc.gov/preserv/preserve.html
LiDo: www.lido.fraunhofer.de/index.html
Lunder Conservation Studio: http://americanart.si.edu/lunder/index.cfm
Midwest Art Conservation Center: www.preserveart.org
Midwest Open Air Museums Coordinating Council (MOMCC): www.midwestmuseums.org
Mid-West Tool Collectors Association: Whatsit Committee: www.mwtca.org/the-gristmill/sample-articles/86-procedure-for-identifying-whatsits.html
Minnesota Historical Society: www.mnhs.org
Mountain Plains Museum: www.mountplainsmuseums.org
MSDS Online: www.msdsonline.com
Museum Pests: www.museumpests.net/default.asp
Museums Association (UK): www.museumsassociation.org
Museums Australia: www.museumsaustralia.org.au
National Academy Press: www.nap.edu
National Archives and Records Administration (NARA): www.archives.gov
National Association for Interpretation: www.interpnet.com
National Association for Museum Exhibition (NAME): name-aam.org
National Association of Government Archives and Records Administrators: www.nagara.org
National Association of Watch and Clock Collections: www.nawcc.org
National Center for Preservation Technology and Training: www.ncptt.npt.gov
National Conference of State Historic Preservation Officers: www.ncshpo.org
National Endowment for the Arts (NEA): www.nea.gov
National Endowment for the Humanities (NEH): www.neh.gov
National Film Preservation Foundation (NFPF): www.filmpreservation.org
National Park Service (NPS) Conserve O Grams: www.nps.gov/history/museum/publications/conserveogram/cons_toc.html
National Trust for Historic Preservation: www.preservation nation.org/about-us
Native American Graves Protection and Repatriation Act (NAGPRA): www.nps.gov/nagpra/mandates/index.htm
Nebraska Museum Association: www.nebraskamuseums.org
Nebraska State Historical Society: www.nebraskahistory.org
Northeast Document Conservation Center (NEDCC): www.nedcc.org/home.php
Old Berwick Historical Society Counting House Museum: www.obhs.net
Philadelphia Museum of Art: philamuseum.org
Phillips de Pury & Company: www.phillipsdepury.com
Preserv'Art: preservart.ccq.mcc.gouv.gc.ca/index.aspx
Preservation Trades Network (PTN): www.ptn.org
reCollections: Caring for Collections across Australia: archive.amol.org.au/recollections/index.htm
Regional Alliance for Preservation: www.rap-arcc.org
Saving Nebraska Treasures: www.netnebraska.org/treasures
Skinner: www.skinnerinc.com
Smithsonian Museum Conservation Institute: si.edu/mci/index.html
Society for American Archivists (SAA): www.archivists.org
Society for the Preservation of Natural History Collections (SPNHC): www.spnhc.org
Sotheby's: www.sothebys.com
Southeastern Library Network (SOLINET): www.solinet.net
Sticky Pad Reader: www.btinternet.com/~ian.hanby/stickypadreader.html
Technical Preservation Services, National Park Service: www.cr.nps.gov/hps
TechniGlove International: www.techniglove.com/nitrile.html
Terra Universal, Inc.: www.terrauniversal.com
Textile Conservation Lab at the Minnesota Historical Society: www.mnhs.org/preserve/conservation/textiles.html

Tippecanoe County Public Library: Resources for Book Care and Repair: www.tcpl.lib.in.us/tech/bookcare.htm

United Kingdom Institute of Conservation (ICON): www.icon.org.uk

United Nations Educational, Scientific and Cultural Organization (UNESCO): portal.unesco.org/culture/en/ev.php-URL_ID=13095&URL_DO=DO_TOPIC&URL_SECTION=201.html

United States Department of Labor: Occupational Safety and Health Administration (OSHA): www.osha.gov

University of Iowa Center for the Book: www.uiowa.edu/~ctrbook/index.shtml

Vidipax: Magnetic Media Restoration: www.vidipax.com

Williamstown Art Conservation Center: www.williamstownart.org/home.htm

World Heritage Center (WHC): whc.unesco.org

Index

About the Authors

Jane Merritt is a textile conservator and conservation administrator who has worked at the Metropolitan Museum of Art, the Textile Museum (Washington, D.C.), and the National Park Service at Harpers Ferry Center, among numerous other prestigious institutions.

Julie A. Reilly is an objects conservator who has worked at the National Museum of American History, the Smithsonian Institution, the National Park Service, and the Colonial Williamsburg Foundation, and was the founding director of the Gerald R. Ford Conservation Center. She is currently the director of development for KANEKO, an exciting new nonprofit in Omaha, Nebraska, dedicated to the exploration of creativity in all of its expressions—art, science, business, and the humanities.

Lucy Lawliss, ASLA, is superintendent for George Washington Birthplace National Monument and Thomas Stone National Historic Site. Ms. Lawliss started with the National Park Service almost two decades ago as the first historical landscape architect for the Southeast Region. From 2001 to 2005, she was the NPS lead for the Cultural Landscapes Program in Washington, D.C.

Rebecca L. Stevens, Architect, AIA, NCARB, is the former Chief Historical Architect, National Park Service, National Capital Region. The practice of historic preservation architecture is her area of expertise.

Made in United States
Cleveland, OH
24 October 2026

46816356R00121